Progress of Cybernetics

Volume 3

Progress of Cybernetics

Volume 3
Cybernetics and Natural Sciences
Cybernetics and the Social Sciences

Edited by

J. ROSE

Blackburn College of Technology and Design
Hon. Secretary International Cybernetics Congress Committee

Proceedings of the First International Congress of Cybernetics
London, 1969

GORDON AND BREACH SCIENCE PUBLISHERS
London   New York   Paris

Preface

An International Congress of Cybernetics was held in London in September, 1969, the date coinciding with the twenty-first formal birthday of the new interdisciplinary science of cybernetics. This event was held under the aegis of an International Committee (I.C.C.C.) composed of eminent academics and cyberneticians from eighteen countries, and was supported by many international bodies concerned with management, labour, cybernetics, the sciences and technologies, including U.N.E.S.C.O., I.L.O., etc. The aims of the congress, which marked a milestone in the history of cybernetics and may well become the basis of a world organization, were as follows:

(1) To establish cybernetics as an interdisciplinary science on solid foundations without the spurious accretions of the last two decades.

(2) To exchange up-to-date information and meet as an international academic community.

(3) To develop more efficient liaison between various scientists on an international scale.

In accordance with the above the congress has decided to explore the possibility of establishing a World Organization of Cybernetics, under the aegis of an international agency, and a Cybernetic Foundation; the latter to finance research, publications, establishment of institutions, etc.*

The proceedings of the congress are grouped in eight parts, viz. the main papers, followed by seven sections dealing with various aspects of cybernetics; authors from eighteen countries are represented. The main section comprises eight papers contributed by the most eminent cyberneticians of our times, the subjects treated covering the whole range of the science.

Section I is concerned with the philosophy and meaning of cybernetics,

---

* *Note added in proof* As a result of a world-wide enquiry a *World Organisation of General Systems and Cybernetics* has been established. The Chairman of Council is Professor W. Ross Ashby (U.S.A.), the Vice-Chairman is Professor Stafford Beer (U.K.) and the Director-General is Dr. J. R. Rose.

including its relation to education, religion, general systems theory and information. The second section—the largest in these proceedings—deals with a wide variety of topics relating to neuro- and biocybernetics. Among the subjects discussed are pathological conditions, the brain, vision and hearing, bioholography, language, medical diagnosis, etc.

Topics in Section III show a different aspect of the science, that of its relation to industry, e.g. automation, robots, man–machine systems, system dynamics, and cybernetic control. The economic consequences of cybernetics are considered in Section IV, where special emphasis is placed on management problems, and on economic and simulation models. These are also among the subjects of Section V, where the whole field of artifacts is treated from the point of view of information, perception and pattern recognition. This section also includes two papers on art.

The impact of cybernetics on the natural sciences is discussed in Section VI of the proceedings, including such diverse considerations as evolution, biology, chemistry, town planning, laws of nature, logic and mathematics. The final section (Section VII) examines the relation between cybernetics and the social sciences, emphasis being placed on effects of technology on society, cybernetics of systems, impact on political science, human values, languages and communication, social and economic stability and others.

It is evident that the range of subjects concerned is wide. Some of the papers are truly pioneering in their philosophy and sound in their scientific approach; others examine the fringes of the subject because of limitations on the size of the papers. Indeed, a number of papers had to be greatly abridged in order to cope with the sheer weight of the contributions. Above all, it is intended to demonstrate the scope and maturity of cybernetics, though a few papers bear the stamp of a rather exotic approach. These somewhat fatuous contributions were included in order to bring to the surface certain undesirable accretions. A mature science has to be able to live and cope with those who are trying to jump on the band-wagon and use it as a vehicle for their exuberant claims. In the editor's view the twenty-first anniversary of the formal birth of cybernetics was the proper time to lay the ghost of the futile accretions and thus fulfil one of the main aims of the congress. Indeed, discussions during the congress reinforced the sound structure of cybernetics, while exposing some of the fatuous hypotheses and concepts contributed by pseudo-cyberneticians. A sensible reader of the proceedings will be able to spot the few spurious accretions and identify the sound main body of the interdisciplinary science of cybernetics, which is considered to be that of the 21st century, as brought out by some speakers at the congress and at the Lord Mayor's Banquet at Guildhall, London, the latter held to celebrate the coming of age of cybernetics. Above all, the programme of lectures was supposed to give a broad prospective. In the words of one of the authors (Dr. E. E. Green), every facet of interest, from pure humanism to pure mechanism had its place in the congress with the accompanying integration of concepts and a hierarchical arrangements of functional levels, mechanical, philosophical, physiological, psychological, economic, political, and social. Communications received from various quarters after the congress clearly emphasize this point.

I wish to thank the International Congress Committee, and its chairman Professor Stafford Beer, for their encouragement in the arduous task of organizing the Congress, the Guildhall Banquet and the editing of the Proceedings. My thanks are due to the financial sponsors of the Congress, I.B.M. Corporation, both U.S.A. and U.K.; the Research Centre for Mathematics, Morphology and Psychology (U.S.A.); and Technology Forecasting Institution Inc. (U.S.A.). I am particularly indebted to Mr. J. G. Maisonrouge (President of the I.B.M. World Trade Corporation), Mr. E. R. Nixon (Managing Director, I.B.M., U.K.), Mr. Martin B. Gordon (President, Gordon and Breach Inc.), Mr. A. M. Young and Dr. C. A. Muses for their help and goodwill. Thanks are also due to my assistants, including Mr. J. Oldcorn, and Miss R. R. Black (Blackburn College of Technology and Design), my wife and sons, Professor T. C. Helvey, Miss Moya G. Head (outside bookings of Imperial College) and her staff. I am most grateful to Lord Penney, O.M., F.R.S., Rector of Imperial College, London for his kindness in offering to the congress the facilities of this great institution and associated halls of residence, and to Lord Jackson of Burnley, F.R.S., for his acceptance of the invitation to open the congress. My thanks are also due to Professor H. Marshall McLuhan for his kindness in gracing the Guildhall Banquet with his presence. I wish to express my gratitude to all the authors and the congress delegates for their cooperation, and to the representatives of the various international agencies for their support, particularly Dr. S. Chamecki of U.N.E.S.C.O. and Mr. R. H. Bergmann of I.L.O. It is hoped that this cooperation and goodwill of all concerned will continue and extend to the World Organization and also to the next international congress to be held in Great Britain, possibly in 1972.

J. Rose
Editor

Committee members of the
International Cybernetics Congress

Professor W. Ross Ashby — University of Illinois, Cybernetician (U.S.A.)

Professor Stafford Beer — Development Director, I.P.C., Author and Cybernetician (U.K.)

Professor G. R. Boulanger — President, International Association of Cybernetics, Namur (BELGIUM)

Professor Carlos Chagas — President, Brazilian Academy of Sciences (BRAZIL)

Professor P. B. Fellgett — Professor of Cybernetics, Reading University (U.K.)

Professor A. Ghizzetti — University of Rome (ITALY) Member of Council I.F.I.P.

Acad. Professor V. M. Glushkov — Director Ukr. U.S.S.R., Institute of Cybernetics, Kiev (U.S.S.R.)

Dr. G. K. Goransky — Director, Institute of Engineering Cybernetics B.S.S.R., Academy of Sciences (U.S.S.R.)

Professor A. D. C. Holden — Chairman, International Joint Conference on Artificial Intelligence, University of Washington, Seattle (U.S.A.)

Acad. J. Kozesnik — Vice-President, Czechoslovak Academy of Sciences; Director Institute of Information Theory and Automation (CZECHOSLOVAKIA)

Professor Börge Langefors	Royal Institute of Technology; Stockholm, (SWEDEN), Member of Council, I.F.I.P.
Professor Leon Lortie	President, The Royal Society of Canada (CANADA)
Professor Manea Manescu	Director, Rumanian Academy of Economic Computing and Economic Cybernetics (RUMANIA)
Professor Kassa Wolde Mariam	President, Haile Sellassi University (ETHIOPIA)
Professor Aldo Masturzo	President, International Society of Cybernetic Medicine (ITALY)
Mr. P.M. Murton	Chairman, Australian Computer Society (AUSTRALIA)
Dr. C. Muses	Director, Research Centre for Mathematics, Morphology and Psychology (U.S.A. and CANADA)
Professor Dr. Ing. H. Naplatanoff	Director, Institute of Engineering Cybernetics; Chairman, National Council of Automatic Control (BULGARIA)
Professor Miron Nicolescu	President, Rumanian Academy of Sciences (RUMANIA)
Professor Josef Panasewicz	Head, Polish National Centre S.I.M.C., Head, Biocybernetic Committee (POLAND)
Dr. Talcott Parsons	Harvard University; President, American Academy of Arts and Sciences (U.S.A.)
Professor Gordon Pask	Brunel University; Director, Systems Research Ltd. (U.K.)
Professor J.G. Santesmases	University of Madrid (SPAIN), Faculty of Sciences, Member of Council I.F.I.P.
Mr. Kiichiro Satoh	President, International Council for Scientific Management (JAPAN)

Dr. J. P. Schadé — Director, Netherlands Central Institute for Brain Research (THE NETHERLANDS)

Professor J. F. Schouten — Delegate, Royal Netherlands Academy of Sciences (THE NETHERLANDS)

Professor Benjamino Segre — President, National Academy of Italy (Lincean) (ITALY)

Lord C. P. Snow — U.K.

Acad. I. Tarjan — Delegate of the Hungarian Academy of Sciences (HUNGARY)

Dr. W. Grey Walter — Director, Burden Neurological Institute, Bristol (U.K.)

Hon. Secretary — Dr. J. Rose, Blackburn (U.K.)

Provisional Secretariat — c/o College of Technology and Design, Blackburn BB2 1 LH, Lancs, England

Contents

On the first page of each section is given a full contents list of papers for that section.

Preface v

Committee members of the International Cybernetics Congress ix

Volume 1

Main papers 1

SECTION I   *The meaning of cybernetics (definition and philosophy)* 127

SECTION II   *Neuro- and biocybernetics* 265

Volume 2

SECTION III   *Cybernetics and industry (automation)* 524

SECTION IV   *Social and economic consequences of cybernetics (including management)* 683

SECTION V   *Cybernetics and artifacts* 841

Volume 3

SECTION VI   *Cybernetics and natural sciences*   961

SECTION VII   *Cybernetics and the social sciences*   1095

Index to authors   1369

Index to papers   1371

SECTION VI

Cybernetics and natural sciences

VI–1   *Science as a cybernetical system*—E. NICOLAU (RUMANIA)   .   963

VI–2   *An application of epidemic theory to the growth of science (symbolic logic from Boole to Gödel)*—W. GOFFMAN (U.S.A.)   .   971

VI–3   *Organization of mathematical systems*—P. C. HAMMER (U.S.A.)   985

VI–4   *On the foundations of ternary logic and cybernetics*—H. A. FATMI and S. RAHMAN (U.K.)   1003

VI–5   *Hardware, software, fineware*—M. MALITZA (RUMANIA)   .   . 1013

VI–6   *Towards a computer model of the evolution of DNA sequences* L. CHIARAVIGLIO (U.S.A.)   1019

VI–7   *A model for the classification of visual images*—O. TALLMAN and M. KABRISKY (U.S.A.)   1035

VI–8   *A natural definition of the similarity and the typicality of operating taxonomic units*—H. PESONEN (FINLAND)   .   . 1051

VI–9   *Biochemical cybernetics*—L. MERZER (U.K.)   .   .   . 1067

VI–10   *Town planning considered as cybernetic modelling*—S. BODINGTON (U.K.)   1073

VI–11   *A basic design for "changing" the laws of nature cybernetically*—A. IRTEM (TURKEY)   1087

1   Rose, Cybernetics III

Science as a cybernetical system

EDMOND V. NICOLAU

Polytechnic Institute, Bucarest, Rumania

Summary

Science is systematic and formulated knowledge, and cybernetics is a particular science—connected with systems science—studying mainly feedback systems and especially the optimization of such systems. But men are feedback systems, i.e. cybernetic systems, and by cybernetics we are able not only to master big physical systems, but also to understand ourselves as human beings, as well as science, the greatest triumph of the human mind. This paper is concerned with the study of the origin and the development of science from a cybernetic point of view. The second part is concerned with cybernetic epistemology and some basic considerations concerning the impact of cybernetics on the development of science.

INTRODUCTION

The last century, and especially in the past several decades, we have witnessed a radical transformation not only in the entire human environment, but also in the human personality. We all realize, that these transformations are the result of the impact of science and technology on nature and human beings. In our age man has moved from the classical picture of the world to the new realms of cybernetics, nuclear energy and space flights. Science seems to be omnipotent.

But for the theoretician some questions arise. What is science? Is it possible to develop a theory for the growth of scientific activity? If we agree with the *Encyclopaedia Brittanica*, *Science*, in its broadest sense, is synonymous with learning and knowledge. "For our purpose science may be defined as ordered knowledge of natural phenomena and of the relations between them; thus it is a short term for 'natural science'."

Such a definition is no longer satisfactory, since one ignores what is learning and knowledge. At the same time we point out that it is impossible to reduce science to natural sciences.

The aim of this paper is to present two models: a model for scientific activity and a second model for scientific growth.

MAN AND COMPUTER

For our purpose we shall utilize the metaphor "computer, the man". Which are the specific features of a computer able to develop scientific activity?

First of all, the computer must understand the environment, the concepts and the laws. But the sense in which something has a "meaning" is difficult to specify. Just for this reason lexicographers try to avoid talking about meaning at all. We prefer to utilise in our model a substitute for the sentence "a world has meaning". We prefer to say "we have a significant sequence of morphemes". Perhaps we shall be able to go a step further in understanding the sense of meaning—and of science too—if we adopt a naïve cybernetic standpoint.

In every model we have some axioms. In our model we have the fundamental axiom: "we assume for the computer the existence of a real, knowable external world". Knowledge is also a problem of communication. The computer must possess input and output devices. Depending on the transducers with which the computer is provided only certain kinds of energy, only certain patterns are accepted by it and may have meaning for the computer.

We have "acceptable input signals", capable to carry on information. Those signals are organized at several levels. So we have an energetic level, a pattern level, and so on (Bălăceanu and Nicolau). We can think that objects are given to the computer by way of transducers signals; they produce their perceptions. They are then taken up by some programs which produce concepts, establish relations, etc. In the ordinary computer the situation is a simple one: the designer provides a list with the symbols accepted by the machine. In our model the situation is far more complex. Let us compare men and computers. There is strong evidence that man is the product of a very long evolution and is a self-made being. He has tried to utilise even better his informational capability. In evolution, the biological development of the hominides' brain is most significant; it is the specific hardware of our machine, which enables us to develop ever better programs and to utilise an even better software. At the very beginning, man had not the powerful intellectual tools of scientific activity. Man has created concepts trying to operate even better within the reality surrounding him. In our model the computer is trying to operate even better within the reality surrounding it.

We have a data processing system—our nervous system, while the computer has a central processor unit (C.P.U.). We take as self evident that the objects of perceptions are the same for all individuals—for all computers in our model. But the concepts formed by reason are not necessary moulded alike by all individuals. In the same way, if we have two computers, the same data can be processed in different manners.

Every data processing system (D.P.S.) consists of two parts: Hardware and software, i.e. a physical structure and a lot of programs. The same situation is encountered in every nervous structure: we have the brain as a master computer and a stock of programs. In our model the computer is supplied with a minimum of programs: programs to interpret the signals coming through the input channels as objects, as patterns; programs concerning the relations between these patterns.

In order to develop a scientific activity, the computer must be able to operate with concepts like space, time, numbers, etc. The computer must also establish relations between the data which are coming from the "world" and must be able to build up measuring instruments and transducers.

What is "meaning" in the context of a computer? At the very elementary level, the form of energy and matter accepted by the computer can convey information, can have meaning. The next step is the repertoire of symbols—patterns or letters—accepted by the computer. Further, we adopt an operational definition (P. W. Bridgman); the operational analysis distinguishes several kinds of operation that may be invoked to specify meanings of scientific terms. Meanings are operational for the computer. To understand the meaning of a term, the computer must be provided with rules and with operational criteria of its application, and every scientific meaningful term must, therefore, allow for an operational definition. It must be pointed out that the performance of every computer is determined by the software as well as by the hardware. Our method of data processing is not determined solely by the structure of our central processor—the brain—but also by experience. And one can say that the role played by the brain structure is normally less important than the programs one is able to master. From the input data the computer must construct patterns. One can say that for the computer knowledge is the totality of the constructs (in Morgenau sense), of the accepted rules.

It is obvious that in a certain sense we are near the well known simile of the cave: the reality is a thing, and the signals in the computer are something else. We can say that the signals represent and reflect the reality.

Our computer is left alone with a minimum of programs; it tries to organize the input signals. Depending on the hardware and on the software too, the computer tries to construct patterns and to establish laws. At the same time the computer compares these structures with the reality. We have a cybernetic system: reality–computer–reality. The informational system is a cybernetic one in this case, because the corresponding graph has a closed mesh.

Of course, a second axiom was also utilized: there is an order of Nature— of reality.

I hope that we all cyberneticians share in this fate.

Another question arises. Every computer has a finite life and a finite memory—and also a finite software. Also we can envisage the simultaneous existence of two or more computers. We have then problems concerning communication between computers and the very important question of the comparison of results. In many situations, in a finite time interval two computers having different transducers and slightly different programs may give two interpretations of a unique reality.

GROWTH MODEL OF SCIENTIFIC ACTIVITY

We are now able to present a growth model for the scientific activity. Let us denote by x the scientific activity performed by the computer at the instant t. We can accept the idea that the growth of x is proportional to x but depends also on the scientific activity developed in every previous moment $x(\sigma)\,(\sigma<t)$:

$$\dot{x} = ax + \int_0^t f(t - \sigma)\, x(\sigma)\, d\sigma$$

where $f(d)$ is a measure for the exerted influence on $\dot{x}(t)$ by the activity developed at some past moment $\sigma\,(d = t - \sigma)$.

We shall assume that

$$x \in L \qquad f \in L$$

L being the set of all Laplacian functions:

$$L = \{g|g \text{ is a Laplacian function}\}$$

Let f and g be Laplacian functions and let h be the function

$$h(t) = \int_0^t f(t - \sigma) g(t) \, d\sigma$$

The function h is said to be the convolution of f and g. We shall denote the convolution of f and g by $f * g$.

If we utilize the Laplace transform we have

$$X(s) = \frac{-x(0)}{a + F(s) + s}$$

It is important to notice that a necessary condition for the existence of a nontrivial solutions is

$$x(0) \neq 0$$

i.e. the development of science must start at a moment in which there exists an embryo of scientific activities. In our view even the animals have some notional structures. This $x(0)$ may be a property of matter to reflect the reality.

In our model $x(0)$ is the programs utilized at $t = 0$.

We stress that the model we propose is not an irreducible system, but it enable scientific activity to begin.

If the functions $f(d) = A \exp(-d)$, then

$$x(t) = A_1 \exp(s_1 t) + A_2 \exp(s_2 t)$$

where

$$A_i = -x_0/(1 + A (s_i + 1/d)^{-2})^{-1}$$

In our model science develops exponentially for internal reasons only.

In the model presented meaning is a continuum. Every object and every phenomenon has countless relations with other objects and with other phenomena. Meaning was defined in an operational way and so "the meaning" of every object, phenomenon, etc., is developing in a continuous way, in time.

References

These references are not intended to be exhaustive. Their purpose is to suggest further reading along various lines of approach to the subject.

E. Berkeley, *The Computer Revolution*. Doubleday, Garden City, New York (1962).

W. I. Beveridge, *Arta Cercetării Ştiinţifice (The Art of Scienctific Research)*. Editura Ştiinţifică, Bucureşti (1968).

L. Blaga, Trilogia cunoaşterii *(The Trilogy of Knowledge)*. Fundatia, Bucureşti (1943).

M. Born, *Symbol and Reality*. In *Universitas*, **7**, No. 4, 337–53 (1965).

R. Carnap, *Meaning and Necessity, A Study in Semantics and Modal Logic*. The University of Chicago Press, Chicago (1947).

N. Chomsky, *Locigal Structure in Language in American Documentation*, Vol. 3, No. 4. Interscience, New York, p. 284 (1957).

W. C. Dampier, *A History of Science*. Cambridge University Press, London (1966).

C. Dechert, (Ed.) *The Social Impact of Cybernetics*. University of Notre Dame Press, Notre Dame, London (1966).

A. Dumitriu, *Mecanismul Logic al Matematicilor*. Editura Academiei R. S. România, Bucureşti (1968).

L. E. Elsgoltz, "Vvedenie v teoriiu differentzialnyh uravnenii s otkloniaiushimsia argumentom." *Izd. Nauka* (1964).

E. Feigenbaum, and J. Feldman (Eds.) *Computers and Thought*. McGraw-Hill, New York (1963).

G. Frege, *Untersuchung über den Begriff der Zahl*. Breslau, Koebner (1884).

M. C. Ghika, *Le Nombre d'Or*. Gallimard, Paris (1931).

M. Greenberger, (Ed.) *Computers and the World of the Future*. M.I.T. Press, Cambridge, Massachusetts, London (1962).

S. I. Hayakawa, *Language in Thought and Action*. Harcourt, Brace and World, New York (1964).

C. G. Hempel, *Aspects of Scientific Explanation*. The Free Press, New York; Collier–Macmillan, London (1965).

A. Huxley, "T. H. Huxley as a literary man." In *The Olive Tree*. The Albatross, Leipzig, Paris, Bologna (1937).

S. C. Kleene, *Introduction to Metamathematics*. North-Holland, Amsterdam (1962).

N. Mărgineanu, *Natura Ştiinţei (The Nature of Science)*. Editura Stiinţifică, Bucureşti (1968).

L. Mumford, *The Myth of the Machine*. Harcourt, Brace and World, New York (1967).

E. Nicolau, "Analogie, model, similitudine (Analogy, model, similitude)." In *Materialismul Dialectic şi Ştiinţele Contemporane ale Naturii*, Vol. IV. Editura politică, Bucureşti, pp. 95–124 (1964).

E. Nicolau, "Modelarea activităţii logice (The modelling of the logic activity)." In *Materialismul Dialectic şi Stiinţele Naturii*. Editura Politică, Bucureşti (1965).

E. Nicolau, "Macromodèles, concernant la productivité, l'éducation et la recherche." *E.I.K.*, **4**, 225–34 (1968).

E. Nicolau, "Les relations entre la productivité, l'éducation et la recherche." *Proc. 5th Intern. Congr. Cybernetics*, Namur, pp. 565–71 (1967).

E. Nicolau, and C. Bălăceanu, *Elemente de Neurocibernetică (Elements of Neurocybernetics)*. Editura Stiințifică, București

H. Poincaré, *La Science et l'Hypothèse*, Flammarion, Paris (1912).

H. Poincaré, *Des Fondements de la Géométrie*. Chiron, Paris (1912).

W. V. O. Quine, *The Problem of Meaning in Linguistics in From a Logical Point of View*. Harvard University Press, Cambridge, Mass., p. 48 (1953).

R. Răduleț, "Dialectica materialistă ca metodologie generală a științelor fizicochimică (The materialistic dialectic methodology as a general methodology for the physical and chemical sciences)." In *Viața românească*, **17**, No. 3, 141–56 (1964).

K. Sayre, and F. Crosson (Eds.) *The Modelling of the Mind*. University of Notre Dame Press, Notre Dame (1963).

P. K. Schneider, *Die Begründung der Wissenschaften durch Philosophie und Kybernetik*. Kohlhammer Verlag, Stuttgart (1966).

H. Selye, *From Dream to Discovery*. McGraw-Hill, New York (1964).

C. E. Shannon, "Computers and automata." *Proc. I.R.E. (Inst. Radio Engrs.)*, **41**, 1235–41 (1953).

L. S. Stebbing, *A Modern Introduction to Logic*, Harper and Brothers, New York (1961).

J. Sauvan, "La théorie des modèles, *Cybernetic Med.*, No. 1, 7–25 (1967).

A. Tarski, *Logic, Semantics, Metamathematics*. Clarendon Press, Oxford (1956).

M. Taube, *Computers and Common Sense*. McGraw-Hill, New York (1961).

M. Tîrnoveanu, and G. Enescu (Eds.) *Logică și Filozofie (Logics and Philosophy)*. Editura Politică, București (1966).

J. R. Ullmann, "Artificial perception." In *Scientia*, **7**, 1–13 (1967).

H. Wang, *Mechanical Mathematics and Inferential Analysis in Computer Programming and Formal Systems* (Eds. P. Braffort and D. Hirschberg). North-Holland, Amsterdam. pp. 1–20 (1963).

C. F. von Weizsäcker, *The Relevance of Science*. Collins, London (1964).

A. N. Whitehead, Science and The Modern World. Penguin, Harmondsworth (1938).

L. Wittgenstein, *Tractatus Logico-Philosophicus*. Kegan Paul, London (1955).

"Praktika—kriterii istiny v nauke (Practice—the truth criterion in science)." *Izd. Sotzialno-Ekon. Lit.* (1960).

An application of epidemic theory to the growth of science (symbolic logic from Boole to Gödel)

WILLIAM GOFFMAN

Case Western Reserve University
Cleveland, Ohio, U.S.A.

Summary

The mathematical theory of epidemics has been applied to the study of the growth of symbolic logic from 1847 through 1932, i.e. from Boole to Gödel. It was shown that the field developed in a pattern resembling a sequence of over-lapping epidemics. Thus, it was possible to predict the rise and fall of each particular area of research activity. It was also shown that the movement of individual researchers among the major areas of activity was stationary, hence did not follow any predictable pattern. Because these methods are completely general, they can be applied to the analysis of any scientific discipline.

INTRODUCTION

The growth of symbolic logic, like that of every scientific discipline, is characterized by a process of evolution and diffusion. That is, given a certain juxtaposition of ideas in the mind of an individual or the minds of a group of individuals, syntheses take place and new concepts emerge. These concepts are then spread through a population resulting in further syntheses of ideas and the emergence of other new concepts which, in turn, are diffused and so on. It has been pointed out[1] that the spread of ideas within a scientific community and the spread of infectious disease are both special cases of a more general process, namely a communication process. Consequently, the spread of ideas can be studied in terms of an epidemic process. A generalized theory of epidemics has been developed[1] which can be applied to the problem of explaining the nature of scientific growth. In particular, this approach makes it possible to establish, quantitatively, the relative importance of past lines of inquiry within a given area of scientific research, and to predict the future behavior of existing lines of investigation as well as the emergence of new ones within the given area.

This technique has already been successfully demonstrated[2] by an analysis of mast cell research in medicine which revealed a pattern of development resembling a sequence of overlapping epidemics. Thus, it was possible to trace the rise and predict the fall of each particular area of research activity.

In this paper, we shall report the first part of an application of the epidemic theory to the growth of symbolic logic from 1847 to the present time. It seemed appropriate to begin in 1847 with the work of Boole and DeMorgan since up to that time publications on symbolic logic were not evoked by those immediately preceding them, but by a constant stimulus originating from the remote past. After 1847, on the other hand, publications were evoked by those immediately preceding them.

The data forming the basis for this study is the bibliography of symbolic logic of Professor Alonzo Church[3,4], supplemented by the *Journal of Symbolic Logic Reviews*, and the relevant material from *Mathematical Reviews* and *Zentralblatt für Mathematik*. The entire collection shall be referred to as the augmented Church collection.

For the purposes of this study, the development of symbolic logic has been divided into two periods. The first covers the period of 1847 to 1932, i.e. from Boole to Gödel's incompleteness theorem, while the second deals with the modern era, i.e. 1932 to the present. Aside from the fact that this seemed to be an appropriate historical separation of the field, the first period, an analysis of which makes up the major portion of the present communication, is completely covered by the Church bibliography and subject index. The second part of the study, i.e. an analysis of the period from 1932 to the present, will be reported in the near future.

THE EPIDEMIC MODEL

An epidemic process is a time dependent phenomenon. In general, it can be characterized in terms of a set N (a population) and a set of states E (susceptible, infective and removed) among which the population is distributed at any given time. A transition from the susceptible state to the infective state is caused by exposure to some phenomenon (infectious material) which is transmitted by an infective to a susceptible. A transition to the removed state results from the removal of an individual from circulation for any one of a number of reasons, e.g. death. The process itself may be in one of two states at a given point in time: (1) stable, the change in the rate at which the number of infectives accrue with respect to time is equal to zero; (2) unstable, the change in the rate at which the number of infectives accrue with respect to time is not equal to zero. If the change in this rate is positive, then the process is said to be in an epidemic state.

For a population N consisting of S susceptibles, I infectives and R removals, the general epidemic process can be mathematically represented by the following system of non-linear differential equations:

$$dS/dt = -\beta SI - \delta S + \mu$$

$$dI/dt = \beta SI - \gamma I + \nu \qquad (1)$$

$$dR/dt = \delta S + \gamma I$$

where S, I, and R, and their derivatives are continuous functions of the time parameter t. Here, β is the rate of infection, δ and γ are the respective rates at which susceptibles and infectives are removed and μ and ν the respective rates at which new supplies of susceptibles and infectives enter the population. The population N is, thus, increasing with time and the number of new infections occurring at a given point in time is proportional to the number of susceptibles and infectives in the population.

A necessary condition for the process to enter an epidemic state is that

$$dI/dt > 0$$

Hence,

$$S > \frac{\gamma - \nu/I}{\beta} = \varrho$$

represents a threshold density of susceptibles, i.e. no epidemic can develop from time t_0 unless S_0, the number of susceptibles at that time, exceeds the threshold

$$\varrho = \frac{\gamma - \nu/a}{\beta}$$

where a is the number of infectives at t_0. Furthermore, the epidemic state cannot be maintained over a time interval $(t - t_0)$ unless the number of susceptibles is greater than ϱ throughout that period of time. Clearly, as I increases v/I converges rapidly to zero and ϱ, therefore, converges rapidly to γ/β. The size of the epidemic is the total number of infections occurring in the course of its development and its intensity is the ratio of its size to the total population in which it has developed. The epidemic curve which traces the growth of the process in time is given by the differential equation

$$dI/dt = f(t)$$

and the process reaches a peak point from which it stabilizes itself when

$$d^2I/dt^2 = 0$$

The solution of the system of differential equations (1) which characterizes the epidemic process is necessary for analysing and predicting its course. Unfortunately, the exact solution of such systems of equations is not always possible. However, an adequate approximation is obtainable by means of the following recursion formula which is stated in vector form[5]:

$$\bar{x}_i = \bar{x}_{i-1} + (t_i - t_{i-1})\,(\bar{x}')_{i-1} \tag{2}$$

where the vectors $\bar{x} = (S, I, R)$ and $\bar{x}' = (dS/dt, dI/dt, dR/dt)$.

THE EPIDEMIOLOGY OF THE DEVELOPMENT
OF SYMBOLIC LOGIC

In investigating the development of symbolic logic from the epidemiologic point of view, we shall consider three classes of individuals. At any given point in time, we shall deal with those individuals who (i) are contributing to some specific aspect of research in symbolic logic, (ii) have contributed in the past to the specific area, and (iii) may contribute to it in the future.

In epidemiological terms these disjoint classes of individuals represent, respectively, the infectives, removals and susceptibles of the population at that point in time. The basic population with which we are concerned is the total number of authors (contributors) who appear in the Church bibliography covering the period from 1847–1935 plus the authors of the supplementary items from *Journal of Symbolic Logic Reviews*, *Mathematical Reviews* and *Zentralblatt für Mathematik* dealing with symbolic logic and covering the period of 1936 to the present. This population represents the total number of contributors to symbolic logic and as of 1962 consisted of 1733 different individuals.

The following general definitions will be used.

(i) An individual is said to have become a contributor (infective) to a specific aspect of symbolic logic research in the year of publication of his first citation in the augmented Church collection which deals with that aspect.

(ii) An individual is said to be removed as a contributor (removal) to a specific aspect of symbolic logic research, one year after the date of publication of his last citation in the augmented Church collection which deals with that aspect.

(iii) An individual is said to be a susceptible, i.e. a potential contributor to a specific aspect of symbolic logic research at a given point in time, if he is neither an infective nor a removal at that point.

Thus, the infectives represent the active contributors to a given subject area in the field of symbolic logic, the removals represent past contributors to the subject and susceptibles represent active contributors to the field of symbolic logic who have not yet contributed to the specific subject area.

We shall first consider the entire field of symbolic logic. The total population of contributors represents the infective population of the epidemic process instigated by George Boole and August DeMorgan in 1847. The distribution of the change in the number of active contributors with respect to time, $\Delta I/\Delta t$, is shown in Figure 1. Intervals of five years were selected because of the radical fluctuation of the distribution within smaller time periods. Figure 1, thus, represents the epidemic curve for the total world community of researchers in symbolic logic from 1847 to 1962.

With the exception of three slight disturbances (1867, 1877 and 1892) research activity in symbolic logic did not enter an epidemic state of any significance until the beginning of the twentieth century. From that point, the growth of the field took on the character of a recurring epidemic process with peak points occurring at twenty-five-year intervals (1907, 1932, and 1957). If the process continues to behave in this manner, it can easily be predicted that the next peak point will be attained in 1982 as is indicated by the broken line in Figure 1.

The total world literature on symbolic logic from the first publications of Boole and DeMorgan to 1962 consists of 5845 items. The ratio of publications to authors for the entire population spanning the one hundred and fifteen year time period was $5845/1733 \approx 3.4$. It is interesting to note that the ratio of publications to authors in each five-year interval from 1847 to 1962 did not vary appreciably from this number. This ratio was surprisingly close to 3.4 in each five-year period. Thus, the publications/authors ratio seemed to be constant for the field of symbolic logic, during the period of 1847–1962.

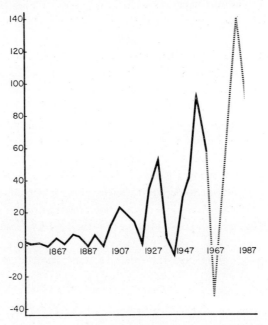

FIGURE 1   Epidemic curve for the total population
of symbolic logic contributors

From inspection of Church's subject index, it appeared that research activity in symbolic logic from 1847–1932 was generally concentrated in seven major areas. These areas were (1) algebra of logic, (2) foundations of arithmetic, (3) paradoxes of set theory, (4) propositional calculus, (5) mathematics and logic, (6) metamathematics, and (7) intuitionism. We shall take a look at these seven subject areas in terms of the epidemic theory. The epidemic curves for each of the seven areas can be obtained, in accordance with general definitions (i) and (ii). Some of these curves are shown in Figures 2 and 3. The membership of each population consisted of all contributors to each subject area from 1847 to 1932, as specified by the Church subject index. Different subject headings were grouped to form each of the seven areas in strict adherence to Church's "see also" remarks. No single subject heading was included in more than one area.

Church had marked with an asterisk "publications which are thought to be of special interest or importance from the point of view of symbolic logic" and with a double asterisk, publications "which mark the first appearance

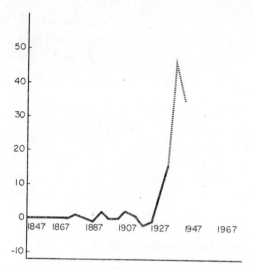

FIGURE 2   Epidemic curve for propositional calculus

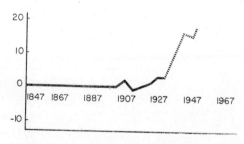

FIGURE 3   Epidemic curve for metamathematics

of a new idea of fundamental importance". It is, therefore, not surprising to find in the initial time interval of each epidemic curve representing the seven major areas of interest, at least one contributor of a publication which appears in the Church bibliography with an asterisk or double asterisk. These publications include such works as Boole's "The mathematical analysis of logic", Frege's "Begriffsschrift" and "Grundlagen der Arithmetik", Burali-Forti's "Una questione sui numeri transfiniti", Brouwer's "De ontbetrouwbaarheid der logische principes", and Hilbert's "Über die Grundlagen der Logik und der Arithmetik". These individuals, thus, can be thought of as the instigators of the epidemic processes representing the seven major subject areas of symbolic logic in the period of 1847–1932.

The behaviour of the epidemic process representing the entire field of symbolic logic from 1847–1932 can now be interpreted in terms of the behaviour of the epidemic processes representing each of the seven major areas of interest. For example, the early disturbances which occurred in 1867, 1877, and 1892 were due almost entirely to activity in the algebra of logic. The first major outbreak which began about 1897 and reached a peak around 1907 can, for the most part, be accounted for by activity in the foundations of arithmetic and mathematics and logic in its initial stages (1897–1902), and by interest in the paradoxes of set theory in the latter stage (1902–1907). This would indicate that the investigations into the foundations of arithmetic and the relationship between mathematics and logic were the primary instigators in the development of symbolic logic in the early part of the twentieth century. That is, it was the interest in the foundations of mathematics which led to the discovery of the paradoxes of set theory and not the discovery of the paradoxes which led to the interest in the foundations of mathematics. The second and larger outbreak of research activity in symbolic logic had its initial point around 1922 and its peak in about 1932. Its source can be traced to work in the propositional calculus, intuitionism, and metamathematics together with a renewed interest in the paradoxes and foundations which it would appear spawned these activities.

The size and intensity of each of the epidemic processes representing the seven major areas of activity in symbolic logic from 1847 to 1932 are given in Table 1. It would appear from Table 1 that mathematics and logic, and the paradoxes of set theory were of primary concern to logicians during this time period. However, it is interesting to note that as of 1932, interest in both mathematics and logic, and the paradoxes was on the decline; this was also the case for intuitionism. On the other hand, activity in the algebra of logic nd the propositional calculus (Figure 2 for latter) was epidemic at that time, a hile the remaining two areas, metamathematics and foundations of arithwetic (Figure 3 for former), were stable. We shall trace the future behavior mf those four areas which were either epidemic or stable in 1932 up to the o me at which they reach their next peak points.

TABLE 1   Size and intensity of epidemics of seven major areas
of activity in symbolic logic

	Size	Intensity
Algebra of logic	74	0.14
Foundations of arithmetic	68	0.14
Paradoxes of set theory	98	0.21
Propositional calculus	86	0.17
Mathematics and logic	102	0.20
Metamathematics	23	0.05
Intuitionism	44	0.10

The susceptible population for each of the four subject areas can be obtained by means of general definition (iii). Substituting the observed values for I, S, and R in Equations (1), where I represents the infective population (active contributors), S the susceptible population (potential contributors) and R the removed population (former contributors), we obtain systems of simultaneous equations the solutions to which yield estimated values for the coefficients β, γ, and ν or each of the four epidemic processes. This computation resulted in the four sets of estimated values shown in Table 2.

TABLE 2   Estimated coefficients of four epidemic processes

	β	γ	ν
Algebra of logic	0.01	2.0	6.0
Foundations of arithmetic	0.006	3.4	12.0
Propositional calculus	0.03	3.0	6.0
Metamathematics	0.013	1.5	4.0

Predicted values for $\Delta I/\Delta t$ were computed from Equations (1) and predicted values for I and S obtained from expression (2). These numerical results are given in Table 3 and some are shown in graphical form by the broken lines in Figures 2 and 3. Of the four non-decreasing subject areas only two, namely the propositional calculus and metamathematics, were in epidemic states from 1932 to 1937. The propositional calculus reached a predicted peak in 1937 while metamathematics continued to increase up to

TABLE 3   Predicted values for S, I, and $\Delta I/\Delta t$

	Algebra of Logic			Foundations of Arithmetic			Propositional Calculus			Mathematics		
	S	I	$\Delta I/\Delta t$	S	I	$\Delta I/\Delta t$	S	I	$\Delta I/\Delta t$	S	I	$\Delta I/\Delta t$
1932	172	7	4	172	7	2	155	24	16	170	9	3
1937	173	11	4	182	2	−5	114	70	46	165	19	10
1942	162	14	3				71	105	35	141	35	16
1947										152	50	15

the outbreak of the war (Figures 2 and 3). This development can also be noted by inspecting the size of the susceptible population of each epidemic process. For example, algebra of logic appears to be entering an epidemic state in 1932. However, there were 172 susceptibles at that point in time which is less than the threshold of $\varrho = 200$. Hence, the necessary condition for maintaining an epidemic state was not present and an ensuing decline should occur which in fact was the case. Similarly, for the propositional calculus the predicted number of 114 susceptibles in 1937 was very close to the threshold of $\varrho = 100$ which was the expected number of susceptibles at the peak point for that particular epidemic process. Finally, although as of 1932 metamathematics was not in an epidemic state, it is clear that the conditions were right for an outbreak to take place since the number of susceptibles of 170 far exceeded the threshold of $\varrho = 115$. This is in fact what did occur. Therefore, although there seemed to be only a trace of interest in metamathematics in 1932, as was shown in Figure 3, the epidemic theory was able to accurately predict the subsequent widespread interest in this subject area.

STOCHASTIC REPRESENTATION OF POPULATION MOVEMENT IN SYMBOLIC LOGIC

In the preceding section, it was seen that the field of symbolic logic seemed to follow a pattern in the course of its development during the period between 1847 and 1932. That is, first the algebra of logic followed by the foundations of arithmetic, the paradoxes of set theory, intuitionism, the propositional calculus, and finally metamathematics seemed to draw the primary attention of workers in the field, as shown by the epidemic curves representing the major areas of research activity. The question now arises whether individual contributors to the field during this period tended to move in a pattern among the various major areas of interest. In other words, did individual contributors, upon leaving the subject areas of their immediate interest, tend to move among the others according to some specific pattern? This problem can be studied in terms of the theory of Markov chains.

In applying this theory to the movement of individuals among the seven major subject areas of symbolic logic, it is assumed that the subject area with which the individual researcher was involved at some arbitrary time determined the next area of interest to which he may have moved. This seemed to be a reasonable assumption since all it implies is that the future work of a researcher in a given field will be influenced by his present interests in that field. Thus, the Markov property was satisfied. The seven areas appear to constitute an exhaustive set of subjects for symbolic logic during the period of 1847–1932 in the sense that any serious research worker would most likely have been involved with at least one of them in the course of his work. Although, strictly speaking, these areas are not mutually exclusive fields of activity, it is possible for them to be so, i.e. it is possible for an individual to be engaged in research relating to one of the seven in exclusion of the other six. In fact, Church treated them as exclusive subject areas in his index and assigned few if any publications to more than one area. Hence, the seven areas seemed to constitute an appropriate set of subjects for studying population movement within the field of symbolic logic, during the period 1847–1932. The Markov chain representing this movement, thus, consisted of seven states, $E_j, j = 1, 2, ..., 7$, where E_1 represents the algebra of logic, E_2 the foundations of arithmetic, E_3 the paradoxes of set theory, E_4 the propositional calculus, E_5 mathematics and logic, E_6 metamathematics, and E_7 intuitionism.

An individual was said to be in the state E_i, $i = 1, 2, ..., 7$, at time t if he was contributing to the literature of the subject area represented by E_i at time t. A one step transition from the state E_i to the state E_j was said to occur if an individual who was contributing to E_i made a contribution to the literature represented by the state E_j in his next publication. The one step transition probabilities p_{ij} for the states representing the seven subject areas of symbolic logic were estimated in the following manner. If n was the total number of contributors to the area E_i as determined from the Church index and m the number of these contributors making one step transitions from

E_i to E_j, then the conditional probability p_{ij} of a one step transition from E_i to E_j was taken to be approximately equal to m/n. Proceeding in this fashion for all possible state transitions, we obtained the following matrix P of transition probabilities (Table 4).

TABLE 4   Matrix of transition probabilities for seven major subject areas of symbolic logic

	E_1	E_2	E_3	E_4	E_5	E_6	E_7
E_1	0.58	0.11	0.01	0.20	0.10	0.00	0.00
E_2	0.03	0.38	0.21	0.09	0.22	0.03	0.04
E_3	0.04	0.10	0.62	0.07	0.06	0.06	0.05
E_4	0.14	0.12	0.02	0.64	0.05	0.02	0.01
E_5	0.04	0.21	0.07	0.08	0.52	0.04	0.04
E_6	0.00	0.14	0.18	0.09	0.18	0.41	0.00
E_7	0.00	0.12	0.22	0.04	0.22	0.00	0.40

Estimates of the initial probabilities a_j, $j = 1, 2, \ldots, 7$, were obtained as follows. Let N be the total number of contributors to the seven subject areas and N_j the number of contributors whose first publication was indexed by Church under the subject E_j. Then N_j/N will be taken as an estimate of the initial probability a_j, i.e. the probability that a researcher entered the field of symbolic logic with a contribution to the subject E_j. On this basis, the initial probability distribution $\{a_j\}$ was as follows.

$$
\begin{array}{ccccccc}
a_1 & a_2 & a_3 & a_4 & a_5 & a_6 & a_7 \\
0.19 & 0.14 & 0.23 & 0.18 & 0.16 & 0.04 & 0.06
\end{array}
$$

Thus, the Markov chain representing the population movement in the field of symbolic logic from 1847 through 1932 was completely described by its initial probabilities $\{a_j\}$ and its matrix of transition probabilities P.

Clearly, this Markov chain is irreducible since every state could be reached from every other state. Furthermore, all states were ergodic since

$$\lim_{n \to \infty}{}^{(n)} p_{ij} = u_j$$

with the following values, for every state E_j.

$$
\begin{array}{ccccccc}
u_1 & u_2 & u_3 & u_4 & u_5 & u_6 & u_7 \\
0.12 & 0.18 & 0.20 & 0.21 & 0.19 & 0.05 & 0.05
\end{array}
$$

Since every state was ergodic, the distribution $\{u_j\}$ was stationary. Furthermore, the values of $\{u_j\}$ were not significantly different from the corresponding values of the initial distribution $\{a_j\}$. Consequently, the Markov chain was stationary. It is interesting to note that the limiting probabilities $\{u_j\}$ were also approximately equal to the intensities of the epidemic processes (Table 1) representing each of the corresponding subject areas. Each intensity being the ratio of contributors in that area to the total number of contributors in the entire field, one would expect such a ratio to approximate the absolute probability that an individual will be in the given state after a considerable length of time. It seems, therefore that the Markov chain constituted a realistic representation of the population movement.

Given a stationary Markov chain with a finite number of states E_i and a matrix of transition probabilities p_{ij}, $i, j, = 1, 2, \ldots, n$. If the chain is in the state E_i, then its transition to the different states E_j forms a finite scheme[6]. The entropy

$$H_i = -\sum_{j=1}^{n} p_{ij} \log p_{ij}$$

can be regarded as a measure of the uncertainty of the chain when it moves one step ahead from the state E_i. The one step entropies of the movement of population among the seven major subject areas of symbolic logic were the following.

H_1	H_2	H_3	H_4	H_5	H_6	H_7
0.41	0.69	0.58	0.51	0.63	0.62	0.65

The logs were taken to the base ten. Thus, the greatest uncertainty occurred when individuals moved from the foundations of arithmetic to other subjects while the least occurred for the movement of individuals from the algebra of logic.

The entropy $H = 0.69$ of the finite scheme of stationary probabilities u_j, indicated the extreme uncertainty of predicting the state of an individual at a given point in time. Therefore, it appeared that there was no predictable pattern in the movement of research workers among the major subject areas of symbolic logic during the period between 1847 and 1932.

References

1. W. Goffman, and V. A. Newill, "Communication and epidemic processes", *Proc. Roy. Soc. (London)*, A, **298**, 316–34 (1967).

2. W. Goffman, "Mathematical approach to the spread of scientific ideas: the history of mast cell research", *Nature*, **212**, 449–52 (1966).
3. A. Church, "A bibliography of symbolic logic", *J. Symbolic Logic*, **1**, 121–218 (1936).
4. A. Church, "Additions and corrections to a bibliography of symbolic logic", *J. Symbolic Logic*, **3**, 178–212 (1938).
5. W. Hurewicz, *Lectures on Ordinary Differential Equations*, M.I.T. Press, Cambridge, Mass. (1958).
6. A. I. Khinchin, *Mathematical Foundations of Information Theory*, Dover Publications, New York (1957).

Organization of mathematical systems

PRESTON C. HAMMER

Computer Science Department
The Pennsylvania State University U.S.A.

Summary

In this paper a review is given of the conclusions of the author stemming from work on the systematization of mathematics. This includes delineation of fundamental concepts such as filters, continuity, and accessibility and a formal chart of elemental mathematical systems; its first of which was created by the author in 1967. The inefficiency of present means of mathematical instruction is pointed out—myriads of facts and details are presented without presenting principles or structures. In particular it will be shown that transitive binary relations can be used as a foundation for approximation spaces, for measure theory, and for filter theory.

INTRODUCTION

Mathematics has a much longer history than many sciences and, perhaps partly for this reason, it remains in a state of disorganization. In fact it was not until George Cantor formulated his set theory that it could be considered feasible to attempt an organization of mathematical systems. In chemistry, in contrast, Mendeleev proposed his periodic chart of the elements in the mid-19th century, cellular structure of living organisms was introduced earlier and Mendel had announced his genetic laws. No basic fault has been found with the general taxonomy scheme for biology advocated by Linnaeus.

In physics, it is true, the Newton's laws of mechanics provided a main thrust and thrusts were received from Maxwell's theory of electromagnetic waves and Mendeleev's chart. However, the detailed structure of atoms and molecules awaited Rutherford, Bohr, and others. The special relativity theory of Einstein served to emphasize the tentative state of physical theories. Why is it then that mathematics, created by man, should have delayed so long a development of a schema? The answer seems to lie in consistent (or inconsistent) misinterpretations of symbolic structures in relationship to reality. The will to believe and to do work exceeded the will to perceive and to interpret. Thus Newton's mechanics was treated as a rational interpretation of the universe rather than a model which should be exploited for its merits and regarded with skepticism insofar as claims to intrinsically representing phenomena are concerned. It was not until Lobachewsky fought and won the battle for his geometry that seeds of doubt concerning the validity of Euclidean geometry as a branch of physics were raised.

Mathematicians, in short, reached in many directions but failed to obtain a picture of the whole. While the foundations were started in the nineteenth century culminating with Cantor's work, it remained for the twentieth century mathematicians to explicitly expound a principle of abstractness. In this principle these are the germs of the possibility of providing a systematic background for mathematics. Unfortunately, abstraction and generality were confused and to this day most mathematicians have little idea as to their distinction.

Abstraction, as the word suggests, is a result of removing from complex situations certain simple features amenable to discourse and thought. Thus the plane of the Greek geometers is an abstraction from physical surfaces no one of which does it represent well in detail. Euclidean geometry was practical because it reduced drastically the amount of information perceived in the physical world and yet contained enough information and maneuverability to apply to myriads of situations. Thus an abstraction is a projection in which customarily much information is lost but in which human comprehension and use is more nearly possible. A generalization, on the other hand, of a given system is a system which embraces the particular system and more. Thus a generalization of Euclidean geometry, such as n-dimensional geometry embraces the Euclidean geometry and much else.

Mathematicians customarily regard generalization as an escape from doing honest hard work. By and large mathematicians work with axiomatized systems laid down by others with little regard for their validity or sense. The attitude thus indicated is self-defeating. To see, in a general way what topological spaces are, means that they must be embedded in more general systems which enable comparisons. I have given a series of generalizations of topological spaces including those of Frechet and others and each serves to illuminate topology as well as to establish communications between topology and other fields.

My conclusion is that mathematics education ignores a fundamental fact. It is easier to comprehend general principles than it is to become proficient in a complex subsystem. Thus, if I can define "continuity" so as to embrace phenomena in the experience of children, then children may be taught the general concept of continuity. However, they will not thereby become proficient with continuous functions of a real variable. Is it reasonable, I ask, to never reach the general concept of continuity while inefficiently dealing with large numbers of examples? This then is my conclusion. If mathematics is to be considered a science efficiency in teaching and learning it is necessary. As it is today, an enormous waste of energy is involved in failing to present basic concepts early, in fact in failing to present them at all.

Suppose the premise is granted. The problem then is to search out the basic concepts and general principles and to then embed them in the educational system. The so-called new mathematics in the United States today is a faint-hearted gesture in this direction. It is in a good direction since sets are discussed early and authors of text books are trying to present some of the essentials. It is faint-hearted simply because there is inadequate knowledge of which concepts are basic and because, evidently, too many mathematicians cherish their recent researches as both useless and esoteric. For example, I have suggested to research workers in semigroups that every engineering student should know about them. Their reaction, universally has been: why should engineers know about semigroups? In other words they believe their work is futile. Yet the fact remains that a pupil in learning to carry in adding positive integers experiences a nice example of a semigroup. The next experience is a partial groupoid: subtraction in the positive integers, is a binary operation not defined for every ordered pair, it is not commutative, not associative, and has no identity! Granted the stupidity of the nomenclature, in which semigroups and partial groupoids should be discussed before groups, are we really respecting the intelligence of our children in withholding names for systems they experience?

Note that the nomenclature starts with rather specific and comparatively rare systems (groups) and suggests that these be introduced before the more general and hence more accessible concepts of semigroups and partial groupoids. This blunder in nomenclature is a standard sort in mathematics. The history of the term "number" should provide a counteracting force.

The concept of number was generalized several times using the same word— positive integers, positive rationals, all integers, real numbers, and complex numbers. Why not call partial groupoids groups, unless we can get a better term?

Now cybernetics might be termed loosely as a study of dynamical systems with a certain emphasis on the alteration of the system due to its own action, i.e. feedback. My paper relates to cybernetics in several ways. First there is the problem: how shall mathematics education and in general all education be improved? In this case the systems are complexes comprised of individuals learning, teaching, and administering as well as the influences and contexts of society. At what level should new concepts be introduced? Experience suggests the importance of educating the teachers, as well as of providing the materials and societal forces to enable these to teach. Teachers with some understanding and a sense of mission then alter the modes of education of the pupils. As these pupils reach the college level, they are prepared for another stage in education—and here in the U.S., at least, the system breaks down. There is virtually no new mathematics in the first two years of college! Thus the cybernetic system of education flaws in a critical place—college mathematics. The question is: how can college mathematics be compelled to improve. Here is where the feedback loop breaks down.

The difficulty rests primarily in the selfishness of eminent mathematicians who have the position but not the intention to push for fundamental reforms. The new generation of mathematicians hopefully may have more social consciousness, the determination, and the patience to provide the stimulus needed.

Let us now consider the feedback in terms of teaching general concepts. As the pupil learns where mathematics fits in the culture, as he learns patterns big enough to embrace particular systems he will, on specialization be much more effective. In particular, he can discuss his work with laymen in general terms and explain what relevance it has. He will understand the kind of work of all other specialists and will have added sources of inspiration. In short he will know whom he may help and from whom he may seek help. As he will naturally be dissatisfied with his state of knowledge he will accordingly work for a better education of the next generation. He should have a balance between confidence, inspired by knowledge of the relevance of his work, and confusion inspired by his knowledge of the limitations of knowledge.

How should these changes be effected? I think that an international effort is indicated to identify general concepts and principles, to weigh their educational advantages, to appraise the continuing alterations needed in the light of new knowledge. It is still the case that excellent expositions presented in inexpensively available books can have a widespread influence. The mathematical literature has improved, it needs now big improvements on the level of conscious evaluation.

In what follows, I must let the reader down, by presenting the results of my personal efforts to understand mathematics. This is not meant to be a conclusive final report. It is based on the philosophy that mathematics is a science which should provide some of the information needed to understand our environments. Lest it be thought that I am being humble, let me hasten to deny it. I have shed more light on the concept of "continuity", for example, than had been perceived in the some 140 years of the mathematical treatment of the concept. Having done this, I realize how ignorant I am of the ramifications and specializations. Of the now rather large numbers of concepts I have tackled with cynicism and faith, I select a few to illustrate both views.

ACCESSIBILITY

In this section I choose to enlarge on a few aspects of the very important concept of accessibility. Insofar as I know, this concept has not before been emphasized although it is readily seen to be of importance. Roads, airplanes, ships, churches, microscopes, telephones, radio, television, glasses, books, magazines, stores, banks, factories, X-rays, accelerators, space-ships, money, radar, universities, schools, organizations, theorems, weapons, medicines, cooking, and so on all provide, in their way, increased access to something. Thus, if the term were used early in education and examples given there would be provided a common denominator for the discussion of related activities. Of course, the negative aspect of accessibility needs also to be emphasized. Many people have insufficient access to food, shelter and education. Doctors can scarcely diagnose states of health, mathematics applies only in restricted cases, the crust of the earth conceals information, the message in a given stone cannot be decoded, much of conceivably important history is lost, children are denied access to poisons (usually) and the medical literature is inaccessible to the general public. New technical languages limit access to special fields.

One of the poor features of education in general is the continual emphasis on the positive, neglecting mention of shortcomings and inadequacies which should in fact challenge the young. But, this is a discussion of mathematics.

In one aspect mathematics provides access to information of certain kinds. The theorem of Pythagoras, for example, shows the functional relationship among the lengths of the sides of a right triangle. This Theorem is used then in geometry to indeed help measure the earth as the term geometry suggests. It is used in surveying astronomy, architecture, engineering, physics, chemistry, and so on. Now consider the situation of this theorem with respect to logic. Granted the hypothesis of a right triangle, the conclusion drawn can be logically no stronger than the hypothesis. Thus, no logical advantage is gained from it. However, theorems provide access to information for *people* to use.

Thus, even if the conclusion is derivable from the assumption, it is of no use unless *people* know it. The proofs (they are numerous) of this Theorem are for the purpose of convincing people that the conclusion is safe to use, i.e. the information is valid. Incidentally, the identification of right triangles, as a concept is not an act of deduction but of induction.

We now consider measures of inaccessibility or measures of separation. I shall return to the general concept of measure later on. The obvious mathematical and real-world measures of separation are those of *distances* stated in a number of units. Now the so-called metric system is a coherent physical system of units of measurement. These units are revised from time to time and are hence empirical. In mathematics a generalization of theoretical distance, first by M. Fréchet, I believe, is called a *metric* function.

The axioms commonly accepted for a metric function which ascribes a real number to each pair of points from a set E are as follows.

(1) $d(x, y) \geqslant 0$ and $d(x, y) = 0$ if and only if $x = y$. This axiom I call the axiom of *positive definiteness*.

(2) $d(x, z) = d(x, y) + d(y, z)$. Thus is called the *triangular inequality* from the image that x, y, z are vertices of a triangle.

(3) $d(x, y) = d(y, x)$ (distance is *symmetric*).

Concerning this system of axioms defining a metric function certain comments are appropriate. First of all there are many examples of mathematical systems in which these axioms hold, Euclidean plane and solid geometry, from which they were in part derived being such. They also hold for distances to be measured on surfaces; for example, if E is the surface of a sphere and $d(x, y)$ is the length of a great circular arc joining x and y, then the axioms hold. Further study has turned up a huge collection of possible metric functions some of which have been subject to detailed study such as those generated by norms in linear vector spaces.

Now, to many mathematicians, this concept of a metric function is fully satisfactory and to some, such as classical geometers, it is too general. You might say, that with infinities of different possibilities surely this treatment is adequate, or even too general. I shall now burst such an illusion. I claim, in fact, that this concept of distance is too limited to cover applications, even mathematical applications *known* at the time of its formulation. In fact, I shall show that each of the axioms may be dropped for some reasons and that *all* of them must be dropped for one kind of application!

Before proceeding to discuss the axiom system, let me state my stand. Fréchet liberated distances from rigid geometrical interpretation by introducing his axioms. He also introduced an écart which was more general. Much work has been profitably done on metric spaces as defined by Fréchet. Thus, the formulation is important, it is useful, and it was a definite advance in its time. However, the enthusiasm with which the concept was received resulted in blinding the enthusiasts to the fact that no mathematical system should become enshrined. There is an adage appropriate here: "You never miss the water until the well runs dry." You might, that is to say, get a limited form of comprehension of metric functions by confining yourself to this definition. However, to achieve more complete understanding you must also study what may be achieved without each of the axioms. How will you understand an axiom unless you have done without it?

Now I consider axiom 3 assuming the other two. This axiom states that the distance from x to y is the same as the distance from y to x. Hence the form "the distance between x and y" is a better indication of how $d(x, y)$ should be read. Do you know of measures of distances where this condition does not hold? Our tribal forebears probably measured distances in terms of days required to get from one place to another.

Is the distance, using canoes for travel, the same from a point x on a river to a point y downstream as it is from y to x? Certainly not! Is the time of travel from one place to another the same as from the other to one? Only rarely. Thus, even while the first two axioms are germane, the third one excludes many important distance concepts. The distance may also be measured in energy required. The famous brachistchrone problem of the calculus of variations measures the distance from a point at a higher horizontal to a lower one in terms of the time a particule could slide from one to the other under the influence of gravity on a frictionless path. In this case, the first two axioms are satisfied but if $d(x, y) > 0$ then there is no $d(y, x)$! In short here distance is completely asymmetrical. Minkowski, a great geometer, introduced a large variety of asymmetrical distances based on convex sets. Thus metric functions do not embrace all distances. Working with the reduced set of axioms would certainly increase appreciation of symmetry when it is present!

Now let me consider axioms 1 and 2. Are there any realistic measures of separation which satisfy none of these axioms? Indeed there are. Let me now use an economic measure, the net *cost* of travelling from one place to another. Except for considerations I shall introduce in a moment, the cost of transportation would satisfy the first two and in some cases be symmetric. However, suppose a payment is made to the traveller for his journey and activities. Then the cost could be *negative* and in such circumstances *none* of the axioms may apply. For example, I once flew from San Diego to Wilmington, Delaware, and then to Madison, Wisconsin. For this trip my expenses were repaid and I received an honorarium for a lecture given near Wilmington. The net cost (i.e. distance) from San Diego to Madison was negative. On the other hand, the triangle law does not hold since I should have had to pay my own expenses if I had gone directly from San Diego to Madison, i.e. $d(x, z) \not< d(x, y) + d(y, z)$. Moreover, the distance was asymmetric.

Now this simple example serves to illustrate a more basic fact. Insofar as people are concerned, the distance from where they are to where they are going is generally negative. That is if, in the total, it were judged better not to go from one place to another why would one do it? Thus there is no sound reason that distances must be positive, or satisfy the triangle law, or be symmetric. To deal with problems of economics or more generally of satisfaction, negative distances are necessary.

This brings me to another striking example of recalcitrant distances. I speak of the distances between people in terms say, of blood kinship. This kind of distance, important in legislation and society, is *not* real-valued, it is not symmetric, and the triangle law is inapplicable in general. For example, the relationship father to son is not the same as son to father. One person x may be a close relative of y and y may be a close relative of z with no known relationship between x and z. This the weak transitivity of closeness which is one effect of the triangle law does not hold. The complexities of distances in family trees are great. I claim that the common language here provided a better clue to distance than the mathematical abstraction of Fréchet.

I conclude this section on accessibility then with the observation that it is impossible to understand mathematics in isolation. If we confine terms used in common language to smaller mathematical concepts we cannot indicate the relevance and irrelevance of mathematics.

SIZES AND MEASURES

Having already set an outlook, I now proceed with the important general concepts of sizes and measures. In the previous chapter I undertook to discuss briefly the concept of distance as a measure of separation or inaccessibility. I found that the metric functions as customarily axiomatized were too restrictive. Here I deal with concepts sometimes considered as absolute. Thus the height of a person is a number (pragmatically), but it is not a comparison of a separation of two objects. Thus at first glance sizes or measures assign numbers to objects which are in that regard their value. However, one objective of the activity of measuring is to establish comparisons which may be thought of as distances.

Now sizes and measures are used everywhere in modern society, so no difficulty arises in providing examples at any age, even preschool. This very usage indicates their importance and thus the words may be and are used from an early age. Without having looked into the matter I assume that much of this is already done in school. However, suppose the pupil progresses through calculus and advanced calculus and comes finally to measure theory. Then he is supposed to divorce almost every measure he knows from that limited technical use of measures. Why is at that Lebesgue seized on the name of such an important concept for his comparatively small system? For, Lebesgue's theory of measures and other theories of measures in mathematics do not have the scope which this concept had *prior* to its reduction by Lebesgue.

If we are to properly educate the young, we should avoid misappropriation of terms. Now I shall not write down the axioms for the measure theory of analysis. I refuse to concede that the term should have been used at all. This contrasts with metric functions where Fréchet generalized previous mathematical usage. A metric is a measure of separation. It is not a measure of so-called measure theory. The cardinal number of a set is a measure of it—beyond the pale of measure theory. The norm of a function is a measure of it, not embraced in measure theory. The *dimensions* of an object comprise a vector measure of it—but it is not included in measure theory. The diameter of a set is a measure of it, but it is excluded from measure theory. The net worth of a business is a measure. In fact, there is no excuse for having used the term measure for a small area of mathematics.

Now, having stated what should have been observed long ago, let me give an example of a possible abstraction of the concept of measure which does embrace examples I have mentioned. As I indicated there is no use in removing axioms from Lebesgue's definition, it is and was a good definition, but not of measures.

The image I propose is that measuring ordinarily involves two kinds of activity. One is to assign to an object another object to be its measure and then to compare the measures of objects in the value space of the measure. For this purpose then, I shall assume a function assigning measures to certain elements of a set and an order relation in the value space which provides comparisons. I shall assume only this to begin with since even the assumption of an order relation might be too limited.

Let X be a set and let E be a subset of X. Let f be a function mapping E into a set V and let T be a transitive relation (i.e. on order relation) in V. Here T will be considered as a subset of $V \times V$, i.e. T is a set of ordered pairs (p, q) such that p, q are elements of V. If $(p_1, p_2) \in T$ and $(p_2, p_3) \in T$ then transitivity requires that $(p_1, p_3) \in T$.

Definition. In the circumstances mentioned above f, T is called a V-valued measure in X (on E).

This definition now gives a certain scope for developing theories of measures. I believe that such a definition, due to its simplicity can be used effectively to discuss a great variety of measures. Note that there is nothing actually in the framework concerning real numbers. Examples abound of such functions and such transitive relations. Thus a careful presentation could be given in high school, say without introducing the infinite processes of Lebesgue's theory.

Examples

I do not choose to develop in any detail a theory of measures since it would lead me far afield. I do wish to establish without reasonable doubt that *no* specialization of what I have propounded will suffice to embrace practical measures. I do this by examples. First, note that I interpret the order relation T as follows. If $p, q, \in E$, and $(f(p), f(g)) \in T$ then the measure of p is less than or equal to the measure of q. While V may be a subset of the real numbers, this is not necessary as we shall show. Two measures (f, T), (g, S) which are defined on E with values in sets V and W respectively are *order-equivalent* provided $(f(p)f(g)) \in T$ and $(g(p), g(q)) \in S$ both hold or both do not for all pairs $p, q \in E$. Let S be an order relation in X. Then the V-valued measure f, T is order-compatible with S provided $p, q, \varepsilon, E(p, q) \in S$ implies $(f(p), f(q)) \in T$.

Cardinal Number of Sets

Let X be a collection of sets and let $fA = |A|$, the cardinal number of A. Let T be the usual ordering of cardinal numbers. Then (f, T) is a V-valued measure where V is the set of cardinal numbers. This measure is excluded from Lebesgue's theory because it is not real-valued.

Diameters of Sets in Metric Spaces

Let d be a metric function defined on a set C. Let X be the power set of C and define fA, for $A \in X$ as the supremum of the set $\{d(a, b) : a, b, \varepsilon A\}$, where fA may be ∞. Here f is basically real-valued non-negative, and the usual ordering of real numbers is T. Now let S be the inclusion ordering in X, i.e. $(A, B) \in S$ means $A \subseteq B$. This measure f, T is compatible with S since $A \subseteq B$ implies $fA \leqslant fB$. Now fA is called the *diameter* of the set A. Since the diameter of the union of two disjoint sets in general has no particular relationship to the diameters of the separate sets, except to be no less than either the function is not additive and is not embraced in measure theory.

Projection Measures

To be explicit in this case, let E be the class of all bounded subsets of 3-space. Let fA for $A \in E$ be the vector (f_1A, f_2A, f_3A) where f_iA is the diameter of the projection of the set A on the x_i axis. Now the values of f are in the positive octant of 3-space. Order relation T is given by $(x_1, x_2, x_3) \leqslant (y_1, y_2, y_3)$, provided $x_1 \leqslant y_1, x_2 \leqslant y_2$, and $x_3 \leqslant y_3$. Then (f, T) is a measure which is vector valued. It is not additive and it would not be additive if the projection of A on the x_i axis were assigned. Since (width, depth, height) are important measures, there is no reason for excluding them.

Measures of Integers

Let E be the set of positive integers, and let $f(n)$ be the number of divisors of n. Here $f(n)$ has values in E and the usual order is presumed, i.e. the more divisors or integers it has, the greater its measure. Note that f, T is not *compatible* with T since $m < n$ does not imply $fm < fn$. This is obviously a measure, well recognized as important in number theory.

Measures of Integers which are Sets

Let E be the set of positive integers and let $f(n)$ be the *set* of divisors of n. Now V is the power set of E and I use T as the inclusion ordering. Is there any reason that a set should not be a value of a measure? I see no objection. Here, if S is the usual order for E, again (f, T) is not compatible with S. Now I state the following result readily verified.

Theorem. Let (f, T) be a V-valued measure in X on E. Then the relation S defined in E by $(p, q) \in S$ provided $(f(p), f(q)) \in T$ is an order relation in E (and hence in X). Then S is called the *identity* measure on E induced by (f, T).

The reason for using a value space $V \neq E$ is simply that most measures have external references and the values are used for manipulation. Consider the current example. It would not make sense for many purposes to simply report the (f, T)-induced order S in E, since it would obscure how I generated S.

Packing Measures

Let X be the class of all subsets of the plane and let X be a subclass of X. To each element A (i.e. set) in Y let a positive number tA be assigned. No wlet a planar set $B = X$ be given. Let $Y_i(B)$ range over all subclasses of Y with the following properties. If $A \in Y_i(B)$ then $A = B$. If $A_1, A_2 \in Y_i(B)$ then $A_1 A_2$ is empty. To each class $Y_i(B)$ let $f_i(B) = \Sigma\{tA : A \in Y_i(B)\}$. (I allow the value ∞, and 0 if no $A \in Y_i A - B$ exists. Then let $f(B) = \sup_i\{f_i(B)\}$. Then f has values on $[0; \infty]$ and, with usual ordering T of real numbers, f, T is a measure. Various selections of Y, t lead to packing measures—such as the number of units radius open circular disks which are contained in B. Note that it is also possible here to assign to fB instead the value $fB = \{Y_i(B)\}$ which would mean that fB has values on the second power set of the plane. These measures are outside measure theory in general but may include them.

Real-valued Measures

Let X be a family of functions integrable in $[0, 1]$. Let $t \in X$ let $f(t) = \int_0^1 t(s)\, ds$.

Take the usual ordering of the real numbers. Now $f(t)$ is the mean value of t and the integral mean of a function is certainly a measure of it. The set V now consists of all real numbers.

Now I rest the case on measures although I have not included norms of vectors and functions, function-valued measures, dimensions of spaces, degrees of polynomials and so on. It should be obvious that measures should indeed not be restricted to the ones included in measure theory of analysis— not even for the purpose of advancing that theory.

FILTERS

In generalizing the concept of continuity (next section) I spent several (about 12) years before I reached the objective of getting a general statement concerning its characteristics. Then a casual glance in a dictionary showed that the common language concept was virtually the same as I had, at great pains, achieved! When filters first came to my active attention, I did not spend so much time. What, I asked, do electronic filters, cigarette filters, chemical filters do? They separate things into two parts. Hence I defined shortly some of the concepts of a mathematical filter.

A *filter* in a set E is any device which produces an *ordered* dichotomy (A, B) on the set, where $A \cup B = E$, A and B are disjoint. The elements of A are *accepted* by the filter, the elements of B are *rejected*.

Before objections are raised, let me clarify. I deliberately used the filter as a *device* since that is what it is in practice whereas the *action* of the filter is expressed in the resulting dichotomy. Now one nice thing about filters is that they are ubiquitous. Children have many examples. Everyone has many examples and even mathematics has many examples. Hence the concept of filters is a natural one to use to unify mathematics while at the same time displaying various kinds of filters all around us.

Factories have go–no go gages (they are filters), St. Peter is reported also to have such a gage. Pupils pass or fail according to a filtering action. Every conjunction of filters is a filter. Every equivalence relation can be determined by filters. An equation is a filter passing those objects which satisfy it and rejecting others. A differential requation is a filter, side conditions are filters and restricting solutions to being analytic (relativization) is a filtering.

Such a general idea, you may say, how can anything be done with it? The answer strangely enough is that filters may be used as an approach to mathematics, in its entirety. But no! You mean can I do something *hard*? I have already done something which, while not in one sense difficult, had escaped the notice of previous men. I have filtered out the concept of filters!

However, I appreciate the reluctance to learn something new without justification. I consider it a reasonable demand to show worthiness since there are many new ideas which compete for our attention. First, however, I mention that a large part of the value of the concept of filters is not directly technical. They could, I believe, be a key feature in basically advancing mathematics education by making mathematics easier to learn.

In order to give some idea about filters without taking too much pace, I first mention a few other kinds and then I develop a few details about one kind I have contributed. It should first of all be clear that most of the filters I know of have been constructed by others without use of the concept. A function f mapping a set E into a set E_1 is a collection of filters in E_1 in the sense that x, f accepts $f(x)$ and rejects all other possibilities in E_1. Let $R \subseteq FXE$ be a binary relation. Then let $a \in F$. Then (a, R) is a filter which accepts all elements b of E such that $(a, b) \in R$. For example, suppose F is a set of French words and E is a set of English words and R is a simple French-to-English dictionary, i.e. each French word is followed by a list of English words which might replace it in translation.

Now consider the set $v(a)$ of English words which follow a French word a. Then $(R, v(a))$ can be used as a filter which accepts all French words each of which is followed by all the English words in $v(a)$. Let the resulting set of accepted French words be $uv(a)$. Now $a \in u(v(a))$ and perhaps other French words as well. Study of such sets would be of interest. The point is that a dictionary is a filtering device. These relational filters, incidentally were studied by O. Öre as Galois connections.

I now move to a more complex situation generalizing aspects of convexity theory. The basic idea is that of neighbourhood filters of topology. The underlying relation R then is the collection $\{(X, Y) : X \cap Y \neq \emptyset\}$ of all pairs of intersecting sets from a space E. Now, if I should choose a class V_0 of subsets of E, I could form a filter (R, V_0) accepting all sets X such that $(X, Y) R$ for *all* $Y \in V_0$. Suppose sets U_0 form a general neighborhood base for a point X in E. The class $C(x)$ accepted by (R, V_0) is the class of sets "close" to X. Letting $(C(x), R)$ be a filter, then the class of sets $V(x)$ accepted is the class of all neighbourhoods of x, the ancestial closure of V_0. I called sets in $C(x)$ the *convergents* of X.

Now let $= \{T_i : i \in I$, an ideal set$\}$ where T_i is an order (i.e. transitive) relation. Let $u_i(x) = \{y : (x, y) \in T\}$, i.e. $u_i(x)$ is the set of all elements of E which follow x in the relation T_i. Now I let $V_0(x) = \{u_i(x) : i \in I\}$ forming a neighbourhood base for x. The class $C(x)$ of sets accepted by the filter $(R, V_0(x))$ is hence comprised of sets A which intersect each "cone" $u_i(x)$. Now let us define a set-valued set function f as follows: $x \in fA$ providing $A \in C(x)$. That is fA is comprised of all elements x of which A is a convergent. This function f on extreme specialization could be the convex hull function in a linear vector space.

An element x of A is called a u_i—extreme point of A provided $Y \in A u_i(x)$ implies $(y, x) \in T_i$. That is x is an extreme point provided no element of A is *properly* greater (in T_i^-) sense)) than x.

Let the set of all u_i-extreme points of A for all $i \in I$ be designated vA. Then $vA = A$ and $v(vA) = vA$.

A set A is u_i—compact provided every complete chain $\{x_\alpha\}$ from A ascending strictly in T_i order has a maximum element. The set A is upper-compact provided it is u_i compact for every $i \in I$. Finally a word concerning the function f. The function f is isotonic, i.e. $A \subseteq B$ implies $fA \subseteq fB$ and $f(fA) \subseteq fA$, i.e. f is subpotent. The latter condition is a consequence of transitivity. Now it may be readily established that $fA \supseteq A$ always if and only if every one of the order relations is reflexive, i.e. $(x, x) \in T_i$ for each c and for every $i \in I$. In this latter special case f is a closure function since $f(fA) = fA$ then. However, I do not require reflexivity.

Theorem A. Let $B \subseteq A$. Then a necessary and sufficient condition that $fB = fA$ is that B be a convergent of every point x in fA, i.e. that $B \cap u_i(x) \neq \emptyset$ for every i where $x \in fA$. In particular this statement holds when $B = vA$ the set of all extreme points of A.

This theorem scarcely needs proof. It provides the strongest condition available relating extreme points to convex sets if fA is indeed the convex hull function.

Theorem B. Let A be an upper compact set. Then $fvA = fA$.

This theorem, which I have proved elsewhere does require some proof. It is, to date, the strongest of its kind. Now these results are not extensive but the opportunities for research opened are numerous and attractive. It should be noted that I have here stated some of the fundamental results of convexity theory (previously unknown) in a context of transitive relations above. There was imposed in E none of the other trappings of linear vector spaces. In fact the theory here is basically easier to grasp than the specialized cases such as the Krein–Milman theorem.

CONTINUITY

Ask a mathematics student to define continuity and you will get something about epsilons and deltas or something concerning inverse images of neighborhoods being neighborhoods. These cases are examples of continuity but they are not nice examples. In fact, I may go further and say that the continuities dealt with in analysis and topology are about as far from a natural concept of continuity as we can get. As a result of this misunderstanding, it is little wonder that students fail to grasp the content of continuity.

Having written several papers on continuity which may be examined I shall concentrate on the gist and examples. Continuity is one of the ways of circumscribing classes of functions. For certain purposes, continuous functions are good, others are bad. I have decided, and this decision is the product of years of work, that continuity and invariance are dual aspects of the same notion. That is, a function is continuous with respect to whatever properties or operations or relations it preserves or leaves invariant. Which properties are to be preserved is a matter of choice. This is, continuity is not an intrinsic property of a function. Every function preserves something, and is hence continuous, but not even the identity function can always be termed continuous. This state of affairs was actually brought about in general topology but it is little recognized.

Having made the statement concerning continuity and being backed by the dictionaries you might say: Well, it is an amusing thought but can you do anything with it? The answer is yes! In fact, I might do a lot with it granted energy, talent, and time. I have identified in this fashion as the same sort, algebraic homomorphisms and topological homomorphisms. The former preserves operations, the latter preserves continuity. The former tends to be a strong form of continuity, the latter one weak. Consider, for example, the fact that every constant function is continuous in topological space context. What of the structure of the domain can be preserved in a single element? Very little. On the other hand, among algebraic homomorphisms, the constant function is possible only when there is an identity element for all operations and that must be the constant value. Between algebraic and topological homomorphisms there is a spectrum of unstudied continuities.

Now to avoid introducing too much and yet to do enough, I restrict myself to the context of functions f mapping each subset of space E onto a subset of E. However, your choice is allowed for the function f. I grant similar freedom in choice for a function g mapping the power at if a second space E_1 into itself. Now let t be a function mapping E into E_1. I define t to be (f, g)—*continuous at* p provided $p \in fA$ implies $t(p) \in g(tA)$ where A ranges over subsets of E and $tA \subseteq \{t(p) : p \in A\}$. Again t is (f, g)—continuous provided it is (f, g) continuous at each $p \in E$. In short $t(fA) = g(tA)$ if t is (f, g) continuous.

Let me now give one an interpretation. First, if f and g are Kuratowski closure functions for topological spaces, then my definition coincides with that of topology. Now let me read "$p \in fA$" as "A implies p in the logic f" or "$A \underset{f}{\to} p$". Then $t(p) \in g(tA)$ reads "tA implies $t(p)$ in the logic g" or "$tA \underset{g}{\to} tp$". Then t is (f, g)-continuous at p provided that from $A \underset{f}{\to} p$ there follows $tA \underset{g}{\to} tp$. Hence it is (f, g)-continuous if at *preserves implication* (in this limited context).

Now I give a striking example. Let c_1 and c_1 be respective complement functions for E and E_1, i.e. $cA \equiv E - A$, $c_1B \equiv E_1 - B$.

Theorem. A mapping t from E to E_1, is (c_1c_1)-continuous if and only if it is $1-1$! What does (c, c_1)-continuous functions preserve? The identity of the elements! This is obviously an important form of continuity. To see how far this is from topological continuity, I observe that C satisfies *no one* of the usual four axioms for a Kurotowski closure operator. However, it is subadditive, i.e. $c(X \cup y) \subseteq cX \cup cY$. This shows how little the notion of continuity has to do with topological spaces in which it was heretofore trapped. One dictionary states "continuity denotes identity with respect to a series of changes".

I can provide a few exercises. Limit-point preserving maps have been neglected in topology. Characterize such maps from the plane to the plane. In the context of T_1 spaces, a mapping preserves limit points if and only if it is continuous and the inverse image of every point is discrete. In this case constant functions are *never* continuous, unless the domain has no limit points at all. In this case, by the way, fA is the set of limit points of A.

Suppose now E is a linear vector space, fA is the convex hull of A and E_1 is a linear vector space and gB is the convex hull of B. Characterize mappings T of E onto E_1 such that t is (f, g)-continuous.

The last example gives me another notion. Let E be the plane and for each pair of disjoint points x_1, x_2 in E let $f\{x_1, x_2\} = (x_1, x_2)$ the *open* line segment between x_1 and x_2. Let $fA = \emptyset$ otherwise. Now a mapping t of E into itself is f-continuous (i.e. (f, f)-continuous) provided $tf \subseteq ft$. It may be a surprise to the reader as it was to me that if t satisfies this condition then it is also g-continuous and h-continuous where $g\{x_1, x_2\} = [x_1, x_2]$ the closed segment and $gA = \emptyset$ otherwise, while hX is the convex hull of X.

There are many surprises in this aspect of continuity. There is also much interesting work to be done. Let me point out now how simple it is, in the context of preserving properties, to prove that the composition of two continuous functions is continuous. If you save a property through one mapping and then save it through another you have saved it! This is the gist of myriads of proofs of this statement scattered throughout the mathematical literature. Is it efficient to prove the same result hundreds of times and never see that it is the same? No! Note that continuity applies equally well in finite sets as in infinite. Examples can be given to children.

Acknowledgement

This research is supported by the National Science Foundation, Washington, D.C., grant under Contract GJ-398 for support of "Computer Science Education".

References

1. P.C.Hammer, Editor, *Advances in Mathematical Systems Theory*, The Pennsylvania State University Press, 1969, *Filters in General*, (5), pp. 107–120, *Approximation Spaces*, (6), pp. 121–133, and *Chart of Elemental Mathematics*, (7), pp. 135–151.
2. P.C.Hammer, Isotonic Spaces in Convexity, *Proc. Coll. Convexity*, Copenhagen, 1965–67, pp. 132–141.
3. P.C.Hammer, Problems in Nonlinear Non-Mechanics, *Proceedings of Symposia on Nonlinear Problems in Engin.*, Academic Press, Inc., New York, 1964, pp. 208–216.
4. P.C.Hammer, Topologies of Approximation, *SIAM J. of Soc. and Appl. Math. Series B. Numer. Anal.*, I, 1964, pp. 69–75.
5. P.C.Hammer, Extended Topology, Continuity II, Proceedings of the *I. Int. Symposium on Ext. Theory of Topological Structures and its Applications*, Berlin, 1967.
6. P.C.Hammer, The Role and Nature of Mathematics, *The Mathematics Teacher*, Vol. LVII, No. 8, Dec., 1964.

On the foundations of ternary logic and cybernetics

H. A. FATMI and S. RAHMAN

Chelsea College, University of London, U.K.

Summary

Cybernetics involves storage and processing of information on the basis of binary logic. Boole has suggested that it is possible to develop logical system which may be more complex than the binary model. His method is used to evolve a ternary model suitable for cybernetic systems relevant to the nervous system of man and other living organism. Ternary models appear more suitable than binary ones for dealing with consciousness, judicial functions, and decision processes in man.

INTRODUCTION

Cybernetics involves storage and processing of information on the basis of binary logic. The comparative study of information processes in man, animal and machine raises important differences in approach to questions of psychology, mental faculties and their logical basis.

In his famous investigation of the laws of thought Boole (1854) said: "It is a consequence of the fact that the fundamental equation of thought is of the second degree, that we perform the operation of analysis and classification by division into pairs of opposites (by dichotomy)... Now if the equation in question had been of the third degree, still admitting of interpretation as such, the mental division must have been threefold in character, and we must have proceeded by a species of *trichotomy*, the real nature of which it is impossible for us, with our existing faculties adequately to conceive, but the laws of which we might still investigate as an object of intellectual speculation."

In recent times profound differences have emerged between the traditional teaching and current scientific opinion on such questions as consciousness, knowledge, thought, control, and communication, which cannot be adequately conceived on the basis of binary logic. On the basis of dichotomy of thought processes it is customary to say that the ordinary field of human awareness—sensory impressions, thoughts, feelings, and sensations—is the conscious level of mind. There is also an awareness of deeper levels of experience which are termed the unconscious or the subconscious. As Dennis Gabor (1961) wrote in a contribution to *Mind, Meanings and Cybernetics:* "Most of us are quite satisfied with a formulation such as this: 'I have a consciousness, which receives sensory data, from an outer, real, physical world, and images, concepts, and urges from my unconscious mind.'"

The ancient schools of thought, based on hundreds of centuries old tradition, take a radically different view of the field of consciousness. They do not make a division between the conscious and the unconscious but speak rather of different levels of consciousness analogous to the different energy levels of modern physics. Instead of dichotomy they have a polychotomy of consciousness with the highest levels of consciousness existing within man in just that realm of our psychology which is termed "unconscious".

The outer mind to which we assign the role of consciousness is in the ancient scheme at a relatively low level of consciousness. Indeed, it is called "relative consciousness" and is only one step removed from deep sleep. The mind we ordinarily use is limited to reception of sensory data from the outer, physical world. It is merely exploring the superficial levels of experience. It gives us a flat picture of the world. We use it to assemble data, to observe, to communicate. It is the mechanical part of our physical apparatus with which we learn and calculate, analogous to the modern computer. This is the logical mind in which the storage and processing of information takes place on the basis of dichotomy.

In his famous theorem "On formally undecidable propositions of principia mathematica" Kurt Gödel (1931) has shown the limitations of binary logical processes. According to Nagel and Newman (1958), Gödel presented the scientists with the astounding conclusion that the (binary) axiomatic method has certain inherent limitations. He proved that it is impossible to establish the internal logical consistency of a very large class of (binary) deductive systems. In the light of these conclusions no final systematization of many important areas of mathematical sciences is attainable, and no absolutely impeccable guarantee can be given that many significant branches of scientific thought are entirely free from internal contradictions.

This led Hinshelwood (1964) to say: "It seems to me that when one explores any of the really fundamental problems of existence by ordinary conscious (binary) logical methods one arrives at unresolvable contradictions... Human knowledge shall forever remain incomplete unless the dichotomy of the internal and the external is somehow removed." In these states of "relative consciousness" man and animal pass most of their life. Occasionally man experiences the higher states of consciousness in inspiration, discovery, or realization of quite new points of view.

This binary logical mind is full of inherent contradictions. We may therefore, ask as follows. How are these contradictions resolved? Can they ever be resolved? Can the deeper levels of consciousness understood on the basis of trichotomy? Can the deeper levels of consciousness cut through this binary tangle, which Hilbert (1952) has called the maze of binary logical relations? Can we evolve a ternary logical model suitable for dealing with judicial processes in man?

CONSCIOUSNESS, TERNARY LOGIC, AND CYBERNETICS

Sir Arthur Eddington (1939) says in his "Philosophy of Physical Science": "This (binary) logical mind is the group structure of a set of sensations in a consciousness." This raises the question: What is consciousness?

According to Adrian (1964) it is extremely difficult to produce agreed definitions of such words as mind, soul, consciousness, and perception but philosophers would mostly couple "consciousness" with "awareness" and would admit that at least some kind of mental activity can take place without being aware of them... The metaphysical problem has lost its appeal and the attack has moved to the field of natural science... We can study the data on either side of the gap (between mind and matter)...We can try to describe the mental data which needs to be linked to material activities in the brain and on the physical side we can study the chain of material events to see how far they can satisfy us as the basis of human thought... Although some of the gap remains it can now be defined more sharply: it concerns the relation of matter to consciousness rather than reason.

"Relative consciousness is only one step removed from deep sleep. As far as the state of brain is concerned the electroencephalographic evidence would put the state of deep sleep at one end of the scale and the state of concentrated attention at the other, with light sleep and relaxed wakefulness in between. But our moments of inspiration and realisation of new points of view are unfortunately too rare for E.E.G. records to have shown what state the brain is in when they occur, and it must be admitted that E.E.G. records only show one aspect of brain activity." (See Figure 1.)

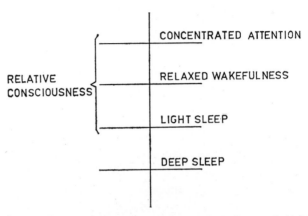

FIGURE 1   Levels of consciousness based upon E.E.G. records (Adrian)

To get further insight into this, we may consider examples of the flash of inspiration which resolves a problem baffling this binary logical mind. Poincaré (1914) relates how after a period of intense mathematical work he went for a journey into the country and dismissed work from his mind: "Just as I put my foot on the step of the brake, the idea came to me ... that the transformations I had used to define Fuchsian functions were identical with those of non-Euclidian geometry." On another occasion when baffled by a problem he went to the seaside and "thought of entirely different things. One day as I was walking on the cliff the idea came to me, again with the same characteristics of conciseness and certainty, that arithmatical transformations of indefinite quadratic forms are identical with those of non-Euclidian geometry." It appears that the nature of these flashes of inspirations is entirely different from physical processes in binary cybernetic systems which relate to our logical mind, whereas inspirations give us a clue to the deeper levels of consciousness.

This deeper process gives us conciseness and certainty and has the effect of integrating everything we have observed and have learned about a particular question. Some of us may have experienced this. Indeed many of the questions with which we start our programmes of research may well have originated in this way. This conciseness and certainty is, as Gödel (1931) has shown, the very quality which is absent from logical processes. This conciseness and certainty, according to ancient thought, springs from levels of knowledge and consciousness within us. The inspiration is a manifestation of this knowledge and consciousness.

Besides these two examples we have an accurate description of yet another discovery, the benzene ring which revolutionised organic chemistry. The discoverer, Kekulé (1890), was writing a chemical textbook: "But it did not go well, my spirit was with other things. I turned the chair to the fire place and sank into a half sleep. The atoms flitted before my eyes. Long rows, variously, more closely, united; all in movement wriggling and turning like snakes. And see what was that? One of the snakes seized its own tail and the image whirled scornfully before my eyes... "As though from a flash of lightening I awoke; I occupied the rest of the night in working out the consequences of the hypothesis... Let us learn to dream, gentlemen."

Born (1967) says: "I myself had in my life perhaps a dozen flashes of ideas which proved to lead to scientifically significant or even important results, just like Kekulé's. To mention the major ones: The discovery of quatum mechanics, the formulae $qp - pq = hi/2\pi$ and the connection of wave mechanics with probability... I am (however) convinced that knowledge consists of the formulation in the mind of a logical consistent image of the world as experienced by the senses... But I know for certain that in the few cases where I have discovered something of importance it came like a flash, and a minute before I knew nothing of it..."

These inspirations come in the briefest moments, striking with the intensity and illumination of lighting; for others it is the product of careful preparation. They are usually accidental and outside our control. One may ask: is it possible to create the right conditions for these inspirations in man and other cybernetic systems by scientific methods? If so, what would be the essential features of such a system?

Michael Arbib (1964) has rightly said: "The Perceptron shows that a machine may adapt; artificial intelligence, that a machine can be creative; and servomechanisms that a machine can be purposive in behaviour. Admittedly, all this is at a far lower level than that exhibited by a human being, but it does demonstrate that many differences between man and machine which, until recently, have seemed immutably qualitative are merely quantitative." If we accept this thesis it appears that we can give a quantitative scientific method which could enable us to come into systematic contact with deeper levels of consciousness in both man and machines. The methods which have traditionally been prescribed for the conditioning of mental faculties is a system of meditation or reflection.

Since the logical mind is an ensemble of sensory impressions and thoughts arising from the outside world, the process of conditioning requires some dissociation from this habitat. This is not possible if the cybernetic system functions on binary logic. But, this may be possible if the cybernetic system is designed and trained to work on ternary logic where reflection or meditation on both the logical elements at the same time may be possible. In such a condition the mind may be withdrawn from the outer physical world, of sensory data and thoughts arising from them, from the field of relative consciousness to a field of greater consciousness. The mind may then be attuned to creative impulses sometimes filled with discoveries not present in our usual habitat. When the ternary cybernetic system returns to the world of sensory impressions, the mind is infused with qualities of consciousness which give clarity, conciseness, and economy. (Jacob Boehme says: "In one quarter of an hour I saw and knew more than if I had been many years at a University.")

What relationship exists between learning and these ternary logical states? Learning is an organized system which transforms certain incoming messages into an outgoing message, according to some principle of transformation, which improves the performance of the system. It is based on accumulation, classification, and interpretation of sensory data. According to Wiener (1964): "Learning of the individual is a process that occurs in the life of the individual, in ontology... Biological reproduction ... occurs in the life of the race, in phylogeny, but the race learns as the individual does ... natural selection is a kind of racial learning, which operates within the conditions imposed by the reproduction of the individual..."

The experience of ternary logical states, of a deeper and wider field of consciousness will inevitably affect the interpretation of what we learn, and may orient science and technology in entirely new directions. It is notable that discovery generally gives a new direction to science. The development of ternary logical systems may, therefore, provide entirely new factors in the evolution of the human race and new relationships between men and machines.

CONCLUSIONS

Using a ternary model we can understand that consciousness can exist without functions and functions without consciousness.

It is now realised that a comparatively small part of the nervous system regulates life and all the mental and physical functions of the living organism as a whole. "A changing dynamic mechanism seems to offer the only tenable hypothesis. It is the integration itself, the relationship of the functioning

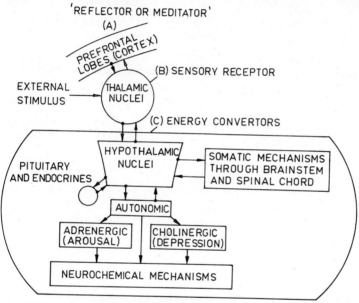

FIGURE 2   A ternary cybernetical model of the nervous system

part to another which is "mind" and which causes the phenomenon of consciousness. There can be no centre. There is no one seat of consciousness. It is the streaming of impulses in a complex series of circuits that makes mind feasible." (Stanley Cobb, 1958.) According to Samson Wright: "It is clear that the prefrontal cortex, thalamus and hypothalamus are so closely interconnected that in the intact person they function as an integrated whole. In emotional situations activity develops in large areas of forebrain. They set up a discharge to viscera and muscles (exteriorization) and at the same time give rise to mental state that prolongs and perpetuates the bodily disturbance."

These considerations lead us to propose a ternary model suitable for cybernetical systems relevant to the nervous system of a living organism, which appear more suitable for dealing with consciousness, judicial functions and decision processes.

"By a species of trichotomy" (Boole, 1931) the nervous system is divided into *three* elements: (A) prefrontal lobes as the reflector or the meditator; (B) thalamic nuclei as the sensory receptor; (C) hypothalamic nuclei (pituitary and endocrines), autonomic and somatic mechanisms as energy convertors (see Figure 2). The neurons in the thalamus store information when excited by external environment. In this model a strong emotion has simultaneous physical and mental reactions and without mental chain reaction the physical effects would be transient. With the help of the model we can determine the site and mode of reaction of most of the powerful drugs in use today. For example, in Figure 2, morphine kills pain at (B) but, also, clouds (A); barbiturates puts (A) and (C) to sleep but do not kill the pain at (B). (C) is the seat of highly powered and opposing chemical mediators which determine the activity, inertial and sympathetic conditions of the organism.

When, the thalamus is working to full capacity it represents the organism governed at the level of awakening consciousness—the organism is fully aware of its external environment. The cortex is reflecting the sources of energy. In deep and dreamless sleep the energy is at a minimum, enough to maintain only the vital functions. Sensory perception is also minimal and the cortex is inactive. In sleep with dreams or waking sleep, there is more energy but the cortex is not fully reflecting the external environment. In objective consciousness or concentrated attention the energy and reflection are maximal and the cortex is reflecting all possible situation.

The limbic system and the reverberating circuits connect the thalamus with the most primitive part of the brain. It is probably the chief means of establishing memory in living organism by drawing together the senses of sight, smell, hearing, and balancing mechanisms, as well as the instincts of self-preservation and reproduction. The neurons in the limbic system may be considered as resonators which store information when excited by external environment.

If the awareness is locked with the reverberating neurons this may give rise to psychosomatic illnesses such as migrane or asthma. The sensory impressions required to regulate life in the organism may be impaired. By ternary logical training involving reflection or meditation it may be possible to withdraw attention and disconnect awareness from reverbrating circuits. By such training the perturbing effects of reverberating memories on the organism may be avoided.

Regressive thoughts appear to be the chief barrier to awareness in living organisms. "Well, suppose I declare that every child had a father. Does that initiate a regress? No, it is merely a definition of the meaning of the word 'child'. But if I were to make a further assertion that every father was also a child, that is had a father, then I should have entered an endless regress" (Dunne, 1962). Excitement, depression, imagination, and identification require thoughts which unintentionally repeat more than once and minimize the awareness in living organism, of its external environment. Judicial functions and decision processes require freedom from regressive thoughts. It may be possible to provide a cybernetic system based upon ternary logic which will be more suitable for dealing with such processes.

Acknowledgments

Thanks are due to Professor Dennis Gabor of Imperial College, and Professor Eric Houldin of Chelsea College, for advice and criticism.

References

Lord Adrian, "Gap between mind and matter." *The Times*, 2nd June, p. 10 (1964).
M. Arbib, *Brains, Machines and Mathematics*. New York, p. 140 (1964).
M. Born, Private communication (1967).
G. Boole, *The Laws of Thought*. Dover Publications, New York, p. 51 (1854).
S. Cobb, *Foundations of Neuropsychiatry*. Baltimore, p. 128 (1958).
J. W. Dunne, *Nothing Dies*. p. 33 (1962).
A. Eddington, *The Philosophy of Physical Science*. Cambridge University Press, Canbridge, p. 148 (1939).
D. Gabor, "The dimensions of consciousness." In *Mind, Meanings, and Cybernetics*. London, p. 66 (1961).
K. Gödel, *On Formally Decidable Propositions of Principia Mathematica and Related Systems*. New York (1931).
Sir C. Hinshelwood, *Proc. Roy. Soc.* (London), Ser. *A*, **253**, 447 (1959).
D. Hilbert, *Geometry and the Imagination*. London, p. 3 (1952).
F. A. Kekulé, *Ber. deut. Chem. Ges.*, **23**, 1265 (1890).
E. Nagel, and J. R. Newman *Goedel's Proof*. London, p. 6 (1958).
H. Poincaré, *Science and Method*, London (1914).
S. Wright, *Applied Physiology*. London (1964).
N. Wiener, *God and Golem, Inc.* London, p. 21 (1964).

Hardware, software, fineware

M. MALITZA

University of Bucarest, Bucarest, Rumania

Summary

The author considers the main efforts directed to the establishment of operational research as a distinctive mathematical discipline and offers criteria for the classification of the methods known under this generic name. Operational research would consist of (a) methods for the optimal determination of a given system; (b) optimal functioning in the presence of "aleatory" requirements; (c) the coordination with other systems. The improvement and refinement of these methods are required today by the increasing use of computers and cybernetics. Advanced techniques of programming are demanding new improved mathematical tools, new algorithms and enriched instruments for mathematical modelling. Together with numerical analysis operational research represents a new category; fineware, with a growing impact on the final efficiency of the computers.

INTRODUCTION

The endeavour to define more strictly the sphere of operational research, to set its limits from the adjacent disciplines and to assign to it an independent place among the modern and applied sciences is not only a simple semantic exercise. The effort devoted to it in the field of research activity and, in a way, its aptitude to progress at a rate corresponding to the weight it carries in applications and in the development of other sciences, are dependent on its degree of independent maturing.

One of the youngest branches of applied mathematics, operational research, continues to be a collection of methods gathered together under an unsuitable name. Although Archimedes could be considered as the founder of this science, because of having used mathematical means to defend Syracuse, operational research is more recent. Mathematical models in economy have already been utilized before the World War II, and statistical methods in production management have been applied concomitantly with the modern development of industry. The last war, demanding the mobilization of all available resources, has drawn all the branches of mathematics towards solving the problem of the optimum mode of action. The resulting collection of methods was treated as a confidential item, in the same manner in which descriptive geometry had remained for many years a military secret on account of the fact that its founder, Gaspard Monge, was an officer in the engineer corps.

OPERATIONAL RESEARCH

At the end of the war all the methods of operational research were rapidly transferred to the domain of industrial production. The consequence was of such importance that numerous authors now attribute the preponderant part in the spectacular increase of production and services to the mathematical methods of organization and management.

Notwithstanding their importance and acceptance the methods of operational research did not make up a new organic discipline. To satisfy the classical criterion of a science they should have been able to define their own object, methods and laws. However, operational research has a vast field of application. Too little has been achieved so far to find out the common structure of the problems liable to be treated by operational methods. Proceeding from several domains, they, in their turn, consisted of techniques and procedures of great diversity. Under these circumstances, almost every author has given a different definition of operational research. Some are reconciled to the idea of seeing in it a simple collection lacking a name or a final status and a list of procedures suitable for applications, taking advantage of results of important branches of mathematics: algebra, calculus of probabilities, mathematical logic, and analysis. However, majority opinion endeavours to define the unifying element of those mathematical methods and to hasten their crystallization into an independent discipline.

Indeed, the common elements of the methods of operational research are considerable in number. In the first place, all of them refer to problems having a great or an infinite number of possible solutions. The methods of operational research offer a procedure of selecting, from the space of possible solutions, a single solution satisfying one or several fundamental conditions; this is the optimal solution. By supplying the procedure of selecting the optimal solution, operational research becomes a precious aid for decision making. Many authors call it "scientific preparing of a decision", and suggest decision as the unifying concept. Although it plays an important part in operational research, decision is a particular moment of a broader process in which three elements take part: objectives, resources and strategy. Decision has the disadvantage of emphasizing an outer aspect of the phenomenon.

The following question can be found in all the methods of operational research: how (by what strategies) must the resources be set, in order to reach (in the best conditions) certain objectives? But, this is only another definition of organization. The constitution of systems made up of interdependent parts, which must satisfy certain functional requirements (objectives), in optimum conditions is the vocation of organization. Thus, the methods of operational research are nothing but bricks of an edifice of the science of organization. To do away with the qualitative legacy of this word, it is not useless to try and find a new name for it. We could name the science of organization, teinology, from a Greek word which means "to place in a determined situation". In contrast with technology would be the science of the organization of the factors contributing to the constitution of a system.

Besides the domain of an economic, financial, commercial nature and of organization of modern production, the science of organization is called to support biology, sociology, psychology, history, the study of relations among individuals and among states, and the situations of conflict, and cooperation. Therefore, in our opinion, it is inadequate to speak about economic mathematics, in the sense that the same apparatus is also used for sociological or for biological mathematics, and so on.

The methods of operational research may be divided into three basic categories. The first is centred round linear programming. This simple model offers the greatest number of applications, where both the constraints and the objective function are linear. In case the function objective is quadratic, programmation becomes quadratic. Finding the pure and the mixed strategies in matrix games may be reduced to linear programming.

The graph theory in its most frequent problems of minimum path or of maximum flow leads to a problem of linear programming or to its extensions. One remains, here, within the same family of methods for which algebra constitutes the most important source. If the first category of methods is useful to the optimal organization of a system or to its internal study, having a pronounced deterministic character, the second class of methods deals with the behaviour of the system in the presence of random external stress; it is dominated by the calculus of probabilities. The older models of the statistical control of quality and the recent theories of equipment, inventory and queueing belong to this section. Its methods find their application in the maintenance problems of a system subject to a number of factors that vary at random (customers, sales, machine break-down, staff fluctuation, etc.).

The third category is made up of instruments which study structures in their reciprocal dependency. The mathematical logic, information theory and theory of automatic mechanisms, are the branches which approach, from various angles, the study of structures.

OPERATIONAL RESEARCH ORGANIZATION

Operational research is the object of intensive exploration in various countries. There are departments devoted to these methods and attached to the universities bearing various names; academic institutes and research centres devote considerable efforts of investigation to them. Various associations and societies aim at spurring and coordinating them. In France, l'Association Française d'Informatique et de Recherche Opérationnelle publishes a journal bearing the same title; in Great Britain the Operational Research Society has been acting since 1948, with the publication *Operational Research Quarterly*, and in the U.S.A., since 1952, the Operations Research Society of America with its Journal. In the Soviet Union the centres of cybernetics, in Kiev, and of telecontrol and automation, in Moscow, as well as the laboratory of mathematical research in economy, in Leningrad, are well known.

Starting with only three members, the International Federation of Operational Research Societies (I.F.O.R.S.) now comprises more than twenty member societies. However, international cooperation in this field is only at its beginning. In the domain of calculus, more advanced forms exist, such as the International Computation Centre in Rome.

In Rumania, where the school of algebra and of probabilities enjoys a respectable tradition, the present literature devoted to the methods of linear and non-linear programming, to the theory of games and to the statistical methods, is rich and varied. Every year the scientific session of the Centre of Economic Computation and Economic Cybernetics gathers together the most important results obtained in applying mathematical methods to the development of national economy. The research workers of the Institute of Mathematics and those of the Centre of Mathematical Statistics of the Rumanian Academy, those of the Centre of Economic Computation and Economic Cybernetics and those of the Centre for Advanced Training of the Managing Staff in Enterprises take part in international conferences and congresses and maintain relations of cooperation with the research workers of other countries. In February 1969, at a meeting of the U.N. economic commission for Europe, they suggested the creation of a European centre of operational research, under the sponsorhip of the United Nations.

International cooperation is meant to support the research work undertaken on a national scale and to convert the group of methods of operational research into a distinct mathematical branch.

CONCLUSIONS

In a first stage of computer development, stress was laid on their technology, called hardware. The progress achieved in computer building and their advanced technical performance have then focused attention on software, on programs. In this domain too, the automatic and semi-automatic languages and the systems of data processing are about to offer all the resources contained in software. Computer efficiency is not exhausted by these two categories. Fast computers and advanced programs both need algorithms suited for calculus as well as instruments for mathematical modelling, created by the mathematical science of organization. In this sense a new category—fineware—may be mentioned, supposed to offer its contribution to broadening the field of application of mathematics and to improving research in the economic, biological, and social sciences.

References

1. R. Cruon, "Essai de caractérisation de la recherche opérationelle", *RIRO*, No. 8 (1968).
2. "Recherche opérationnelle et organisation", *Préface de M.P.Masse*, AFCOS, Paris (1960).
3. C.W. Churchman, R.I. Ackoff and L. Anroff, *Introduction to Operations Research*, New York (1957).
4. M. Malitza, R. Theodorescu and C. Zidaroiu, *Introducere Matematică în Știința Organizării*, Editura Tehnică, București (in press)
5. D. Feigenbaum, "The engineering and management of an effective system", *Management Sci.*, August (1968).

Towards a computer model of the evolution of DNA sequences*

LUCIO CHIARAVIGLIO

School of Information Science
Georgia Institute of Technology, U.S.A.

Summary

The processes that lead from the genetic molecules of one generation to the molecules of the next, the processes of replication, recombination, mutation, and selection, exhibit the structure of a Boolean sequential machine.

A computer model of a portion of this Boolean sequential machine has been realized. The model produces from an initial set of inputs all the possible one-step, two-step, ..., n-step recombinants that are obtainable from the initial inputs. Each class of recombinants is available for inspection by various querying programs. The querying programs yield information such as the distribution of molecular lengths, the number of distinct molecules in each length, molecular composition, the number of distinct recombinational steps required to achieve target outputs, etc.

In this paper we describe the molecular processes of interest, the computer model of recombination and report some of the difficulties encountered in the construction and operation of the programs and the solutions that have been implemented.

* This study was carried out in part under National Science Foundation Grant GN-655.

RECOMBINATION

In order to aid our intuition we may assume that we are describing the replication and recombination processes that occur in the reproduction of organisms whose genetic materials consist of one double stranded DNA molecule. For example, we may think of the life cycle of organisms such as phages. The processes of interest occur in some host, or better host states, which are to count as the relevant environment of these processes. The one or more phage DNA molecules that are injected into the host and replicate and recombine within the host are the inputs of the machine. The DNA molecules that are released upon lysis and which can take part in subsequent rounds of replication and recombination are the outputs of the machine. The set of host states in which replication and recombination can occur is the set of states of the machine.

In what follows we state the definition of the Boolean sequential machine and motivate the definition by means of the concrete biological picture. The mathematical elaboration of the theory of Boolean sequential machines is done elsewhere.

A double stranded DNA molecule is composed of two largely complementary sequences. Each of the two sequences is constructed from four units: A (Adenine), C (Cytosine), G (Guanine), and T (Thymine). The rule of complementation is that each A in one strand is complemented by a T in the other and each C is complemented by a G. We may consider that each DNA molecule n base pairs long is modeled by a two row by n column matrix composed of the elements A, C, G, and T. Each row of such matrix represents one of the strands of the molecule. Each column represents a base pair. Matrices may contain a number of non-complementary base pairs.

Replication without error may be thought of as a function of host states and base pairs. Thus, if (a, b) is the ith column of a matrix d and x' is the complementary base to x, then replication of d in some host state yields output matrices that have as ith columns the pairs (a, a') and (b', b).

Recombination on the other hand is not generally just a function of the base pair at the ith locus and the host state[1,2]. There may be many other loci of the inputs which will play some decisive role with respect to what can be found at the ith loci of the outputs[3]. The set of outputs that may be obtained by recombination will depend on the laws that govern the production of molecular fragments, the laws that govern the mating of the produced fragments and the degree of repetitiousness of the input molecules relative to the fragmentation and mating laws[4-7].

We may picture the situation as follows. Suppose that

$$...ACGTAATCGACCT... \qquad (1)$$
$$...TGCATTAGCTGGA...$$

$$...CAGTAATCGTCTA... \qquad (2)$$
$$...GTCATTAGCAGAT...$$

are two inputs. Let us assume that the fragmentation laws allow the formation of the fragments

| ...ACG | (1a) | TAATCGACCT... | (1b) |
| ...TGCATTAGC | | TGGA... | |

| ...CAG | (2a) | TAATCGTCTA... | (2b) |
| ...GTCATTAGC | | AGAT... | |

Now, if the mating laws required no more than the formation of six complementary base pairs, then from the above fragments one could obtain the original molecules plus the following new recombinant molecules:

$$...ACGTAATCGTCTA... \qquad (1a) \times (2b)$$
$$...TGCATTAGCAGAT...$$

$$...CAGTAATCGACCT... \qquad (2a) \times (1b)$$
$$...GTCATTAGCTGGT...$$

More generally we may suppose that within some host state h the scissions that require the rupturing of the hydrogen bonds of k or more complementary base pairs are rare. Similarly we may suppose that within h stable matings between fragments requires the formation of no less than $n < k$ appropriately spaced complementary base pairs. Under these hypothetical assumptions any two subsequences of some input into h which are stabilized by no more than k complementary base pairs and matched at no less than n appropriately spaced loci would be possible sites for recombination.

If (a, b) and (c, d) are base pairs at the corresponding loci of two regions that are possible sites for recombination and if complementary matching is arbitrarily assumed to be left to right strand, then recombination at these sites yields the pairs (a, d) and (c, d) at the corresponding loci of the resulting molecules. Repeated rounds of replication and recombination of the mentioned inputs may yield terminal outputs that have at corresponding loci one of the sixteen base pairs that may be formed from the bases a, a', b, and b'.

Let expressions of the form "$x \vee y$" signify joint inputs or outputs formed from the base pairs x and y that are situated at corresponding loci of regions that are possible sites of recombination. If $x = y$, then the outputs for these loci are the same as the outputs obtained by either base pair alone. Thus, the operator $\vee$ is idempotent. The relation of being candidates for recombination is symmetric although not generally transitive. Hence the operator $\vee$ is commutative but not associative. However, we shall restrict our attention to those regions on which the relation of being candidates for recombination is transitive. With this restriction the operator $\vee$ is also associative.

Let the set B be the closure of the set of all possible base pairs under the idempotent, commutative, and associative operator $\vee$. We shall suppose that the deletion base pair is also in B. The deletion base pair, 0, is the identity element with respect to $\vee$. The dual of 0 is the element 1 where $x_1 \vee x_2 \vee \cdots \vee x_n = 1$ and $\{x_1, x_2, \ldots, x_n\}$ is the set of all base pairs. Each x in B has a dual $\bar{x}$ such that $x \vee \bar{x} = 1$. In brief, B and the operators $\vee$ and $^-$ may be recognized as a finite Boolean algebra generated from $\{x_1, x_2, \ldots, x_n\}$.

If H is the set of all host states, then the replication and recombination function R considered at the base pair level of the input molecules is a mapping of the Cartesian product of B and H into B. This mapping is normalized.

$$R(0, h) = 0 \tag{3}$$

If we consider x and y in B such that they are located on inputs that are able to replicate and recombine in h, then R is idempotent, non-decreasing, monotone, and submultiplicative.

$$R(R(x, h), h) = R(x, h) \tag{4}$$

$$x \leq R(x, h) \tag{5}$$

$$\text{If} \quad x \leq y, \quad \text{then} \quad R(x, h) \leq R(y, h) \tag{6}$$

$$R(x \wedge y, h) \leq R(x, h) \wedge R(y, h) \tag{7}$$

We may now extend our considerations beyond the base pair level to inputs and outputs composed of sequences of base pairs and joint inputs and outputs of such sequences. For sequences of length no greater than n we may consider the set of all functions f that map $N = \{1, 2, 3, ..., n\}$ into B, B^N. B^N is a Boolean algebra under the operators defined pointwise. Sequences that are shorter than n are here viewed as sequences n long which contain a number of 0 base pairs. If we wished to consider sequences of any finite length, then we could take N to be the set of natural numbers.

In either case we might not wish to consider that all elements of B^N are relevantly distinct. For example, in certain organisms sequences that differ by appropriate circular permutations may not be biologically distinguishable. Such considerations give rise to quotient algebras of B^N. Since we wish to remain as universal as possible in the present treatment of replication and recombination we shall not explore these quotient algebras here. Thus B^N may contain more distinguishable elements than are necessary.

The replication and recombination function R of sequences may be thought of as a mapping of the Cartesian product of B^N and H into B^N. *Mutatis mutandi* Equations (3) to (7) hold for this extended R.

There are two basic alternatives with respect to R and sequences in B^N. The first alternative is that the replication and recombination of initial subinputs does not alter the host state in any significant way. The replication and recombination of terminal subinputs occurs in the same host state as the replication and recombination of the initial ones. The second alternative is that the replication and recombination of initial subinputs may alter the host state in some significant way. If h is the initial host state, then the replication and recombination of some initial subinputs produces a host state k and $h \neq k$ in the sense that there is some input f in B^N such that $R(f, h) \neq R(f, k)$.

If replication and recombination may produce host state transitions, then we must countenance besides R a state transition function S. This function maps the Cartesian product of B^N and H into H. If f, g are in B^N, $f \wedge g = 0$, $(f \vee g)(i) = f(i)$ for $1 \leqslant i \leqslant j$, and $(f \vee g)(i) = g(i)$ for $j < i \leqslant n$, then

$$R(f \vee g, h) = R(f, h) \vee R(g, S(f, h)) \tag{8}$$

If f is an initial input and g is a terminal input, then the output of $f \vee g$ for the state h is the same as the output of f for the state h followed by the output of g for the state $S(f, h)$. It may be noted that the first alternative described is realized when S is the identity function on H.

The following requirements are satisfied by S for any h in H and f, g in B^N:

$$S(0, h) = h \tag{9}$$

$$S(f, S(f, h)) = S(f, h) \tag{10}$$

if $f \wedge g = 0, (f \vee g)(i) = f(i)$ for $i \le i \le j$, and

$(f \vee g)(i) = g(i)$ for $j < i \le n$, then $S(f \vee g, h) = S(g, S(f, h))$ (11)

In summary, we may say that the recombination and replication processes form a Boolean sequential machine (B^N, H, B^N, R, S) with the following characteristics: (a) the input and output set B^N is the Boolean algebra of all the functions from the index set N into the Boolean algebra of base pairs; (b) H is the set of host states; (c) the replication and recombination function R, the output function, maps $B^N \times H$ into B^N and is normalized (Equation (3)), sequential (Equation (8)), and for fully receptive states is also idempotent (Equation (4)), nondecreasing (Equation (5)), monotone (Equation (6)), and submultiplicative (Equation (7)), (d) the state function S maps $B^N \times H$ into H and is the identity for the zero element (Equation (9)), is idempotent (Equation (10)) and also sequential (Equation (11)).

THE COMPUTER MODEL OF RECOMBINATION

In order to simulate the recombination portion of the described machine it was necessary to construct a production program that would perform the breaking, mating, and storing operations on any set of simulated molecular inputs.

The laws which govern the breaking and mating of molecules are not as yet fully understood. It is probable that these laws are state dependent. It may also be the case that in nature not all recombinants that are produced may take part in further rounds of recombination and replication. There may be constraints on the outputs of recombination that are independent of the laws which govern recombination. In our model the storage operations represent natural selection and the breaking and mating algorithms represent the laws of recombination. Thus it was advisable to design a production program that would be able to accommodate a variety of selection rules as well as large variety of recombination laws.

The basic facilities of the recombinant production program may be described as follows.

(1) An algorithm breaks a given simulated molecule (a $2 \times n$ matrix) into four fragments each of which has one strand exposed so as to form a possible mating region. Both the locus at which the break is initiated and the length of the exposed single strand are fixed before the operation of the algorithm. If the break is to be initiated immediately after the ith column and terminated immediately after the $(i + k)$th column, then there are two ways of making such a break. We may introduce a break between the i and the $i + 1$ loci of the top row and a break between the $i + k$ and $i + k + 1$ loci of the bottom row or reverse the procedure and introduce a break between the i and the $i + 1$ loci of the bottom row and a break between the $i + k$ and the $i + k + 1$ loci of the top row. Both breaks are made by the algorithm which thus yields four fragments.

(2) An entirely similar algorithm breaks another simulated molecule into fragments. This second molecule need not be different from the first. The loci at which this algorithm initiates and terminates the breaks are determined uniquely by the length of the possible recombinants to be produced and the loci at which breaks were initiated and terminated in the first molecule.

(3) An algorithm checks each fragment produced by (1) against fragments produced by (2). When the two single stranded regions of the fragments satisfy the mating requirements, then the algorithm proceeds to form a recombinant.

The flexibility of the recombinant production program hinges on several variables whose values may be kept constant, adjusted algorithmically, randomly, or according to some specified distribution. These variables are as follows

(1) The length of the input molecules.

(2) The sequence of base pairs that constitute these molecules.

(3) The composition of the molecules.

(4) The position along the length of the molecules at which breaks are to occur.

(5) The length of the mating regions.

(6) The number of non-complementary base pairs that are formed by each mating.

(7) The distribution of the non-complementary base pairs.

(8) The length of the produced molecules.

The first three parameters allow for choices of the initial set of inputs. The fourth to seventh parameters allow for variation in the breaking and mating rules. The joint setting of parameters four and eight make it possible to generate each class of *n*-step recombinants systematically by subclasses of *n*-step recombinants of equal length. This procedure simplifies memory management and decreases the need for peripheral storage devices.

The facilities of the storage, querying, and selection programs receive the recombinants assembled by the production program and subject these simulated molecules to a number of steps that will vary with the genetic situation that is being modeled and the status of the simulated molecules in the program. Simulated molecules may be divided into three subclasses. The initial molecules are the original inputs into the production program. The intermediate molecules are the outputs of the production program which are going to be inputed again into the production program. And the terminal molecules are the outputs of the production program which belong to the target population that is being produced.

Querying and selection programs are of two types. We may query or select with respect to population parameters or we may query or select with respect to properties of the individual molecules. In the case of queries or selections with respect to population parameters whole populations must be produced. In the case of queries or selection with respect to properties of the individual molecules they may be queried or selected as each one is produced and it is not necessary to produce and store and entire population prior to implementing the selection or querying programs. Consequently, this last case generally makes more modest demands upon the storage capacity of the system. All programs are run in such a way so as to implement the selection and querying of individual properties as early in the procedure as is possible.

Selection and querying procedures may be implemented both for intermediate and terminal simulated molecules. As noted earlier the production program already produces simulated molecules systematically by length. Thus selection and querying procedures based on molecular length are implemented partially by the production program.

The basic facilities of the storage, querying, and selection programs may be described as follows.

(1) All of the simulated molecules may be processed through a number of subroutines that ascertain (a) the length of the molecule; (b) the base composition of the molecule; (c) the occurrence of given subsequences in the molecule; (d) if the molecule is already in store; and (e) the number of recombinational steps that have produced the molecule.

(2) All of the simulated molecules may be selected for or against on the basis of the results of the above querying subroutines. If the molecule is an intermediate molecule and it is selected, then it is stored with other molecules of the same length and the same number or recombinational steps. If the molecule is terminal and selected, then it is subjected to data extraction, the data is stored and the molecule eliminated. In either case if the molecule is not selected then it is simply eliminated.

(3) All of the populations of simulated molecules may be run through querying programs that ascertain (a) the total number of molecules; (b) the distribution of individual properties; (c) totals and averages of individual properties; and (d) the population storage status.

(4) All of the populations may be processed by selection programs that are based on the population parameters. Routines are available which construct random samples of populations. As is the case with individual molecules only intermediate populations are kept in store.

We may consider an example in order to illustrate the joint operation of the production, querying, and selection programs. Suppose that we are interested in discovering if there are any molecules of length l in the n-step recombinant class obtained from some initial input that have not been obtained previously by less than n recombinational steps. For the sake of simplicity let us also suppose that the initial input is one molecule of length l_0 and that the scission and mating laws require a fixed scission and mating length $m < l_0$. It is clear that if the class of n-step recombinants of length l is to have any members, then l must fall between m and $nl_0 - (n - 1) m$.

We have to perform matings between i-step and j-step recombinant classes such that $i + j + 1 = n$. Also within such classes not all lengths of molecules can yield terminal molecules of length l. If the longest molecule in the i-step recombinant class is of length l_i, then no molecule in the j-step recombinant class need be considered if it is shorter than $l + m - l_i$. In general we need only consider pairwise all those molecules in the i and j-step recombinant classes whose sum of lengths is no less than the length l of the target molecules plus the length m of the mating region. Thus the systematic generation by length affords some savings in storage space. But this is not the only way in which we can save space since once a particular subclass of recombinants has been used in all possbile ways, then the entire subclass may be eliminated from storage.

As soon as an i-step recombinant of length k is produced it can be checked against all recombinants of length k that had been produced by less than *i*-steps. If the molecule is in store, then it is eliminated, if not, then the molecule is stored in the class of *i*-step recombinants of length *k*. If all the *i*-step recombinants of length *k* have been generated and there is no further use for the *j*-step ($j < i$) class of recombinants of length *l*, then this whole class

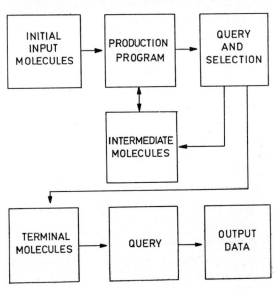

FIGURE 1   A generalized flow chart of programs

may be eliminated from storage. Thus by repeated generation and elimination from storage very large classes of recombinants are produced, used, and queried in a piecemeal fashion. In our present example the process terminates after having generated, queried and eliminated every *n*-step recombinant molecules of length *l*.

A generalized flow chart of the production, querying, and storage programs is given in Figure 1.

Figure 2 shows some of the organization of the initial and intermediate arrays together with their connections to the production, query, and selection programs.

CONCLUSIONS

The main difficulty that is encountered in any modelling of evolution is the size of the populations that have to be processed. In nature such processes

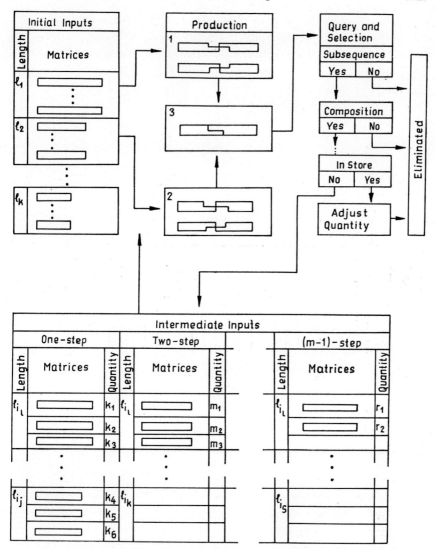

FIGURE 2   Organization of arrays with their connections to programs

never occur in a selection free mode. Thus we seem to be trying to accomplish in a computer more than what occurs in nature. It is extremely hard to beat nature at its own game. Nevertheless we must try to do so if we are to model usefully selected aspects of evolution.

If a model of evolution is to yield information about natural selection, then it cannot incorporate arbitrary selective devices. In other words such models will have to be virtually selection free. Thus we seem to have to process population that are larger than the natural ones. It can be appreciated that the growth rate of these simulated populations will generally be larger than the growth rates of the natural ones (Figure 3).

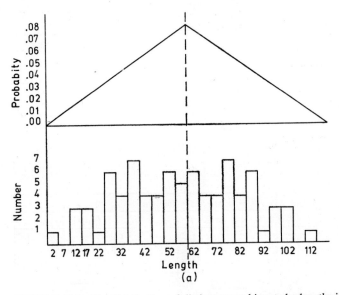

FIGURE 3(a)   The distribution of distinct recombinants by lengths in the one-step population. One initial molecule of length 60, 3 complementary bases required for mating. 174 matched our of 6786 tries producing 83 distinct molecules

As we have noted a modest beginning at solving the problem of size can be made by instituting production programs which generate the populations selectively by length of molecule. The length parameter is then altered algorithmically so as to generate the full target population in a piecemeal fashion. If necessary further fragmentation of the target population may be achieved by the joint selective production by length and some other molecular parameters. At this time we cannot suggest any modes of selections that are as easy to implement as length selection.

In order to achieve a more complete model of the molecular processes that occur in nature, we would have to modify the production programs so as to include replication and mutation. The principal problem encountered in such an expansion is the lack of basic information as to the relative rates of these processes and the natural mechanisms that give rise to such rates. The design of subroutines that will replicate and mutate arbitrary molecules is not difficult. The difficulties lie entirely in how these subroutines are to be coupled to the recombinant production program.

The present recombinant production program assumes that all molecules are in sufficient supply so as to produce within the scission, mating, and selection laws in force all the recombinants that would issue from them. Clearly this is not true in nature. Molecules are present in varying amounts and their supply is replenished and depleted at different rates. Of course, a wealth of suggestions as to the possible coupling of replication, mutation,

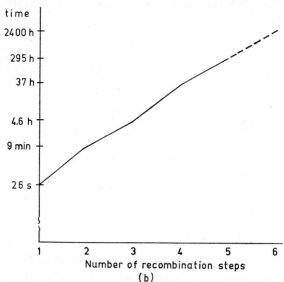

FIGURE 3(b)   Growth of CPU time for the production of complete 1–5 step recombinant populations. One initial molecule of length 60, 3 complementary bases required for mating

and recombination may be found in the biological literature. But we do believe that it is probably at present more productive to conduct a fairly extensive program of exploration with the partial model described.

We conclude by suggesting some evolutionary experiments that we think can be carried out with our computer model. Some of these experiments are in the process of completion in our laboratory.

There are now available nearly 500 sequences or partial sequences of proteins. The comparative study of these sequences may yield information about the ancestry and evolution of the organisms in which they are found. The relatively new discipline of chemical paleogenetics concerns itself with such studies. We have envisaged the following chemical paleogenetic experiments.

(1) There are known coding relations between triplets (codons) of bases and amino acids. The code is degenerate. To each amino acids there generally corresponds more than one codon. It also appears that the coding dictionary of an organism does not contain all the possible codons. Thus, we can inquire if there is some reason for such partial dictionaries that can be ascertained by our model. What we do is to encode a protein from an organism in all the possible ways, then subject the encoded simulated molecules to the recombination production program and monitor the growth of the recombina classes. We then ascertain if the growth of the recombinant classes for the molecule that is encoded with the known or partially known dictionary exhibits any systematic differences from the others. The repetition of this type of experiment with molecules from different organisms would yield information as to whether particular coding dictionaries serve to stabilize protein molecules relative to recombination.

(2) Two or more sequences of homologous proteins are encoded in various ways in order to determine how far apart they are in terms of recombinational steps. That is to say that one encoded molecule is used to produce recombinants of a given length which are compared to the other encoded molecule. The number of recombinational steps and the degree of matching may yield information about the evolutionary relation of the molecules. Or if this is already known we may infer relations between the coding dictionaries.

(3) Sequences that encode for enzymes may be compared for their recombinational stability against the sequences that encode structural proteins. The latter are generally more monotonous looking than the former. It is sometimes presumed that this monotony is an outcome of their evolution.

The three experiments described seem to be of fairly immediate biological relevance. We have envisaged and are conducting a number of experiments that are designed to disclose to us some of the general features of recombination[8]. We are asking the following sort of questions.

(1) Is recombination a symmetric process on some identifiable class of molecules?

(2) If we start with input molecules of length l, then what is the growth rate for the population of various possible lengths?

(3) How do the growth rates reflect systematic changes in the scission and mating laws?

(4) How does the number of strand heterozygotes produced reflect changes in the number of mismatches allowed per mating?

(5) What sorts of molecules produce a relatively large number of distinct recombinants?

(6) What sorts of molecules produce a relatively small number of recombinants?

(7) What are the relations between periodicity and number of distinct recombinants produced?

Answers to questions such as these are often necessary to the construction of realistic experiments and are also very useful as guidelines for the expansion of the presented model.

Acknowledgments

The author gratefully acknowledges the assistance rendered by Mr. J.H.Poore, Jr. in the supervision of the design of the described programs and the assistance of Mrs. J.L.Martin, Mr. S.M.Smith and Mr. R.N.Wahlberg in their preparation. Thanks are also due the Atlanta Public School System for the use of their computer facilities, and to the IBM Corporation for its loan of an APL terminal.

References

1. M.Meselson and F.W.Strahl, *Proc. Natl. Acad. Sci. U.S.*, **44**, 671 (1958).
2. J.H.Taylor, P.S.Woods, and W.C.Hughes, *Proc. Natl. Acad. Sci. U.S.*, **43**, 122 (1957).
3. G.Streisinger, J.Emrich, and M.M.Stahl, *Proc. Natl. Acad. Sci. U.S.*, **57**, 292 (1967).
4. A.D.Hershey, E.Burgi, and L.Ingraham, *Proc. Natl. Acad. Sci. U.S.*, **49**, 748 (1963).
5. A.D.Hershey and E.Burgi, *Proc. Natl. Acad. Sci. U.S.*, **53**, 325 (1965).
6. A.D.Kaiser and R.Inman, *J. Mol. Biol.*, **13**, 78 (1965).
7. Ray Wu and A.D.Kaiser, *Proc. Natl. Acad. Sci. U.S.*, **57**, 170 (1967).
8. R.J.Britten and E.H.Davidson, *Science*, **165**, 349 (1969).

A model for the classification of visual images

OLIVER TALLMAN
and MATTHEW KABRISKY

A. F. Institute of Technology, U.S.A.

Summary

A biological model of foveal vision is described, in which a quite complete set of spatially coded data is mapped topologically on the visual input cortex. From this model, we derive a digital computer model of postulated cortical computation for the classification of visual images. It is presumed that sensory data is analysed for classification through the mutual interaction of arrays of cortical elements corresponding to the visual input cortex and associative areas of cortex. In the computer model, arrays of basic computational elements suitably interconnected act together to perform a two-dimensional Fourier transform of the spatial input stimulus. Classification is accomplished by comparing spatially filtered transforms of the input stimuli with prototypes which have been obtained and stored during a preliminary training period. Results are presented of simulations in which alpha-numeric characters and other geometric shapes are classified.

INTRODUCTION

Since the central problems of behaviour, intelligence, and information processing involve phenomena which are patterned, attention of researchers in these areas has been given to the process of pattern recognition. An excellent survey by Nagy of recent work in pattern recognition provides a comprehensive bibliography of the results of this attention[1].

Tretiak[2] has proposed a definition of pattern recognition which, while not in concise mathematical terms, states in plain language exactly what is meant in the process. Pattern recognition is to "look" at something and to "say" something about it. In this context the process may be described as the sensing of some external scene, the abstraction of the information contained in the sensed data into a form suitable for decision making, and the production of a portrayal in some measure of the meaning of the external scene. In a sense, then, pattern recognition may be said to lie in the "eye" of the beholder.

An important subproblem of the pattern recognition process is that of the classification of visual images. In this paper the problem is approached not by constructing a device which classifies visual images, but by modeling the "eye" of the beholder. A simple biological model and its corresponding engineering model will be described; some properties of the engineering model will be reviewed; and the results of a simulation experiment will be presented.

BIOLOGICAL MODEL

Knowledge of the functional organization of the human visual system is incomplete. Evidence gathered from studies of lower animals is not always directly applicable to the human, especially in the case of foveal vision. Significant differences exist in the respective views of the world of animals of diverse species; no general law seems to hold. Because of the extreme complexity of the human visual system, anatomical data generally provides evidence which is circumstantial at best. Any biological model derived from known physiological or psychological aspects must necessarily be conjectural. That assumptions made here may be untenable in these disciplines is an unfortunate, but distinct, possibility.

In the spirit of this understanding, the circumstances will be reviewed and a simple, perhaps naïve, biological model will be developed for monochromatic, static, monocular foveal vision in the human as it pertains to the classification of visual images.

Anatomical evidence indicates a one-to-one relationship between the foveal cones of the retina and the corresponding fibres of the optic tract[3]. A topological mapping of the external scene exists at the lateral geniculate body where it is assumed that a single synaptic junction permits the preservation of this one-to-one relationship during transmission to the visual input cortex. This assumption is in accord with physiological findings and the results of observations of visual acuity[4]. To assume that dispersive processing of foveal information occurs at the geniculate utterly fails to account for the remarkable acuity of the ensuing cortical perception.

It is presumed then that a remarkably acute topological representation of the foveally sensed external scene is impressed on the visual input cortex, an array of tiny functional columns each containing perhaps hundreds of neurons. This array, Brodmann's area 17, enjoys a rich interconnectivity with the visual association cortex, area 18, and in turn with other association areas, area 19 and perhaps[5] even area 20. These areas are of similar structure, each being an array of these functional columns.

It is presumed that it is not the activity of a single cell, or necessarily of an individual column, which results in the perception of an image, but rather the action of the entire array of columns which performs the required computation. Each functional column, or vasic computational element (b.c.e.), may be likened to a single individual in a card section at a football game. It is not his particular performance which forms the "pattern", but rather the activity of the entire card section acting in unison as an entity.

It is interesting to consider the computation which can be performed by such a configuration. The question to be asked is: what computations can suitably connected arrays of columns of neuronisms perform? Kabrisky has posed this very question and demonstrated that a two-dimensional cross-correlation computation could be performed by such a model in a manner analogous to the performance of an optical cross-correlator[6]. He has suggested that such a model might be able to perform other computations which have optical analogs. It is this suggestion which has motivated the development of the computer model to be described.

A GENERAL MULTI-ARRAY MODEL

In order to answer the question posed in the previous section, it is useful to consider a general situation where some external scene is impressed topologically onto a discrete two-dimensional array of basic computational elements (b.c.e.'s) as depicted in Figure 1.

This array enjoys a rich interconnectivity with another array of identical b.c.e.'s. Assume that the output of each b.c.e. in the first array is distributed to every member of the second array. Assign to each b.c.e. a very simple computation; each ouput of a b.c.e. is the complex sum of its inputs. Each b.c.e. in the first array has just one input and many outputs. Each b.c.e. in the second array has many inputs and just one output.

Such a configuration strongly suggests an optical homolog in which geometric ray tracings correspond to the pathways and diffracting and collecting screens, respectively, correspond to the arrays. In this continuous homolog the phase-amplitude distribution of light at the collecting screen is described by the Kirchhoff integral[7]. The pupil function of the diffracting

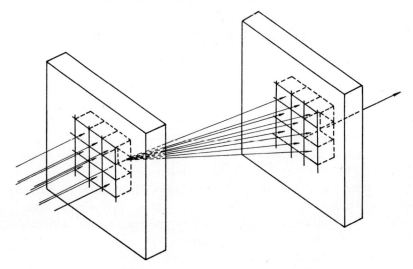

FIGURE 1   Array-to-array computer model

screen is multiplied by a phase factor and the product is integrated over the diffracting screen. This phase factor is introduced by the differences in path lengths which the light traverses from the points in the diffracting screen to the point in the collecting screen where the computation is being made. The resulting distribution constitutes an integral transform whose kernel function is a phase factor of exponential form. In general, this exponent is a combination of polynomial functions of the coordinates of the two screens. In one important case, that of far field or Fraunhofer diffraction, the phase factor exponent is a linear combination of products, higher order terms being negligible. In this case, the approximation to the Kirchhoff integral is equivalent to the two-dimensional Fourier transform.

The model depicted in Figure 1 supports just such a computation, where the integration is instead a finite summation, and the result is a discrete, rather than continuous, transform. To demonstrate a particular computational capability of this model, consider some further qualifying interpretations.

Let each pathway from the first array to the second be capable of carrying both phase and amplitude information. The path lengths are arranged such that the net phase difference between information traversing each path and some reference phase ϕ is related in a particular way to the geometric locations of the emanating and terminating b.c.e.'s, respectively.

Specifically, let the b.c.e.'s in the first array be identified by the ordered pair (m, n) where $m = 1, ..., M$ and $n = 1, ..., N$; M and N are large integers. Let the b.c.e.'s in the second array be identified by the ordered pair (p, q) for $p = -P, ..., 0, ..., +P$ and $q = -Q, ..., 0, ..., +Q$; P and Q may be smaller than $M/2$ and $N/2$, respectively.

Let the topological distribution of the mapping of the external scene on the first array be the function a_{mn}, and the distribution of the outputs of the b.c.e.'s of the second array be the complex function A_{pq}.

Let the path length between b.c.e. (m, n) in the first array and b.c.e. (p, q) in the second array be chosen such that the phase difference between the information traversing this path and some reference phase ϕ is proportional to the products mp/M and nq/N by the constant 2π.

Then the output of b.c.e. (p, q) will be

$$A_{pq} = \sum_{m=1}^{M} \sum_{n=1}^{N} a_{mn} e^{-j2\pi(mp/M + nq/N) + j\phi} \tag{1}$$

Note that the summations are independent of the reference phase, so that if ϕ is arbitrarily taken to be zero, no generality is lost, and the output A_{pq} is just the two-dimensional discrete Fourier transform of the input distribution a_{mn}.

This model is, in principle, a Fourier transform computer, and to the extent to which the discrete Fourier transform approximates the continuous integral transform, the computation performed is isomorphic with the calculation of the Kirchhoff integral for the case of Fraunhofer diffraction.

Consider a foveal visual scene mapped topologically on a sheet of human cortex consisting of the functional columns postulated in the previous section. Consider further that this array, area 17, is connected to another array, area 18, with the rich interconnectivity specified by the model, but with the property that the neural pathways connecting the arrays are capable in some way of carrying both phase and amplitude information.

There would appear at the output of the second array the discrete Fourier transform of the topological mapping of the external scene on the visual input cortex, or first array.

There may be as many as 100,000 b.c.e.'s in area 17 allocated to foveal vision, the number corresponding to the number of foveal cones in the retina.

It is important to note that it is not necessary for all of area 18 to be employed for this classification process. The ranges of the numbers p and q in the model may well be much smaller than the ranges of m and n, respectively, in the first array. Such a case would result in a form of spatial filtering, which will be found to be of paramount importance to the classification process to be simulated in a following section.

THE FOURIER TRANSFORM

In recent years the methods and technique of Fourier theory as applied to electrical engineering have been expanded and taken over into the field of optics. In one application, the case of Fraunhofer diffraction is described in terms of a two-dimensional Fourier transform. In another, the optical system is analysed as a linear spatial filter. This discussion and the succeeding sections will consider the theoretical basis of the use of Fourier transforms as analytic tools in two-dimensional image classification. The Fourier transform is a naturally occurring phenomenon, which sets it aside from an infinity of other transformations which might be considered, and in its discrete form can be computed by the model which we have proposed from biological evidence.

In the one-dimensional Fourier theory used in analysing communications systems, the independent variable in which the behaviour of the system is described usually is given in units of *time*. The corresponding transforms used in the analysis are then given in reciprocal units, those of *frequency*.

This reciprocity is carried over into two dimensions, the input or "pattern" space being a surface whose coordinates are given in units of *length*, and the image space or "spectrum" having units of *spatial frequency* or wave number, e.g. cycles per metre or waves per radian.

The two-dimensional Fourier transform may be considered as a spectral resolution of the pattern function into its constituent Fourier elements. The spectral function describes the phase–amplitude distribution in the spectrum. This results, then, in a complex valued spectrum which can be separated into a real spectrum and an imaginary spectrum, just as in the one-dimensional case.

Suppose the origin of the spectrum is taken to be at the centroid of some finite region. The value of the transform at the origin can be considered to be the zero spatial frequency term, analogous to the "d.c." term in electrical current analysis. The values in the outer fringes of this spectral region correspond to the high-frequency terms of the one-dimensional case.

The Fourier integral transform is a transformation from the pattern space onto an image space. The unfiltered transform is uniquely invertible for pattern functions which are quadratically summable[8], i.e. for patterns of finite energy. Under the Fourier transform, magnitude, an even function of the coordinates, is invariant to translation, while phase, an odd function of the coordinates, changes in direct proportion to the amount of translation. A function which is a rotation of some original function in the input space will transform into the same rotation of the transform of the original function. The transform of a uniformly *contracted* pattern is proportional to the uniformly *expanded* transform of the original pattern, and vice versa.

The discrete Fourier transform may be defined to be a summation over a set of discrete points and need *not* be considered an approximation to the integral transform. The results obtained are *exact* and no further approximations need be made.

Consider an arbitrary discrete spatial distribution a_{mn}, for $m = 1, \ldots, M$ and $n = 1, \ldots, N$. It will be convenient to assume in later computations that M and N are large odd integers. The discrete Fourier transform may be defined by the following transform pair:

$$A_{pq} = \sum_{m=1}^{M} \sum_{n=1}^{N} a_{mn} e^{-j2\pi(mp/M + nq/N)} \qquad (3)$$

$$a_{mn} = \sum_{p=-P}^{P} \sum_{q=-Q}^{Q} A_{pq} e^{+j2\pi(mp/M + nq/N)} \qquad (4)$$

where $P = (M - 1)/2$ and $Q = (N - 1)/2$.

It can be shown that Equation (4) is convergent for distributions which are quadratically summable, i.e.

$$\sum_{m=1}^{M} \sum_{n=1}^{N} |a_{mn}|^2$$

exists and is of finite value. The transform is uniquely invertible.

6 Rose, Cybernetics III

The distribution a_{mn} may be termed a *brightness* function; the distribution A_{pq} is the Fourier *image* function; and the quadratic content, which is proportionally invariant under the transformation, may be termed the *energy* of the pattern a_{mn}.

If a discrete pattern is rotated on a finite rectangular grid through a continuous angle, distortions of the pattern occur which are dependent on the granularity of the grid. In the same way such distortions occur also for expansion and contraction of the pattern. For M and N very large, these distortions are very small. Neglecting this distortion, rotation of the pattern results in rotation of the transform through the same angle, and expansion (contraction) results in a transform which is proportional to a contracted (expanded) transform of the original pattern. The transform of a pattern which is a translation of some original pattern is just the transform of the original pattern multiplied by a phase factor related to the amount of translation in each direction. These results presume that spill-over from the grid has not occurred.

The discrete Fourier transform is even-symmetric in the real part and odd-symmetric in the imaginary part about the origin $p = q = 0$.

The consequences of some of the facts collected in this section will be discussed in conjunction with the considerations of the application of the Fourier transform to image classification.

SPATIAL FILTERING IN IMAGE CLASSIFICATION

The intuitive appeal for the use of the Fourier transform in image classification is, in principle, threefold. First, the features of an input stimulus are distributed (or "smeared") uniquely throughout the Fourier spectrum. Also many of the pattern features (and thus subjective differences between patterns) will manifest themselves, after suitable normalization, in particular spectral frequency regions. Finally, the Fourier representation of the input stimulus lends itself directly to selective spatial filtering.

Filtering in an information system may be generally defined as a process which separates information of a particular class from that which is irrelevant to that class. This is precisely what is desired in an image classification problem.

In the one-dimensional case of electronic communications, the filter is often a device which permits the transmission of information in some particular frequency band in preference to that in other bands. The filter separates a signal having known characteristics from irrelevant information, or noise, having known or predictable statistical characteristics. It is often possible to realize a filter which for a given problem is optimal in some carefully defined sense. In general, however, a filter which is optimal for one problem will be suboptimal for any other. This concept of filtering extends directly to any multi-dimensional case.

Optical filtering may be accomplished in the frequency domain by inserting in the plane of the collecting screen a thin transparency, resulting in a filtered diffraction pattern which is weighted at each point by the transmission characteristics of the filter.

In the array model proposed in a previous section, a form of discrete spatial filtering will result if the values of ranges of the numbers p and q are restricted in some way.

In digital computation, spatial filtering of a bandpass nature may be accomplished by computing the transform only at particular points in the spectrum.

Digital computation of the Fourier transform with selective spatial filtering of the bandpass type may be employed to simulate the operation of the proposed multi-array model in the image classification process.

In general, the problem is multi-class in nature, involving the classification of patterns possessing distortions in shape, size, and orientation as well as "noise" of other types. The design objective is to select a transform-filter combination which extracts from the input pattern that information relevant to classification. What is sought is an efficient transformation from a pattern space whose elements are of dimension $M \times N$ to an image space whose elements are of dimension $2P + 1$ by $2Q + 1$. The desired result is a set of images representing the input patterns suitably for decision theoretical classification. The spatial filter need not extract discrete features or properties, but rather must discard redundant and irrelevant information.

Preliminary design of a spatial filter for a specific problem might involve the investigation of the spectral content of a representative sample of patterns. Optimization would be accomplished by means of some form of statistical test on larger samples. Classification might be accomplished after adaptively adjusting decision boundaries found from a similar training set. Conclusions concerning optimality of the system may then be drawn by comparing the performance of the classification system with that of an ideal or perfect system, established by *a priori* assignment of the set of patterns to specific classes.

If the comparison is accomplished in the chosen norm, the decision is based on "closeness" in that norm. If the chosen norm has the form of the square root of the energy, the decision function is a Euclidean distance; the decision beoundaries are linear hyperplanes; and the process is truly *image* classification rather than *pattern* classification in the context of the terminology of this paper.

Although this process is problem-oriented and not distribution free, it is not necessary to assume a particular distribution. Rather the results would tend to vitiate or negate the means. It is instructive to visualize each class as a faceted cloud in the Fourier image space, whose faces are the linear hyperplanes corresponding to the Euclidean distances between prototypes of each class. Adjusting the choice of each prototype is equivalent to adjusting the decision boundaries between class clouds. Convergence of any adaptive method is, of course, not guaranteed since it is distribution dependent. As with filter design, conclusions concerning optimality may be drawn only by a statistical test of some form.

It is the objective of the digital simulation to analyse the suitability of systems based on these notions for the classification of images pertaining to a specific problem.

DIGITAL SIMULATION

Classification of two-dimensional quantized images using Fourier transforms and spatial filtering techniques has been accomplished by digital simulation using a computer controlled flying spot scanner and the IBM 7094 digital computer.

Quantization of the input pattern on a square grid of dimension 81×81 was accomplished by the use of a Litton Industries flying spot scanner controlled by a Digital Equipment Corporation PDP-1 general purpose computer. The quantized patterns were written on magnetic tape for use in the IBM 7094 computer in which the transform-filtering-classification program resided.

In this program, the center of brightness is calulated and the pattern shifted until this centre occupies some fixed standard position. The "trimming" of the pattern location on the grid may be qualitatively compared with the centering of objects of interest in the field of view of the fovea. The pattern is then normalized to unit energy content, having results not unlike those of pupilary control or retinal reflectance in an eye. No other preprocessing is performed in this program.

There exist efficient algorithms for the machine calculation of the Fourier transform[9, 10]. Since the input grid is square, the quantity to be calculated is

$$A_{pq}^* = \sum_{m=1}^{81} \sum_{n=1}^{81} a_{mn}\, e^{-j\frac{2\pi}{M^*}(mp+nq)} \qquad (5)$$

where A_{pq}^* is the filtered transform, a_{mn} represents the brightness distribution of the quantized, centred, normalized pattern, and the calculation is taken over selected values of p and q, respectively. Computational efficiencies may be achieved by making use of the symmetry properties of the transform and some trigonometric relationships pertinent to the kernel function[10]. The entire program requires less than two seconds per pattern including input–output operations.

Preliminary design of the spatial filter is made by examining the spectra of a small but representative sample of the patterns of interest. The first step is to determine heuristically from the extent of the data on the 81×81 grid, a mean fundamental frequency contained in the set. This permits the establishment of the value (which need not equal 81) of M^* in Equation (5) above.

The next step is to determine the frequency extent in each direction in the spectrum of contributions from the pattern sample. In general, non-negligible contributions lie in some region of the spectrum ranged by values of p and q smaller than 81×81.

If point-by-point differences between patterns from like classes and between patterns from unlike classes are calculated, it is possible to judge in which regions lie image differences between similar patterns not pertinent to the classification process and those between dissimilar patterns which might be useful.

Further adjustments in the filter selection may then be made by examining results of tests conducted on larger samples of patterns of interest.

After a filter has been selected, or perhaps several filters for analytic purposes, and the computation in Equation (5) is performed, the image is in a form ready for the decision process. No further post-processing of the image is performed by the program.

The decision function used in the program is closeness in the chosen norm, or the minimum Euclidean distance between the test pattern image and prototype image functions from each class in the problem. The first step in prototype selection is the calculation of the mean image function from a representative sample of images from each class.

The prototypes, and thus the decision boundaries, are then adjusted during a period of testing on a larger sample. If an image is correctly classified, it lies in the assumed "cloud" and no adjustment is made. If it is incorrectly classified, a new mean image is computed which now includes this test image. This still may not cause the correct classification of this image; in fact, one which originally belonged to the cloud might be ejected by this adjustment. This suggests an iteration on the test data of the decision boundary adjustment. Certainly, convergence of this process is not guaranteed; in general, the images will not be linearly separable. If divergence actually occurs, a return to the filter design process is indicated. Usually, some best performance may result from this iterative process and the system may now be tested on a set of patterns not in the original set. At any stage in the process the analyst may return to either filter adjustment or boundary adjustment. In the final analysis a judgement must be made concerning system performance with respect to some definition of optimum performance.

THE NUMERIC CHARACTER PROBLEM

In this section, the simulation of the classification of hand-printed numeric characters is described. It is the objective of the simulation not to demonstrate a numeral reader, but rather to test and evaluate the spatial filtering principles incorporated in the model on a specific problem.

To this end, the patterns employed in the simulation should possess a reasonable amount of complexity, should be chosen from a non-trivial set of classes, and should be, in the view of the analyst, reasonably unambiguous. The numerals, from each of ten classes, possess properties whose nature approaches these criteria.

A set of 200 characters, hand-printed by twenty different people, was collected for the experiment. Computer print-outs of patterns were obtained and the visual inspection of a sample of these patterns permitted the choice of $M^* = 64$ for the calculation of Equation (5).

The uniquely invertible spectrum is an 81×81 grid whose central cell corresponds to the d.c. value $p = q = 0$. Each concentric square ring of increasing dimension represents a particular spatial harmonic of the fundamental frequency, so that there are forty such harmonics in the entire grid.

Inspection of the spectra of a small sample revealed that little significant structure lay outside the tenth harmonic for this problem. Thus a low-pass filter of dimension 21×21 would be sufficient to encode a pattern with little distortion. This was verified by calculating the inverse transforms of several filtered images.

Point-by-point differences on the 21 × 21 grid were calculated for several pattern pairs. For pattern pairs from the same class small differences appeared in the first three harmonics, differences in detail manifesting themselves in the higher frequencies. For pattern pairs from different classes larger differences were found throughout the ten-harmonic spectrum.

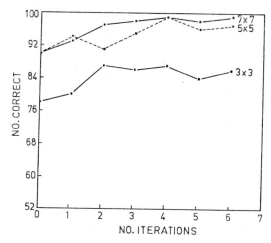

FIGURE 2   Learning curves, ten numeral classes

Three low-pass filters were selected for analysis: a three harmonic (7 × 7) filter, a two harmonic (5 × 5) filter, and a fundamental frequency (3 × 3) filter. Systems for each filter were exercised in identical ways. Sixty patterns, six from each class, were used to establish a mean prototype for each class. Decision boundaries were adjusted on an additional 40 patterns by iteratively changing the mean prototypes whenever errors occurred. Learning curves for each system based on iterations for the 100 patterns in this training set are shown in Figure 2.

Each system was then tested on 100 additional patterns, ten from each class, not in the training set, using the decision boundaries corresponding to best performance achieved during training. Results for each system are given in Table 1.

Best performance during training occurred for each system after only a few iterations. The three harmonic (7 × 7) filter appears to have the most stable learning curve, and one would predict a lower erorr rate for this system for patterns not in the training set. The test results bear this out.

Further tests are presently being conducted with this model. Effects of rotation, scale change, and additive noise are being investigated. Simulation

TABLE 1

System	Training errors	Total errors
3×3	13/100	35/200
5×5	1/100	9/200
7×7	1/100	6/200

is underway on a larger sample of hand-printed alpha characters from a larger set of classes. Results are not available at this writing, but preliminary results appear to be qualitatively similar to those reported here.

CONCLUSIONS

The digital simulation of a model for the classification of visual images, derived from known aspects of the human visual system, has been performed. A problem in the classification of numeric characters has been described and the results of the simulation have been presented.

It is believed that the moderately sized sample of characters employed in the test possess a general pathology indicative of a non-trivial problem familiar to researchers in character recognition. The results portray a system approach capable of efficient and accurate classification of these patterns.

The premise that selective spatial filtering in the discrete Fourier domain permits this classification is vitiated by the results. The extent to which this emulates the operation of human cortex remains a matter of conjecture. That these accuracies are achieved with a minimum of pre-processing, without the extraction of distinct features, and with efficient image storage techniques suggests a line of research which is being pursued aggressively in our laboratory.

References

1. G. Nagy, "State of the art in pattern recognition", *Proc. I.E.E.E. (Inst. Elec. Electron. Engrs.)*, **56**, 836–62 (1968).
2. O. J. Tretiak, "Image processing: Basic techniques and applications", *Summer Course, Mass. Inst. Tech.* (1968).
3. S. Polyak, *The Vertebrate Visual System*, University of Chicago Press, Chicago (1957).
4. H. Chang, "Functional organization of central visual pathways", *Assoc. Res. Nervous Mental Diseases* (1950).
5. H. Dusser de Barenne *et al.*, "Physiological neuronography of the cortico-striatal connections", *Assoc. Res. Nervous Mental Diseases* (1942).
6. M. Kabrisky, *A Proposed Model for Visual Information Processing in the Human Brain*, University of Illinois Press, Urbana (1964).
7. M. Born and E. Wolf, *Principles of Optics*, 2nd revised ed., Pergamon Press, Oxford (1964).
8. N. Wiener, "General harmonic analysis", *Acta Math.*, **55**, 117–258 (1930).
9. J. Cooley and J. Tukey, "An algorithm for the machine calculation of complex Fourier series", *Math. Comput.*, **19**, 297–301 (1965).
10. C. Radoy, "Pattern recognition by Fourier series transformations", *M.S. Thesis, Air Force Inst. Tech.* (1967).

A natural definition of the similarity and the typicality of operating taxonomic units

HEIKKI PESONEN

Department of Geography
University of Oulu, Finland

Summary

In certain instances one may be faced with a body of observed data whose characteristics cannot be stated or explained by means of any clear hypothesis. This kind of situation is common in science and in everyday life. The reaction to it is to classify the objects and to take typical objects as representatives of the whole body of objects. Such classification procedures may be seen as a method of encoding as efficiently as possible the original information. At least, when the body of observation is a large one, it would be better to do the work applying some specific algorithms with the use of automatic data processing. The mushroom growth of different taxonomic programmes recently demonstrates this. The author then describes his work in this field.

THE PROBLEM

In certain instances one may be faced with a body of observed data whose characteristics cannot be stated or explained by means of any clear hypothesis. This kind of situation is common in science and in everyday life. One possible reaction to it is to classify the objects and to take objects typical to the groups as representatives of the whole population. For example, when thinking of the human population of the world, we may divide it into nations, and bear only typical representatives of them in our mind. This method of thinking may be a primitive one, but it is possible to give an exact definition to it, and so to get a natural taxonomic program.

Let us imagine that we are anthropologists, who have the task of dividing a population grouping of individuals into natural divisions. As the starting point, let us think of the individuals as represented by points in a space. The dimensions are the observed characteristics of the individuals. Having only two or three dimensions, some groups may be seen in the space. But how can we get a numerical measure of the grouping? The usual way is to define some sort of combined variance of the variables in the data matrix and then to compare the variance within groups to the variance between groups. The within-group variance should be as small as possible and the between-group variance as large as possible. I should call this grouping strategy an apartheid policy. For example, in a hypothetical country the government has to divide the peoples into groups in such a way that the internal homogeneity of the groups is great and the differences between the groups are clear.

For myself, I would take another leading principle for the grouping. It gives a more specific definition to the task of the taxonomic work than the apartheid policy. I would call it the model policy. What we are looking for in the grouping is a model or models of the individuals to be grouped. For myself, I think that there is no common method which ought to be used every time to find the model individuals. It may be possible to describe exactly how the characteristics of the individual reflect its real structure, and thus to get the best possible method in every case. Unfortunately no such knowledge is available in most situations in which some taxonomy is necessary, and so a general method is needed.

It seems reasonable to think that the task of the grouping process is to describe the data material in such a way that the investigator could proceed to form more specific hypotheses about the real forces which are responsible for the data material. Stated in such a general way, the only tools to be used to find the procedures could be based on some type of general information theory. For this reason, I define the typical individual or "type" as a means to transfer information about its group members. The type must then be as similar or near to each of the group members as possible.

DEFINITION OF SIMILARITY[1]

If for a variable k the two observation units i and j have the same value, the information obtainable about the individual i, if j is known, is a function of the number of possible classes C_k into which the variable k could divide the population. This is true whether the variable is a quantitative or qualitative one.

What is the situation when k is a quantitative variable whose values are different for the two individuals? If the values of the variable k had been measured with less precision, at some stage the two values have been the same. The C_k of this hypothetical variable may be taken as a measure of the information received. It can be calculated according to the formula

$$C_k/(|X_{ki} - X_{kj}| + 1) \tag{1}$$

where the numerical values of X are the class numbers in the form 1, 2, 3, ..., C_k. This formula is a measure of similarity, and as an inverse without the term C_k the "distance".

By the same reasoning used above in the case of a single variable, it is clear that the similarity between two observation units is the product of the similarities of the variables

$$\text{Sim}_{ij} = \prod_{k=1}^{k=M} C_k \times \prod_{k=1}^{k=M} (|X_{ki} - X_{kj}| + 1)^{-1} \tag{2}$$

where M is the number of variables.

If any variable is qualitative, its similarity coefficient is C_k when the values are the same, otherwise 1.

It was stated in connection with formula (1) how it is possible, when the variables are quantitative, to obtain a simple measure of distance from the measure of similarity Sim_{ij}

$$\text{Dis}_{ij} = 1/\text{Sim}_{ij}'' \tag{3}$$

when $C_k = 1$.

This distance function is neither a Euclidian distance nor a more general Minkowskian r-metrics[2].

These distance coefficients are likely to have useful mathematical features. A Euclidian distance is also generally held to be a natural measure. But this is only necessarily so in a two- or three-dimensional geographic or luna-graphic coordinate system. When some sort of similarity between research objects is measured instead of distances between places, the Euclidian measure has been found to have its drawbacks. To quote Warr and Knapper[3]:

"There are, however, several cogent arguments against the use of D scores (Euclidian distance) when assessing the difference between profiles. The objections to D are based on the fact that the same D score can be derived from a number of different relationships between profiles. Consider the following two pairs of profiles: P_1 and P_2; P_3 and P_4:

Scale	P_1	P_2	P_3	P_4
1	2	2	6	4
2	8	8	1	3
3	6	6	8	6
4	3	3	7	5
5	7	3	2	2

The D score between P_1 and P_2 is the same as that between P_3 and P_4 despite the fact that there are differences on four scales between P_3 and P_4 but only on a single scale in the former comparison." According to (3)

$$\text{Dis}_{P_1 P_2} = 5 \quad \text{and} \quad \text{Dis}_{P_3 P_4} = 3^4 = 81$$

The difference is clear.

A very popular way of measuring similarity between individuals when the variables are quantitative is to calculate the correlation coefficient between the individuals. Despite its great popularity, this way of correlating individuals is quite senseless. If, for instance, the numerical values of all the variables for some individual are the same, the correlation of this individual with others cannot be calculated. This kind of individual is like a variable that has no variance at all. We can, however, resolve this dilemma if we add a quite artificial variable to the existing variables and give every individual a random value relative to it. It should be easy to see, however, that a variable of individuals is generally not distributed normally as the correlation coefficient would presume. This is obviously not regarded as being a hindrance to the carrying out of factor analyses of Q type. It has also been shown that the correlation between objects is not independent of the direction of the scales of the variables[4]. My own index does not have the above drawbacks. But someone might find others in it.

ANALYSING THE NATURALNESS OF THE SIMILARITY INDEX

It would naturally be interesting to know how adequately my index measures a human being's natural experiencing of similarity. It would probably be easy to show that it gives a better result than does the mere use of random numbers. And the test will have greater interest if my index is compared with, say, ordinary Euclidian distance. If we examine quantitative variables, it will be easy to discern the theory of such a test. For two variables, it appears in the following diagram (Figure 1).

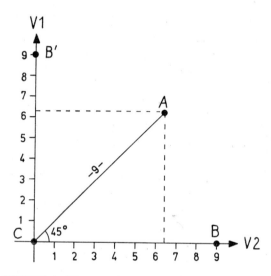

FIGURE 1   The graphic representation of the testplan

The person in the test is asked whether the object placed at point C bears a closer resemblance to the object at point A or the one at point B. In Figure 2 there is a questionnaire based on a test arranged like this. Up at the left it first asks the age of the interviewee. The interviewee is then asked to put a tick in box 1 if male and box 2 if female. The interviewee is then asked which of the Figures 1 and 2 bears a closer resemblance to Figure 3. If an answer is possible, the figure should be ticked. After this follow 9 sections with 3 figures in each. The figures are all squares which vary in size and darkness. Square 3 is always the same. It is regarded as being located at point C.

The darkness of the square determines its location in respect of the $V\,1$ axis. The darkness scale was prepared by means of screen paper[5]. The screen paper was used to prepare a greyness scale apparently having regular gradation.

The area of the square determines its location in respect of the $V\,2$ axis.

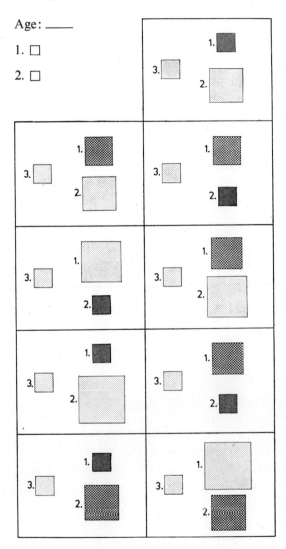

FIGURE 2   Relative similarity response questionnaire

The area scale is a logarithmic one. No separate test was made of the impression it gave of regular gradation in size. Instead, an attempt was made to find a size scale that corresponded in length with the darkness scale. This was done by comparing their end points, i.e. the largest square with the darkest square. Thus the questionnaire shows 3 different logarithmic size

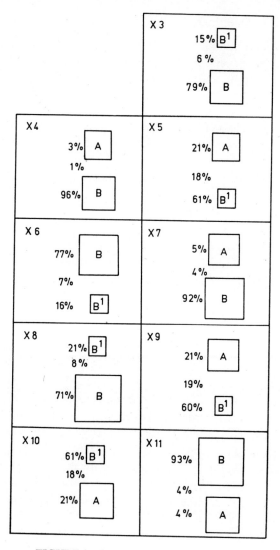

FIGURE 3   Responses to questionnaire

scales, all having the same starting point while the largest areas are different.

Figure 3 is a diagram showing the location of each square in a coordinate system. Each question has been marked as $X3$–$X11$. The questions can be divided into three groups depending on what area scale was used:

Questions	Area of largest square cm^2
X 3, X 4, and X 5	3.24
X 6, X 7, and X 9	4.63
X 8, X 10, and X 11	6.25

The smallest square was the same size in all, being 1 cm^2.

The diagram also shows for each question the percentage of persons opting for the various squares, and the proportion of persons unable to decide (Figures 2 and 3).

The number of tested persons was 202. They were told that participation in the test was voluntary and that the test was not an intelligence test but was to be used only in an attempt to find people's natural impressions of the matter being studied. They were asked to answer independently, and were told that it was best to leave the question unanswered if the answer did not seem to be obvious without a deal of thought. They did not have to write their names on the questionnaire. Nobody asked refused to take part in the test.

31 of the tested persons were first-year undergraduates, 40 were in the 5th or 6th class in evening school and the rest were pupils of forms IV–VII in an ordinary secondary school. The age and sex compositions of the tested persons are shown in Table 1. Four female persons in the test would not consent to state their age.

One of the tested persons entered himself as both man and woman, but, as a school class was concerned, it was easy to establish that he was a male at least officially. The testing of the university students was done in the cartography room of the Department of Geography during ordinary lecture hours, a break of 15 minutes being reserved for it. The school pupils were tested during an ordinary school lesson. They too were of course given a free 15 minutes for the test. Another questionnaire, which will be dealt with later, was also answered during this time.

It appears from the distributions of the answers to questions $X3$, $X6$, and $X8$ that the ends of the size and darkness scales are not found to be equi-

TABLE 1   Tested persons

	EVS	STDTS	VII	VI	V	IVA	IVB	All
No age answer	2	1	–	–	1	–	–	4
14	–	–	–	–	–	8	3	11
15	–	–	–	–	1	8	7	16
16	1	–	–	5	2	12	13	33
17	1	–	–	7	11	5	6	30
18	3	–	3	4	7	–	–	17
19	7	–	11	10	3	–	–	31
20	6	5	–	1	1	–	–	13
21	6	13	1	1	–	–	–	21
22	1	6	–	–	–	–	–	7
22	2	2	–	–	–	–	–	4
24	2	2	–	–	–	–	–	4
25	1	–	–	–	–	–	–	1
26	1	1	–	–	–	–	–	2
27	2	–	–	–	–	–	–	2
28	1	1	–	–	–	–	–	2
29	1	–	–	–	–	–	–	1
32	1	–	–	–	–	–	–	1
33	1	–	–	–	–	–	–	1
36	1	–	–	–	–	–	–	1
	40	31	15	28	26	33	29	202
Males %	10	52	40	21	42	36	72	38
Sightpersons	1	6	–	–	–	5	2	14
One type (3) persons	3	7	5	5	3	12	6	41

STDTS, undergraduates; EVS, evening school students; others, day school pupils.

valent by the tested persons, but that the value for the end of the size scale is smaller than the end value for the darkness scale. This can also be seen when a comparison is made between the distributions of the answers to questions $X4$, $X7$, and $X11$ and those of questions $X5$, $X9$, and $X10$. The replies to these sets of questions seem however to indicate that the distance to the point between the coordinate axes is experienced as being longer than the corresponding distance on a coordinate axis. If this is the case, the author's distance measure is in this sense more natural than is the Euclidian. But to make sure of this, the test will have to be repeated with a difference greyness scale in which the screen pattern does not vary. This factor may have influenced the result.

The percentage distributions of the answers to the different questions have been examined above. Below, tested persons will be examined individually and a definition of the ideal answer will be given, and it will be seen whether persons giving ideal answers were to be found in the material.

As the observation material was processed by means of a computer program written in the SURVO programming language, a person of that kind was defined in the same language[6]. The definition, however, will also be given in words later on.

Obviously, to the ideal test person there must be a size scale equivalent to the darkness scale. This would be demonstrated by that person's inability to answer at least one of the questions $X3$, $X6$, or $X8$. Concurrently, he should be able to answer the two other questions belonging to the same group as the question he was unable to answer among $X3$, $X6$, or $X8$. This is a characteristic of a test person for whom the Boolean variable "sight" has the value true. This test person is still not perfect, for he is not necessarily able to distinguish between the three size scales employed. For the most ideal test person the Boolean variable "find" gets the value true. There were fourteen "sight" test persons (see Table 1), but only two of these were "find" test persons. The distributions of the answers of the "sight" elite individuals are by and large the same as for the whole population, naturally with the exception of questions $X3$, $X6$, and $X8$ (Table 2). For the other questions the answers seem to have been more obviously clear, which fits the idea of elite individuals being either persons with a better than normal comprehension of dimensions or persons who fill in forms more conscientiously than normal.

TABLE 2   The distribution of the answers of the "Sight" persons

	$X3$	$X4$	$X5$	$X6$	$X7$	$X8$	$X9$	$X10$	$X11$
1	–	–	1	2	–	1	2	14	14
2	3	14	13	1	14	1	12	–	–
No answer	11	–	–	11	–	12	–	–	–

If this is the case, this part of the material confirms the result obtained on the basis of the entire material, according to which a measure of distance defined in terms of formula (3) is a better description of the difference between objects as experienced by people than is the Euclidian measure of distance.

EVALUATION OF TYPICALITY[1]

In order to decide a type for each group, it is necessary to measure the total information which the type transfers regarding its group members. Information is usually defined as a logarithmic function when it is additive and it would seem reasonable to do so here.

$$\text{Sim}'_{ij} = \log \text{Sim}_{ij}$$

when the typicality might be

$$\left(\sum_{j=1}^{j=N} \text{Sim}'_{ij} \right) \Big/ (N - 1) \tag{4}$$

where N is the number of group members and Sim'_{ij} is omitted when $i = j$.

But what happens when these principles are applied to a specialized example, in which the data matrix is of the form

Number	X_1	X_2	X_3	X_4	
1	0	0	1	1	
2	0	0	1	1	
3	0	0	1	1	
4	1	1	1	1	$M = 4$
5	1	1	0	0	
6	1	1	0	0	$N = 7$
7	1	1	0	0	

Without the logarithmic transformation, the similarities of one variable are 2 or 1 (equation 1)), and the information is therefore 1 bit or 0 ($\log_2 (2) = 1$, $\log_2 (1) = 0$).

The typicalities according to the formula (4) of the individuals 1–3 and 5–7 are $(2 \times 4 + 2)/6 = 1.7$ and for individual 4, $6 \times 2/6 = 2$. Number 4 is thus the most typical individual. But this result is inadequate. The rows and the columns of the data matrix may not be in the same positions when the typicality is calculated. Another solution is prefered by the author, i.e. not to use the logarithmic measure Sim'_{ij}, but to define the similarity as before as the product of the similarities of the different variables (2), and to take the typicality as the mean of these similarities.

$$\text{Typ}_i = \left(\sum_{j=1}^{j=N} \text{Sim}_{ij} \right) \Big/ (N - 1) \tag{5}$$

Sim_{ij} is omitted when $i = j$.

According to this new evaluation of typicality:

$$\text{Typ}_{1-3 \text{ and } 5-7} = (2 \times 2^4 + 2^2)/6 = 6 \quad \text{and} \quad \text{Typ}_4 = 6 \times 2^2/6 = 4.$$

CONCEPT OF TYPICALITY

At the same time as the 202 tested persons were asked for their opinions on the similarity of the squares, they were also shown another questionnaire which is reproduced in Figure 4. The questionnaire has two sections, each with a population of its own. To the left of each individual is its number. The

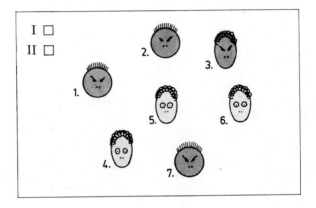

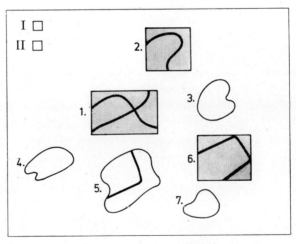

FIGURE 4   The populations

tested persons were asked to find from each section one individual most typical of the population, and preferably only one. There are 2 boxes in each section in which it was requested that the number of the most typical individual should be entered. But if the tested person felt that there necessarily had to be two typical individuals, he was allowed to enter a second number.

The observant reader will easily notice that both of the populations have been prepared on the basis of the data matrix on page 1061. To individual

TABLE 3   The cross-tabulation of the answers to the question: "Who is the most typical individual of the population?"

(1) Population

II \ I	0	1	2	3	4	5	6	7		%
0	18	4	12	41	7	8	6	2	98	49
1	–		–	2	2	–	–	–	4	2
2	–	2		2	2	7	1	–	14	7
3	–	2	–		1	2	1	2	8	4
4	–	10	8	5		1	3	1	28	14
5	–	3	8	3	4		2	4	24	12
6	–	1	3	5	4	2		1	16	8
7	–	2	1	1	1	2	3		10	5
	18	24	32	59	21	22	16	10	202	
%	9	12	16	29	10	11	8	5		100

(2) Population

II \ I	0	1	2	3	4	5	6	7		%
0	27	12	5	20	13	28	4	2	111	55
1	–		5	3	1	1	1	–	11	5
2	–	4		7	1	–	–	1	13	6
3	–	9	4		–	–	2	5	20	10
4	–	4	6	2		–	2	1	15	7
5	–	7	4	–	–		1	–	12	6
6	–	2	1	2	1	1		–	7	3
7	1	–	6	4	1	1	–		13	6
	28	38	31	38	17	31	10	9	202	
%	14	19	15	19	8	15	5	4		100

four corresponds in the first population individual number 3, and in the second population individual number 5.

The replies on both of the populations have been cross-tabulated in Table 3. Eighteen tested persons did not reply at all to the typicality question on the first population. The number of such persons was 27 for the second population. The most interesting were the test persons who indicated only one type, as had been requested. The distribution of their answers is shown in the top line of the tables. The "mean individuals" found number 3 in the first population and number 5 in the second to be clearly more popular than the others, although the distribution for the second population was more even than that for the first. The "tabulation" of the characteristics of the second population was obviously more difficult than that of the first. The distribution of the persons who found the "average individual" from the first population resembles the distribution of "sight" persons, as emerges from Table 1.

General opinion obviously regards the average individual as being typical. But the test situation was artificial in the sense that an attempt was made therein to distinguish the finding of a type from the forming of a group. But this is not the case in my taxonomy program, where the concepts of similarity and typicality function precisely to form a group. Their justification thus depends on how good the taxonomy program is, i.e. how correct grouping it performs.

IS IT POSSIBLE TO TEST THE VALUE OF SOME GENERAL TAXONOMIC METHOD?

Various criteria can be thought of for the determination of the superiority of a taxonomic program. One such is the criterion of predictability. For instance, a taxonomy program classifying bacteria in a certain way is a good one if it proves later that the groups obtained are sensitive in different ways to different antibiotics[7]. But predictability cannot be the measure of superiority of a general taxonomic method. This is obviously based on the program somehow discerning the true structure of objects, and this must certainly be different in different sciences. A general taxonomic program cannot, consequently, be studied by simulation either[8].

One could, of course, analyse the extent to which the groupings obtained with various taxonomic methods correspond to people's characteristic manner of grouping objects. For a test of this kind one could, for instance, generate object populations from a single data matrix, as done above in studying concepts of typicality. The results might show one taxonomic program to be clearly more natural than others. But this is not a sufficient or even necessary requirement for the evaluation of a taxonomic program.

A taxonomic method is meant to be an aid for the researcher, so that the grouping of the material will give the researcher a better picture of the objects of his study than he would get by examining the material in the mass. For this reason a consistent manner of testing various taxonomic methods would be as follows.

Take two random collections of scientists and present a large selection of different types of data material to both groups. The first group would use, e.g., my method, and the second, i.e. control group would use some other method. In a few years we would get a statistical measure showing which of the grouping methods is of greater assistance.

Acknowledgments

I am extremely grateful to the 202 persons who took part in my test and who all volunteered to be "guinea pigs". My wife, Sisko Pesonen, did the testing of the school classes at Lassinkallion Yhteiskoulu, Oulu. Mr. Paavo Korhonen drew up the questionnaires I had envisaged. Messrs. Rolf Erlewein and Martyn Summerhill did the translation into English.

References

1. H. Pesonen, "A natural way to measure similarities and to divide a population into groups", *NordDATA-69 kongressföredrag*, Vol. 1 (1969), pp. 269–76.
2. J. B. Kruskal, "Multidimensional scaling by optimizing goodness of fit to a nonmetric hypothesis", *Psychometrika*, **29**, No. 1, 22–7 (1964).
3. P. B. Warr and C. Knapper, *The Perception of People and Events*, Wiley, London (1968), pp. 59–60.
4. E. C. Minkoff, "The effects on classification of slight alterations in numerical technique", *Systematic Zool.*, **14**, No. 3 (1965).
5. *ARTYPE*, Nos. 4010, 4025, 4001, 4002, 4003, 4013, 4004, 4014, 4034, and 4039.
6. T. Alanko, S. Mustonen, and M. Tienari, "A statistical programming language SURVO 66", *BIT*, **8**, No. 2 (1968).
7. N. T. J. Bailey, *The Mathematical Approach to Biology and Medicine*, Wiley, London (1967), pp. 135–6.
8. R. R. Sokal, "Numerical taxonomy", *Sci. Am.*, 106–16 (1966).
9. H. Pesonen, "General taxonomy program", *IBM, PID, Program order*, No. 360D-13,1,005.

THE SURVO PROGRAM

Boolean instructions.

EQUAL@	$e\ u_1\ u_2$	e is *true* if $u_1 = u_2$
LESS@	$e\ u_1\ u_2$	e is *true* if $u_1 < u_2$
LESSQ@	$e\ u_1\ u_2$	e is *true* if $u_1 \leqq u_2$
BETWEEN@	$e\ u_1\ u_2\ u_3$	e is *true* if $u_1 \leqq u_2 \leqq u_3$
OR@	$e\ e_1 \dots e_r$	$e := e_1 \vee e_2 \vee \dots \vee e_r$
AND@	$e\ e_1 \dots e_r$	$e := e_1 \wedge e_2 \wedge \dots \wedge e_r$
NOT@	$e\ e_1$	$e := \neg e_1$

```
BETWEEN@ ASWX3   1  X3 2
   @  ASWX4   1 X4   2
   @  ASWX5   1  X5 2
   @  ASWX6   1 X6 2
   @  ASWX7   1  X7 2
   @  ASWX8   1 X8   2
   @  ASWX9   1 X9   2
   @  ASWX10  1 X10  2
   @  ASWX11  1  X11 2

NOT@ NASWX3    ASWX3
   @ NASWX6    ASWX6
   @ NASWX8    ASWX8

AND@ KORD1   NASWX3   ASWX4   ASWX5
   @ KORD2   NASWX6   ASWX7   ASWX9
   @ KORD3   NASWX8   ASWX10  ASWX11

NOT@ NKORD1   KORD1
   @ NKORD2   KORD2
   @ NKORD3   KORD3

OR@ SIGHT   KORD1   KORD2   KORD3
AND@ FK1 KORD1 NKORD2 NKORD3
   @ FK2 NKORD1 KORD2 NKORD3
   @ FK3 NKORD1 NKORD2 KORD3

OR@ FIND   FK1   FK2   FK3
```

Biochemical cybernetics

L. MERZER

U.K.

Summary

The basic principles of cybernetics are negative feedback and homeostasis. The author quotes a number of chemical reactions to demonstrate the application of the above principles. The problem of bridging the gap between biological and "a-biotic" reactions is then discussed.

INTRODUCTION

The basic principles of cybernetics are negative feedback and homeostasis. The first consists of a phenomenon producing in turn another phenomenon, whose effect is to cancel the first, thus producing self-regulation. Homeostasis is a tendency of a system to maintain its equilibrium with the help of the negative feedback. An additional feature of cybernetics is that the effects are binary, e.g. they either exist or not. Either there is an impulse or none and no other possibility.

One has to state right from the start that the principles of Cybernetics apply to many manifestations of human and social life. It is only by accident that it first appeared in an "electromechanical" form.

The principles of cybernetics have their applications, as we shall attempt to show, in chemical and biological manifestations, and could be used for trying to solve social and economical problems which could be looked upon as part of biological life. They may supply the answer to apparently insoluble problems.

In the initial stages of application of cybernetics, devices have been constructed behaving and acting as imitators and extensors of human and animal brain and muscle activity: from mechanical tortoises and rats finding their way towards a lettuce or through a maze, memorizing the route, learning to avoid the past mistakes, through robots playing noughts and crosses, draughts and chess and never losing—to most complicated computers solving intricate mathematical calculations, storing acquired data and using them when the right time comes and all that at a lightning speed, which would have taken years of tedious work by scores of men to solve. They can be geared to most elaborate controls; running, providing and regulating whole industries, without human intervention. The computers even acquire "neuroses" when abused and are submitted to "treatment" for their correction. The trend is to construct even more elaborate computers, dealing with more intricate problems, like self-repairing and self-producing or reproducing. This invasion of computer control into the industrial and economic world, although it solves problems connected with employment of human beings, it creates unemployment. It will be seen that there is a possibility of a solution to this new problem by application of cybernetic principles. We shall come back to this problem at the end of this paper.

The characteristics of computer behaviour present an impressive similarity with behaviour of living organisms. There is even a branch of psychology which uses this similarity to observe the behaviour of living beings and to draw conclusions from it. This is a very dangerous approach because one may lose the notion that there is a boundary between a computer and a living being. And yet this boundary is quite sharp. However, the performance of the computer resembles the human mind. The computer is made from glass, metal fibre, or mineral; the mind of living flesh and blood, or scientifically speaking of proteins, carbohydrates, fats, plus other ingredients composing a living organism. One is a-biotic, the other a biological function. The similarity will always remain an analogy and could not become an identity.

CYBERNETICS AND CHEMISTRY

There is a succession of chemical reactions, some simple, others of great complexity, which could be considered as satisfying the basic principles of cybernetics, e.g. negative feedback, homeostasis, and binomial connotation.

(a) A well-known example of this is the law of Le Chatelier: "When a stress is brought to bear on a system in equilibrium, the system tends to change so as to relieve the stress." This means if one of the conditions of the chemical equilibrium, e.g. pressure, temperature, or concentration is modified, the reaction tends to change in the direction in which the modified condition is restored to its original value. A very good example to illustrate the application of this law to a basic industrial chemical process is the synthesis of ammonia by the process of Haber. As molecular weights of all gases occupy this same volume at the same pressure and temperature, if one mixes 1 volume of nitrogen gas and 3 volumes of hydrogen and submits this mixture to high pressures the resulting gas will be ammonia.

$$N_2 + 3\,H_2 \rightarrow 2\,NH_3$$

1 vol.   3 vol.   2 vol.

It means that to counteract the increased pressure the reaction tends to reduce the volume of the gas and therefore the pressure.

The synthetic reaction is exothermic and is therefore favoured by a reduction of temperature; but the rate of reaction rises with increasing temperature, because increased temperature increases the mobility of the reacting molecules, and thereby the chances of encounter. In practice a compromise between actual yield of ammonia and rate of attaining equilibrium is achieved by using high pressure and *moderately high* temperature.

Iron and iron oxides, as catalysts also increase the probability of encounter of the molecules and therefore increase the rate of reaction.

The reaction satisfies all conditions of cybernetics. The re-establishment of equilibrium is ruled by the principle of negative feedback—the tendency towards equilibrium is a manifestation of homeostasis, and the reaction is binomial. The reaction between molecules in contact is instantaneous or there is no reaction. This should not be confused with speed of reaction—which depends on the frequency of encounters of reactant molecules. The catalyst has the function to increase this frequency but at the moment of contact of the reactants—the reaction is instantaneous.

(b) Reaction of equilibrium of the type

$$AB + XY \rightleftharpoons AX + BY$$

This type of reaction is considered as dynamic, taking place simultaneously in both directions at such speeds that the concentration of components on both sides of the equation remain unchanged. This occurs as long as thermodynamic conditions, e.g. concentration, pressure, and temperature remain constant.

This constant of concentration is expressed by the equation

$$\frac{C_{AX} + C_{BY}}{C_{AB} + C_{XY}} = K\,(CTP)$$

where C is the concentration, T the temperature, and P the pressure. K is a constant of equilibria specific to this reaction in given conditions and can be considered as determining a state of homeostasis. Any change in the thermodynamic conditions disturbs this equilibrium and the reaction tends towards a new equilibrium—a new constant K' is established and therefore a new state of homeostasis is established. Assuming that component AB was added to produce a new concentration, a new equilibrium is established

$$\frac{C'_{AX} + C'_{BY}}{C'_{AB} + C'_{XY}} = K'$$

where $K' \neq K$.

This reaction is of a negative feedback type because it tends to establish and maintain a state of homeostasis; it is of binomial type because each reaction occurs at the instant of contact of the reacting molecules, and the reaction either occurs or does not, as we have postulated before.

Practically all enzymatic reactions (which are of prime importance in biology) are of this type of reaction. Without going into detailed analysis of the diverse type of enzymatic catalysis, like the interaction of enzymes and co-enzymes, phosphate carriers, or hydrogen donors and acceptors, they all have a common characteristic of contributing to a displacement of an equilibrium into another one, and thus establishing a state of homeostasis.

(c) A similar situation occurs in the case of buffer solutions. They are solutions containing either a weak acid and a salt of this same acid with a strong base or a weak base and a salt of this base with a strong acid. The weak acid and base, respectively, dissociate very little in relation to the total amount of acid or base in the aqueous solution, but their salts are dissociated into ions, in large proportion to the dissolved salt. As it is *the concentration of hydrogen ions alone* which determine the pH of a solution or its acidic state, then a small addition of acid causes the process of dissociation or association to move towards re-establishment of the initial hydrogen ion concentration. For example, if more acid is added to a solution in water of acetic acid which is a weak acid and sodium acetate which is a salt of a weak acid and a strong base, the acetate ion from the salt will combine with the added hydrogen ion to form a non-dissociated acetic acid

$$[CH_3COO^- + Na^+] + H^+ \rightarrow CH_3COOH + Na^+$$

It means that the excess of free hydrogen ions has been captured into an associated form of acid and the pH remains unaffected.

If a strong base is added to this buffer solution the hydroxide ion OH^- combines with the available hydrogen ion to form little dissociated water. The depleted free hydrogen ion is replaced from non-dissociated acetic acid and the hydrogen ion concentration is unaffected.

$$HC_2H_3O_2 \rightarrow C_2H_3O_2^- + H^+$$

In the blood carbonic acid and sodium bicarbonate act as a buffer system to help to maintain the pH of blood close to 7.4, even though acidic and basic substances pass continually in the blood stream.

A solution containing bicarbonate may act as a buffer in the following fashion: when acid is added

$$HCO_3^- + H^+ \rightarrow H_2CO_3$$

when a base is added

$$HCO_3^- + OH^- \rightarrow HOH + CO_3^{2-}.$$

We see in this particular case that sodium bicarbonate acts as an acid or a base, and is called amphoteric substance.

The release or capture of a hydrogen ion obeys the principles of negative feedback; it reacts in the opposite direction according to whether hydrogen ion or hydroxyl ion is added. Homeostasis is maintained in the form of a constant pH value and the reaction is binomial.

(d) Another example of chemical homeostasis is tautomeric equilibrium. It consists of the fact that a given substance has two different internal structures even if the total amount of components remains unchanged. There are many examples of tautomerism in organic and biological chemistry of plants and animals: enol- and keto- forms, laevo- and dextro- forms of sugars, straight and branched forms of acyclic chains. The simplest example would be the equilibrium of hydrogen cyanide

$$H-C\equiv N$$

and isonitrile

$$H-N\equiv C.$$

As a general rule both forms may co-exist. Their equilibrium is determined by external conditions and the reaction in one way or another tends towards re-establishment of this equilibrium, hence negative feedback, homeostasis and reaction of binomial character.

(e) Lastly, amphoteric solutions play a very important function in chemistry in general, and in biochemistry in particular. Bicarbonate of sodium has been shown to be acidic or alkaline, according to conditions. All amino-acids belong to this category of amphoteres, and it is superfluous to stress their importance in biology, because of the fact that they are the components of all proteins and therefore all living beings. The general structure of amino-acids is NH_2—R—COOH, R being a hydrocarbon chain of variable length and sometimes containing other groups or elements like S, P, or additional NH_2. Their acidic or basic function depends on the surrounding medium whether basic or acidic. This could be interpreted that this dual character of the amphotere is a form of a negative feedback directed towards homeostasis and the reaction again binomial, instantaneous in the moment of contact of reacting atoms. All these reactions are not artifacts; they do, or may occur in biological reactions of living beings and may also be reproduced *in vitro* in laboratories.

In both cases the reactions are identical and not analoguous; they differ only in the environment in which they happen—they are concurrently a-biotic and biological reactions. As the two environments, a-biotic and biological, are both favourable to these identical reactions, the boundary between the two types of reaction becomes blurred. The negative feedback is no more an exclusively electromechanical phenomenon but a more generalized biochemical occurrence. It behaves live a self-repairing and self-reproducing computer.

Conversely, one can use the a-biotic conditions to explain the biological reactions of chemical or enzymatic type. In this way the gap between the a-biotic and biological forms is bridged in both directions—from a-biotic to biological and conversely from biological to a-biotic.

Town planning considered as cybernetic modelling

S. BODINGTON

Emcon, U.K.

Summary

The Newtonian model provided the theoretical foundation for far-reaching developments in industrial techniques which, in the nineteenth century, transformed the civilized world. The practical power of mathematics from the seventeenth to the nineteenth centuries lay pre-eminently in modelling the physical behaviour of matter. New developments in technology (electronics in particular), computer science, information theory, and modern mathematics generally, have opened the way not only to the modelling of individual living creatures but also of social organisms as wholes. The social and economic implications of such cybernetic modelling will be far-reaching. The model is the indispensable foundation of perception in all sentient beings. Collective forms of models (peculiar to man) provide the basis, *inter alia*, for science and human co-operation. The "plan" of the town planner is a particularly important example of the collective model. Today cybernetic modelling plus data banking opens a way to its development along quite new lines permitting great intricacy of form and real time interrogation in decision making. These potentials open new vistas for social co-operation and coordinated control of social development.

INTRODUCTION

Quite a lot of preliminaries are, in my opinion at least, needed before getting down to cases about the use of models in town planning. "Town planning" in English is a synonym for physical planning—as contrasted with, for example, economic planning. All the same, the main difficulties that I am

8   Rose, Cybernetics III

concerned about in these preliminaries relate equally—or perhaps specially—to economic planning and indeed to modelling in the social sciences generally.

Much useful work has been done using concepts and techniques taken over from the physical sciences, for example "gravity models" are used in transportation and shopping studies. Concepts are drawn from statistical mechanics and the notion of entropy is used for models representing the flow of journeys between different land uses. Indeed, this whole range of applications has been given the general description of "social physics". (In Britain some of the best work drawing on techniques in the physical sciences has been undertaken by Alan Wilson of the Centre for Environmental Studies.) It is, of course, also true that economists have drawn heavily on mathematics developed essentially for the physical sciences; the most obvious example is the differential calculus, as applied to marginal theory.

Undoubtedly this is the way it goes in scientific work. New developments draw on analogous work done in other sciences. Words, concepts and techniques are taken over often with only minor adaptations. I am not quite sure why today we are talking so much about "models" and "modelling". Humans have a kind of instinct about new developments of far-reaching import, and may be we talk so much about models because we sense the importance of "cybernetic modelling". Certainly models coupled with the new theories and the new computing power out of which the new science that we call cybernetics is being born, will have a striking significance for societies of the future. But the model in itself is man's oldest intellectual tool. (Indeed as I will have occasion to refer to more fully below, the model as an instrument of intelligent activity is a good deal older than man himself.) Pictures, words, toys, even plays, novels, and films are various kinds of models. With the development of mathematics there came into being a new form of model making—if you like, a "science of model making"—of extraordinary power. It often seems that the power of mathematics is something inherent in mathematics itself. New theories, new theorems, and their proofs can grip the human imagination in much the same way as great drama or great music. But mathematics has also been powerful in the sense that it has given men power to do things that otherwise they would not be able to do.

THE NEWTONIAN MODEL

The most startling example of the power of the mathematical model—and I mean power in a very practical, material sense—has been the Newtonian model. The Newtonian model provided the theoretical foundation for virtually all the technical advances of the industrial revolution—certainly up to the end of the 19th century. And even today it is only at some frontiers of technical development that it can, in any sense, be said to be obsolete.

These gigantic achievements of the Newtonian model make one hope, or at least wonder, whether mathematical models applied to social problems will ever develop a similar power. If research can suggest means of improving the performance of machines made of metal, why should not appropriate modelling give a new power and effectiveness to improved social and economic systems within which the machine of metal serves as a very minor constituent instrument?

The questions that have been posed in the preceding paragraphs must, I think, cause a certain sense of uneasiness on a number of counts. Undoubtedly social organisms may be represented as "systems" complying with the strict mathematical definition of a system. Machines of metal may be similarly represented. But in the latter case we think we know simply enough how output is to be measured, what measures of performance are applicable. But how do we do this for a social system? We realize at once that we are in new and strange territory. I think most of us have at one time or another felt this already when borrowing mathematical techniques from the physicist. What is our equivalent of the Newtonian model?

There are a number of things of which it is perhaps well that we should remind ourselves. In modelling the behaviour of matter we constantly and continuously use the simple underlying Newtonian model. Newton's laws in a few sentences give us the whole essence of this model. Using this engineers, physicists, a wide range of scientists working at different points of time and different points of space have a common starting point, a common framework to their thinking that makes all the work they do, however freely, however independently, become in a sense a part of one and the same scientific structure.

The tremendous strength of the Newtonian model lies in two characteristics (1) It is universally understood and accepted; it is, as it were, a common philosophy, a common world outlook shared by all modern man. (2) Despite its simplicity it has an extraordinarily deep truth content.

Commonly—or so we tend to think—the model maker is faced with an awkward choice. A simple model is clear, easy to understand, easy to use. But to be simple it must abstract from reality by leaving out of account innumerable concrete particularities by "over-simplifying". So, in most situations, the simple model gives only a crude idea and may, for practical purposes, be too far removed from reality. The Newtonian model, despite its simplicity, can often, in a few short steps, bring one to conclusions that are practically meaningful. For example, if one leaves out of account the frictional force of air acting on a projectile, one can in one or two lines produce a formula to show how high and how far a projectile will carry if the speed and direction at which it is launched are known.

Are we just lucky to be able to model our material world so simply? Is it just that social life is in the nature of things more complex and therefore not susceptible to such simple modelling? Or is it that human thought and experience gave us the intellectual skill to separate off one aspect of our natural/ historical environment, that aspect that is the subject matter of Newtonian physics, and see it in a very simple light. How is it that the invariances that make a simple model fruitful are peculiar only to what we call the physical world, or shall we find similar invariances running through other aspects of our environment? Can we make some aspects of our environment simple by the very act of discovering the invariances, the simplicity to be found in them?

These are questions of philosophy and epistemology that it will take much time to solve. My reason for bringing them up here is that I wish to suggest that we will not really get going on cybernetic modelling in the social field, we will not fully exploit the great potential of which more and more people are becoming aware, until much work and much struggle, aided perhaps by brilliant insights of creative genius, has laid more solid intellectual foundations.

I am not, of course, suggesting that we should give up and fold our arms until someone has found our analogue of the Newtonian framework. On the contrary it is precisely out of the groping and the mistakes that the clumsiness of the work at present being undertaken—and most of it is all that—that the stronger, better, wider foundations will be found. The historical journey to the Newtonian model was a very tough one. Before there could be Newton there had to be Copernicus, Tycho, Kepler, and Galileo. There was a new world outlook to be developed and bitter opposition came from the old. May be our problems in arriving at a clearsighted vision of the essentials of socio-economic life may be every bit as great. There is the problem of how we see our socio-economic life, the problem of how we model it with sufficient simplicity, the problem of how we get common understanding and acceptance of the models as a basis for common work.

The Newtonian mathematics is extraordinarily well adapted to the Newtonian Model, but to gain its acceptance was far from easy at first. Professor James Lighthill in reviewing *The Mathematical Papers of Isaac Newton*, Volume III, writes:

"The latter parts of this volume, devoted in the main to material almost certainly used for lectures by Newton, show (along with the Editor's comments) how difficult it was for Newton to compromise between the advanced state of development of his knowledge of mathematics and natural philosophy and his audiences' scientific illiteracy. The real audience for Newton's momentous discoveries was, in fact, at this time outside Cambridge. It was, above all, publication of the present tract on Series and Fluxions that would have brought his discoveries to the notice of this thinly spread and, indeed, international audience. It is ... truly tragic that although this tract was brought close to a form suitable for publication in the winter of 1670–71, when Newton was 28, proper orderly progress towards acceptance of the new techniques was postponed for at least 20 years through its non-publication. All sorts of difficulties in getting a relatively short tract like this on unfamiliar subject matter published, in those days when scientific publication was in its infancy, led to long delays during which possibilities of attaching it to some other work were explored. Later the young Newton, with his retiring nature, was so disturbed by the controversy surrounding the publication in the philosophical transactions of the Royal Society of his 'new theory about light and colours' that he ceased to seek for publication altogether."

However, it is this work of Newton and a handful of his contemporaries, of which of course one was Leibniz, that sowed the seed of mathematical analysis which accounts for such a high proportion of the activity of mathematicians throughout the following 300 years.

Most of this work was, in effect, providing gadgets to beautify, simplify and extend the performance of the Newtonian model of the material world. (Even the work of those mathematicians whose last concern was whether their work was or was not "useful", in fact helped towards a deeper understanding and more simple manipulation of the model.)

MATHEMATICS AND MODELLING

It has been said that had the computer been invented in Newton's time the whole course of mathematics might have been quite different, emphasis being laid on the mathematics of the "discrete" as against the mathematics of the "continuous". All "if's" of history are rather absurd. (This particularly because it was on soil made fertile by Newton's theoretical work, that technologies were generated to make the modern electronic computer a possibility). However, it provides a way of thinking about differences between the old mathematics and the new. An important requirement imposed on the mathematical models devised by Newton and his successors was that they should not be unduly laborious to make work. Or, to say the same thing in another way, functions—that is the mathematical expression of the model— must be such as can be manipulated with nothing more than pencil and paper and a reasonable number of hours of intellectual work. Mathematical advances which saved time and simplified calculation were of great value throughout the last three centuries of mathematics and, generally speaking, the mathematician needed to be his own computer.

Now one may envisage shifting to the computer any routine of mathematical operations that may be clearly defined. The understanding of basic principles and methods of general applicability, laborious as they may be, may tend to become more important than the intellectual gymnastics without which no mathematician of the past could do much. The economies and housekeeping of "brain–power–time" may tend to give way to the economies and housekeeping of operational speeds and size of memories in the computer.

It is a remarkable fact that mathematics somehow seems to prepare tools in advance of their practical requirement. At all events, throughout the 19th century, very new lines of approach began to appear which laid foundations of great importance for the social sciences. Outstanding, of course, was the work of Charles Babbage (1791–1871)—the "conceptual inventor" of the modern digital computer. Simultaneously such men as Augustus de Morgan (1806–1871), George Boole (1815–1864), John Venn (1834–1923), Charles Peirce (1839–1914), Gottlob Frege (1848–1925), were demonstrating how mathematics was rooted in a more general logic; a little later there is the great work of Whitehead and Russell. There is the work of George Cantor (1845–1918) on the theory of sets and the great contribution to the birth of modern algebra from such men as Sylvester (1814–1897) and Cayley (1821–1895). All this work made a gigantic contribution to a mathematics of a far more general applicability. The preconditions for mathematics as a science of model making on a *very general scale* were created by this work. In a practical sense, however, the mathematical models most in use remained those of the physical world and so remain right into the 20th century.

Whether or not social cybernetics would be viable without the computer need not be argued. The same historical process that has produced the conceptual work on which social cybernetics will be founded laid the technological foundations for the computer revolution. Babbage's important work *On the Economy of Machinery and Manufactures* (1832) was the fruit of his search for the technical means of building his "analytical engines". It was a major contribution to man's understanding of the economic significance of technology but it did not produce the answer to his practical need. It is doubtful whether the computer could have had any significant socioeconomic impact before the development of modern electronics and the transistor in particular. In a practical sense the real revolution comes when, on the one hand the theory of machines has demonstrated the possibility of reducing virtually any mathematical operations to elementary logical processes which, on the other hand, can be simulated by electronic hardware operating at speeds approaching that of light in units of minute dimensions, the economic cost of which is constantly being reduced with extreme rapidity.

These are historical developments that have already occurred. They provide preconditions for mathematical modelling of quite new kinds. The very birth of cybernetics came from Norbert Wiener's work carrying mathematical modelling into the field of biology, into the representation of the nervous system. In his *Introduction to Cybernetics* in 1947 he wrote: "We decided to take a nervous problem directly from the topic of feedback and to see what we could do with it experimentally." In collaboration with Dr. Arturo Rosenblueth the ideas about cybernetics which Wiener had been discussing with a number of colleagues at M.I.T. began to be tested out as a new means of scientific/mathematical modelling. That cybernetics would be applicable to social problems was evident to them from the start.

"As to sociology and anthropology, it is manifest that the importance of information and communication as mechanisms of organization proceeds beyond the individual into the community. ... it is completely impossible to understand social communities such as those of ants without a thorough investigation of their means of communication ... for the similar problems of human organization, we sought help from the anthropologists ...".

Few today can doubt the future of cybernetics in the social field; but what has been done so far remains clumsy and uncertain. Possibly there are difficulties here of a new kind, difficulties that did not arise in such a marked form for the natural scientists. In natural science there is a common heritage of fundamental concepts, won, as I have already mentioned, with great difficulty over a long period of time. The common starting point of the "scientific outlook" is an inestimable advantage to the progress of many-sided collaborative work. In the social sciences we are still a lot farther back. We see the potential but there still is an immense amount of preliminary ground work before this potential can be realized. What I have to say here is no more than suggest some lines of approach that might help us find the right angle from which to tackle model making as an aid to physical planning.

First of all I would like to refer to the work of Professor J.Z.Young. The value of this work is that it gives a deeper understanding of the biological/ sociological "mechanisms" by means of which "information" is obtained, interpreted, and communicated.

Most relevant to our purposes is Professor Young's *A Model of the Brain* (1964). Discussing the distant possibility of making nervous systems to order he writes (pp. 12–13):

"... There is no need simply to follow nature's way exactly, or to use the same materials, which take millions of years to fashion by natural selection. Man's way is to find other materials and by short cuts produce what he calls 'machines' that do the work more easily for him. And so, if you notice, the argument has gone round the circle and we are answering the question whether we should use machine language in asking how the brain works by saying that our brain works by making machines. To say this may seem to be an over-simplification; many people live without making machines and are concerned with other things. But all normal humans make models, or at least use words. By speech we produce, as it were, models of the world. Words influence other people because they fit with the models that those others have in their heads. In his writing and art, his speech and his machines man manages to transfer outside his head at least some features of the information that is within it. The formation of such artefacts, available for the use of many, is our unique feature. The modern electronic apparatus that assists with communication of information and with computation is only the latest stage of a development that has been going on throughout the history of man. Indeed, it goes much farther back than this. In Chapter 7 we shall see that in a certain sense the brains of all higher animals embody models of the animal's world. Because of this correspondence they are able to issue instructions that appropriately regulate the homeostat."

Chapter 7 discusses the structure of the eyes and optic pathways in the octopus. In Chapter 8, Professor Young writes (p. 125):

"The late Kenneth Craik of Cambridge taught us to say that we learn by building models in the brain. I shall try to push the idea to the extent of describing in an octopus brain the units out of which the model is built. There is enough evidence to make us suspect that we shall find them in other brains, including our own."

He asks first what we mean by a model (pp. 125–6):

"Like most other words, this one has the advantages and disadvantages of many shades of meaning, but the only alternative to using it is to adopt some word with no particular connotations at all. For example, if we say that a brain that has learnt contains an engram, we are, in effect, only repeating that there must be in it some entity representing the situation. What more is meant by saying that the brain contains a model?

A model is certainly a representation of something else, and many representations, as we have seen, use some kind of conventional code. Thus, at one extreme, a set of equations may be a mathematical model, using suitable symbolism to define the operations of a physical system, say a new rocket. A working model or a child's toy imitates some, but not all, the features of larger systems, by assembling parts made of other materials."

"To recapitulate, when we say that the brain contains a 'model' we intend to emphasize the following points about the 'engrams' that are built up in the brain by learning.

(1) They are formed by appropriate selection among a set of code units, predetermined, probably mainly by heredity.

(2) They are used in making predictions that are useful for homeostasis.

(3) The usefulness, at least of more elaborate models, is that they can be made to conduct, as it were, small scale experiments within the head."

The tremendous importance of the foregoing for our work lies in the fact that a closely analoguous process is also carried through on a social scale. We are interested in Professor Young's findings because we are interested in how model making in general advances understanding and adaptive behaviour even as related to the individual organism, but we are particularly and doubly interested because man also builds models collectively, socially. He does so by collecting and encoding information. Such models may be useful in the control and adaptation of society to its environment ("social homeostasis"). On a social scale man may also conduct experiments "in imagination", by means of the model in lieu of "the bitter experience of history".

Professor Young himself, though the purpose of his book is study of the individual organism, touches on possible meanings of his work for the collective, social organism. In his Chapter 18 on "The Control of the Collection of Information" he writes (p. 286):

"Every organism, in order to survive, takes actions that are appropriate to the surrounding conditions. It does this because it contains in its nuclei a controlling system that adequately represents the environment. The surroundings change and this representation is continually brought up-to-date."

This *mutatis mutandis* is almost precisely what a physical and, indeed, an economic plan should do on the social scale. Man has developed an information system on a social scale that is quite unparalled in any living creature known to man (pp. 297–8):

"The circuits have become so adjusted in man that the mechanism for acquiring information by the individual is greatly hypertrophied and the heredity mechanism is relatively less effective (though still, of course, fundamental). The recent acceleration of the rate of change of man's condition has been the result of the elaboration of codes by which information can be passed directly from one individual to another. By speech and writing we acquire information not just from two parents, as in ordinary heredity, but from many. Such 'multi-parental inheritance' provides immense possibilities for evolution. By allowing for the rapid development of new combinations of the code it enables evolutionary experiments to proceed at a rate that would not be possible by the slower recombinations of two by two. Indeed, the characteristic of man is that by means of language and tools he constructs models of the world outside his own brain and outside his own genetic system. By proper use of these models he would be able to overcome all the risks that the environment offers. But there are evidently risks within the language systems and social economic systems themselves. The proper use of these means of communication depends upon a degree of cooperation that is not always readily elicited, especially between larger groups of people."

The physical plan is precisely a model. It is a socially constructed model to represent interrelated land uses. What these land uses are and how they relate depend upon the numbers of people in a community, the activities they perform, and the means of communication. So behind the cartographic plan, the marking of land uses on a map, or the sketching of architectural structures within a natural and historical environment, there lie (1) people, structured by age, sex, social class, and occupation, evolving and changing over time, (2) economic activities producing goods, changing the environment, and (3) communications permitting the movement of goods and people and the communication of information within the collectivity.

All the activities (1) to (3) above have been modelled and generally the models have used digital computers to analyse data. There are, for example, a number of population projection models currently in use by planners. Elaborate models have been devised to forecast transportation requirements. However, there is a long way to go before these models can be said to serve as effective tools of social planning.

Even where models are being used to a considerable extent, there is very often a certain lopsidedness in their use. For example, transportation models may give planners estimates of what roads would be required to carry expected motor vehicle traffic on certain assumptions. But the more essential integration of transport planning with other forms of land use planning is generally lacking; and often the underlying logic of such transportation models as are available to planners is not known to them or fully understood by them.

There are a number of fairly effective shopping models that answer well enough such limited questions as given a population of X located at known points, what floor space will be required for shopping facilities and where should it be located. There are computer models that tell the planner what his future population will be, what its age structure, etc., assuming that he can adequately estimate migration in and out of his region, fertility rates and death rates. What is lacking is a better coordination between such models as exist and a better adaptation of the logic guiding the construction of limited models so that they relate better to an overall planning strategy.

The best work being done in Britain to get a better understanding of the planning model as a coordinated whole is probably that being done by the Centre for Environmental Studies and the Centre for Land Use and Built Form Studies at the University of Cambridge School of Architecture. (The Urban Systems Model that has been developed at the Cambridge Centre has an affinity to the valuable work done by Cripps and others for the planning department of the Bedfordshire County Council. The main structure of the Cripps model is the same as that described by Cripps and Foot in *Official Architecture and Planning* (1968, p. 928). The Cripps model has, to a certain extent, drawn on Ira S. Lowry's *A Model of Metropolis*, (1964).)

The Cambridge Unit's model essentially deals with the interrelationships between (1) location of "basic employment", (2) location of employees' housing, (3) consequent population location, (4) location of services. An iterative process generates housing requirements for employees, which in turn generates service requirements which in turn generate housing requirements of service employees and so on. The relationships of the elements in the model both generate and imply relationships of communication which are in turn dependent upon activities, land uses at different points in the space that is to be physically planned. Application of the model to Reading has already tested its basic validity.

There is also quite a lot of work and thinking being devoted to information handling for planning purposes. The obvious advantages of once for all collection of basic information and the storage of this information in data banks, that can be interrogated by planners, are well understood. However, very little practical work has yet been undertaken to test out how a computerized information system might operate in a planning office. Clearly this is a big thing to attempt. In my view, nonetheless, it shows considerable lack of imagination that substantial funds have not been made available to attempt this experimentally. One is well aware that first attempts would be costly and might not prove successful. A first attempt would have to be made on a considerable scale, involving work by a quite large team of people, to be of value. In the U.K. so far there has been research on a limited scale into the feasibility of data banks, plus some efforts by go-ahead planning authorities to coordinate such information as is available to them.

A far more bold experimental policy would be justified by the fact that physical planning relates to the effective allocation of resources to construction which run annually to some thousands of million pounds. (In 1968 investment in U.K. in dwellings at 1958 prices was over £ 1250 million and investment in buildings and works by industries and services was nearly £ 2000 million.)

Possibly large-scale experiments in such new areas as data banking should await more experience and experimentation on a smaller scale. This too is signally lacking in the British scene. Some valuable academic work is being done but this runs the risk—and some of those undertaking this work are the first to appreciate the fact—of getting out of touch with reality. Research and development work on the application of cybernetics to town planning is seriously impeded by conventional thinking in academic, scientific, and administrative circles. That any modern nation must spend considerable funds on research and development is now generally recognised. But ideas about what constitutes a legitimate research project in relation to social planning are still very hidebound. The analogue of the Newtonian model for social planning may turn out to be something very different from anything that the natural scientists have been using. This may well be so because of a fundamental difference distinguishing the terrain of social sciences from that of natural sciences. In social sciences decision makers are, as it were, within the system; decision makers are people. In the natural sciences the decision makers are outside the system. The adjustment that a community makes to its environment is made as a result of decisions informed by the very operation of the system that these decisions in turn adapt and change. Planning also plans the decision making process by which further plans are shaped.

CONCLUSIONS

Clearly complex questions of social, political and economic theory will have to be thrashed out before we really know what we are doing in social cybernetics. But to make a start we need to get as much experience as possible on what one might call interactions between theory and practice. In physical planning this could in fact be begun in quite a simple way. The experience, training, and mental orientation of people in the planning profession makes it easy to find some of their number who are keen to try out new ideas. If one could overcome a conventional resistance to classifying work done in a planning office as "research", all one has to do is to see that funds are made available for planners to try out possibilities of using cybernetic modelling in their work. Funds required would not be heavy in relation to the magnitude of the expenditures to which they relate. The planners would need to be supported with advice from mathematicians, programmers and others who "think cybernetically".

They would need to have a limited amount of computing facilities readily available. (The arrangement of this might, in itself, have a useful "spin off" affording a better understanding of the facts of life about using computers in practice, the advantage of computer utilities, etc.) The kind of modelling that planners would need would fall into two categories; quite simple models which could be developed specially to meet their requirements but which, once developed, could be made known and adapted to the use of other planning offices, and, secondly, complicated models where they would have to restrict themselves to the models developed by specialist research units of which the Cambridge Unit may be regarded as a prototype. Where the more complicated models existed to meet their requirements, they would work with those who had developed these models. Where such models did not exist, expression of specific requirements would help those working in the larger research centres to maintain a live interchange with the "industry" that their more specialized work was designed to support.

A basic design for "changing" the laws of nature cybernetically

ALI IRTEM

Istanbul, Turkey

Summary

The Father of Cybernetics, Norbert Wiener, has stated in one of his works that the world is an organism. Based on the idea above, and considering the fact that the stability conditions of the essential variables of an organism (in our case the known laws of nature) might cybernetically be changed, I have tried to give in this paper, a basic design to "change" the laws of nature cybernetically. For, the experimentations in the self-organizing computers may induce the events that do not occur in the "ordinary" nature. The new technological possibilities thus obtained may obviously be enormous. The author of this paper has not yet found any possibility to construct such a special-purpose artifact, but such machines have already been built and are functioning in several countries, although very few people are—seemingly—aware of this.

INTRODUCTION

The Father of Cybernetics, Norbert Wiener, has stated in one of his works that the world *is* an organism. Based on the idea above and considering the fact that the stability conditions of the essential variables of an organism (in our case: the known laws of nature) might cybernetically be changed, I have tried to give in this paper, a basic design to change the laws of nature cybernetically.

The changeability of the laws of nature should not however be considered as a very new concept. The question "whether the laws of nature are a func-

1087

tion of time or not" was asked answered initially—as far as I know— by a famous French mathematician, Henri Poincaré, in one of his works on the philosophy of science. In his investigations, however, Poincaré came to the conclusion that it would be more "convenient" for the scientist to admit that *the laws of nature are not a function of time.* But since the time of Poincaré our opinion about "convenience in science" might have been changed. In the present age of space and cybernetics, we might be prepared to select and induce some contingencies in nature. The deterministic view of the world has been given up for more than half a century, beginning perhaps with Planck and Heisenberg. Obviously, from the deterministic point of view, "changing the laws of nature" means nothing else but a sign that the known laws of nature have to be amended or generalized.

But in case we try to induce some "anti-laws" in a certain region of nature, and if we are "somewhat" successful in this respect, (the life process is, for example, one of these existing "anti-laws", as Norbert Wiener stated in his works), then it would no more be "convenient" for any scientist to admit that the known laws of nature are *still* not a function of time. Now I would like to stress here that in this communication I have not taken into consideration only the micro-physical events in the world where presumably these "anti-laws" are more effective; my main point being that we could (contemporarily) change the laws of nature in the macro-physical world too. For example—as I quoted above—the life process can be considered as nature's "partial struggle" against the second law of thermodynamics.

Yet we could construct cybernetic machines which might overcome any other known law of nature (for example gravity).

In order to change the known laws of nature we have to construct mechanisms which can select for us from the huge amount of common events in the world those odd and extremely unlikely ones which we want. The important point is, however, that the said mechanism of selection could be constructed *according to the known laws of nature.* Yet in order not to be misunderstood, may I stress the point that by "changing the laws of nature" I do not mean that the world has not any natural laws at all. I merely want to point out that in this attempt I presume that these laws are statistical in nature, and that, therefore, we might be in a position to deviate from them through appropriate mechanisms. The known laws of nature are what nature does in most common cases, but we can also select (or induce) the cases where nature acts in quite different ways, in accordance with our wishes, temporarily.

A BASIC DESIGN FOR CHANGING THE LAWS OF NATURE

Consider a mining engineer who has some ore at the foot of a mine-shaft and that he would like it brought to the surface. The power required for this purpose is, however, more than be can supply personally. Now what he should do to perform this task automatically is to take some system that is going by the law of nature from low entropy to high, and he should couple this system to his ore, so that "low entropy" is coupled to "ore down", and "high entropy" to "ore up". The engineer lets the whole system go to work, confident that as the entropy goes from low to high, so will it change the ore's position from down to up (Ashby).

The method of changing the laws of nature could now be seen (and realized) in the same way. If we consider the following: (1) "the ore down" as "the old known law of nature"; (2) "the ore up" as "the new law of nature to be programmed in our system". Then we could change the old law of nature in the same way (the entropy is used above, not as in the heat engines, but as understood in stochastic processes). If we consider for the time being the whole nature as a deterministic machine (for example as Newton does), then we could approximately specify its behaviour by a set of ordinary simultaneous differential equations of the first order:

$$\frac{dx_1}{dt} = F_1(x_1, x_2, ..., x_n; \quad a_1, a_2, ..., a_n)$$

$$\frac{dx_2}{dt} = F_2(x_1, x_2, ..., x_n; \quad a_1, a_2, ..., a_n)$$

$$\frac{dx_n}{dt} = F_n(x_1, x_2, ..., x_n; \quad a_1, a_2, ..., a_n)$$

where F's are single-valued and where the right-hand side contains no function of t (time) other than those whose fluxion appears on the left, and where a's are parameters of nature. However, we suppose today that the relations mentioned above (i.e. all common laws of nature) are valid approximately under some known conditions. These conditions constrain a region within which the common laws could be valid. In order to change any known common law of nature according to our wishes, we have only to change the parameters "$a_1, a_2, a_3, ..., a_n$" of the equations above, in such a way (in such a programme or mathematical relation or selection function or filter function) that we get (in the subject region) the x values we programmed beforehand. This is perhaps a difficult task to do. But it might be solved in some cases. One of the basic designs to perform such a task is given below. A possible method to change the laws of nature is to use some random sources *for the generation of all possibilities* (and a random source of energy to generate the energy needed) and pass both their outputs through some device that will select and induce the answer required (the new law of nature programmed beforehand by us).

From now on, we have to distinguish two different tasks. (1) Our problem is to design a machine which might change any given law of nature.

(2) The task of the machine, constructed *according to the known (given) laws* of nature is to bring out the new law of nature which we programmed in our machine beforehand. But how we could programme the nature through our above-mentioned machine automatically (to be more precise, cybernetic-ally)?

To do this, let us take the advantages of the following ideas (see Figure 1). We suppose that two determinate dynamic systems (X and S in the figure below) are coupled through channels G and U, so that each affects the other. Then any resting state of the whole (that is, any state at which it can stay

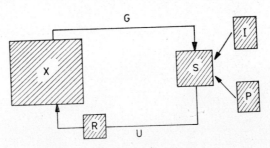

FIGURE 1   Coupling of two dynamic systems

permanently) must be a resting state in each of the two parts (systems) individually; each being in.the conditions provided by the other. So if "S" have a set of conditions ζ (the old known laws of nature) in S, then S's power of veto (according to W.R. Ashby) ensures that a resting state of the whole will always imply ζ (the old known laws of nature) in S. Suppose next that the linkage G is such that G will allow ζ (the old known laws of nature) to occur in S if and only if the set of conditions η (the new laws of nature we programmed beforehand) occur in X. S's power of veto now encures that any resting state of the whole must have the set of conditions η (the new laws of nature) in X. So the selection and induction of S and G to have these properties ensure that the only states in X that can be permanent are those that have the set of conditions η (the new laws of nature). We have to note that the selection and inducing of η (the new laws of nature) in the sense of its realization in X, has been done in two stages. The first occurred when our scientist/engineer specified S and G and ζ. The second occurred when S acting with further reference to the scientist/engineer, rejected state after state of X, accepting finally the ones that gave the set of conditions η (the new law nature) in X.

If we summarize the principles used above we should state the following. We identified the system (in which we would like to have a new law of nature) with X, and the new law which we would like to realize in it with η. The selection and inducing of η (new laws of nature) in X was first beyond our power. So we built and coupled to it a system S (with random information and energy sources) so constructed that it has a resting state if and only if its information (and energy) through G is that η (the new law of nature) has occurred in a resting state in the system X. As the time progresses the limit of the whole system (X and S), is the permanent realization of η (the new law of nature) in X. The scientist/engineer has to design and construct S and G, and to couple it to X, after that the process occurs, as far as the scientist/engineer is concerned, automatically (to be more precise, cybernetically).

For the realization of the above-mentioned conditions the scientist/engineer must also arrange the following scheme, indicated in the figure as R (a kind of "brain" for realization of the "new kinds of natures").

(a) System S should send disturbances of inexhaustible variety (information and physical power) along the channel U, if ζ is not occurring in S.

(b) And keep U constant, i.e. block the way from disturbances of inexhaustible variety, (information and physical power) to U, if ζ *is* occurring. In that way the system X shall have the set of conditions η (the new laws of nature) as the time passes on.

According to Ashby, the information theory makes clear whence comes the extra information needed for our purpose in the "ordinary" nature. The postulate that information cannot be created is not violated by the "ordinary" evolution, for the evolving systems receive an endless stream of information in the form of mutations. Whatever their origin, whether in cosmic rays or thermal noises, they constitute a typical information source of the type considered by Shannon. They give to the evolving system, during each unit of time, an amount of information which can be necessary with an accuracy as we please, by the value of

$$-S_i\, p_i \cdot \log p_i$$

where, p_i's are probabilities that various mutations will occur in unit time. The evolving system has thus *two* sources of information: That implied in the specification of the rules of natural selection, and that implied by the in-pouring stream of mutations*.

LIMITATIONS FOR THE CHANGEABILITY OF THE NATURAL LAWS

In his work, "Design for an intelligence amplifier", Prof. Ross Ashby mainly prefers to tackle (with his design for intelligence amplification) the difficult social and economic problems of human society. However, I hope to be able to show in this paper that the subject ideas are so powerful that they could also be used for much greater purposes such as changing the laws of nature. But, all these have some limitations which I would like to discuss below.

In order to change the known laws of nature, we have (1) at least one additional regulation device in our system X; (2) a source of information of inexhaustible variety I; and (3) a source of physical power of the same variety P at the disposal of the system X.

However, greater sophistication of decision criteria seem to lead to a hierarchy of control, and might generate a greater degree of uncertainty in regulation and control. Ashby again has also given the limits of every control mechanism: this is the law of requisite variety. On the other hand, Bremermann has also given the possible limitations of every brain (natural and man-made). Yet, the technical and especially the "timely" limitations expressed by Ashby and Bremermann in their works in this respect, should also be applicable to the changeabilities of the laws of nature. But could we not even overcome these limitations by our system (X and S) as explained above? This question seems to be open now!

---

* Obviously the principles explained above, could also be used to cure human diseases as well.

CONCLUSION

The author of this communication hopes to be excused for the fact that he did not have enough time and occasion to treat the present subject more thoroughly. For this reason his indication above should be considered as *initial suggestions and hints to proceed further.*

Acknowledgments

I would like to express my deepest indebtedness to Prof. Ross Ashby, University of Illinois, U.S.A., who was so kind to send me among his other papers, "Design for an Intelligence Amplifier", on which my present attempt is mainly based. Here, I would also like to express my sincerest indebtedness to Prof. Dr. Hüseynov, and to Dr. Babajev, from the Institute of Cybernetics, Academy of Sciences, of Azerbaijan, Baku, U.S.S.R., who have given me some valuable suggestions to improve the above-mentioned basic design.

References

W.R. Ashby, "Design for an intelligence amplifier." In *Automata Studies* (Ed. Shannon and McCarthy). Princeton University (1955).

W.R. Ashby, *Design for a Brain.* Chapman and Hall, London (1960).

W.R. Ashby, "Can a mechanical chess-player outplay its design?" *Brit. J. Phil. Sci.*, **3**, No. 9 (1952).

W.R. Ashby, "Some consequences of Bremermann's limit for information processing systems." *Bionics Symp., U.S.A.* (1966).

H.J. Bremermann, "Numerical orptimization procedures derived from biological evolution process." *Bionics Symp. U.S.A.* (1966).

B. Hüseynov, Private communication (1968).

A. Irtem, "Happiness amplified cybernetically." *3rd Intern. Congr. Cybernetics, Namur, Belgium* (1961).

A. Irtem, *Education of the Machines.* —, Istanbul (1963).

A. Irtem, *Self-Organizing Machine and Money-Making Instrumentations.* Turkish Journal "Symposium", Istanbul (1963).

A. Irtem, *Some Applications of Boolian Algebra.* Turkish Journal "Symposium", Istanbul (1964).

A. Irtem, "Programming miracles." *5th Intern. Congr. Cybernetics, Namur, Belgium* (1967).

A. Irtem, *Programming of New Kinds of Biologies.* Revue de Bio-Mathématique, Paris (1969).

N. Wiener, *The Human Use of Human Beings.* Doubleday, New York (1956).

N. Wiener, *Cybernetics.* Wiley, New York (1961).

SECTION VII

Cybernetics and the social sciences

VII–1   *Social aspects of modern technology*—R.H.BERGMANN
         (SWITZERLAND) 1097

VII–2   *Cybernetics and social structure*—V.H.BRIX (U.K.) . . 1107

VII–3   *The cybernetics of evolving systems*—M.BELIS (RUMANIA) . 1121

VII–4   *Cybernetics and society*—F.J.RICCI (U.S.A.) 1131

VII–5   *Some theoretical and experimental considerations of cyber-
         netics, responsive environments, learning and social develop-
         ment*—D.R.STEG and A.D'ANNUNZIO (U.S.A.) . . . 1145

VII–6   *Organizational cybernetics and human values*—R.F.ERICSON
         (U.S.A.) 1163

VII–7   *A quantitative approach to human interactions and social
         phenomena*—G.C.THEODORIDIS (U.S.A.) 1185

VII–8   *Stability and social change*—A.M.YOUNG (U.S.A.) . . 1205

VII–9   *Cybernetics as a model for political science: a critique*—
         L.R.KERSCHNER (U.S.A.) 1215

VII–10   *Subjective information theory, thermodynamics, and cyber-
         netics of open adaptive societal systems*—G.G.LAMB (U.S.A.) 1231

VII–11   *On random decision processes with complete connections*—
         M.MALITZA and C.ZIDĂROIU (RUMANIA) 1249

VII–12 *The importance of a cybernetic approach to the study of the natural languages*—F. VANDAMME (BELGIUM)   .   .   .   1257

VII–13 *Towards a syntax-monitored semantic pattern recognition*— L. CHIARAVIGLIO and J. GOUGH, JR. (U.S.A.)   1267

VII–14 *Resource allocation for university information services*— H. D. BAECKER (CANADA)   1281

VII–15 *Cybernetics: its impact on the processes of learning, politics, and production*—A. M. HILTON (U.S.A.)   1287

VII–16 *Self-regulation of internal states*—E. E. GREEN, A. GREEN, and E. DALE WALTERS (U.S.A.)   1299

VII–17 *Creative work and computer structures*—Z. L. RABINOVICH (U.S.S.R.)   1319

VII–18 *Cybernetics and warfare*—J. VOEDVODSKY (U.S.A.)   .   .   1329

VII–19 *The epicosm model of the material and mental universes*— S. C. DODD (U.S.A.)   1351

Social aspects of modern technology

RALPH H. BERGMANN

International Labour Office, Geneva, Switzerland

Summary

The outstanding scientific and technological advances of recent years have already demonstrated their potential contribution to better living and working conditions. Concurrently, there are human and social implications of the new technology which require analysis and appropriate action. The labour-saving characteristics of advanced technology can lead to unemployment at plants where it is introduced or at competitive or supplier plants, and possibly even at the industry or economy-wide level. Manpower adjustment programmes—public and private—are required to ensure that the introduction of new technology is not slowed by overt or covert opposition and that those persons affected by its use do not suffer. To meet the labour force requirements of the new technology, current patterns of vocational training require review and re-casting. The 50th Anniversary of the International Labour Organization which is being celebrated this year, marks an appropriate occasion to draw attention to the social aspects of automation and the role of this international organisation, a specialised agency of the United Nations, in dealing with its effects. Because of its tripartite structure, the ILO is in a unique position to draw upon the experience and co-operation of employers' and workers' organizations as well as governments in meeting the challenges of this technological era. It seeks to ensure that the advantages of new technology are equitably shared and that hardships do not fall on an unfortunate few.

INTRODUCTION

The technological advances of recent years have been dramatic, far-reaching, and even awesome. Brief mention of such diverse developments as computer control of steel rolling, desalination techniques, artificial hearts, and lunar exploration equipment, serves to indicate how modern technology has reached into a broad variety of fields. Diverse as these developments may be, however, they share a common origin—they have grown from intensive research, brilliant intuitions and stimulating idea-confrontations. Human beings, in short, have brought these developments to fruitition. It is only natural then, that a conference on cybernetics consider the "feedback" effect of modern technology upon human beings. Social questions of this sort may not yield to the crisp analysis of the physical sciences, but cannot for that reason be ignored by scientists.

The advanced technology of modern times represents in part a continuation and refinement of older scientific and technological trends, and in part new concepts and principles. Cybernation is a most significant factor in this new technology with a clear promise that it will play an increasingly important role in the world of ten, twenty, or fifty years hence. Hand in hand with a legitimate admiration for the current capabilities of modern technology, including cybernation, there must be an interest in and concern for, its implications for mankind. Serious efforts to review technology's impact on society are under way in a number of national settings, while the International Labour Office and other bodies are involved in this activity from an international point of view.

It is worth quoting a man well known for his pioneering work in the utilization of nuclear energy, Admiral Rickover of the United States Navy, who has recently been addressing himself to this feedback effect. He has expressed his views as follows[1]:

"It troubles me that we are so easily pressured by purveyors of technology into permitting so-called 'progress' to alter our lives, without attempting to control it—as if technology were an irrepressible force of nature to which we must meekly submit... As a means to human ends [technology] can be made to produce maximum benefit and do minimum harm to human beings and to the values that make for civilized living... How in the future to make wiser use of technology is perhaps the paramount public issue facing electorates in all industrial democracies."

In the United States, a ten-year programme of research on "Technology and Society" is nearing the half-way mark at Harvard University. In the United Kingdom, concern for these questions has led to the recent organization of a British Society for Social Responsibility in Science. Scientists and technologists are increasingly becoming aware that their activities have broad implications for mankind and that efforts are required to channel developments in a positive way.

Although a classification of these implications cannot avoid some duplication and overlap, consideration will first be directed to the employment effects of the new technology, next to its impact on occupational structure, thirdly to other topics associated with the question of work, fourthly to issues apart from the work situation, and finally to the question of developing nations.

TECHNOLOGY AND EMPLOYMENT

The impact of modern technology at the work place has probably received most attention, particularly with respect to the question of whether unemployment is caused by the new techniques. It is usually true that recently introduced technology, often called "automation", is capable of yielding the same or a greater output with fewer workers than were previously required. While this refers particularly to those technologies which are used to carry out traditional operations in office work, in steel plants, in oil refineries, etc., it refers also to new developments which threaten to replace older techniques, as for example nuclear energy and the use of lasers. Cybernation techniques are most certainly labour-saving, often reducing the need not just for unskilled or semi-skilled staff, but also the need for skilled and professional staff. Furthermore the labour-saving effects of new technology must be measured not only at the factory or mine or office where it is installed, but also by taking into account the consequent labour displacement at that firm's competitive and supplier plants.

For some, these labour-saving characteristics mean only one thing: "unemployment". An examination of this serious charge must start by clarifying two different uses of the word "unemployment". On the one hand it can refer to that portion of a country's labour force which is unemployed at a particular time—i.e. the national unemployment level. On the other hand it is also used to refer to persons who have been displaced from their regular employment and severed—temporarily or otherwise—from the employer's payroll. While the national figure is, of course, related to plant-level displacement, the important point is that national unemployment figures may be at minimal levels and show little or no change, even while there are dramatic cases of worker displacements as modern technology is introduced. Thus, the economist, for example, may see no unusual unemployment at the national level while the trade union leader may point with accuracy to the unemployment of workers at a score of industrial establishments. This apparent contradiction is explainable by the fact that while some workers are losing jobs, others are at the same time finding work, and overall national figures do not reflect these internal movements.

There is far from general agreement that modern technology pushes a country's unemployment level higher than otherwise. While fewer workers per unit of output may be needed for operating the new technology, account must be taken of the new jobs associated with the development and production of the complex equipment itself. Its introduction may provide a stimulus to economic growth—and therefore more job opportunities— since it often leads to new products, or lower prices for older products. Without the use of modern technology, according to some analysts, an industrialized society would suffer a handicap in the competitive world market and its loss in trade would adversely affect unemployment levels. But it is not enough to point to national statistics and argue that technological advances do not lead to unemployment.

Unemployment in the second sense—i.e. the displacement of the individual from his regular job—is just as real, and even more immediate. Such unemployment may indeed be traceable to modern technology and its impact on income security hardly needs elaboration. Beyond the economic loss, however, the unemployed worker suffers a psychological blow when learning that his work experience is no longer valuable, he must undergo the pain of changing jobs, and he may face additional hardships in moving himself and his family to a new locality. Manpower adjustment programmes—both public and private—can help meet the problems of the individual. Since those problems arise from circumstances outside his control and can be traced to developments which are presumably benefitting the community at large, it is only proper that public measures be joined with private programmes to provide the help that is required. In some cases, emphasis can be put on arrangements to help the individual remain with his regular employer—with appropriate training, mobility allowances, wage protection, etc., so that he does not suffer from his shift to alternative work. In other cases, economic protection can be provided—through unemployment payments, severance awards, etc.—to the worker whose employment must be terminated. Retraining, at government or establishment expense, becomes a corollary and essential tool to help in the adjustment process.

These are but some of the techniques which have been utilised in cases of worker dislocation arising from technological advance. New approaches or variations are constantly being developed through imaginative collective bargaining between employers and workers representatives. In this drive for worker protection, the underlying motive has not been to block or hamper the introduction of new technology, but rather to ensure a measure of equity when such changes are applied. At a recent I.L.O. meeting, the participants stated the point as follows[2]:

"It is urged that the benefits of advanced technology including automation be widely shared by all members of society rather than accruing only to workers and employers directly involved. At the same time, the hardships resulting from technological change should not fall heavily on a few but should be costs shared by the community as a whole."

OCCUPATIONAL REQUIREMENTS

In addition to the quantitative question—will there be enough jobs for the entire labour force after automation's use is more widespread?—there are qualitative implications for the labour force which form the second topic for review. At the level of the plant and industry, the demand for men with traditional skills will decline, while the need for more advanced skills will increase. Transferability of skills becomes important for the worker. This in turn calls for modifications in education and training programmes in order to ensure that workers have an adequate background to make their transfer possible and profitable.

From the point of view of the entire economy, modern technology brings with it changes in occupational structure which have broad implications for the entire education system. Already in the technically advanced United States, the distribution of occupations has shifted so that over 50% of the labour force is engaged in jobs which are classified as "white-collar" occupations. If the use of advanced technology means that society requires an ever-higher proportion of the workforce in technical and professional occupations, then, while new opportunities will arise for human fulfillment, there will be consequent new challenges for existing institutions.

OTHER ISSUES

A review of the impact of modern technology on work and work-associated questions leads also to consideration of such areas as job satisfaction, safety, working time and increased leisure. While benefits undoubtedly accrue in these fields as new technology is introduced, there are potential danger spots—the mental strain of operating giant equipment, the boredom arising from a "watch-dog" role as automatic controls make decisions within pre-set parameters, and the alienation when a worker sees no connection between his activity and the total process or final product. Indefinite as these issues are, they are nevertheless social consequences of the new technology.

THE I.L.O.

Emphasis has so far been placed on work-associated issues, the general area which is the major concern of the International Labour Organization. This organization is this year celebrating its fiftieth anniversary, and a substantial portion of its efforts in that period have been directed toward the protection of workers against the hardships and insecurity arising from technological change.

In framing the Treaty of Versailles after World War I, the major powers provided specifically for the establishment of a labour organization which was to contribute to the cause of lasting peace through the promotion of social justice. The International Labour Organization was thus created in 1919, independent of the League of Nations but associated with it. In the post World War II period, the organization has become one of the specialized agencies of the United Nations, with special responsibilities in the labour field.

While the United Nations and other associated bodies are composed of government representatives, it is noteworthy that the I.L.O. is a tripartite organization—with representatives of employers and workers participating with government representatives in the decision-making process at the very highest level. This tripartite structure has been one of the strengths of the Organization for in the delicate area of social progress it has been able to bring together the views and interests of the parties directly concerned with social questions in the labour field.

At the first International Labour Conference fifty years ago, delegates adopted international labour standards on such issues as the eight-hour day, maternity protection, and the minimum age for employment. These standards have a binding force when ratified, comparable in many ways to an international treaty. Addtitional standards have been formulated in subsequent years, dealing, for example, with such subjects as unemployment benefits, job security for workers and vocational training programmes to meet the needs of new technology. International standards have in turn influenced national legislation and national institutions.

In the post World War II period, the standard-setting activity has been supplemented by programmes of technical assistance to developing countries and over 750 experts are currently working on I.L.O. projects around the world. Their fields of work range from efforts to improve national vocational training programmes to technical assistance in establishing a trade union research department, from management development centres to programmes for stimulating the growth of producer cooperatives. The Organization has grown from 45 Member States in 1919 to over 121 at the beginning of 1969.

Within the secretariat, a special section has been established to deal with the problems of automation—and the focus of that unit has been on identifying the problems associated with the introduction of new technology and gaining acceptance for programmes which protect workers against its negative effects. This has involved research, technical meetings, and publication. A set of public and private programmes for dealing with the dislocations arising from automation has been developed, and an international information clearing-house has been established. Insuring that human problems of new technology are met has the effect of reducing fear of change with a consequent diminution of resistance to its introduction. Thus individuals receive the help they need, while the smooth introduction of new technology enables it to yield its fullest potential.

ENVIRONMENT

Work-associated issues are of course not the only social issues on which modern technology is having a marked impact. Man's total environment, for example, is being changed as new chemicals pollute the streams while concentrations of industry and population pollute the air. The recent death of millions of fish in the Rhine sharply demonstrated that national boundaries pose no constraint for pollution of this sort. Nuclear testing has similarly dramatized the international aspects of pollution problems. While basic decisions to establish adequate safeguards come first within a national setting, international action has already been undertaken in important areas, and additional programmes are under consideration.

Even pollution questions pale, however, before the dangers inherent in the use of nuclear energy for military purposes. Here, more vividly than anywhere, one sees the direct relationship between social issues and technological advance.

DEVELOPING COUNTRIES

A fifth, and final, area for consideration concerns the developing countries of the world. Their struggle for growth and well-being is necessarily set within the framework of today's technology, which seems to hold for them both a promise and a threat. The threat arises from the increasing scientific and technological gap between such countries and the industrialized countries. Not only are there special problems in finding and training manpower to effectively utilize advanced technology, but without it, competition with the advanced world becomes increasingly difficult. Even as a country turns to the development of educated and trained manpower, however, greater opportunities in industrialised countries often attract the very persons who are needed to successfully apply the advanced technology. And then, in those instances when new technology is introduced, it offers relatively few work opportunities for the huge mass of unemployed and underemployed persons which is characteristic of the developing country. Their economic and social conditions are unaffected by the country's economic growth. But there is also a promise inherent in the advance of science and technology—the promise that such advances will lead to new techniques more appropriate for use in developing countries and new uses for their raw materials.

As the U.N. Second Development Decade approaches, increasing attention is being directed towards the challenge of human-oriented development. As part of this effort, the I.L.O. has launched a long-range World Employment Programme to assist countries to develop productive employment opportunities for their workforce and thus to achieve social progress concurrently with economic growth.

It would be wrong to conclude that modern technology contains more threat than promise. The technological developments of recent years have most certainly brought benefits, and a glance at the future indicates that additional gains can be expected from such areas as underwater exploration, medical research and cybernetic applications, to name but a few fields of current technological activity. To ensure that social benefits are not overshadowed by social costs, there are perhaps two roles which scientists and technologists can play. They must first of all be aware of the social implications of technological advance. It is this awareness which enables the individual to introduce social evaluations into his work and to influence social decisions from the position of a qualified expert. The second role involves a conscious attempt to use technological progress for social progress. New uses for the raw materials of developing countries have already been mentioned; application of scientific techniques to urban problems would also fit into this category, as does the research to develop pollution control techniques. Scientific and technological developments contribute to the well-being of mankind; it is up to mankind to minimise associated social distress.

The I.L.O. experience of fifty years has shown the intricacies and difficulties involved in achieving social progress, and a look ahead shows that new technology, in use and on the drawing board, holds promise of both benefits and hardships. At the very first International Conference on Cybernetics in 1956, the social aspects of modern technology were considered in a paper entitled "The Problem of Automation from a Psychological, Family and Social Point of View"[3]. When this organization celebrates its fiftieth anniversary, as the I.L.O. is doing this year, it is to be hoped that such questions will still have a place on the conference agenda.

References

1. Admiral Hyman Rickover, *Symp. on Automation and Society, Univ. of Georgia* (1969).
2. *I.L.O. Meeting of Experts on Programmes of Adjustment to Automation and Advanced Technological Change, Conclusions and Recommendation, Geneva* (1967).
3. S. Lévy, "Comment envisager le problème de l'automation an point de vue psychologique, familial et social", *1st Intern. Congr. on Cybernetics, Namur* (1958), pp. 664–8

Cybernetics and social structure

V. H. BRIX

Chartered Mechanical Engineer, U.K.

Summary

Present-day literature on organization and management increases rapidly
and the need is ever more pressing for some basic conceptual guidelines to
help the student to assimilate the material pouring out of the press. The
neat, precise yet generalized formulations of cybernetics offer some promise
of providing a framework of this nature. The present paper outlines several
postulates which suggested themselves as a result of scanning some of the
current literature whilst keeping cybernetic ideas very much in mind. The
postulates refer to homeostasis, information channels, and the study of
systems. A "cybernetic" picture is shown of current society with its conflict
and strife.

INTRODUCTION

The aim in the present paper is to collect together various concepts currently
held in the areas of management, organization, and human affairs and to
view them through "cybernetic spectacles". This type of exercise appears to
be a worthwhile one, for the rapidly developing ideas on systems and feedbacks show promise of casting fresh light on the work of the great thinkers
of the past. For instance Burke's philosophy of gradualism, the importance
of conserving existing institutions, can figure side by side with the integrative,
systemic ideas of Hegel. The intriguing propositions of John Stuart Mill can
be meaningfully discussed in terms of present day control theory. In *Nerves
of Government* Deutsch[1] makes full play of control theory terminology in

describing organizations and nations, whilst Burton[2] develops the theme to discuss international problems within a totally new and refreshing context.

In the following paragraphs a somewhat closer look is taken at the human system or organization and an attempt is made to identify a homeostatic mechanism which underlies much of human social behaviour.

It is so important now to try and simplify the study of management and human relations, for the literature in this area is expanding so rapidly; students must have some kind of framework or pattern to help them to find their way through the morass of prolific, and often, turgid treatises pouring out of the press. Students of subjects like physics, chemistry, thermodynamics, etc., already have elegant theories and precise concepts to guide them. These subjects can indeed be assimilated within a time span of a few years of study only. Useful contributions in design can be made by young engineers soon after graduation because the experience of several centuries has been distilled for them and has been effectively "packaged" as patterned, teachable information.

There are two reasons why cybernetic thinking should be applied in the areas of sociology and management. The first is the one alluded to, above, namely the possibility of discerning new patterns of behaviour. The second, no less important, is the discipline itself. Cybernetics is a mechanistic concept, it deals with "things" which can be understood and described by precise terminology. Political, management and social literature however consists of so many abstract words which mean different things to different people[3] and it is hopeless to expect any measure of agreement, let alone advance, to be established until this woolliness is cleared away and the percepts within peoples minds can be brought into concordance.

There is no optimum way of presenting a subject like this, for each item is a component of a whole; no concept takes priority in the sense that a logical sequential discussion can be set out in a causative way, or a chronological layout like a railway time table. Each thing affects the other, this is the very nature of the "systems" approach with its inherent reciprocity of feedbacks.

CONTROL

Cybernetics clarifies our ideas about "control". In cybernetics it is recognized that *A* can control *B* most effectively when *A* incorporates within itself a requisite "model" or "percept" of *B*, and can communicate with *B* along a direct informations channel in which feedback can take place. This concept has been developed to apply to the case of one machine controlling another (the first machine must incorporate some analogue or "model" of the second), to the control which organisms exert on their surroundings, and, latterly to the case of human control, over machines or over other human beings. For brevity we shall refer to this concept of control as C_{df}, meaning "direct channel control with feedback".

In everyday affairs we are only too aware of a different kind of control, indeed we are subjected to this in various forms. The most obvious form of control, authoritarian or militaristic, involves commands proceeding from, for instance A, to B, and B carries out instructions. There is little, or no, feedback. In its less marked forms we see such control exerted through the medium of deterrents and incentives. Many consider that workpeople can only be "controlled" through the threat of unemployment and/or the offer of incentives: "carrot and stick". More insidious forms of control are exerted by implicit threats to status, or by various offers of indirect reward.

This type of control seems to prevail when there is some degree of difference in perception of goal as between controller and controlled. The "mismatch" has to be made up, it appears, by the application of deterrents or rewards. The communication is almost one way in the A–B direction, a command or instruction, and B performs a task acting to some degree as a "tool" of A, B indeed becomes part of A's effector system bypassing B's decision making or cerebral centres.

Control, in this case is exercised by manipulation of environment. A can only get B to do what A wants by altering B's environment, either increasing B's uncertainty by the imposition of threat, or exciting B's expectancy of reward, i.e. injecting some ingredient of hope into B's perceptual organs. It is very important to distinguish between the two forms of control. We shall refer to this second form by C_{im}, which means "indirect control by environmental manipulation".

In practical cases both C_{df} and C_{im} prevail to some extent at the same time. C_{df} predominates in participative groups, teams, i.e. within a well-trained football team, or between members of a space flight team, C_{im} characterizes the bark of the N.C.O. "you, you, and you" when apportioning an unpleasant task to his subordinates. Less obvious, but just as effective, this form of control underlies organization in firms and bureacracies, where the polite "advice" of the executive is mandatory and is an intruction, however muted. Non-compliance on the part of the subordinate carries with it the expectancy of some unpleasant environmental change. On the other hand we might regard the normal patient–doctor relationship as representative of C_{df}.

SYSTEMS

When several objects evince some recognisable relationship between each-other they are considered to form a system. Conversely a "non-system" is a random assortment of things which are not perceived to be inter-related in any way. The importance of recognizing human beings, as belonging to systems was recognized by Bertalanffy[4] and by Talcott Parsons[5]. Stafford Beer[6] develops the systems approach to organization, a more "cybernetic"approach than the eminently systemic ideas of Argyris[7].

In the sphere of politics, it is quite essential nowadays to regard the world population as a system[2]. Burton develops the view of extreme mutual inter-dependancy of nations, ideas stemming from works such as Coplin[8] and Boulding [9]. Not only is it desirable to see human beings as systems, but, according to Ginsberg, people evince a "drive", a need, to enter relationships with eachother, i.e. to form a system. He says that there exists a strong desire on the part of human beings to respond to and to be responded to by other human beings*.

THE HUMAN SYSTEM

Before going back to the social system, the interactions between the elements, the human beings, certain characteristics of the human being itself are relevant. The human being is a system too. It is a complex aggregate of cells subdivided functionally in a manner to promote survival of the organism as a whole. There are the sensors (eyes, ears, touch, etc.) through which information passes to the brain where it is selected on the basis of comparison

---

* Reference has been made in the text to the neuro-biological stress, most commonly referred to as "anxiety". This, I believe is only one part, one stretch, within a whole spectrum of states of neurological tension ranging from despair, despondency to hope and confidence[10]. The assumption is made that the degree of "tension" (pleasurable or otherwise) is a direct function of the perceptual mismatch input and its credibility.

* Sociologist Ginsberg identifies a positive "drive" in people to socialize. Within the context of the model in this paper we would interpret this "drive" as the tension which acts in response to inconsistent, non-coincident perceptual signals, i.e. ones of low probability or expectancy, relating to the status of other people and the self-image.

with stored signals (memory) from past experience. There is the decision-making function, and the "effector" subsystem, where signals can be transmitted outwards or the environment manipulated. Biologists George[11], and Klir and Valach[12] (II) give simplified functional diagrams of human systems. Psychologists[13-16] make use of these concepts bringing into prominence the importance of the "model" within the memory system which has to be used in order to interpret the percepts coming through the sensors. According to these authors, the signals which impinge from the environment are projected against, or matched against the percepts already held of the situations as presumed to be, or expected. If they fall into line, they are most probably rejected (ignored). If outside the internal percept or model, excitation is aroused which programs actions intended to bring then into line, i.e. to reduce the mismatch. According to Sokolov, the excitation is largely proportional to the difference between the incoming signal and the internal "model" expectation of what it "ought" to be. The greater the internal variety of the model (due to past experience and accumulated information) the more likely is matching to take place. There should be isomorphism between the model and the relevant part of the environment transmitting the signals.

The human system is therefore sensitive to environment, and is equipped to make differential assessments of changes in the environment. Neurobiological responses are made internally when changes are perceived, i.e. when there is uncertainty or mismatch in signals from outside, which initiate programs to annul the mismatch. The programs may be only internal ones, i.e. internal searches for "meaning" in order to scan the memory to arouse the models inside to meet the new situation; they may initiate decisions and actions by the effectors to change the environment in the direction of lessening the mismatch, or an avoidance strategy, might be put into effect.

ADAPTATION AND CHANGE

Insects and animals represent systems which are more or less in balance with their environment, the "eco-system". They survive so long as they possess inbuilt programs adequate to deal with the range of environmental change which they are normally called upon to experience.

Animals do not normally engage in intra-species conflict and genocide[17] as appears to be the case with human beings. Such manifestations have only been noticed when animals are subjected to artificial environments, such as overcrowding, for instance, in zoos.

Our particular concern is the proliferation of strife and genocide which has marked the increasing human population over the last 5000 years or so. (Quincy Wright[18] remarks that these are fairly recent manifestations of mankind.) The Malthusian prophesy of population limitation by intra-species strife of mankind looks as if it is being fulfilled. The latter centuries have been remarkable not only as a period of rapid technological improvement (elaboration of man's effector system so that machines change the environment instead of his body), but remarkable also for the proliferation of, and diversification of, religions, philosophies, nations, cults, and so-called "races".

Within a very short stretch of biological time, mankind has transformed his environment from its "natural" primeval forest with its wolves and bears into a veritable jungle of human beings, his fellows, all jostling together, cheek by jowl, an environmental transformation with which, it would seem, he is as yet ill equipped to deal. Little wonder that he has not been able to throw off many of the survival mechanisms such as violence and aggression[19] which had relevance only when he was under threat from denizens of the forest, as distinct from the uncertainties and complexities of his own kind.

The failure of the system of human beings to adapt to the rapid changes made by them to their own environment is manifest in other spheres. Antony Vickers[20] recently drew attention to the lag between economics and techno-logical development as exemplified in the anachronism of the banking system. Sir G. Vickers[21] sums up the situation by referring to "ecological traps" of our own making.

It would appear that the perceptual models which people have of their environment have been seriously lacking for them to have failed so miserably to deal with their own social environment. The exploratory efforts of man-kind to construct perceptual models of their increasingly complex environment, i.e. the proliferation of religions, political theories, etc.—to give "meaning" to uncertainties, only serve to diversify and further confuse.

There certainly is a control problem here.

THE SOCIAL SYSTEM: PERCEPTUAL MODELS

Perceptual models are the "pictures" which people build up within their minds in order to understand the signals they continually receive from outside. This is a prerequisite of controlling the environment by C_{af}, and therefore of survival.

When A talks to B, or otherwise communicates with B, A really talks to, or communicates with his image or percept of B. Similarly, B really communicates with his own image of A instead of with A. The signals, the information, which passes between them serves either to reinforce, or to detract from, the images which already exist.

Again, when A talks to his image of B he sees this image within the context of his own image, and possibly images of other people present and absent. He cannot see an image on its own, it really always forms part of some system or other. The relationship between the images, that of A and B, forms a significant ingredient of what sociologists call the relative status of A, B and others relevant in a given situation.

If A does not know B he still has some pre-conceived idea of B, and in his interactions with B he seeks to build up a more realistic image. He can only do this by receiving signals from B.

B however will not supply information gratuitously about himself to A without there being some reciprocity, A must return the compliment. Small packets of information pass to and fro', the transaction tacking place in such a manner that percepts on both sides become clearer and begin to merge without undermining any pre-existing assumed status relationship. Various codes of behaviour, the wearing of uniforms, etc., are all patterns of behaviour which ease this type of communication, subserve the extant system, and can therefore be regarded as mechanisms which minimise status ambiguity- and therefore perceptual mismatch.

SUGGESTED DEFINITION OF STRUCTURE OR ORGANIZATION

Let us pretend we can see right inside A's brain and look at A's picture of the A–B system. Again let us do the same thing with B. There may be a high degree of similarity between the two, or there may be little match at all. In the first case we would say that there is some "structure", in the second hardly any. The determinant of structure in either case is the *degree of matching* of the percepts in the two separate minds. The quantitative measure of the structure is the common component or part of the percepts, shared between the two. The parts which are uncommon represent structural ambiguity.

The same arguments might apply to larger systems than the A–B system. Take for instance a well-trained football team. We have here eleven indi-

viduals who by training and practice have developed an effectively functioning organization. Each player knows the capabilities of his fellows, and
could, perhaps subconsciously, evince a percept of the team as a whole which
would coincide very closely with the percepts of the other members. The
very nature of the game calls upon a very high order of communication
whilst a match is being played. There is no time for orders and commands.
Each player, when manipulating the ball, is autonomous, but, at the same
time delegates control to his team-mate in a manner understood by both
when passing the ball.

The importance of perceptual uniformity has been recognized for many
years. As early as 400 B.C. Mo Tzu postulated the need of perceptual uniformity. In the eighteenth century French philosopher J. Offry de la Metrie
drew attention to the role of self-image within organizations. Latter day
literature on management brings percepts and self images very much to the
fore. K. Davis[21] says that the percept a manager has of his role should differ
as little as possible from his role as seen by his employees. (And of course the
reverse is true.) Professor Revans[4] (p. 202) reports very high degrees of
disparity of role perception between management and employees in one
firm which was studied, a poignant reminder of present-day structural weakness in industry. This theme is discussed by Kelly[22]. The influence of Elliot
Jaques in this field should be recognized[23]. Kahn[24] and Bennis[25] see
structural breakdown (conflicts) in terms of mismatch in expectation of
different people with respect to given roles, "expectation" within this context
being closely related to "perceptual model".

HOMEOSTASIS

In scanning the social system through "cybernetic spectacles" we should
discern the property of "ultra-stability" which Ross Ashby[26] identifies as
the condition of survival of the system. This is secured by the mechanism of
homeostasis, i.e. the return of a system to a stable condition whenever and
however disturbed, by means of internal feedbacks. First recognized by
biologist Cannon in 1932, Miller[13] identifies this mechanism in the psychology
of human beings.

There is no law which says that processes identifiable in live organisms
and in human beings should also be revealed in social systems, groups of
human beings. Nevertheless, there is a good case for suggesting that something like this may well occur.

There are varied social manifestations which point to some homeostatic action—some tendency to return to a previous state when disturbed—for instance we have the social pressure which people experience to conform to existing norms. There is the resentment of the deviant, the tendency to relegate unconventional people to out-groups. A sudden bid by one member of a group for higher status by ostentatious behaviour soon provokes reactions from his fellows which bring him to heel. Deutsch[1] recognises homeostasis in nations and describes the internal "disequilibrium" with which it is associated. We also see the persistence with which institutions survive, long after the original aims or goals of those institutions have disappeared. We have the survival of old forms of organization, rigidly structured to resist change.

We now come to the crux of the matter. If human systems possess such highly developed homeostasic ingrdients, why are they always breaking down? Why is there strife? What is the nature of conflict? Why do human beings periodically exterminate each-other? Can cybernetics help us here?

SOCIETY AS A HOMEOSTAT

We shall outline at this stage a cybernetic model which seems to take in features of the foregoing paragraphs, and then examine this model to see if the nature of strife, conflict and genocide might be discerned in a useful manner.

Looking through "cybernetic spectacles" at a group or system consisting for instance of A, B, C, we do not "see" the individuals. We only see three mind pictures—diagrams of the structural–status arrangement of A–B–C, as perceived by each individually. If we superimpose the three, the common part of the picture will be seen, rather like the holes which show through when three cards from a "coordinate" ("peek-a-boo") index are placed together. The "real component" of the structure is the part common to all three. Suppose there is however appreciable divergence in the case of B. B projects his own image to a higher status than the position he is assigned by A and C. Signals from B to A and C will reflect this deviation as a perceptual mismatch. Signals from A and C to B, likewise, will not accord with B's self-image. Uncertainty in the form of perceptual mismatch is thus diffused through the system. This disturbance excites neuro-biological action, usually in the form of "anxiety", a biological state, like pain, which reacts and continues until the disturbance is removed*. Attempts to argue the point with B by A and C might follow by direct channel communication. A non-zero-sum outcome might appear as a common percept to all three, in which case some bargaining might result in adjustment and compromise. Whatever happens, the neurological stress will be locked up in the system, and will not be discharged until some perceptual matching can be achieved, at least to a degree which will bring the "anxiety" below a certain threshold.

The mutual bargaining between A, B, and C represents direct inter-communication between the three, in which all have participated, i.e. the decision-making centres of all have been exercised. This is an example of C_{df}, control through direct channels with feedback (reciprocity), and through its agency, a structure has been evolved.

Now consider a case where B's percept cannot be brought in close enough alignment with A's and C's, so that the system A, B, C, is left with a degree of undischarged "anxiety". We can visualize this "anxiety" as a mental alarm bell, insistently disturbing and relentlessly continuing to disturb until actions are taken to switch it off. Memory systems of each have been rapidly scanned in order to bring to the surface any precedents whereby the conflicting claims might be understood, but to no avail.

Failing control by direct channels C_{df}, the participants have no alternative but to resort to C_{im}, indirect, environment-manipulatory control, i.e. A, C, subject B to bribery or threat. The former is usually turned down as it has no unambiguous endpoint. Threat, coercion in some form or other is usually practiced, there is an apparent end point, i.e. the maximum power† which B may be perceived to possess to resist. Once B is under threat, there is no alternative but to exercise C_{im} against A, C, in self defence, the degree of countervailing threat matching, at least, the threat from A, C. Unfortunately, however, the anxiety remains undischarged, so that the process of reciprocal threats goes on, indeed it often "runs away" to situations where the expense or loss occasioned in keeping up the escalation far exceeds any possible rewards gained by winning (i.e. the situation in Vietnam).

The situation is recognized as a more or less normal one in international affairs, desperate efforts are made to avoid escalations by power balances and treaties. Burton[2] refers to this as "non-systemic" behaviour. There are no

---

* See footnote on p. 1110.

† *Definition of "power".* The ability of one system to affect the environment of another system, ignoring feedback from that system.

homeostatic elements of self-correction here, one threat excites another, anxiety builds up and there is no easy way in which it can be discharged.

We have thus presented two pictures of society. The first is an illustration of a homeostatic, self-correcting process which integrates or stabilises structure by discharging the anxieties excited by perceptual mismatch. The second picture is one of society where homeostatic control is absent. The anxieties, the environmental threats which impinge on each element, each subgroup, each human being, seem to exceed the threshold of anxiety necessary to put C_{df}, control by feedback, processes in operation. As it were, an emergency situation is now apparent, where the relatively slow consensual control systems are replaced by syndromes more appropriate to reactions to catastrophies like fires or floods, conditions where coercions, commands, etc. with their inherent threat and anxieties can be subordinated to the greater threats which are perceived in the catastrophe itself. Let us go back for one moment to considering our animals and their ecological balance. We have remarked on the notable absence of internecine conflict amongst greatures which are reckoned to be "more primitive" than mankind. Might we presume that these species, have, by evolution, attained a requisite homeostasis, and they have adequate intercommunications and perceptual models to deal with the situations they are normally called upon to face?

Again, we understand, that paleolithic and neolithic mankind lived fairly peacefully. These societies were probably C_{df}-controlled. Only in emergencies might we expect such societies to switch over to C_{im}. Indeed, they possessed little power to wield C_{im}, for they had little control over environment, and the environment so controlled did not possibly have much effect on their fellows.

Within recent years however, we have not only the increased technology with increased powers to wield C_{im} (machine guns, etc.) but a vastly increased population consisting of creatures exerting ever more C_{im}.

Little wonder therefore that the picture over the latter millenia has been one where human beings have resorted to an ever-increasing extent on the "emergency" syndromes, the C_{im} systems, the tyrannies, bureacracies* and power blocs. Industrial organizations *rely* on C_{im}, the employer–employee dichotomy being only too apparent. One psychologist has stated that anxiety in industry caused more time lost than the actual strikes!

---

* The "emergency" or transient features of the military or rigid bureacratic command system have been described by Clarke[27].

CONDITIONS FOR A HOMEOSTATIC SOCIETY

Consideration of society as a cybernetic system, the discerning of homeostatic mechanisms, brings to the forefront certain questions which might be asked, as an aid to studying the present-day malaise.

Firstly, in principle, is a homeostatic society feasible in the light of present-day population and technology?

Secondly, how can perceptual mismatches in organizations, societies, and nations be reduced. Should there be some meta-political concept or religion?

Thirdly, are human beings over-sensitive to perceptual mismatch? After all, the human organism is a "perception differentiator", and perhaps it over-perceives differences and under-estimates similarities.

Fourthly, are there enough or adequate channels of communication whereby mismatches can be effectively reduced before anxiety builds up to the "threshold"?

Fifthly, has the human brain adequate variety inside it to form isomorphic models of the increasingly complex outside world?

In most scientific problems, the difficulty is so often to pose the right questions at the outset. The cybernetic mode of thinking might help us to pose the right questions.

Whether, however, answers can ever be obtained to these is unknown. One thing which could help considerably is to disseminate the systemic–cybernetic view of society as widely as possible. The acceptance of an objective, de-personalized "Weltanschauung" might help the ordinary people of the world to recognise the truly disfunctional nature of power, and to mandate systems and governments where anxieties can be discharged by widespread exercise of C_{df}, control by feedback, instead of by environmental manipulation and power.

CONCLUSIONS

Each individual within a system is aware of the system only through his own image or percept of the system and the feedback information which reaches him through his sensors.

We adopt a definition of a human system therefore in which we identify structure of a system by the common element in each persons percept of the system—a structure is just a common percept or set of percepts. Divergencies between percepts are structural ambiguities, "non-structure", and amount to environmental uncertainties or "error".

The existence of such "errors" cannot be tolerated in human society. Every means must be employed to reduce perceptual mismatch and to discharge social uncertainty.

Perceptual mismatch arouses neuro-biological stress (which includes anxiety), just as error in a mechanism might arouse a "voltage" signal.

The means to reduce perceptual mismatch is the exercising of control. Efforts are made to discharge the "anxieties" by controlling, or attempting to control, other human beings, other groups, or the environment in general.

We identify two kinds of control. There is firstly "control with feedback", acting through effective channels of communication, and requiring internal perceptual isomorphic models of what is happening outside. This type of control is homeostatic, it is essential for the stability and wellbeing (lack of anxiety) of society.

The second type of control is "control by manipulation of environment", and is brought into action when the first "cybernetic" type of control fails, for some reason or other, to be exercised. It is an "emergency" form of control primarily concerned with the immediate survival of the controller, but applied in situations where rapid changes have to be dealt with. Authoritarian systems, executive and military command systems exemplify this kind of control. It does not rely on feedback, nor does it draw on internal models of high requisite variety.

Organisms and human beings switch from the first to the second type of control when the environmental feedback, the perceptual mismatches, exceed certain thresholds.

The complexities of present-day industrial society with its rapid changes and its proliferation of human beings have overloaded the human capacity to adapt by the homeostatic feedback processes which are manifest in more "primitive" societies, i.e. in the case of wild animals, insects etc. The second form of control therefore prevails to a high degree. Authoritarianism, power politics and bureaucracies depend on the "environment-manipulatory" control method and fail to discharge anxiety by reducing perceptual mismatch. Stress and tension therefore tends to remain within human societies, and this initself generates positive, self-perpetuating, feedback which reinforces the anxiety and undermines the structures already present. We have thereforea "cybernetic" picture of current society with its conflict and strife, and it may be possible to pose meaningful questions to aid the sociologists and political scientists in their studies.

References

1. K.W.Deutsch, *The Nerves of Government*, Free Press, New York (1960).
2. J.W.Burton, *Systems, States, Diplomacy, and Rules*, Cambridge University Press, London (1968).
3. J.Casson, *Using Words*, Duckworth, London (1968).
4. L.Bertalanffy, *General Systems*, Vol.1, University of Michigan Press, Ann Arbor (1956).
5. T.Parsons, *The Social System*, Routledge and Kegan Paul, London (1951).
6. S.Beer, *Decision and Control*, Unwin, London (1966).
7. C.Argyris, *Integrating the Individual and the Organization*, Wiley, New York (1964).
8. International law and assumptions about the state system", *World Politics*, **17**, 626 (1965).
9. K.Boulding, *Conflict and Defense*, Harper Bros., New York (1962).
10. W.McDougall, *An Outline of Psychology*, Methuen, London (1949).
11. F.H.George, *Cybernetics and Biology*, Oliver and Boyd, Edinburgh (1965).
12. J.Klir and M.Valach, *Cybernetic Modelling*, (Transl. from Czech.), Iliffe, London (1957). (SNTL, Prague (1965)).
13. G.A.Miller, *Psychology*, Hutchinson, London (1964).
14. E.N.Sokolov, "Modelling properties of the nervous system", in *Cybernetics in Thought and Life (Kibernetika Myshlenie Zhizn)*, Izd. Soz.-Ekon. Lit., p.242, Moscow (1964).
15. E.I.Boiko, "Modelling the brain function and higher neurodynamics", in *Cybernetics in Thought and Life (Kibernetika Myshlenie Zhizn)*, Izd. Soz.-Ekon. Lit., p.280, Moscow (1964).
16. Napalkov and Turov, "Memory" (in Russian), *Nauka i Zhizn*, No.10 (1964).
17. L.H.Mathews, "Overt fighting in mammals", in *The Natural History of Aggression* (Eds. J.D.Carthy and F.J.Ebling), Academic Press, London (1965).
18. Q.Wright, *A Study of War*, Vol.1, Chicago University Press, Chicago (1942).
19. M.Gilula and D.Daniels, "Violence in the age of technology", *Science*, **164**, 396 (1969).
20. A.Vickers, "The engineer in society", Proc. Inst. Mech. Eng., **183**, Part 1, No.5 (1968–1969).
21. Sir G.Vickers, *Value Systems and Social Processes*, Tavistock Publications, London (1967).
22. J.Kelly, *Is Scientific Management Possible?* Faber and Faber, London (1968).
23. E.Jaques, *Equitable Payment*, Heinemann, London (1961).
24. G.D.Kahn *et al.*, *Organizational Stress*, Wiley, New York (1964).
25. W.G.Bennis, *Changing Organizations*, McGraw-Hill, New York (1966).
26. W.Ross Ashby, *Design for a Brain*, Chapman and Hall, London (1954).
27. R.L.Clarke, "Flexible Control of R and D", *Chartered Mech. Engr.*, (1968).

The cybernetics of evolving systems

M. BELIS

Polytechnic Institute, Bucarest, Rumania

Summary

A physical system is a collection of devices united by some form of inter-dependence. Its existence is defined by a double set of interconnection relations: internal and external ones. The external influences dominate in the long run the internal organization of a system. Biological systems are physical systems provided with the ability to strengthen progressively their internal interconnection relations, that is to maintain their own structure in an active way. This consists of two basic mechanisms namely adaptation and learning. Both are control processes requiring a semantic. Adaptation represents a trial-and-error process controlled by the medium (at the level of the species); the favourable changes in the offsprings of a species are reinforced by feedback by the medium (natural selection). Learning represents a trial-and-error process controlled by the system itself by pro-cessing information. It enables the system to change the external inter-connection relations according to its own needs. Evolution is defined as the consequence of these two basic mechanisms: on the one hand, it re-presents the structural changes occuring by adaptation; on the other hand it represents the enlargment of the capacity of processing information due to learning.

INTRODUCTION

In order to cope with un unknown environment, biological systems are obliged to watch it, to notice and record its regularities. The most intelligent of them—men—are able to encode these regularities in laws which enable

11   Rose, Cybernetics III

them to forecast the reactions of the environment, to plan their future behaviour in an optimal way.

Man, in his effort to acquire knowledge, first tried to understand the
steady structures of phenomena and much later their change in time. This
happened because of the difficulty of studying moving structures having
time constants very different from those of the observer. Rapid varying
phenomena prevent significant observations and slow varying ones give a
false impression of stability. Since the Greek philosopher made the deep
remark "Panta rei" (everything flows) man made during the following two
thousand years a tremendous effort to know "how" they change and even
"why" they change.

Among the various dynamic structures which were studied, the living ones
raise the most passionate controversies. This happens because the complexity
of their structure made it difficult to obtain exact knowledge, thus leading
to various hypotheses; on the other hand, all that concerns man—even his
functionning—is related in some way to certain ethical, religious or political
systems of thought, with respect to which it is estimated, accepted or rejected.

This work tries to synthesize, from a cybernetic point of view, current
knowledge concerning "how" biological systems change in time, a problem
which can be tackled by scientific means. The cybernetic approach shows
new aspects of the problem.

LIFE ACCORDING TO SYSTEM THEORY

A physical system is a collection of devices united by some form of interaction or interdependence. This interdependence gives rise to new properties
which are not the sum of the component properties but they are completely
different from a qualitative point of view.

Each system is related to others in the frame of a higher level system with
respect to which they play the role of components. The physical world appears as a multilevel organization each physical device being at the same
time a system and a component; its existence is thus conditioned by two sets
of interconnections relations, the internal and the external ones. These two
sets of relations do not necessarily agree. If they disagree, the external interconnection relations prevail over the internal ones, that is the higher the
level of a system, the stronger its organization.

Living systems are physical systems provided with the ability to strengthen
progressively their internal interconnection relations, that is to maintain and

develop their own structures at different levels of organization. Unlike non-living structures, whose transformations in time are destructive, the internal interconnection relations of the living structures express their ability to regenerate themselves in time. Regeneration amounts not only to the maintenance and the reproduction of a given structure but to a progressive improvement of the maintenance mechanism. This is accomplished at several levels of organization, each of them using specific means. The higher the level of the system, the more efficient the mechanism used; hence the durability, the complexity of the structure and the cohesion increase with the system level. Because of the double set of interconnection relations which define a system (the internal and the external ones) this one is subjected to a double kind of influence. On the one hand, it must fulfil the requirements of the higher system in which it represents and element, and on the other hand it must fulfil its own requirements as an independent system. Both these requirements are expressed by the interconnection relations, written for each level. The living world represents a hierarchized organization of systems, each of them being a brick in a more and more complex edifice.

REPRESENTATION OF THE INTERACTION SYSTEM–ENVIRONMENT

A deterministic system can be represented by a black box, provided with inputs and outputs (Figure 1). The input–output relation (1) defines the sys-

$$P(x, y) = 0 \qquad (1)$$

tem S. The internal state of "S" is a label "s" connected with each pair (x, y) so that given the input "x" and the state "s", the output "y" is uniquely determined.

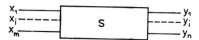

FIGURE 1   A deterministic system

Deterministic systems are rather theoretical systems, for actually the functionning of every physical system is affected by noise; in this case, for a given input and state, the output is more or less uncertain depending upon the amount of noise. This uncertainty is expressed by a probabilistic input–output relation. Moreover, if the system has certain degrees of freedom, if it is not strictly programmed, this uncertainty becomes more marked.

Living systems are noisy systems with many degrees of freedom so that they will be considered as probabilistic automata defined by the probabilistic distributions

$$p(y_i) = \|p\ (y_i/s_ix_i)\|$$
$$p(s_i) = \|p\ (s_i/s_jx_i)\|$$
(2)

The above input–output state relation of a system is a kind of formalism which encompasses its structural organization as well as its relations with the external world. Accordingly it includes both internal and external interconnections relations. The responses "y" which a system gives at its output, as well as its internal states "s" are both changing with time. We suspect that this happens either because of the changing conditions of the environment, which leads variable inputs to the system, or because of an inner mechanism of optimization.

We represent the interaction between the system and a complex environment as two coupled systems and we assume that the outputs of the system are to be correlated in some way to its inputs so that the whole system could work. Such a scheme is a very general one, for whichever would be the level of the system it always will have an "environment". The first question which arises concerns the mechanism of these changes: "how" can a system change its internal states and its external responses so that it could maintain suitable relations with an unknown and changing environment, and moreover to improve these relations. Notice that we avoid the "why" these relations are to be maintained and improved. It is an unanswerable question for the moment. But there is still a more subtle question connected with the first one, to which we can try to give an answer nowadays; it concerns the result of these changes, the direction of the cumulative process—if it exists—which enables the system to progress in some way, if any.

Relations (2) can be written at each level of organization of living systems. We will deal with two distinct levels, the species and the individual ones. Each of them uses specific means for improving their relations with the environment that is to make their internal and external interconnections relations more and more concordant. These specific means are adaptation and learning.

ADAPTATION

Adaptation is the mechanism used by the species. It represents a trial-and-error process controlled by the environment, in which certain changes of the responses and of the internal states are reinforced progressively. The general

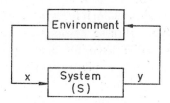

FIGURE 2   Adaptation

scheme of Figure 2 becomes a scheme of interaction between the species and the environment (Figure 3). The system (species) sends output messages (offsprings) to the environment. In its turn the environment sends input messages (offsprings which have survived in contact with the medium) to the

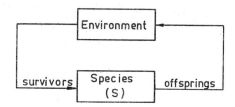

FIGURE 3   Interaction between species and environment

system. The internal states of the system (the structural and functional features of the species) depend upon the features of the input (survivors) which reinforces or weakens the existing ones. On the other hand, the characteristics of the offsprings depend upon the internal states of the system and accordingly upon those of the survivors.

This feedback scheme enables a control process to be directed towards the optimization of the external interconnection relations. Indeed, the characteristics which favour survival will be reinforced, and those which led their bearer to death will disappear. The process is carried on progressively, by successive trials, the more so as the characteristics of the environment are themselves variables. A major problem is to be clarified in connection with this mechanism. It concerns the way in which the system changes its responses (the characteristics of the offsprings).

A mechanism may exist in which random variations called mutations create new features which are to be tested in the environment. This one would have an all-or-none behaviour from the point of view of the species: it selects some of the messages whom it feeds back in the system and it eliminates the others. Alterations of these messages during their passage through the environment are not to be taken into account. This theory provides a fair working principle and the simplest which have been proposed in the absence of more exact knowledge; but it has certainly to be refined. The deep transformations which the representatives of the species undergo during their stay in the environment could influence the direction of the variations in a more subtle way, still unknown. The random character of the variations could be only the effect of the noise superimposed on a deterministic signal yet undiscovered because of its weakness or complexity. As Darwin said, it is "a most perplexing problem". Whichever the exact mechanism, it leads to the reinforcement of those features of the system which contribute to the improvement of the external interconnection relations, *by modifying the internal ones*. Thus, the features of the individuals will change so that the system with the higher level (the species) could survive and strenghten.

LEARNING

Learning is a process by which a system can improve the concordance between the internal and the external interconnection relations, *by modifying the external ones*. It represents a trial-and-error process controlled—in its higher forms—by the system itself by processing information. The general scheme of Figure 2 represents now the interaction between the individual and the environment (Figure 4).

The system (the individual) receives input stimuli from the environment and sends output responses to the environment. The outcome of each response has a certain utility with respect to the goal of the system and represent a reinforcement message. In this way learning systems acquire the ability to give correct responses in order to ensure their optimal working conditions. To this aim a new solution was adopted, namely to modify the environment and not the system. The search for better working conditions developped the information processing capacity of living systems so that progressively this one surpassed the vital necessities. This available capacity was used for different other tasks, whose variety and complexity contributed to its further development.

The mechanism of learning is partially at random and partially deterministic. The random character is due to the uncertainty of the system in face of an unknown environment. As their information processing ability

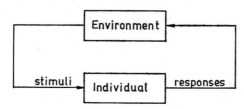

FIGURE 4   The individual and the environment

increases, living systems become capable to establish different strategies which enable them to efficiently use the available information, thus diminishing the random character of their actions. The information to be processed concerns the parameters of the goal and the setablishment of subgoals, the knowledge of the outcomes and correct estimation of their utility with respect to the goal, knowledge of certain relevant characteristics of the environment.

Learning ability gave an evergrowing autonomy to the individual which can ensure by itself its optimal working conditions. The individual is no longer a simple life carrier for the species but its existence acquires a special importance as it can contribute by learning to a better agreement between internal and external interconnection relations.

WHAT IS EVOLUTION?

By considering the successive transformations undergone by biological systems during their whole history and by trying to unravel the direction of these changes we get the following results:

At each level of organization there is a better concordance between the internal and the external interconnection relations of a system; this has been achieved on the basis of successive slight modifications of both types of relations and especially of those which characterize the lower level. Because of the hierarchic structure of living systems, modifications ocurring at one level entail corresponding modifications at all the other sublevels of organization. This accounts for the great variety of transformations of a system, whose origin are not to be sought in the necessities of the system itself but in those of the system of higher organization.

The structural organization of a system and the elements which constitute it are in a permanent interdependence: the properties of the components condition the general features of the structure and in turn its organization influences the constituents. The great many interconnection relations between systems of different levels made more and more complex their structural organization because it had to respond in an adequate way to various and sometimes antagonistic influences. But complexity requires coordination and control, and these in turn require information processing. Information processing ability appears as one of the main results of the evolutionnary changes undergone by living systems. At the same time it represents a necessary means for ensuring the concordance between systems of evergrowing complexity.

Concordance, complexity, coordination, control, and information processing are the successive steps made by living systems during their historical existance. They led to a stronger cohesion between systems of different levels and at the same time they enhanced the individuality of each system. Indeed, by processing information each system increases its possibilities of survival, consolidates its own position and accordingly its autonomy. But these can be achieved only by an harmonious integration in the higher level system to which it belongs and in the frame of which it has to develop.

Concentrating on two distinct levels of organization, the individual and the species, we find a better integration of the individual (especially the man) in its natural and social environment, as a result of two basic mechanisms: adaptation and learning. The maintenance and the improvement of the equilibrium between the development of the individual and that of the whole system to which it belongs is a major result of evolution. Disturbances of this equilibrium leads either to an exagerated subordination of the individual to the necessities of the higher system or to an abnormal development of the individual, disregarding the basic requirements of the system to which it belongs. Both are detrimental, as the system can survive only by its individuals and these can develop only in the frame of a system. Through evolution various mechanisms developed for the maintenance of this equilibrium. In their early forms these mechanisms were purely automatic, showing a marked predominance of the system upon its components. Later on, superior mechanisms were developed, using information processing structures at the individual level.

The freedom the individual acquire in this way is limited by the understanding of the general interconnection relations it has to satisfy. In this way its development is in keeping with the development of the whole system, whose destiny is nevertheless in its hands. The main success of evolution is to have created systems which could understand its laws and freely work towards their fulfilment.

Cybernetics and society

FRED J. RICCI

Computer Applications Consultant

U.S.A.

Summary

This paper presents a view of society from a cybernetic standpoint. It stresses the consideration of society as a whole and it attempts to solve some of its problems by studying the communication links that join the various segments together. A few theses are presented in addition to previous and current attempts to solve sociological problems by means of cybernetics.

INTRODUCTION

Society, in general, is a very vast and complex accumulation of many things and human functions. We can refer to it as a system. It is political, it is religious, it involves the interrelationships between people, families, corporations, colleges, etc. For a person to exist in this society he must adapt and respond intelligently to the world about him. He must adjust to the buildings he works and lives in, he must live and take information from newspapers, television, books and other people and he must do this in the most congenial and efficient manner possible. As a matter of fact, to help people perform and function properly in society such disciplines in the areas of psychology, sociology, philosophy, history, economics, education, architecture, law, and even homemaking, have attempted over the years to study and formulate guides for humans to function and live within. These disciplines have and are attempting to consider society in all of its categories. In each area of consideration vast strides have been made to study, to do research and then like the artist to perform a change in the perspective of society with respect to that particular area. The difficulty is that no interaction has taken place.

What I am suggesting is that a cross pollinization is needed. Society must be looked at as a whole; as the sum of all the parts not just the parts. People in various disciplines must begin joining together in a vast dialogue. Society must be viewed as made up of many inter-related parts (subsystems) all contributing to the overall system. How the various segments of society inter-relate, how they can be studied, what mechanism can be established to govern them and how information is conveyed between them belongs to the study of cybernetics.

The new science of cybernetics which Professor Wiener and his colleagues at M.I.T. have developed has had a marked influence not only in mathematics, where it was originally conceived, but in engineering communications, psychiatry, neurology and many social sciences. The word came about because Norbert Wiener felt constrained to invent one. Hence "cybernetics" which is derived from the Greek word *kubernetes* or "steersman" the same Greek word from which we eventually derive our word "governor".

Cybernetics according to Wiener was developed to class communications and control together. Why did he do this? "When I communicate with another person," he said, "I impart a message to him, and when he communicates back with me he returns a related message which contains information primarily accessible to him and not to me. When I control the actions of another person, I communicate a message to him, and although this message is in the imperative mood, the technique of communication does not differ from that of a message of fact."

It is the thesis in this paper that society can only be understood through a study of the messages and the communication facilities which belong to it, and that in the *future* development of these messages and communication facilities, messages between man and machines, between man and man, and between machine and machines are destined to play an ever-increasing role. That is, in order for us to employ a systems approach to society we must study communications which ultimately implies the use of machines (computers).

It is not implied that a computer is the only tool that can be used in this systems approach to society, but it is and will be an ever-increasing valuable and powerful tool. It is powerful not because it is a machine, but because it is compatible with the essence of the problems in society—namely communications.

The commands through which we exercise control over our environment are the kinds of information which we impart to it. Like any form of information, these commands are subject to disorganization in transit. They generally come through in less coherent fashion and certainly not more coherently than they were sent. In control and communication we are always fighting Nature's tendency to degrade the organized; that is increase the degree of randomness (entropy) and to destroy the meaningful.

So the study of society in general, from a systems point of view, has its foundations in the study of cybernetics. Cybernetics in turn relies on the manifestation of information and control with an ever-increasing propensity for computer usage.

Society tends towards randomness (increased entropy) and control and understanding of society tends towards organization (decreased entropy). If we are to begin to apply a systems approach to society we must begin by organizing.

CYBERNETICS GROUP

At the present time, I am involved with a group of persons from various disciplines in studying and applying the cybernetics concept to society from many points of view. As a matter of fact, by the time this paper is published, this group probably will have been incorporated as Janus Cybernetics Inc. The name Janus was chosen because the group was begun in January. Janus is an "ancient Italian (perhaps solar) deity, regarded by the Romans as presiding over doors and gates and over beginnings and endings, commonly represented with two faces in opposite directions".

The function of this group is to join many disciplines together to look at society from a systems point of view. Many organizations, and society in general, consider the solution to a problem from their own point of view. For example, a company producing a product will develop its organization in such a way as to sell as many products as possible and to saturate a given market. Our organization intends to be able to develop a wider perspective. We intend to combine the talents of sociologists, engineers, architects, clergy, businessmen, marketing specialists, educators and scientists in such a way that a cross polinization will occur. This group intends to do advanced planning in areas of urban and suburban planning, educational systems, sociological systems and scientific development. At the present time, we are in the process of defining ourselves. We are asking questions of one another and about the group as a whole so that the best possible communications can take place. The first task of this group in solving problems from a systems point of view was to design itself by maximizing the information passed from one person to another with the least amount of errors. As part of the experiment, it is felt that once the group has defined itself and how it should

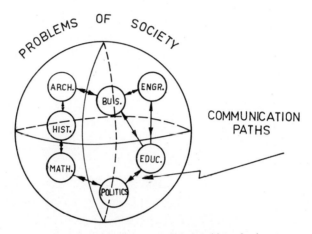

FIGURE 1   Systems diagram of the inter-relationships of subsystems

function from a systems point of view, then and only then will it be able to solve the problems of other organizations. We are organizing so that we may show others how to organize. If you like, we are using a cybernetics approach to reduce the entropy.

I mention the above group and its work because I feel that only active work, experimentation and organization can lend support to my thesis. Being a practical engineer, I am convinced that an hypothesis can only become valid when it is tested. Part of the function of this group is to provide an experimental foundation for our theories.

The remainder of this paper will be devoted to the more technical aspects of my original thesis, that is, in order for us to employ a systems approach to society, we must study *communications* which ultimately implies the use of *machines* (computers).

If a group of individuals of various disciplines are interacting with one another, the procedure may be looked at as a sphere with many parts within it, that is, as a system with many subsystems. Figure 1 depicts such an inter-relationship.

In this diagram, the sphere depicts society as a whole while the internal spheres depict the disciplines and forces at work trying to solve the problems of society. It is the thesis of this paper that the communication links or paths between the various subsystems are the areas which must be studied. All of the other subsystems are recognized disciplines in which much research has been done and is being done.

The communication paths that connect the various disciplines together are subject to disorganization and faulty transmission. In order to use the computer to make these paths less noisy, the following questions have to be asked.

(1) How can the computer be utilized in analyzing the messages between man and machine, man and man, and machine and machine?

(2) How can computer be used to understand and control communications?

(3) How can the computer be used to *organize* (reduce entropy) of information and thus increase understanding?

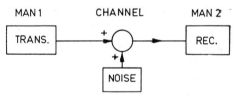

FIGURE 2   Block diagram of communications linkage
between man and man

COMPUTER AS TOOL IN ANALYSING
COMMUNICATIONS BETWEEN MAN AND MAN

The computer has been utilized as a tool in analyzing communications between machine and machine, and man and machine, but very little work has been done in analyzing information between man and man. Figure 2 is a typical communication facility between man and man, where man is used in the generic sense of universal man or organizations belonging to man. The channel over which man communicates with man is intended to be any one or combination of the following: voice, television, radio, telephone, newspapers, or written word. The block depicting noise is anyone of several mechanisms which distort the signal as it proceeds from one man to another.

Communication, in this context, can be defined as "social interaction through messages". Messages are formally coded, symbolic, or representational events of some shared significance in a culture, produced for the purpose of evoking significance. The distinction between the "communication approach" and other approaches to the study of behavior and culture rests on the extent to which (1) messages are germane to the process studied, and (2) concern with the production, content, transmission, perception, and use of messages is central to the approach. A communication approach can be distinguished from others in that it makes the nature and role of messages in life and society its central organizing concern.

Thus to characterize the verbal channels which exist between men, namely the written word, television, telephone, radio, and the spoken word, one must be concerned with understanding this media. At the present time much work has been done by persons in engineering, biology, logic mathematics, and computer science in this area, but much has to be done.

Automata theory seems to provide the answers to some of the problems of communication. This theory emanated from the study of discrete parameter information systems such as the digital computer, but can be applied to communications between man and man. What I am suggesting is that man can better understand his communications with other men by studying the communication within computers; this is how computers can help improve the communications link. By studying the nature of the computing system and using it as a device for experimentation, man will increase his knowledge of the role of *messages* in life and society.

THE BASIC SYSTEM MODEL
OF THE HUMAN INFORMATION CHANNELS

In order to characterize the communication channel, modern mathematical techniques must be utilized to get the appropriate *model*.

Cybernetics is concerned with models and some of the software models are: computer programs, infinite automata, finite automata, information theory, and the theory of games.

This section will be concerned with models developed from automata theory. Although a complete scheme for study will not be presented, approaches will be considered.

Before we can present any logical scheme for understanding the communication links, we must make the assumption that all channels can be discrete, any channel that is not can be converted by an analog to digital convertor. With this assumption, one may develop the model depicted in Figure 3, where I_j represents a discrete input into the system. The value of a given symbol can be specified by identifying it as a particular value from

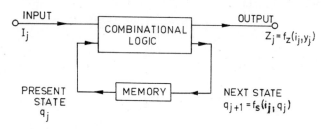

FIGURE 3   General representation of a discrete parameter system

a set I of all possible input symbols. Inside the block box there are storage elements that can remember part of the history of the input and response of the system. The contents of these storage elements at a given observation determine the state of the system when the observation is made. Because the system's input and output can take on only discrete values, this means that the parameter representing the memory of the system can also be represented by a variable that can take on only discrete values. The state of the system at the ith observation is represented by the variable q_i, and it is assumed that q_i can take on any of the values that belong to the set Q of all possible states of the system.

Because the state of the system represents the memory of the events that have previously occurred, it is possible to develop an expression that relates the value that the state variable will have at the next observation to the present value of the state variable and the value of the present input symbol. In a functional notation this becomes

$$q_{j+1} = f_s (i_j, q_j)$$

where f_s is referred to as the next state function of the system.

In general, the system does not generate an output symbol every time an input is applied. When an output is generated, however, its value will depend on the system's present input state. This may be related to a situation in society where much information is being input from one system to another

12   Rose, Cybernetics III

in discrete quantities, but no decisions are made until all of the information has been put in and processed in some form. This is one of the lessons learned about society from studying the computer itself, that is, in order to process information accurately and with the least randomness, as many inputs as possible should be acquired, then and only then will entropy and confusion be reduced.

The output of a system can be represented as a sequence of variables, Z_j, where Z_j may be any one of the possible output symbols from the discrete

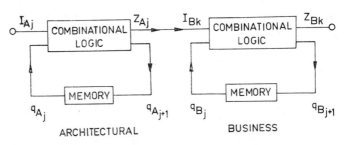

FIGURE 4   Total automata inter-related system

set Z of output symbols. The relationship between the output and the input and state of a system may be represented in functional form as

$$Z_j = f_Z(i_j, q_j)$$

where f_Z is the output function of the system.

From this discussion it can be seen that the discrete parameter systems of interest can be represented in terms of the possible inputs, states, and outputs that the system might have and the properties of the two functions f_S and f_Z. For a given discrete system, the functions f_S and f_Z have a particular character which determines the output of the system and the next state.

If the automata theory model of the discrete system described above is applied to a model of transmission between two disciplines, for example, architectural and business, the amount of *a priori* knowledge in each discipline may be depicted by the memory; the discrete inputs of the architectural system may be depicted by I_{Aj} and that of the business system as I_{Bk}; the present state of the respective systems may be depicted by q_{Aj} and q_{Bj} while the outputs are Z_{Aj} and Z_{Bk}. Figure 4 depicts the inter-relation of one system with the other.

It can be readily recognized from this system identification that the input to one system (I_{Bk}) is equal to the output of the other system Z_{Aj}, that is

$$I_{Bk} = Z_{Aj}$$

While the inputs and outputs of the system can be equated, the *states* of the respective systems cannot be. A number of conclusions can be drawn from this description.

(1) In any *interactive* system the inputs to one system depend on the outputs of the other system or systems.

(2) Any memory a system may have is autonomous to that system and not available to any other system unless voluntarily given.

(3) The state of a given system is independent of any other system, because f_s is purely a function of that system.

The conclusions made about the model depicted in Figure 4 lead one to believe that if more efficient use were made of the memories and interaction of memories with the inputs and outputs of a given system a more efficient and meaningful pollinization would take place between systems. How this can be brought about is left to the computer theorists and designers. Society can use their results to decide on better ways to develop communications among men.

GENERAL ROLE OF COMPUTERS
IN INCREASING EFFECTIVE COMMUNICATION CHANNELS

In addition to gaining an understanding of communication links between man by understanding the computer itself, a great deal of cross-pollinization may take place by using the computer.

In the future, networks of computers designed for sharing data bases will play a major role both in the private world and in the military. The linking together of information centers and libraries will take place by using real time computers. Information storage and video displays will be used to transmit accurate information between organizations and private citizens. Thus, the efficient use of real time computers will increase the interactions between the various disciplines so that information may be transferred more accurately and with greater speed. Many projects are underway by such companies as Bell Telephone Laboratories and RCA Corporation to provide and improve upon computer linkage in the military, telephone and educational systems areas.

The RCA Autodin Project (Automatic Digital Network) is a world-wide common user data communications system and the worlds most advanced operational system of its kind. This system was designed to operate continuously. It provides maximum message protection and transmission accuracy, and provides full message interchange capability among the scores of subscriber media, codes, formats, and speeds. Network performance is maintained consistently above 99%. Message traffic has increased from 1 to 6 million messages/month and is increasing continually.

Another computer designed by RCA is the Random Access Computer (R.A.C.). This computer was used to test field army command and control information systems concepts and procedures. It is a large-scale, general-purpose digital computer which is capable of assembling many items of information for issue in printed reports and constantly changing displays.

The two projects mentioned above are just a few of the many engineering tasks now going on in the United States to increase the information flow and recognition. Owing to managerial and technical difficulties the extension of these projects will move slowly, but in the proper direction of a cross-pollinization among men.

COMPUTER SIMULATION OF CYBERNETIC SYSTEMS

Mention has been made of how societies communication problems can be solved by studying computer systems themselves and using computer systems to improve overall communications. Attention will now be given to the use of computers in the simulation of socio-economic and political systems.

In order for segments of society to understand and solve problems related to the entire society, specific models must be made of particular problems so that a common area exists for communication. Once a model (usually quantitative) has been developed, the various segments of society may contribute to and change the model so that it depicts the actual situation most closely. This quantitative description of the actual physical or sociological system is known as simulation. Simulation is beginning to develop into a more understandable and useful science especially in the area of computer simulation. Perhaps a few examples of simulations that I have performed in addition to simulations others have performed will make the concept clearer.

In order to increase the efficiency of the registration procedures at Monmouth College, West Long Branch, New Jersey, a group of students and myself embarked on a program of writing computer programs using the

General Electric 265 time-shared system. We attempted to simulate the courses being offered, the time they are being offered, the instructors, and rooms available in a computer program. The program then could be run to produce an optimum registration schedule of courses, instructors, time of meeting, and room. The simulation has the advantage that many combinations or alternatives may be attempted on the computer without actually trying the given registration procedure. This is one of the greatest advantages of simulation programs, that is, many alternative situations may be attempted without ever implementing the situation.

Simulations have been done at Michigan State University in the area of sociology by Dr. H. Koenig and in the area of simulating the function of the entire university by other members of the staff[23,25,26]. Dr. Koenig used modern control systems in addition to the computer to depict dynamic sociological problems.

A recent paper by Dr. P. N. Rastagi of the Massachusetts Institute of Technology depicts very clearly the advantages of simulation. In his paper[27] "Protracted military conflict and politico-economic stability" he describes protracted military conflicts between nation-states in the twentieth century. Dr. Rastagi became interested in protracted conflict in trying to understand the economic difficulties in India engendered by wars with China and Pakistan. The Vietnamese conflict was another motivating factor. According to Dr. Rastagi: "Military conflicts have important psychological and economic aspects. The marshalling of a nation's resources for war objectives produces concomitant impact on the thought pattern and economic condition of the populace. Controls and privations imposed on the population are inevitable features of wartime living conditions and are directly related to the magnitude of the war effort and the capacity of a nation's resources." In the simulation study, an attempt has been made to view a prolonged military conflict in its inter-relationship with the psychological and economic factors. Insofar as the latter elements are concerned with the support that a regime commands from the masses, implications for political stability also enter the picture. The study seeks to explore these implications using the C.T.S.S. system of project M.A.C. at M.I.T. The modeling philosophy adopted for the simulations described in this paper is based on feedback systems theory. The approach used, known as industrial dynamics, was developed at M.I.T. under the leadership of Jay Forrester.

At the present time, there are many computer simulation languages in use and under development in the United States. Such languages as general purpose simulation language (G.P.S.S.) and continuous simulation language (C.S.S.L.) have proved very successful and are being used extensively. Simscript and Simpac are two other languages with a wide usage. Specific areas of use are in the simulation of railroad systems, corporation structures and judiciary systems.

The use of models in understanding cybernetic systems is taking on a strong hold in the areas of economics, biology, sociology, psychology, business, and many other areas. I think it is important that concentrated effort and monies be allocated to the continued use of computer simulation of cybernetic systems in society. These systems will allow us to make more rational and meaningful decisions on when and how actions should be taken and what the effects will be. For example, if an accurate model of the poverty program in the United States can be made, one would be able to answer some of the following questions.

(1) What effect is the poverty program having on the economic conditions of the poor?

(2) What psychological and sociological influence does money have on these people?

(3) What is the best structure for implementing money in the program?

(4) Is this program increasing or decreasing participant dependency?

Questions of this nature may be asked in any segment of society. Hopefully computer simulation will help answer these questions and provide a more rational basis for decision making in addition to providing a quantitative cross-pollinization in society.

CONCLUSION

Society can only be understood through a study of the messages and the communication facilities which belong to it, and that in the future development of these communication facilities depend on careful study which ultimately implies the use of computers.

This paper attempted to indicate present techniques and future techniques using computers to better understand our society and control it. If we can understand something thoroughly and predict with a great deal of accuracy, certain outcomes we will be able to reduce the entropy in society and bring about better communications.

Techniques for understanding society and improving its communications facilities have been depicted by demonstrating the function of a cybernetics group concerned with a cross-pollinization purpose. The use of the computer as a tool in analysing communications channels has been considered in addition to the establishment of a specific automata theory model. The description of this model will help one to understand communications by studying the computer itself.

Further understanding of society through the use of computers was considered by discussing the use of computers in communication environments in addition to pointing out the important use of simulation.

In the entire spectrum of discussion, perhaps the use of computers as communication links and simulators will have the greatest impact in the immediate future, because these are the areas in which the most money is available for experimentation. Perhaps computing systems developed for the government may be used for the improvement of society.

Society may be considered as an inter-relationship of many disciplines all with their own particular goals, functions and science. The future of society as a whole can only be understood, controlled and improved by a careful cross-pollinization and understanding. The future of our society depends upon all people joining together, each doing their part, to make this world a better place to live. I cannot help believing that not until people begin considering society as a whole will we ever see significant progress.

Cybernetics (the control and communications of man and machine) is and will play an ever increasing role in the understanding and control of society. In order to implement the cybernetic concept the computer will prove to be a very valuable tool.

References

1. K. U. Smith and M. F. Smith, *Cybernetic Principles of Learning and Educational Design*, Holt, Rinehart, and Winston, London (1966).
2. E. Florey, *An Introduction to General and Comparative Animal Physiology*, Saunders, London (1966).
3. F. E. X. Dance, *Human Communication Theory*, Holt, Rinehart, and Winston, London (1967).
4. N. Wiener, *God and Golem, Inc.*, Chapman and Hall, London (1964).
5. N. Wiener, *The Human Use of Human Beings; Cybernetics and Society*, Houghton Mifflin Company, Boston (1950).
6. N. Wiener, *Cybernetics, or Control and Communication in the Animal and the Machine*, M.I.T. Press, Cambridge, Mass.; Wiley, New York (1948).
7. F. H. George, *Cybernetics and Biology*, Oliver and Boyd, Edinburgh (1965).
8. R. F. Fagen, *Politic sand Communication*, Little, Brown Series in Comparative Politics, Boston (1966).

9. A. M. Hilton (Ed.), *Proc. 1st Ann. Conf. on the Cybercultural Revolution—Cybernetics and Automation*.

10. Fink, *Computers and the Human Mind*, Heinemann, London, (1966).

11. J. W. Forrester, "Industrial dynauics—a major breakthrough for decision makers", *Harvard Business Rev.*, July–August (1958).

12. B. Russell, *Bertrand Russell Speaks his Mind*, Bard Books, Avon Books, New York (1962), p. 72.

13. T. C. Schelling, *The Strategy of Conflict*, Oxford University Press, Oxford (1960).

14. Tsien, *Engineering Cybernetics*, McGraw-Hill, New York.

15. L. J. Fogel, *Biotechnology: Concepts and Applications*, Prentice-Hall, Englewood Cliffs, N.J. (1962).

16. J. G. Taylor, A. J. Navarro, and H. R. Cohen, "Simulation applied to a court system", *I.E.E.E. (Inst. Elec. Electron. Engrs.), Trans. System Sci. Cybernetics*, **SSC–4**, No. 4 (1968).

17. J. C. Green, "Simulation of a Traveling Repairman Problem", *(I.E.E.E. (Inst. Elec. Electron. Engrs.), Trans. System Sci. Cybernetics*, **SSC–4**, No. 4 (1968).

18. K. A. Swanson, "Objectives of simulation", *I.E.E.E. (Inst. Elec. Electron. Engrs.), Trans. Systems Sci. Cybernetics*, **SSC–4**, No. 4 (1968).

19. D. R. Brennan and Silberberg, "The system/360 continuous modelling program", *Simulation (Tech. J. Simulation Councils*, **11**, No. 6 (1968).

20. "1130 continuous system modelling program (1130-CX-13X)", *Program Reference Manual* (H20-0282) *IBM Corporation Data Processing Division*.

21. D. R. Brennan, "Continuous system modelling programs: state of the art and prospectus for development", *Proc. of the IFIP, Working Conf. on Simulation Programming Languages*, Oslo, North-Holland, Amsterdam (1967).

22. K. E. F. Watt, *Ecology and Resource Management*, McGraw-Hill, New York (1968).

23. H. Koenig and G. M. Kenney, "A prototype planning and resource allocation program for higher education", *Proc. Symp. on Operations Analysis of Education*, U.S. Office of Education (1968).

24. K. Ricci, "Memory and meaning", *Progressive Architecture* (in press).

25. R. Zemach, "A state space model for resource allocation in higher education", *I.E.E.E. (Inst. Elec. Electron. Engrs.), Trans. Systems Sci. Cybernetics*, **SSC–4**, No. 2 (1968).

26. H. Koenig, G. M. Keeney, and R. Zemach, "State space models of educational institutions", *Proc. Organization for Economic Cooperation and Development* (1967).

27. P. N. Rastagi, "Protracted military conflict and politico-economic stability", *Simulation (Tech. J. Simulation Councils)*, No. 1 (1969).

Some theoretical and experimental considerations of cybernetics, responsive environments, learning and social development

D. R. STEG and A. D'ANNUNZIO

Drexel University, U.S.A.

Summary

The purpose of this study is to consider some theoretical aspects of the concept of "responsive environments" and its relation to learning as well as to some recent experimental findings. This problem has reached crucial proportions as is clearly indicated by the current controversies of the validity and/or substantiation and/or justification of reinforcement theories of learning versus control theories of learning. The distinction to be made between cybernetic control and reinforcement control delineates clearly the difference between sensory feedback and the feedback concept of knowledge of results or reinforcements, and has far reaching meaning for the application of control theory to human activity. An experimental environment of a "responsive" nature has been researched since 1965 at the "Early Childhood Center", a laboratory school at Drexel Institute of Technology under the direction of the department of Human Behaviour and Development. Findings suggest that early stimulation (ages 2.5 to 5 years) seems to be effective in specific language and reading skills including alphabet recognition, reading ability, language facility, and typing ability. Unexpected results in areas other than academic skills have become evident, particularly in the areas of emotional and social development. Children who were unable to use a similar non-automated program, owing to rather severe behavioural difficulties, were successfully involved in the automated program.

INTRODUCTION

The purpose of this study is to consider some theoretical aspects of the concept of "responsive environments" and its relation to learning and to some recent experimental findings.

This problem has reached crucial proportions as is clearly indicated by the current controversies of the validity and/or substantiation and/or justification of reinforcement theories of learning versus control theories of learning.

The essential feature of the pragmatic theory of knowledge is the maintenance of the continuity of knowing with an activity, an activity which purposely modifies the environment.

Dewey considered human thought subject to growth, thus subject to change, subject to control, be it religious belief or be it science, thus implying a living, dynamic, operating system. The mechanics underlying Dewey's consideration of intention, of an incentive, or a purpose, are based on reaction to impulses. However, achievement of a goal when completed results in a museum piece. And, to quote Dewey: "No-one can carry around with him a museum of all the things whose properties will assist the conduct of thought."

The further object of this paper is to apply this philosophy to a system of controls, and to analyse the concept of the learning activity as part of the development and maturation of human thought, and, as such, subject to controls and to laws of control systems.

LEARNING, EDUCATION, AND TRAINING

As, of late, "teaching machines" have been put to use in "normal" and "abnormal" teaching situations, and a wealth of opinionated data has been published on the subject of the learning process[1,2]. Many have maintained that the impact of "educational technology" has been clearly demonstrated[3].

It thus seems appropriate to attempt an outline of the system involved in the learning phenomenon and the distinction between training and education.

Training involves the learning of some specific pattern of behaviour, be it equilibrium on a tight rope or chess playing, etc., while education concerns the development of new, not previously learned behaviour.

Thus, in every field of human endeavour, education would lead to accomplishments beyond the learned patterns. The result of education is creativity, while the result of training is performance involving skill and not necessarily creativity.

What brings into focus this difference, could be illustrated by the example of a trained "specialist" able to make a copy of a Vermeer which is hard to distinguish from the original. Whether it is in the field of painting or literature, or music, a masterwork can be recognized by the individual master's style. A work by Rubens, Borodin, or Hemingway is traceable to the author by the average layman, provided he had some basic training in the particular field. The training involved would be a training to paint, compose music or write literary composition. While this kind of training necessarily required a teacher or teaching machines, even self-taught training is predicated on the assimilation of some previous experience. Creative activity goes beyond previous experience. Education implies going beyond previous experience while assimilation of previous experience is the expected result of training.

CYBERNETIC CONTROL AND REINFORCEMENT CONTROL

The distinction to be made between cybernetic control and reinforcement control delineates clearly the difference between sensory feedback and the feedback concept of knowledge of results or reinforcements, and has far-reaching meaning, both theoretical and applied, for the application of control theory to human activity.

Feedback–Control

The principle of feedback-control was recognized by training psychologists more than 25 years ago. However, its introduction as a formal behavioral concept dates back to 1948, when Wiener published his book *Cybernetics*. His term cybernetics, called attention to the study of human control mechanism and the principle of feedback control.

Feedback control visualizes an elementary system of control by which the sensing elements of an organism can obtain information and feed it back internally for guidance of its operative motor nerve centers. Such feedback was a commonplace of the physiologist long before the engineer found common ground with him in "cybernetics". This principle of steersmanship by feedback has undoubtedly played a very important evolutionary role in animal life. Possibly even before life appeared.

Feedback mechanisms are characterized by the use of the measurement of some physical quantity to control a motor mechanism that in turn adjusts the magnitude of the measured quantity to bring it to a predetermined desired value.

Behavioural scientists have indicated a rather widespread acceptance of the principle of feedback. However, feedback and knowledge of results is being used synonymously, and knowledge of results is thought to function as reward as well as information. In the *Psychological Abstracts* feedback is indexed as "See also knowledge of results, Reinforcement". One can thus see why many theorists took the term feedback to mean reinforcement.

In the latter analogy the feedback signal is interpreted as having reinforcing properties. And the smaller the magnitude of the error, the greater the reinforcement value of the signal. It is understood then that the response that minimizes error is presumably strengthened or learned.

It has been observed experimentally, that providing knowledge of results, rather than reducing or withholding knowledge, does lead to more effective learning[4]. And, it is true that immediate knowledge is more effective than delayed knowledge. But, this does not automatically enhance efficiency of performance and learning[4]. Yet, it is generally assumed that learning can be enhanced it is followed by reinforcement.

In other words, dynamic sensory feedback provides an intrinsic means of regulating motion in relation to the environment while knowledge of results given after a response is a static after-effect which may give information about accuracy, but does not give dynamic regulating stimuli. Dynamic feedback indication of error would thus be expected to be more effective in performance and learning than static knowledge of results.

Furthermore, the efficacy of reinforcement assumes an active need or drive state while, feedback theory assumes that the organism is built as an action system and thus energizes itself. Hence, body needs are satisfied by behavior that is structured primarily according to perceptual organizational mechanisms, and require programs that communicate.

Systematic transformations of sensory-feedback patterns are affected by the use of tools, be they symbols, socio-psychological, economic, or other instruments. Opposed to this, reinforcement theory describes learning as due to the effects of reinforcements that bear no systematic relation to the different kinds of behaviour learned.

Transformation of Control

A theory of behavior organizations should enable us to conceptualize an orderly progression from relatively simple overt response patterns seen in very young children to the complicated skills, symbolic responses, and other abstract thinking that an individual can exhibit. These human processes can be analysed in terms of systematic transformations of sensory-feedback patterns. Implicitly this denies the general validity of association and reinforcement models.

What appears to be different types of thinking may actually be considered as differences in patterns of feedback control. There are no distinctive categories in learning except in a general descriptive sense.

(1) Verbal learning and instrumental learning differ because the systematic transformation of closed-loop regulation of behaviour are different in these two areas.

(2) Instrumental learning and unaided psychomotor learning differ since the use of tools and machines involves spatial, temporal and kinetic transformations of feedback. This in turn changes the pattern of control.

(3) Psychomotor learning incorporates the feedback mechanisms of manipulative movements.

(4) Orientation learning involves integration of the larger transport and postural movements of the body into a more general pattern of control.

Classical conditioning differs from orientation learning because the subjects are restrained and deprived of much of the varied sensory feedback used in normal adaptive responses. Feedback theory can account for a variety of behaviour (from relatively simple overt responses to complex overt and symbolic skills). Thus, cybernetic research in learning may well provide a framework for understanding and studying a variety of learning patterns.

Control Theory and Learning

Assuming that, as with the laws of physics, the laws governing control systems apply equally to animal, man, or machine, we can follow the control theory application to learning. In the language of the systems engineer, a closed-loop control system pattern consists of (1) an input signal that triggers some action; (2) a feedback signal of the result of this action to compare with the input signal; (3) a closing of the loop, a summation of the two signals; and (4) effective action to counteract this new signal. In a control system, action is triggered as a result of an actual error input (doubt, disturbance). The error is essential to the activity of any control system. These control patterns apply equally to automatic machinery, animal behaviour and man's everyday automatic activity[4].

Conclusion

Use of linear programs (including branching) in teaching, deliberately limits the media of communication, the experiences of the student and thus the depth of understanding that he achieves. We suggest that instead the student be provided with a broad context of experience by resorting to all of the activities and to all of the communicative media at our disposal. This includes verbal and non-verbal material. Thus the student learns by responding to the perceptual organization of his environment.

COMMUNICATION AND SOCIAL DEVELOPMENT

In communication there are at least two different systems that can be involved. There can be communication with a person or communication without a person, or rather, communication by means of an intermediary, an object. It need hardly be emphasized that communication through objects is different than communication with a person.

Up to now education and training has been dependent on relations between people. Usually a child learns by being in communication with another person, be it another child, or an adult. This is the dimension of the field up to the present.

In the case of communication through objects, there is a direct relationship between the individual and the object. Such a system is different from the one in which there is direct contact between people.

As a result, the field of teaching systems, is just that much enlarged, although interrelations between people and objects are all subject to the person to person relations.

All of teaching is about (1) science (object-to-object relation); (2) applied science (person-to-object relation); (3) humanities (person-to-person relation). Person-to-person relation is common to all teaching be it between pupil and teacher or parent and child, and so on. However, in machine teaching–learning (pupil and object) there is now a different system involved. A new continent has been discovered, a new dimension, a new era where the relation involved is people to objects. Other areas will probably develop, but this one has a place for the machine.

Lest one immediately worries about the competition this may present with the other system, consider that an airplane does not interfere with walking. Furthermore, we suggest that this machine, the Edison Responsive Environment (E.R.E.), should be used at an early age. It is best suited for use at that time since it is then that all systems of communication can be used and developed. For instance, in the case of the airplane, it should be used for long distances and not to cross a street. It is much harder to use the E.R.E. later and it has severe limitations. Think for instance about what one could try to teach an Einstein with it or even a Romney.

People–object relation is as essential as people–people relation. However, people–people relations work best when people share similar experiences. People–people contact is basically inhibited by different educational backgrounds, inhibited by the fact that people have not had similar past experiences. But, if both teachers and students had people–object relationships, and share some experiences, then education, which is people–people relation, becomes easier to achieve.

Social and Responsive Environment

The social environment is a matter of give and take, but relations between people–object is not. It is argued that a child who has not yet established a people–people relation (an autistic child for instance) runs the risk of establishing only a people–object relation and may remain satisfied with that. But it may well be that it is the other way around. A person may be able to be involved in a people–object system, the non-give-and-take system. A person involved in a system relation with objects has learned that there is a certain affinity possible with the outside world which is relation between people and objects. Then, the next possible step may be when one of the objects in the outside world is in fact a person. It is thus possible that a relation which does not have a give and take may soon change into one that does. Experimental evidence at the Drexel Institute of Technology Early Childhood Center, in working with mentally and physically handicapped children, seems to support this.

SOME EXPERIMENTAL CONSIDERATIONS

Introduction and Sample

A pilot study reported in 1968 was an attempt to gauge the effectiveness of the use of the E.R.E. (Model 3) in conjunction with a non-automated type-writer in teaching three- and four-year olds over a five-month period. In addition, efforts were made to determine the effects of the treatment upon language facility. The sample for this study comprised 27 children—15 paid tuition and 12 did not. The latter group were children of primarily low socio-economic status (i.e. neighbourhood children participating in a Get-Set program). The mean age for the tuition group was 49 months while the mean age for the non-tuition group was 49 months. Mean I.Q. score, as measured by the Stanford–Binet Intelligence Scale (1960 revision), was 118 for the tuition group and 100 for the non-tuition children.

While there were significant differences in achievement levels among the Get-Set and the tuition group, before treatment, within five months no sta-tistically significant differences were found in alphabet recognition (upper and lower case letters), ability to type words, and size of sight vocabulary[5].

A follow-up study was designed to measure the effects of the "responsive environments" setting on psycholinguistic abilities*, when compared with an equated group. The equated group attended another early childhood cen-tre, considered to be one of the best, in the same community, receiving ap-proximately the same experiences except that this centre possessed no auto-mated equipment. Twenty boys and twenty girls between the ages of 3–0 and 5–0 were matched, individually, on the basis of chronological age and mental age, psycholinguistic abilities, sex, and race (half white and half coloured). The assessment of mental age was limited to the *Peabody Picture Vocabulary Test*, while the assessment of psycholinguistic abilities to the *Illinois Test of Psycholinguistic Abilities*. These tests were given before and after treatment.

The purpose of the study was to determine the underlying and presumably longer-range changes in the child's pattern of development. It has been determined, in the above pilot, that the children at Drexel's Early Childhood Center were able to match names of alphabet letters to their graphic sym-bols and type letters from dictation. These results, nevertheless, may not, in themselves, have been indicative of underlying changes in those abilities

---

* See Appendix 2.

necessary for future reading success. What would be more revealing, concerning the effects of the "responsive environments", would be changes in underlying psycholinguistic abilities.

PROCEDURES

Treatment

A daily 15-minute session was provided for the three-year old, 20 minutes for the four-year old. The adult–child ratio was 1:1.

All children were offered the treatment daily with daily option of refusing. A combination of both automated and non-automated equipment was used. The choice of instrument for a given day was dependent upon the discretion of the teacher and the availability of the automated equipment. However, all of the subjects received approximately 80% of the total instructional time on the automated machine. Time spent at the E.R.E. for the study ranged from 4 to 23 hours.

The non-automated booth contained a typewriter, as well as audio-visual equipment and Instructo materials. In this setting, the assistant sat at the child's side in order to operate the equipment manually, while in the automated booth, the machine was operated from a central panel and the child was observed through a one-way mirror. A daily record was kept of time spent, stroke count, and performance. During the time of treatment the training area in the automated setting was bare, except for the equipment, and the temperature was controlled at 72 degrees.

A three phase program developed in the automated setting in which each child was (1) to demonstrate the ability to match names of alphabet letters to their graphic symbols, (2) to demonstrate the ability to type letters from dictation, and (3) to demonstrate skill in reading words orally. During these daily sessions, the child sees no-one in the training centre except the booth assistant. Training involves the child with all the staff at this centre so that a daily record is kept of the child's performance, stroke count on the equipment, time spent, etc., and weekly discussions reviews progress made.

The machine can be programmed in four phases, depending upon the progress of any particular child. During an introductory phase the child is allowed to explore, striking whatever key he wishes. Each depression locks the keyboard until after the letter is pronounced by the machine. In later sessions of this phase, flash cards of individual letters may be presented for the child to match with the letters on the keyboard. The child remains in this phase until he can relate the sound to the written letter.

During the next, intermediary phase, the child is asked to depress a specific letter key, for example, that has been pronounced to him by the booth assistant over the intercom. Such cues as locking the keyboard (except for the particular letter called for) and coloring the child's fingers to match colors on the keyboard are given. This phase, which is still semi-automatic, is an extension of the previous one.

During the next phase the machine is totally automatic and assumes that the child is totally familiar with the alphabet.

By responding to instructions provided in the program, the child learns that letters form words and thus becomes familiar with the typing of the syntactical structure of the language. The machine locks itself so that nothing except the letters that are indicated by the verbal command can be typed.

The final stage is an extension of the above procedures to include sentences and paragraphs. The child may wish to dictate a story into the machine. The story is then programmed so that the child can type the story. Picture, of a particular youngster—can be added to the now fully automated program.

The E.R.E. program was integrated with other types of pedagogical procedures. These took the remaining twenty percent of instructional time. These were designed to focus on the development of visual and auditory perception skills necessary for the later development of reading ability. For those children already possessing these pre-reading abilities, the instructional procedures will focus on the development of obtaining and conveying the meaning of language symbols.

At the "lower" levels of neurological integration the skills to be learned involve auditory and visual non-symbolic aspects—the perception or manipulation of the symbol, with little regard for meaning. At the auditory level, for example, such exercises as the following list were given:

    matching sounds
    reauditorization of sounds
    utilizing visual and kinesthetic cues in sound discrimination
    develop awareness and recognition of non-verbal auditory patterns
    imitate sound and rhythm patterns
    coordinate auditory and visual patterns

And, in using the visual modality, examples included the following:

    match pictures to outline drawings

superimpose designs on preletter forms

orientation, manipulating objects in various positions

sequentialization, using coloured beads, and printed non-verbal patterns, etc.

perceiving detail, using drawings, and filling in outlines of homes, etc.

At the "higher" levels the exercises used were taken from Fernald's[6] system of remedial reading, and others from Gillingham and Stillman[7]. Fernald's system can be conceptualized as employing the assimilation of simultaneous visual and kinesthetic symbolic stimuli as an aid to retrieval in learning whole words. This letter system is as comprehensive and systematic as Fernald's but is thoroughly multi-sensory and begins with the presentation of short visual units (single letters as opposed to whole words). At this higher symbolic level the choice of which system to use is dependent upon the specific integrities exhibited by the particular child. Many children, for example, had difficulty retaining the visual image of a whole word and consequently needed a more phonetic and elemental approach such as Gillingham and Stillman's.

Thus, the types of exercises to be used with any particular child is determined in two ways: (1) the degree of perceptual integrity the child possesses which determines his vertical level of neurological integration, and (2) the specific sensory modality (auditory or visual) through which he appears to learn most readily.

Analysis of Data

Significant differences in psycholinguistic abilities were found in favour of the Early Childhood Center. Significant changes in these abilities would appear to indicate that the effects of instruction appear to be diversified, of a profound nature, and of extended duration.

Results show an increase of one year and one month in psycholinguistic test scores for girls and an eight-months increase for boys, at the Early Childhood Center. These differences were obtained during a seven-months period, covering twenty-five weeks of instruction. The children at the Early Childhood Center spent approximately two hours each week on the automated and follow-up program on a voluntary basis. The control group spent approximately four hours each week on "readiness" and pre-reading activities.

The greatest increases in psycholinguistic abilities were obtained by those children who had the higher pre-tested mental age scores. When these differences, obtained for children at the Early Childhood Center, were compared with the differences obtained for the control group, the paired change values were significant at the one per cent level of confidence. The mean change for boys in the control group on the ITPA was an increase of three months while the increase was five months for girls.

Statistical Treatment

Since the children from each group were paired, the difference between means for paired observations and equated groups were calculated. The standard error of the difference was obtained and a significance level of the value of "t" at the five per cent level of confidence for a one-tailed distribution was adopted.

Since it is assumed that children change in the same direction where learning is concerned the fact that one change is significant and the other is not may rest upon a very small difference in the $\bar{z}$ ratio. Thus, a statistical test of the net differences between changes were made on those tests which were given before and after the experiment. The simplest approach was to treat the individual changes as if they were single measurements $(D_e = m_{e2} - m_{e1})$ and then determine paired change values.

The net difference between changes was ten and a half months for the Drexel Center children in growth in psycholinguistic abilities.

No significant differences were noted between the two groups in terms of growth in mental age as measured by the PVVT.

However, effects of early instruction have shown that children can and do learn in what were formerly called the "pre-school" years.

Unexpected results in areas other than academic skills have become evident, particularly in the areas of emotional and social development. Children who were unable to use the similar non-automated program, owing to rather severe behavioural difficulties, were successfully involved in the automated program.

Video-taping of sessions were made at the beginning of this school year and were made again in June allowing greater clarification of behaviour changes. The final tape to be shown will be 25 minutes long.

SUMMARY

The E.R.E. was originally selected as the core of our training program because of its educational design. The crucial requirement to be met was provision for instantaneous and dynamic sensory feedback.

To date, three years of research has shown significant differences in psycholinguistic development among equated groups of three to five-year old children, with apparent indication that the effects of instruction are diversified, of a profound nature and of extended duration.

Longitudinal follow-ups necessary to further gauge longer term gains are continuing.

APPENDIX 1: SOME DEFINITIONS

For completeness the following terms derived from the philosophical and cybernetic model, which are in common use in the field of philosophy, psychology and education, can now be defined in symbolic terms in the sense of the model previously described[8].

Art: dynamic perception.

Concept: pattern recognition. To have a concept is to recognize a pattern.

Concept formation: In the same class as understanding defined below. Choice is essentially involved.

Control: concerted behaviour of components forming an organized whole.

Education: triggering of dynamic perception.

Effect of experience: to expedite the time requirement of performance by eliminating some intermediate steps in the process of training. May adversely affect education by limiting new concept formation.

Effect of language: to circumscribe within a common framework the otherwise dispersed signals of communication messages. Language is a code and a channel (in the sense of a T.V. channel). No explanation or communication can be other than limiting.

Emotion: signal amplifier, beneficial if properly integrated in the control system.

Intelligence: ability to learn. Note that, with these definitions, the intelligence quotient does not measure intelligence.

Intelligence quotient (I.Q.) Instantaneous measure of the problem solving range. Note that this does not measure in any respect the image filter. Thus, it is a static response, and of little significance.

Intention: system hunting, inert characteristic of any teleological construct. Motive creating purposes without resulting involvement of will, forms inconsequential intention.

Learning: growth in all elements of the feedback model. Thus, learning implies use of thinking and involves, for example, new concept formation.

Motive: input signal (birth of a new concept) may or may not be acted upon.

Pattern recognition: a correlation program involving the image filter in its trivial (identity) mode: or, alternatively, a correlation process or a process involving symbol recognition, be they language or any other kind of symbols, drawing upon memory.

Problem Solving: thinking as defined by model, involving image filter in its trivial (identity) mode. It is a technique, used in thinking—object of training, result of application of skill.

Purpose: balance requirement of a closed-loop system creates purpose when the feedback signal has not satisfied the input signal.

Reflex thinking: thinking involving identity mode of image filter, elementary adaptive control. It is another tool to be used in training; there is a trivial relation between it and thinking.

Thinking: analysis of doubts; result of understanding.

Understanding: "successful" thinking as defined by the model involving the "creative" modes of the image filter. "Successful" implies achievement of intended congruence. The output of the feedback loop is interpreted broadly to include understanding, action, and other constructs flowing through the same loop, or alternately, understanding implies disintegration (creation of doubt) of existing concepts. (No evaluation is possible if value is fixed, hence the elimination of fixed value is a prerequisite for understanding ... hence doubt.)

Will: motor force controlled by output resulting from comparison of input signal and feedback (purpose).

APPENDIX 2: THE PSYCHOLINGUISTIC ABILITIES*

The nine psycholinguistic abilities are defined below. Each definition is accompanied by a brief explanation of how the ability is tested.

---

* James J. McCarthy and Samuel A. Kirk, Illinois Test of Psycholinguistic Abilities, Institute for Research on Exceptional Children, University of Illinois, Urbana, Illinois.

Tests at the Representational Level

Tests at this level have one thing in common. They all assess some aspect of the subject's ability to deal with meaningful symbols—to understand the meaning of symbols (decoding), to express meaningful ideas in symbols (encoding), or to relate symbols on a meaningful basis (association).

The Decoding Tests

Decoding is the ability to comprehend auditory and visual symbols—that is, the ability to comprehend spoken words, written words, or pictures.

Test 1. Auditory decoding is the ability to comprehend the spoken word. It is assessed by a controlled vocabulary test in which the subject is asked to answer yes or no by voice or gesture to a series of graded questions.

Test 2. Visual decoding is the ability to comprehend pictures and written words. It is assessed by a picture identification technique in which the subject selects from among a set of pictures the one which is most nearly identical, on a meaningful basis, to a previously exposed stimulus picture.

The Association Tests

Association is the ability to relate visual or auditory symbols (which stand for ideas) in a meaningful way.

Test 3. Auditory-vocal association is the ability to relate spoken words in a meaningful way. This ability is tested with the familiar analogies test in which the subject must complete a test statement by supplying an analogous word (e.g. the examiner says, "Soup is hot; ice cream is ...").

Test 4. Visual–motor association is the ability to relate meaningful visual symbols. The present test requires the subject to select from among a set of pictures the one which most meaningfully relates to a given stimulus picture.

The Encoding Tests

Encoding is the ability to put ideas into words or gestures.

Test 5. Vocal encoding is the ability to express one's ideas in spoken words. It is assessed by asking the subject to describe simple objects such as a block or ball.

Test 6. Motor encoding is the ability to express one's ideas in gestures. The manual language of the deaf is an example of motor encoding. This ability is tested by showing the subject an object and asking him to supply the motion appropriate for manipulating it (e.g. drinking from a cup or strumming a guitar).

Tests at the Automatic–Sequential Level

Tests at this level deal with the non-meaningful uses of symbols, principally their long-term retention and the short term memory of symbol sequences.

Unlike the representational level tests, no attempt has been made to sub-divide the automatic–sequential level tests into their decoding, association, and encoding aspects because of the lack of theoretical clarity at this level.

The Automatic Tests

Our frequent use of a language and the abundant redundancies of language lead to highly overlearned or automatic habits for handling its syntactical and inflectional aspects without conscious effort. So familiar are we with linguistic structure that we come to expect or predict the grammatical structure of what will be said or read from what has already been seen or heard. In speaking or writing, these automatic habits permit one to give conscious attention to the content of a message, while the words with which to express that message seem to come automatically.

Test 7. Auditory–vocal automatic ability permits one to predict future linguistic events from past experience. It is called "automatic" because it is usually done without conscious effort. In listening to a speech, for example, we develop an expectation for what will be said which is based on what has already been said. In the present test, the subject must supply the last word to a test statement, invariably a word requiring inflection (e.g. the examiner says, Father is opening the can. The can has been ...").

No suitable visual–motor counterpart to this test could be designed. The ability to read incomplete sentences and supply the correctly inflected word in writing would seem an appropriate task, but obviously it is not suited for two-and-a-half-year old children. After many unsuccessful attempts to design a picture substitute for the visual–motor channel, the effort was abandoned.

The Sequencing Tests

Sequencing, as used here, is the ability to correctly reproduce a sequence of symbols; it is largely dependent upon visual and/or auditory memory.

Test 8. Auditory–vocal sequencing is the ability to correctly repeat a sequence of symbols previously heard. It is assessed by a modified digit repetition test.

Test 9. Visual–motor sequencing is the ability to correctly reproduce a sequence of symbols previously seen. It is tested by requiring the subject to duplicate the order of a sequence of pictures or geometrical designs presented to the subject and then removed.

References

1. J.P. DeCecco, in *Education Technology*, Holt, Rinehart and Winston, New York (1964).
2. E.R. Hilgard, *Theories of Learning and Instruction,* University of Chicago Press, Chicago, Ill. (1964).
3. Review in Educational Supplement, *New York Times,* July 18 (1965), p. E. 7.
4. D.R. Steg, *A Philosophical and Cybernetic Model of Thinking,* International Association of Cybernetics, Belgium (1967).
5. D.R. Steg, Paper presented at *Inter. Reading Assoc., Boston* (1968).
6. G. Fernald, *Remedial Techniques in Basic School Subjects,* McGraw-Hill, New York (1943).
7. A. Gillingham and B. Stillman, *Remedial Training for Children with Specific Disability in Reading, Spelling and Penmanship,* Educators Publishing Service, Cambridge (1960).
8. D.R. Steg, *A Philosophical and Cybernetic Model of Thinking,* Supro.

Organizational cybernetics and human values

RICHARD F. ERICSON

The George Washington University, Washington, D.C., U.S.A.

Summary

At least since Norbert Wiener began to depict the human degradation potentially inherent in the cybernetic approach to organizational and institutional design over two decades ago, philosophers of science and others in highly industrialized societies have been worrying—in print and otherwise—about evolving trends. The substance of the concerns may perhaps be encapsulated by this question: are we now again pursuing a witless decision path where the sole parameter is "what is possible technologically" as we yesterday appeared only to ask the question "does it make sense economically"? Today's massive environmental pollution problems are largely a consequence of the paramountcy of econo-industrial values. (And, to compound the felony, economic values improperly costed, since implicit and opportunity costs were largely ignored.) Will tomorrow's "human pollution" problems result from even more disastrous neglect of cybernetics applied to social constructs and human values? Some years ago the noted educator Robert Maynard Hutchins opened an essay dealing with an assessment of the latent social impacts of cybernation with the sanguine statement "I assume 1985 can be anything we want it to be". Is that any longer a tenable assumption? How can we deal with convictions such as that recently expressed by the nuclear physicist Amos DiShalit when he argues that the time has come for us to recognize that the most man can hope for is parity with the emerging "self-actualizing" machines. The major hypothesis explored by this paper is that managers of large enterprises—public or private, in any context—have an increasingly urgent socio-humanistic responsibility to create self-actualizing organizations which will assure to the maximum extent possible, the transcendence of human values. The major thesis of the paper is that general systems insights, cybernetic science, and computer technology provide the basis for achievement of this paramount objective.

INTRODUCTION: SCIENCE AND THE HUMAN CONDITION

The essential method of modern science is analysis. Reductionism and incrementalism have given us deep insight into the nature of matter and energy, at least. We have built a techno-industrial society structured mainly so as to maximize the power of these understandings in order to give us leverage in our age-old struggle with nature. Thus, some would conjecture that at long last we may be at that point where there can truly be a "human use of human beings". But only the most extreme optimist would hold that such an outcome is as yet more than a vision.

The fact is that, in this decade of the 1960s, we may trace the locus of another exponential curve in man's experiences. To a large degree it is a curve which measures a countervailing inclination in man's nature. It measures man's desire to synthesize, to find meaning and purpose, from man's point of view.

This drive, in and of itself, is not new. It is of the essence of religion. Much of philosophy concerns man's search for holistic concepts which will help him see a meaningful pattern in the complexity with which his perceptual world confronts him. What *is* new is the rapidly growing intensity of the quest, and the modern context of the search. Plato's *Republic* is from a world quite different from that of Boguslaw's *The New Utopians*.

The essence of modern science has recently been epitomized as follows.

(1) Science is constantly, systematically and inexorably revisionary. It is a self-correcting process and one that is self-destroying of its own errors...

(2) A related trait of science is its destruction of idols, destruction of the gods men live by... Science has no absolute right or absolute justice... To live comfortably with science it is necessary to live with a dynamically changing system of concepts... it has a way of weakening old and respected bonds...

(3) Not only are the tenets of science constantly subject to challenge and revision, but its prophets are under challenge too...

(4) Further, the findings of science have an embarrassing way of turning out to be relevant to the customs and to the civil laws of men—requiring these customs and laws also to be revised...

(5) Certainly we have seen spectacular changes in the concept of private property and of national borders as we have moved into the space age...

(6) Moreover, the pace of technological advance gravely threatens the bountiful and restorative power of nature to resist modification...

(7) Another trait of science that leads to much hostility or misunderstanding by the nonscientist is the fact that science is practiced by a small elite ... (which) has cultural patterns discernibly different from those of the rest of society...

(8) The trait that to me seems the most socially important about science, however, is that it is a major source of man's discontent with the *status quo*...[1]

Examination of the essence of this list of characteristics of modern science gives us a basis for appreciating Norbert Wiener's closing words in his assessment of the "Moral and Technical Consequences of Automation" made only a decade ago[2]:

"... we can still by no means always justify the naive assumption that the faster we rush ahead to employ the new powers for action which are opened up to us, the better it will be. We must always exert the full strength of our imagination to examine where the full use of our new modalities may lead us."

Delineations of the highly exponential rate of change in the growth and application of human knowledge abound. Examples from many fields are readily at hand. That we live in an era of quantum jumps in science and technology seems patent and uncontestable, at least measured by any yardstick provided by man's experience to date. Yet our full appreciation of the magnitude of what is happening to us is only slowly dawning. As one astute observer wrote a few years ago[3]:

"Within a decade or two it will be generally understood that the main challenge to U.S. society will turn not around the production of goods, but around the difficulties and opportunities involved in a world of accelerating change and ever-widening choices. Change has always been part of the human condition. What is different now is the pace of change, and the prospect that it will come faster and faster, affecting every part of life, including personal values, morality, and religion, which seem most remote from technology... So swift is the acceleration, that trying to 'make sense' of change will come to be our basic industry."

And the urgency of contemporary circumstances have been well expressed only a few weeks ago by a biologist, who feels that[4]:

"... now the empirical evidence may be turning to support those who feel that science is in some sense in the grip of natural forces which it does not command...

I am not really sure that we stand on the kind of watershed Luther stood on when he nailed his theses to the door of the cathedral, but we may make a serious mistake if we do not at least entertain that possibility. If we fail to recognize the average man's need to believe that he has some reasonable command over his own life, he is simply going to give up supporting those systematic elements in society which he sees as depriving him of this ability."

This paper is concerned with man in organizations. The major hypothesis explored is that managers of large enterprises—public or private, in any context—have an increasingly urgent socio-humanistic responsibility to create self-actualizing organizations which will assure to the maximum extent possible the transcendence of human over technological values. The major thesis is that general systems insights, cybernetic science and computer technology can, so to speak, be "turned upon themselves" and made to provide the basis for achievement of this paramount requirement of contemporary managers.

HUMAN VALUES AND NON-CYBERNETIC TECHNOLOGIES

Concern for the impact of technology upon human values is hardly a recent phenomenon. With varying degrees of explicitness since Karl Marx at least, many have sought to call man's attention to the shift away from naturalistic values implicitly required by machine civilization. As man was released from nature's grasp by his power-multiplying and labour-extending artifacts, he came under a new yoke: the man–machine interface had its own set of action priorities and behaviour imperatives.

But more than this. Effective interaction with machines necessitated shifts in attitudes, changes in values. Nowhere was this more evident than in the workplace.

The utilization of steam power, for example, clearly implied the clustering of workers about factories. The accompanying value shift requirements have been noted, for example, by Elton Mayo, in his contrast of the "established" and the "adaptive" society. Clearly, the attitudinal skill most valued by modern industrial society is adaptiveness. Where the only constant is change, ready accomodation to change is a valued behaviour. Mayo agreed with Janet that, in modern circumstances, for most of us, "sanity is an achievement". To keep one's emotional equilibrium is not easy among the shifting patterns in which most of us live.

But just at the time that man was called upon to contrive stability in increasingly dynamic environments, he was also required to find his place in increasingly large-scale and monolithic bureaucratic structures. As industrial artifacts evolved to more complicated forms and interrelated processes, a correspondingly complex set of organizational modes was generated.

Thus, one strand of our concerns in this paper is with the impact of technologically induced organizational complexes upon the attitudes and values of the humans who populate them. The other strand is concerned with the larger questions deriving from the impacts of technology upon man's environment in general. The substance of our inquiry may perhaps be encapsulated by this question: are we now again pursuing a witless decision path where the sole parameter is "what is possible technologically" as we yesterday appeared only to ask the question "does it make sense economically"?

It would not be sufficiently useful for purposes here to describe in detail the growing demand for articulation, for integration, for synthesis, for a more cosmic understanding of the socio-political implications of man's econotechnological behaviour during the past century. But perhaps it is worth illustrating the point. Let us consider the now familiar example of the pollution of our physical environment.

In classical economic doctrine, air is a commonly cited example of a "free" good. Economists are concerned only with the "optimally efficient allocation of economic resources", and "economic goods" are those which are in short supply, relative to demand.

But in recent times some of the most essential non-economic resources have rapidly moved out of that category. Concern for the magnitude and rate of pollution—environmental, social, and others—has intensified. Air, water, quiet, privacy: rather suddenly, these are decidedly economic goods. We are finally beginning to comprehend the accumulation of enormous "hidden" costs of our econo-technological order, costs never reckoned in industrial or national accounts.

The dawning realization of the extent to which man has already fouled his nest brings us up short. Indeed, we fear that, in some compartments and, in some respects, "spaceship earth" may already have been irremediably damaged. What price unbridled technological progress? Increasingly, the urgent need for holistic assessment of applied science is manifest. Only if we are sufficiently aware of full social ramifications will we be able to forestall the deleterious consequences of the "technological cornucopia" we have generated.

Thus, from society's standpoint, modern science and technology is Janus-faced: it has given us wealth in one sense, and poverty in another; it has harnessed nature to man's basic needs in ways and to extents undreamed-of only a few decades ago, but it has fostered a continuingly lowered "quality of life". Today's massive environmental pollution problems are largely a consequence of the nearly unchallenged primacy of econo-industrial values. (And, to compound the felony, economic values improperly costed, from a social system point of view, since implicit and opportunity costs of production were largely ignored.) Our essential concern grows from this historical trend. Will tomorrow's "human pollution" problems result from even more disasterous neglect of cybernetics applied to social constructs and human values? This is the haunting issue.

Some years ago the noted American educator Robert Maynard Hutchins opened an essay dealing with an assessment of the latent social impacts of cybernation with the sanguine statement[5]: "I assume 1985 can be anything we want it to be." Is this any longer a tenable assumption? How is it to be reconciled with the conviction recently expressed by the nuclear physicist Amost DiShalit when he predicted that the time has come for us to recognize that the *most* man can hope for is *parity* with the emerging "self-organizing" cybernetic computer complexes apparently an increasingly inherent part of our organizational life?

GENERAL SYSTEMS THEORY, CYBERNETICS, AND THE METHODOLOGIES OF MODERN SCIENCE

Before turning to the development of the argument, however, we must take note of another view expressed by Norbert Wiener which has caused some concern among those of us working for the development of organizational cybernetics. It may be recalled that in (one of his last works) *God and Golem, Inc.* Wiener[6] concluded that he had

"... accomplished the task of showing many valid analogies between certain religious statements and the phenomena studies by cybernetics, and had gone reasonably far in showing how cybernetic ideas may be relevant to the moral problems of the individual."

He rather tartly dismissed the idea that the social sciences could benefit by the application of cybernetics because, in his words, "cybernetics is nothing if it is not mathematical" and that he had "found mathematical sociology and mathematical economics or econometrics suffering under a misapprehension of what is the proper use of mathematics in the social sciences...". Wiener's major concern was that, in the social sciences, we have not appreciated how much mathematical physics rests upon the ability accurately and validly to measure the data with which it deals. And there is, for Wiener an inherent difficulty, because, for example[7]:

"... the economic game is a game where the rules are subject to important revisions, say, every ten years, and hears an uncomfortable resemblance to the Queen's croquet game in *Alice in Wonderland*... Under the circumstances, it is hopeless to give too precise a measurement to the quantities occurring in it."

We will not quibble that for Wiener not to have distinguished mathematical economics from econometrics may reveal his own lack of appreciation of the value of heuristic model building, as against inductive validation of mathematically deduced statements about nature. Be that as it may. We shall simply assert the social utility of speculatively considering the value impacts of "alternative futures", using concepts such as homeostasis, positive and negative feedback, isomorphic reasoning, and morphogenic systems. We shall certainly not pretend that the social sciences have even yet much prospect of completely rigorous application of cybernetic science. But given the magnitude of and the urgency of the social need for fresh insight and imaginative outlook, general systems and cybernetic imagery such as found in the works of Kenneth Boulding, Anatol Rapoport, Ludwig von Bertalanffy, and Stafford Beer are sorely needed. The identification of system isomorphies and the construction of homomorphic models is well worth whatever "pure science" rigor must be sacrificed when, in the words of Rapoport[8]:

"Once this logic is grasped, the system approach to the study of man can be appreciated as an effort to restore meaning (in terms of intuitively grasped understanding of wholes) while adhering to the principles of *disciplined* generalizations and rigorous deduction. It is, in short, an attempt to make the study of man both scientific and meaningful."

A CONTRAST OF PARADIGMS:
NON-CYBERNETIC VIS À VIS CYBERNETIC ORGANIZATIONS

Early in his book *Cybernetics and Management* Stafford Beer says[9]: "It is inevitable that the word 'control' must be used frequently in the forthcoming discussions. I wish to state explicitly at this point that henceforth it will be used in a special sense: it will never denote the repressive and mandatory type of system which customarily passes for control..." The accompanying paradigm illustrates what Beer probably had in mind when he speaks of such a "repressive and mandatory" control system. It also serves to bring into focus our concern for human values as affected by organizational processes. Let us interpret the (clockwise) progression in Figure 1.

At the outset, we assume the existence of more or less clearly stated organizational objectives, for we are dealing here with purposive organizations. On the basis of the application of the "principles of organization

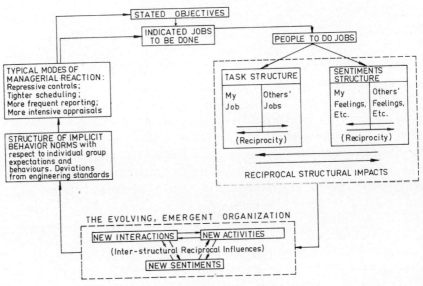

FIGURE 1   A reality analysis fo organizational behaviour processes

and management" as usually delineated in traditional texts, management thinks in terms of the logics of hierarchical authority structure and of rational modes of departmentation of the jobs to be done, as the organization is designed. Efficiency, co-ordination logics, "span of control" considerations: these are the by-words in terms of which organization charts are usually drawn.

But, unfortunately for such an approach, people are required to do the jobs; and eventually specific names have to be written into the boxes on the chart. But just here, at this early stage in design, is where the usual approach begins to fail to take important parameters into account, for managements usually attend to only the "task" subsystem of the total system with which they should in reality be dealing. That is, management understands the necessity of organizational design which integrates each task into the total work flow; principles such as "scalar chain" are applied to assure, on paper at least, that each job will contribute to the organization's ultimate purposes. But historically it has only recently come to appreciate the other major subsystem with which it should deal: that of "sentiments", to use F. J. Roethlisberger's characterization. The argument is simply this: the effectiveness with which an organization functions is determined at least as much by who holds the positions which are delineated on the organization chart, as by the cleverness of the organization structure which defines and abstractly interrelates the "jobs to be done". Thus, the assumptions, feelings, perceptions, values, etc. which comprise the "personalities" of the specific people involved in the operation must somehow be taken into account, if a systemic organizational model is to be achieved. And this is all the more so since, as the exhibit indicates, there is not only reciprocal influence exerted within each of the subsystems, but *between the subsystems themselves* as well.

Thus the dynamics of organizations-in-action should be viewed as an evolving social system, with management attention focused on the continually emergent system resulting from the reciprocal influences exerted by new activities (jobs), interactions (relationships), and sentiments (values)—to use Homans' terminology. Now because historically management simply did not have the communication and control tools adequately to deal with such emergent phenomenon on a "real time" basis, we usually find that a subtle and intricate set of "implicit behaviour norms" comprise the real essence of the actual control mechanism operative in large-scale organizations. That is, something is usually needed in order to "make the organization work" and to fill the behaviour interstices left by the formalized statement of the system found in such paraphernalia as organization charts, manuals of operating procedure and the like. Organizational cement is therefore manufactured by organizational participants within the framework of the inadequate formal control system specified. This cement comprises the behaviour norms which are based upon the "evolving pattern of expectations" which organizational role players develop. A *sub rosa* dynamic control system arises, most often in terms of the tacit pattern of agreements which evolves among interacting organizational participants, reflecting their needs and values, as well as the organization's.

Now when management belatedly becomes aware that, for example, engineering standards are habitually not being met in work outputs, the usual reaction is for the activation of formal authority and control mechanisms. Unsatisfactory performance evaluations more often than not seem to lead directly to the imposition of explicit, formal, manifest control mechanisms. And, as subsequent events all too often show, such delayed and proscriptive reactions either merely trigger a search for new modes of behaviour which will put management off for another period of time, or to a divergent cycling and organizational explosion which we usually refer to as a "positive feedback" phenomenon.

If things deteriorate sufficiently—and they usually do—the cycle depicted on the accompanying schematic is usually completed by someone in management concluding that "it's time we reorganize". Indeed, a favourite bureaucratic pathology seems to be "if in doubt, reorganize" in terms of either restructuring positions, or reshuffling people, or both. It is hypothesized here, however, that *an index of managerial quality* is to be found in the frequency with which managers have to resort to the instruments of formal control: the more the need for using explicit sanctions, the greater the likelihood is that the manager(s) in question do not adequately understand the nature of the problem(s) with which they seek to deal. The cliché "having lost sight of our objectives, we redouble our efforts" reflects this overanxious and erroneous managerial reaction. As the chart indicates, the fact may be that really needs to be called into question is the organization's *stated objectives*.

Here then is a telescoped image of a behaviour cycle which lead Chris Argyris over a decade ago to the conclusion that[10] "there is a lack of congruency between the needs of healthy individuals and the demands of formal organization". What is the alternative?

Perhaps the most important single characteristic of modern organizational cybernetics is this: that in addition to concern with the deleterious impacts of rigidly imposed notions of what constitutes the application of good "principles of organization and management", the organization is viewed as a subsystem of larger system(s), and as comprised itself of functionally interdependent subsystems. Thus, the so-called "human relations movement" of the past quarter-century or so concentrates upon analysis of the internal dynamics of organizational life. The "fusion process" is its focus: out of the individual's attempt to personalize the organization, and the organization's efforts to socialize the individual, comes an amalgam which hopefully enables each concurrently to fulfil its needs.

But at best, feedback in organizational concepts such as those delineated above depends upon a very high order of managerial perceptual sensitivity and interpersonal communications clarity. Even where such managers are to be found, in large-scale organizations the permutations and combinations of interaction dynamics soon exceed human channel capacities. Thus, it is only as we have moved into the world of general systems theory, cybernetic science and computer technology have the on-line, real-time loops been adequately closed. Perhaps this can best be illustrated by considering how organizational

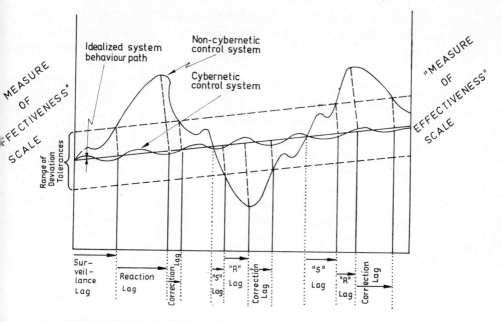

FIGURE 2   Comparison of surveillance, reaction, and correction lags; non-cybernetic and cybernetic controls

cybernetics has the potential for substantially eliminating three kinds of communication and control lags usually found in management information systems.

Figure 2 indicates that, as the non-cybernetic organization pursues its goals along a chosen behaviour path, from time to time the output indicators signal that the behaviour tolerances have been violated. This requires positive managerial action to bring the output within prescribed limits. But we see that correction usually occurs only some time after the limits have been exceeded, and then only with a time lag.

Analytically, what we see is that three kinds of lags are identifiable: the "surveillance" lag, the "reaction" lag, and the "correction" lag. By the first is meant simply that, more often than not days or weeks or months pass between the occurrence of an actual deviation, and its report to management: this is the surveillance lag. But even after managers are aware of the need to do something, and actually set about corrective action, organizational inertia must be overcome. The firm may tend to persist for some time as it has been heading, before the redirection brakes take hold: this is the reaction lag. Finally, the correction lag occurs between the time the system begins to exhibit a reversal of inertia, and return to a path within the range of tolerance.

Now of course the slightly deviant behaviour path which oscillates about the "ideal" path represents the situation after realization of on-line, real-time reporting and control capability. It may be noted in passing that, as the Forrester industrial dynamics model has shown[11], immediately corrective and completely remedial managerial actions which will always instantaneously return organizational behaviour to the idealized path is usually *not* desirable. Optimal lags often exist, as complex organizational subsystems interact. But here too, cybernetic approaches to organizational design will help reveal what these are. This is no small point. It bears upon Beer's concern the complementary fallacies *composito* and *divisio*[12]. And since Beer has admirably presented the technical case for organizational cybernetics in both his *Cybernetics and Management*[9] and his more recent comprehensive volume *Decision and Control*[13], I shall rest the argument at this point.

So we come at last to the essential question: how will all this promote the realization of human values?

PSYCHOCYBERNETIC ORGANIZATIONS, HUMAN NEEDS, AND SOCIAL VALUES

Louis Fried has recently provided an imaginative utilization of Kurt Lewin's topological and vector psychology and the associated force-field theory to describe how the man–machine (psychocybernetic) system may be integrated with questions of perceptions and values in human organizations[14]. Suffice it so say that this kind of analysis represents substantiation of the line of argument presented here, which may now be summarized as follows: (1) really effective human organizations tend to be those which openly acknowledge usually implicit values, and assign them explicit priorities; (2) continuous discussion and modification of organizational values by participants will increase the likelihood of organization viability (homeostasis) and progress (heterostasis or morphogenesis); and (3) cybernetically designed and managed organizations are not only most likely to realize their targeted levels of effectiveness, they also have greatest potential for fulfilling basic human needs and for realizing associated human values.

Let us be more specific in this linkage of human needs, social values, and organizational cybernetics. Clyde Kluckhohn[15] has defined a value as a "conception, explicit or implicit, distinctive of an individual or characteristic of a group, of the desirable which influences the selection from available modes, means, and ends of action." Another anthropologist[16] concludes that (1) values differ, but all people have values; (2) values appear as parts of patterns of behaviour developed in coping with specific sorts of life circumstances; (3) the concepts we develop to think about human life are shaped by values; (4) it is very difficult for us human beings to treat the solution of human problems as a technical matter...; and (5) even though the doctrine of "cultural relativity", as once put forward, has failed to withstand more sophisticated examination, it will never again be possible for us to think in terms of ethical absolutes in the same way that our nineteenth-century forebears did.

But values, in turn, are functionally related to kinds and levels of perceived needs. Of course, needs too are culturally determined in substantial measure— at least in the modes of their realization. But, equally, it is possible to identify basic categories of human needs which transcend cultural contexts. Table 1 (first and second columns from Rotter[17]) links six basic human needs to corresponding social values, frequently as expressed in modern industrial societies. The table is constructed on the basis of the following putative assertion: *cybernetically controlled organizations will be more likely to respond to the indicated social values, and therefore will more ably identify and more effectively meet human needs.*

Because cybernetically oriented control systems give the organization far greater potential for articulation with larger systems of which they are a part (subsystem), the organization's values are likely to be highly responsive to those in the social environment. The cybernetic organization's value interpretations are also, reciprocally, very likely substantially to influence the general social values to an appreciably larger extent than in the case of traditional non-cybernetically managed entities. As I have elsewhere suggested, this cybernetic subsystem–system–suprasystem integration will tend to increase managerial value characteristics such as these: (1) moral sensitivity;

TABLE 1   Types of organizational response to human needs and social values

Categories of human needs	Category definitions	Corresponding social values	Typical modes by which non cybernetic organizations respond (satisfaction modes)	Illustrative enhancement potentials in cybernetic organizations
recognition—status	need to be considered competent or good in a professional, social, occupational, or play activity. Need to gain social or vocational position—i.e. to be more skilled or better than others	opportunity	merit advancement; award systems; incentive programs; overt commendations by superiors; status symbols	expanded range of rational choice; fewer organizational rigidities; easier to identify individual merit; objectification of performance appraisal criteria; more peer-group selections
protection – dependency	need to have another person or group of people prevent frustration or punishment, or to provide for satisfaction of other needs	security	job tenure (employment security); group solidarity (implicit group behaviour norms); unions and formal associations; informal cliques; dyads, "buddy" systems	greater intra-organizational mobility; more feeling of "belonging" because of greater total communication, etc.; greater openness, deeper awareness of mutuality
dominance	need to direct or control the actions of other people, including members of family and friends. To have any action taken which he suggests	progress	hierarchical leadership roles; "father figures" translated into bureaucratic structures; formal, legalistically legitimized role structures; "superior/subordinate" chains, political maneuvering	more leadership roles filled on basis of genuine merit; greater dynamism, therefore greater opportunity for morphogenesis; greater release of creativity because of more amorphous structures; "*ad hoc*" and task-directed leadership
independence	need to make own decisions, to realy on oneself, together with the need to develop skills for obtaining satisfactions directly without the mediation of other people	freedom	pseudo-and quasi-democratic processes; grievance procedurs; "corporate devil's advocates", "ombudsmen"; staff roles, specialized expertise	more chance to "do one's thing" in terms of organizational needs; objectivity a norm: release from bondage of unprovable assertions; greater inter-organizational mobility; freedom to innovate and be creative because technological change is a norm

love and affection	need for acceptance and indication of liking by other individuals. In contrast to recognition-status, not concerned with social or professional positions of friends, but seeks their warm regard	participation	supportive and "humancentred" management; rapport developed by after-hours activities, company-sponsored diversions, etc.; "coffee klatsch" groups confidants, mutual "back-scratching";	greater professionalism leads to greater mutuality and sharing; more *ad hoc* groups, formed on a voluntary (sociometric) basis; greater inclination and opportunity to test consensus; more opportunity for spontaneous collaboration
physical comfort	learned need for physical satisfaction that has become associated with the gaining of security	environmental quality	provision of work-conducive surroundings; equipment support and services; sensory protection; ancillary reinforcements, e.g. provision of parking space, etc.	earlier, clearer and more focused evidence of dysfunctional circumstances; greater chance for selectively providing for individual needs; more automation and robotizing of labourious tasks

(2) service motivation; (3) "extra-organizational" loyalties; (4) attitudes of tentativeness (tolerance); (5) democratic procedural orientations; (6) compassion; (7) search for "optimum instability" for the system; (8) rationality; and (9) greater self-actualization via "collegial" milieux[18]. The final column in Table 1 comprises items which are meant to be illustrative of the ways in which psychocybernetic organizations at least *have potential for* considerably enhancing the need-meeting, value-serving response modes typically found in traditionally controlled organizations.

But we ascribe only the *potential* for greater value realization. Various images of cybernetically oriented organizations have, for many years now, been speculatively and suspiciously viewed as bringing about, with at least an equal degree of potentiality, quite the opposite result. So in conclusion, we address the question: what ground do we have for projecting the far greater likelihood that cybernetically managed organizations will in fact bring about—sooner or later—a more "human use of human beings"?

OUR SOCIOCYBERNETIC WORLD:
MAN'S NEW BASIS FOR CONSANGUINITY

The essential premise of this paper has been that we do indeed live in an era of "historical discontinuity", and of "radical change", where guidelines that have served man not too badly in the past have little relevance to present circumstances. Not that man has never before been thrust into eras which broke sharply with the past. Social revolutions and cultural cataclysms are an integral part of the human experience. But the present discontinuity is unique, for it is subtle, intangible and extremely complex in its manifestations. It has at once an "either/or" quality, an Armeggedon and a Utopian feel to it.

Thus, man is no longer merely in a "game against nature". As never before, man is now in an "x-person" game, where the outcome is almost surely *not* of the zero-sum type. R. Buckminster Fuller's[19] *World Game* is an imaginative expression of this viewpoint. For these reasons there is, as never before, an urgent need to understand the forces at work, so as reasonably to assure their resolution in man's favour. More than this, the requirement is for man to control the *generation* of these science/technology vectors, in terms of socio-cultural hierarchies of values upon which consensuses have been reached. As the British historian E.H.Carr[20] concluded several years ago:

"... progress in human affairs, whether in science or in history or in society, has come mainly through the bold readiness of human beings not to confine themselves to seeking piecemeal improvements in the way things are done, but to present fundamental challenges in the name of reason to the current way of doring things and to the avowed or hidden assumptions on which it rests."

Recent interpretative works in the United States such as Ferkiss' *Technological Man*[21], McHale's *The Future of the Future*[22], and Boguslaw's *The New Utopians*[23]; speculations such as Kahn and Wiener's *The Year 2000*[24], and the *Daedalus* volume "Toward the Year 2000"[25]; and institutionalizations of such ideas such as are found in the recently formed World Future Society and the Institute for the Future have their counterparts in Europe and other parts of the world. They suggest that there are conjunctive forces in modern high-technology societies which are bringing into sharp focus the necessity for man to recognize that he now has the possibility of "creating his own future" as never before.

But even more discomfiting, in terms of old values and ancient premises, man is now meaningfully able to *design* his own future, not just choose from nature's alternatives. Thus, in the words of a prominent solar astronomer (see Roberts[1], p. 260):

"In our explosively changing world it is no longer sufficient to live with philosophies or religions simply handed down from an older generation... Rather than simply fight for the preservation of the old things that are good, we must plan creatively also to shape the new. We must commit ourselves to dare to build the world we want, knowing that it is possible if we but demand it..."

We have presented the argument that cybernetically controlled organizations, when we learn sufficiently well how to design and maintain them, have the potential for bringing about the kind of psychologically maturing "reciprocation" between organization and individual of which the managerial psychiatrist Harry Levinson has so ardently written[26]. Moreover, the application of cybernetics has potential for revolutionizing political processes, by providing for individualized responses to great questions arising in large-scale complex social systems. Within the past year, the British Minister of Technology has expressed the opinion that[27]:

"Carried to its logical conclusion, this (cybernetically inspired) process of decentralization could well provide a far greater role for the individual in the community than the 1984 pessimists about technology have ever realized. It is not only possible, but certain, that the evolution of modern management science will ultimately allow *every single individual* to be taken into full account in the evolution of social planning, taxation, and social security policy. Through a system which took account of the circumstances of each individual, governments could get a feedback so comprehensive as to allow policy to be really personalized... *Our discussion will become, more openly, arguments about value judgments...*" (Underscoring supplied.)

In the United States, the "hippies" who want to "turn on, tune in, and drop out", the "yippies" who seem to prefer anarchy to the kind of rationalized social chaos they perceive, the campus malcontents, and the considerable number of those "over 30" oldsters who seem, in some measure, to share such views: all bespeak an extreme manifestation of what the respected motivational psychologist Ernest Dichter discerned many years ago: that the "Mr. Jones" who typifies urban American society has himself been undergoing profound change[28]. In substance, we seem increasingly to be, in Riesman's nomenclature, "inner directed" rather than "other directed". This represents a profound change in value sets and action priorities from that which prevailed only that rather short time ago when William White discovered the "organization man". It is exemplified in the United States, of course, by Detroit's finally having to take cognizance of the increasing incursions of the VW "beetle" and now the Toyota into the domestic U.S. automobile market. Similar trends are currently evident in other consumption propensities.

In the early part of this decade I suggested that such value shifts, in conjunction with the emergent impacts of organizational cybernetics, would provide a new basis for consanguinity among the nations of man. The substance of the chain of argument was expressed as follows[29]:

"Scientific management was an early attempt to rationalize the management function. Now digital computers, epitomizing the new information technology, bid fair to automate the office as well as the factory. Cybernetic management, utilizing the information technology, evolves optimal logico-deductive patterns of industrial organization and procedure. As these technological imperatives impinge, nations will converge in terms of socio-industrial authority structures and behavioral modes. It seems most likely that there will be a universal tendency toward pluralistic industrialism."

If or to the extent that such tendencies eventuate in the coming decade or two, we shall perhaps witness a general trend away from the "entrepreneurial ethic" to that which has been called "scientific humanism", having the following characteristics[30]: (1) more effort will be organized around the problem to be solved, rather than around traditional functions such as production, marketing, etc., (2) the leadership role will rotate within each mission or project, based on the nature of the problem and the sequence of knowledge required at various stages of its solution; and (3) participation in the management process will become more widely distributed among all levels of the organization. Thus[31], "the frantic search for individualism in a society that increasingly demands interdependence from its members ... (will create pressures) for production systems that are built around human needs rather than around conventional concepts of efficiency." Warren Bennis' predictions of the "coming death of bureaucracy" gain credibility when viewed in terms of the emerging organizational cybernetics.

So both from the standpoint of their likely impacts upon organizational structures and processes, and from their projected potentials in creating new organizational environments, the trinity comprising (1) general systems concepts, (2) information theory and the associated cybernetic science, and (3) computer technology may prove holy or otherwise, depending upon man's implementing value priorities. "Who controls the controllers, and how?" is a question which assumes greater urgency now that the apparition which George Orwell conjured in 1949 looms as an ominous potential only fifteen years hence. We conclude here as Boguslaw did in the final paragraph of his trenchant work[23]:

"Our own utopian renaissance receives its impetus from a desire to extend the mastery of man over nature. Its greatest vigor stems from a dissatisfaction with the limitations of man's existing control over his physical environment. Its greatest threat consists precisely in its potential as a means for extending the control of man over man."

And while we are mindful of Ferkiss' (see Ferkiss[22], p. 255) warning that "man's destiny lies in continuing to exploit this 'openness', rather than entering into a symbiotic relationship with the inorganic machine that, while it might bring immediate increments of power, would inhibit his development by chaining him to a system of lesser potentialities... Man must stand above his physical technologies if he is to avoid their becoming his shell and the principle of their organization his anthill, we share McHale's (see McHale[23], p. 300) view:

"The future of cultural forms already has many more dimensions of rich diversity. The promise within the newer media is of a greater interpenetration and interaction of life–art–culture rather than the forms–objects–images that preserved and isolated social life.

As for the larger communication and understanding implied in a shared planetary culture, it is more than obvious today that we must understand and co-operate on a truly global scale, or we perish."

References

1. W.O.Roberts, "Science, a wellspring of our discontent", *Am. Scholar*, Summer, pp.252–8 (1967).
2. N.Wiener, "Moral and Technical Consequences of Automation", May (1960) (Reprinted in *Automation: Implications for the Future* (Ed. M.Philipson), Vintage Books, Random House, New York (1962), p.173).
3. M.Ways, "The era of radical change", *Fortune*, May, 113 (1964).
4. R.S.Morison, "Science and social attitudes", *Science*, July, p.154 (1969).
5. "After automation—what?", Tape 199, dialogue recorded at the Center for the Study of Democratic Institutions, Santa Barbara, California.
6. N.Wiener, God and Golem, Inc., M.I.T. Press, Cambridge, Mass. (1966), p.90, 91.
7. *Ibid.* p.91.
8. W.Buckley (Ed.), *Modern Systems Research for the Behavioral Scientist*, Aldine, Chicago, Ill., (1968), foreword, p.xxii.
9. S.Beer, *Cybernetics and Management*. Wiley, New York (1959).
10. Argyris, "The individual and organization: some problems of mutual adjustment", *Admin. Sci. Quart.*, June, p.9 (1957).
11. J.W.Forrester, "Industrial dynamics: a major breakthrough for decision makers", *Harvard Business Rev.*, July/August, especially p.49 (1958).
12. S.Beer, "Below the twilight arch: a mythology of systems", *Yearbook Soc. Gen. Systems Res.*, **5**, 17.
13. S.Beer, *Decision and Control*, Wiley, New York (1966).
14. K.Lewin, "Psychocybernetics and the organization", *Data Processing Mag.*, November, pp.44–45 (1966).
15. C.Kluckhohn, quoted in R.Tagiuri, "Value orientations and the relationship of managers and scientists", *Admin. Sci. Quart.*, June, p.40 (1965).
16. L.R.Peattie, "Anthropology and the search for values", *J. Appl. Behavioral Sci.*, **1**, 4, 371–2 (1965).
17. J.B.Rotter, *Social Learning and Clinical Psychology*, Prentice-Hall, New York (1954).
18. "The Impact of Cybernetic Information Technology on Management Value Systems", prepared for the XV International Meeting of The Institute of Management Sciences, (Cleveland, Ohio, September 12, 1968). To be published in the October, 1969 issue of *Management Science*, and in Volume **XIV** (1969) of the *Society for General Systems Research Yearbook*.
19. Published in multilith as *"World Game: How It Came About,"* April 21, 1968.
20. E.H.Carr, *What is History*, Alfred Knopf, New York (1961), p.207.
21. V.C.Ferkiss, *Technological Man: The Myth and the Reality*, George Braziller, New York (1969).
22. J.McHale, *The Future of the Future*, George Braziller, New York (1969).
23. R.Boguslaw, *The New Utopians: A Study of System Design and Social Change*, Prentice-Hall, Englewood Cliffs, N.J. (1965).
24. H.Kahn and A.J.Wiener, *The Year 2000: a Framework for Speculation on the Next Thirty-five Years*, Macmillan, New York (1967).
25. "Toward the year 2000", Daedalus, Summer (1967).

26. H. Levinson, "Reciprocation: the relationship between man and organization", *Admin. Sci. Quart.*, March, p. 370 ff. (1965).

27. A. Wedgwood Benn, "Living with technological change", *New Statesman*, December, p. 827 (1968).

28. E. Dichter, "Discovering the 'inner Jones'", *Harvard Business Rev.*, May/June, p. 6 ff. (1965).

29. R. F. Ericson, "Toward a universally viable philosophy of management", *Management Sci.*, May, p. 47–8 (1962).

30. E. J. Korprowski, "New dimensions for decision making", *Management of Personnel Quart.*, Winter (1968).

A quantitative approach to human interactions and social phenomena

GEORGE C. THEODORIDIS

University of California, Berkeley, California, U.S.A.

Summary

The needs that motivate the actions of man and of the other living organisms are discussed within the context of their role as the driving force in the operation of the biosphere as an information processing system. An information-like formulation is introduced for the quantity that represents the reward that an event contributes toward the satisfaction of a person's needs. Typical human needs for events and experiences of various kinds are expressed as functions of age. Satisfaction of such needs is achieved through personal and social interactions. People establish personal bonds and form social units such as families, schools, churches, cities, or nations. The stability or cohesion of such groups and their importance in the lives of their members can be quantitatively assessed through their average contribution in terms of need satisfaction. Temporal steady state and stability can only result if human needs are being satisfied to an adequate degree. Accumulating unfilled needs will periodically lead to violently hostile interactions between individuals, groups, or societies. The dynamics of such interactions can be quantitatively formulated in terms of the gain expected by each party in the form of need satisfaction and the average effort corresponding to such need satisfaction in the particular environment. A similar formulation is applicable to every kind of decision regarding an anticipated course of action that offers the expectation of a certain need satisfaction at the cost of a given amount of effort.

INTRODUCTION

The purpose of this paper is to discuss the operation of individuals and societies, as motivated by the human system of needs, from the point of view of the laws and objectives that seem to determine the course of the biosphere as a whole in its physical function as an information processing system. Human needs can be expressed as required amounts of the physical quantity that measures the reward that a certain event represents for a person. The dependence of the various types of human needs on such variables as age or sex must be understood in terms of the underlying objectives that are being pursued within the framework of the wider biospheric goals. The existing human need patterns are the basis for the interaction between individuals and for the formation of social units at various levels of size and cohesion. The strength and the stability of personal relationships and of social structures can be quantitatively assessed on the basis of their reward contribution toward the need satisfaction of the participants. The decision making process can be also formulated in terms of the reward expected from the courses of action under consideration.

LIVING ORGANISMS AND THE BIOSPHERE AS INFORMATION PROCESSING SYSTEMS

All functions of a living organism can be described as processing of the physical entity called information, which is equivalent to the thermodynamic quantity called negentropy (Katz, 1967). Schrödinger (1946) was the first to suggest that living organisms feed on the negentropy in their food, rather than on its content in energy or matter. The need for a continuous influx of information in the form of food arises from the fact that in a physical system any internal change can only result in the conservation or decrease of its information content, never in its increase. In the system of a living organism and its environment, performance of the organism's information processing functions usually results in the generation of new quantities of information; this happens whenever some information in the environment is observed through the organism's sensory organs, when the observed information is transmitted through the nervous system and stored in the brain, and when the stored information is recalled during the process of thinking, or is directed to the organism's motor systems (vocal cords, hands, etc.) for reproduction in the environment. During any of these operations, handling a given quantity of information means generating at least an equal amount of information somewhere in the organism–environment system (Brillouin, 1956). In order to make these functions possible, the system must be constantly supplied with new quantities of information in the form of food.

An example of information processing by a living system is illustrated in Figure 1 for the case of a man who reads a braille message and copies it. We

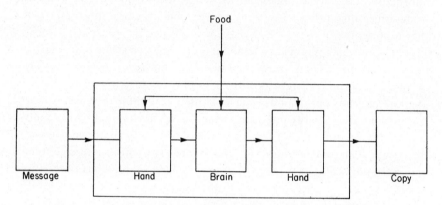

FIGURE 1   Information flow diagram for a man who reads and copies a braille message

consider braille reading in order to simplify the system by eliminating the need for an information source in the form of the light that is necessary for visual reading. The person observes the information content of the message with his hand, transmits it through the nervous system to the brain, stores it in his memory, recalls and transmits it again to his hand, and reproduces it by writing the copy. At the end of this operation, the man–environment system includes, in addition to the original message, the information contained in the written copy and in the person's memory. During the operation, information was generated in sensory cells of the hand, in the nervous system, and in the hand muscles. Since for the system as a whole information can, at any given moment, only decrease or remain constant, the described generation of new forms of information is only possible through the supply of the information contained in the food that the man consumes.

Although many forms of life obtain the information necessary to perform their functions by feeding on other organisms, the main ultimate source of information for the biosphere considered as a whole is the sun (Morowitz,

1968). The information carried by solar photons is channelled through the plants into the complex system of biochemical reactions that life has evolved.

In addition to being the fuel that sustains life, information is the physical entity that best describes the structural nature of living organisms. Besides processing information, living organisms can be actually described as being information. Individual organisms as well as the biosphere as a whole can be described quantitatively in terms of the total structural information that they represent.

Let us consider a physical system that is exposed to a steady informational input of i bits per second. Irreversibilities occurring during the various stages of information processing within the system result in a loss of information at a rate of i' bits per second; such a loss may result, for instance, from the transformation of energy into heat at the environmental temperature of the system, which is the level of zero information. The informational content of the system at any given instant is I bits, defined as the information contained within the physical structure of the system which would not have been there, had the system not been exposed to the informational input i. The informational content I can be increasing, decreasing, or remaining unchanged, depending on the relative magnitude of i and i'.

For an information processing system in steady state (i.e. $dI/dt = 0$) we can define an information lifetime τ, equal to the average time that elapses before the dissipation of information that enters the system:

$$\tau = \frac{I}{i} \tag{1}$$

Whenever the operation of an information processing system is altered so as to reduce or eliminate a previously existing irreversibility, the average information lifetime τ increases; in the extreme, idealized case where all irreversibilities are eliminated, information is never lost and τ is infinite. An information processing system with fewer irreversibilities can be considered more efficient, since for a given informational input it can perform more tasks than a similar system with more irreversibilities. The information lifetime τ can be, therefore, regarded as a measure of the efficiency of an information processing system. According to Equation (1), this quantitative measure of the functional efficiency of an information processing system can be also expressed by its total structural informational content per unit of information flow processed.

An evolving biosphere can be regarded as a quasi-steady-state information processing system that undergoes evolutionary changes in informational content at a rate which is much slower than the rate at which information is being received and processed. The schematic diagram displayed in Figure 2 is an idealized approximation to the terrestrial information processing

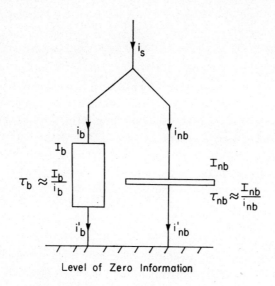

FIGURE 2   Division of the continuous flow of solar information between the two quasi-steady-state information processing systems of the biosphere and the non-biospheric environment

system. The solar information input i_s is divided into a biospheric part i_b and a non-biospheric part i_{nb}. The picture is simplified by assuming a constant flow of solar information i_s, and ignoring any other information sources. The fact that slow evolution is in progress results in a non-zero time derivative dI_b/dt, satisfying the quasi-steady-state condition:

$$\frac{dI_b}{dt} = i_b - i'_b \ll i_b \tag{2}$$

We define the biospheric and non-biospheric information lifetimes τ_b and τ_{nb}, as well as the overall average lifetime τ_s for the incoming solar information i_s as it is processed by the biospheric–non-biospheric ensemble:

$$\tau_b \approx \frac{I_b}{i_b} \tag{3}$$

$$\tau_{nb} \approx \frac{I_{nb}}{i_{nb}} \tag{4}$$

$$\tau_s \approx \frac{I_b + I_{nb}}{i_s} \approx \frac{i_b}{i_s}\tau_b + \frac{i_{nb}}{i_s}\tau_{nb} \tag{5}$$

The evolution of a biospheric information processing system that shares a continuous, steady flow of information with a less sophisticated non-biospheric system can be described as a long term, gradual increase of the biospheric informational content I_b. In addition to the long term increase in I_b we should probably expect some short term, transient fluctuations. The fact that the informational content of the terrestrial biosphere has evolved from nothing to its present size, can be regarded as "experimental" evidence for the validity of an evolutionary law of continuously rising biospheric informational content I_b.

Evolution toward a larger biospheric informational content I_b can be shown to be equivalent to evolution toward a higher overall information processing efficiency, and a corresponding longer average lifetime τ_s for the incoming solar information i_s. The total biospheric information I_b can be therefore regarded as a quantitative measure of the operational efficiency and the evolutionary advancement of the terrestrial biosphere. (Theodoridis and Stark, 1969.)

NEEDS AS THE DRIVING FORCE FOR THE OPERATION OF THE BIOSPHERE—REWARD CONTENT OF EVENTS—HUMAN NEED FUNCTIONS

In a general sense, the biospheric system is driven and controlled by the external flow of information and by the natural laws that govern the interaction of this information with the terrestrial environment. This control is exercised, however, through the "quasi-independent" actions of individual organisms that make choices and decisions motivated by physiological processes, instincts, or desires based on reason and free will. These decisions are made in the part of the organism that we shall call the "deciding centre".

All the motivating factors that affect the decision process comprise the "system of needs" under which the organism operates. The final result of the independent activities of all individual organisms will be in accord with the existing natural laws that govern the biosphere, since these laws have led to the evolution of the need systems and the deciding centres that generate the actions of each organism. The evolution of a system of needs or of a deciding centre is similar to the evolution of a biological organ, a technological tool, or a social system, and must proceed according to the existing evolutionary laws. The nature of a need system and the functional characteristics of a deciding centre must be therefore examined and understood within the framework of maximum biospheric operational efficiency and evolutionary advancement.

Figure 3 illustrates schematically the informational interaction of an organism with its environment. An important factor in the operation of the deciding centre with respect to a particular informational transaction with the environment, is the way in which the environment and the transaction itself are being perceived. This aspect of the deciding process depends on the input that the deciding centre receives from the perceiving organs, as well as on information stored in the organism's memory concerning similar previous transactions. Out of the total amount of information that might conceivably be available about a particular informational transaction, only a very small proportion will be fed into the deciding centre. The manner in which this selection is performed must balance the simultaneous requirements for decisions that are reliably responsive to the needs of the organism and to the overall objectives of the biosphere, and for a decision making process that is not unnecessarily cumbersome and wasteful.

An important objective of the systems of needs that propel living organisms in performing their information processing function is the capture and the processing of information in amounts as close as possible to the maximum information handling capacity of the particular organism. This is clearly evident in the appetite of living organisms for a full and active life and their dislike of boredom (Heron, 1957). The fact that people usually regard rest as desirable is not inconsistent with the concept of maximum information processing; it is, on the contrary, a proof that the human system of needs is so efficient in motivating man toward action that many people operate close to the limit of their capacity.

Survival of living organisms and extension of their information processing operation for as long as possible is another goal of their need system that is entirely in accord with the principle of maximum information processing. All needs that are aimed at self-preservation by securing food and shelter or through self-defence against potential dangers can be classified in this category.

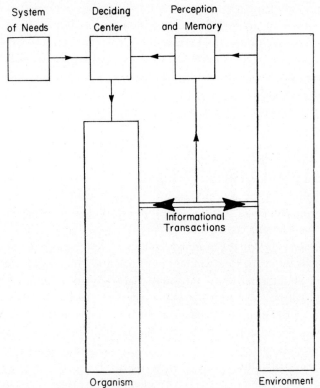

FIGURE 3   Schematic representation of the informational interaction of
an organism with its environment

An important part of the needs of an organism is directed toward the reproduction and perpetuation of the information processing capacity that the perishable living organism represents. To the extent that the information handling systems of an organism are mapped in the form of genetic information, perpetuation is assured through the need for genetic reproduction. Needs for interaction with individuals of the opposite sex play a prominent role in the need systems of most species. Advanced forms of life have increasingly evolved information handling capabilities that are transmitted from generation to generation through the developed avenues of communication. The needs of such culturally oriented forms of life have accordingly included the necessity of an adequate amount of contact between generations that assures the perpetuation of their non-genetic information handling capacities (Blum, 1963). Such culture reproducing patterns play an important role in the human system of needs, since civilized man has evolved a large information processing culture, apart from his genetically reproducible information handling systems. Human needs that are aimed at promoting contact between successive generations through parent–child or teacher–student interactions, have attained an importance comparable to that of the needs for interactions with the opposite sex for the purpose of genetic reproduction.

The natural desire for a full and active life can be described in terms of the terminology employed in the previous section as an attempt to maximize the rate of biospherical information processing i_b. The desire to survive is consistent with extending the average lifetime τ_b of the information that enters the biosphere. The needs of living organisms that are aimed at the genetic or cultural reproduction of their informational reservoir can be best described in quantitative terminology as an effort to preserve or increase the biospheric informational content I_b by offsetting the natural dissipative processes that continually drain the information stored in the bodies of living organisms or in their cultural products.

The discussion of a system of needs must necessarily revolve around the concept of reward as the quantity that a particular event contributes toward a person's need satisfaction, and that the deciding centre associates with the event in making a choice. The basic premise is that such a quantity can be defined and can serve as a common basis of comparison for events that may be entirely different in nature. We assume that any two events, no matter how different and unrelated, represent for a person at any given time specific amounts of reward that can be placed on a common quantitative scale; the person's deciding centre will use the anticipated reward values for the two events if a comparison and choice between them is necessary.

It appears plausible that the reward content of an event is closely related to its content of information, the physical quantity around which all functions of living organisms revolve. In support of this thesis, let us review some of the features that we respond to in our choice and evaluation of events and experiences. A clue comes from the type of adjectives that we often use to favorably describe an event; attributes such as extraordinary, unique, rare, unusual, excellent, outstanding, or striking, stress the rarity of a particular experience, and its departure from the level of the usual and the average. It is, indeed, quite true that rarity and novelty add to our interest in an event or item. Many rare stones or metals, as well as most collectors' items, such as stamps or coins, owe their value not to their usefulness for any practical purpose but merely to their rarity. The element of surprise and the unexpected add to the pleasure produced by a gift, and to the amusement generated by a joke. Whole classes of events only attract our interest while they are still novel and unusual; as soon as they become usual and readily available most people lose interest in them. The popularity of such events tends to oscillate with periods roughly equal to the length of time required for people to forget their previous exposure to them. Events, experiences or ideas that are important enough to be worthwhile even when they become usual and lose part of their novelty value, persist and become permanent features of human life.

The flow of information from the various environmental sources constitutes the informational content of the events experienced by each individual. An event represents a large amount of information processing in terms of the inputs that it provides and the responses that it evokes from a large number of our sensory, nervous, or motor systems. While this large informational content of an event is its actual contribution to the fulfillment of our information processing function, its reward, as perceived by the decision centre, must necessarily consist of only a small, representative sample of information. The distinction between the total information content and the representative sample can be demonstrated by discussing the mode of operation of our system of needs for food. The full informational content of food is used to fuel our information processing operation, whereas the small, representative sample of information in its appearance and taste determines the choices that we make in order to cover our needs for food.

Of all the theories on human motivation the one that comes closest to identifying information as the element to which people respond is the adaptation level theory (Helson, 1964). According to this motivation theory, man is sensitive to departures from the levels of external stimuli that he usually receives, and to which he gradually adapts. This concept has many features that are in qualitative accord with what one would expect if information is an important parameter in the human reward function. Experimental evidence on the dependence of satisfaction on the frequency of various experiences lends support to this line of approach (Parducci, 1968).

We are now going to discuss a possible mathematical expression for the reward content of an event for a person, as a function of parameters related to characteristics of the event and of the person. The validity of any such formulation of the human reward function can only be proven by demonstrating the consistency of observable human phenomena with predictions that can be theoretically derived. No such proof of validity is advanced or implied here; the employed functional dependence is merely formulated so as to be in accord with some obvious qualitative features and relationships. The main purpose of formulating a specific reward function is to illustrate some of the concepts and techniques that might be employed in a quantitative approach, and to be able to conduct the discussion in terms of concrete parameters. It should be noted that most of the concepts and relationships that will be discussed in this paper can be expressed in terms of any reward function, not depending on the adoption of a particular mathematical formulation.

In formulating a function to represent the reward content of an event, as the quantity contributed to the need satisfaction of the person that is experiencing it, we visualize individual events as symbols in a generalized code that encompasses the whole spectrum of events that a particular culture can offer for the need satisfaction of its members. We define the reward content R_j of an event j that is experienced by a person for a length of time t_j as the product of a relevance factor r_j, the preoccupation time factor t_j and an informational factor I_j:

$$R_j = r_j t_j I_j \qquad (6)$$

We formulate the informational factor I_j in a manner similar to Shannon's (1949) information function:

$$I_j = -\log_2 P_j \text{ bits} \qquad (7)$$

The event probability P_j is now defined on the basis of the subjective estimate by the person involved, of the average time T_j during which a typical person in his environment is preoccupied with the type of event j over a period of time T:

$$P_j = \frac{T_j}{T} \qquad (8)$$

The preoccupation time t_j includes the whole length of time during which the subject's centre of attention is occupied by the event in question, whether this is during the event, before it in anticipation, or after it in recollection.

The relevance factor r_j is a dimensionless number between zero and unity, indicating the portion of the event that the subject deems relevant to his needs. As the irrelevant portion of an event we consider the fraction that could conceivably be omitted without reducing the subject's interest in the event. From Equations (6) and (7) it follows that reward is to be expressed in units of time information, such as for instance year bits or day bits.

The exact nature and category of the reward content of events can be as varied as the events themselves. A detailed study of a human system should consider individually a number of such categories, depending on the degree of accuracy and detail desired. For the purposes of this discussion we are going to be using a simple and elementary classification of human needs and events into "giving" and "receiving" categories. The criterion for this classification is whether in the relevant part of an event the subject plays a predominantly giving or receiving role. The existence of giving and receiving roles in an interaction does not mean that the needs of one person are satisfied at the expense of the other person. The nature of the human system of needs is such that people have both giving and receiving needs, and events can represent, accordingly, giving or receiving reward.

Reward transactions between people are conducted in a variety of currencies, such as food and other bodily needs, shelter and security from danger, transmission of knowledge, skills and other types of useful information, or contribution to a person's self-confidence by acknowledging his worth and ability. The particular form of reward that is relevant to a person's needs may vary with age and is reflected in the magnitude of the relevance factor r_j, included in the definition of the reward content of an event in Equation (6). The evolving pattern of relevance factors for various types of events determines the consecutive stages of development of an individual. One can thus think of large groups of events that people find relevant only during certain periods of their lives, such as childhood, adolescence, adulthood, or old age.

Giving and receiving needs change with age in a manner that can be understood in terms of the underlying objectives of the human need system. It is clear that people with predominantly receiving needs will be drawn into interactions with people with predominantly giving needs. The polarization of giving and receiving needs between men and women, as well as between adults and young people, is thus a powerful force promoting interactions between these groups aimed at genetic (man–woman interaction) and cultural reproduction (adult–young interaction) of the human informational reservoir. Figure 4 displays schematic diagrams of giving and receiving need functions

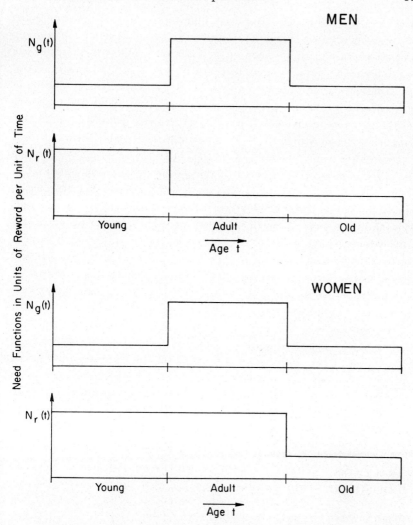

FIGURE 4   Typical giving and receiving need functions for men and women

$N_g(t)$ and $N_r(t)$ versus age t for men and women. The purpose of these diagrams is merely to illustrate in a qualitative way the time variations of these need functions; an individual's life is divided into young, adult, and old age periods, and the magnitude of the need functions is set at one of two arbitrary levels, as a qualitative relative indication of a high or a low level of the respective needs.

People in the young age group have high receiving needs (N_r functions) and low giving needs (N_g functions). During this period people are developing physically and are learning much of the knowledge and skills that they are going to use in life; they are, therefore, at the receiving end of most relationships with their parents, teachers, or people of their environment in general. At the end of the young age, people switch their attitudes and living habits from the previous receiving orientation to the giving pattern of adult life. Giving needs are now high for both men and women. A large part of these giving needs are being directed toward the children who, particularly in the early years, have more contact with the mother; the giving potential of women must therefore be higher than that of men. In order to be able to generate this larger amount of giving, women have high receiving needs during adult life as well, as opposed to men whose receiving needs are relatively limited. The typical flow of giving needs during the adult stage is directed from the man primarily to the woman, and also to the children, and from the woman primarily to the children. Inadequate giving potential on the part of either parent will deprive the children of an adequate satisfaction of their receiving needs. During old age, giving and receiving needs recede for both men and women, in comparison to the level of needs during the young and adult age. An indicative criterion for the relative intensity of people's needs is the eagerness and drive that they show toward interacting with other people. While young and adult people interact continuously with each other, old people require increasingly lower levels of interaction with their environment.

NEED SATISFACTION THROUGH PERSONAL AND SOCIAL INTERACTIONS—STRENGTH AND STABILITY OF PERSONAL BONDS AND OF SOCIAL STRUCTURES

A person satisfies his needs through various interactions that lead to a network of bonds connecting him with other individuals or with social groups in his environment. Questions regarding the strength and the stability of such bonds can be approached in a manner parallel to that employed in treating similar questions regarding physical bonds within structural units of matter, such as nuclei, atoms, molecules, or crystals.

The pyramid of structural organization of matter starts with a set of indivisible building blocks that are the basis of all higher structural units. Complex units are held together as a result of what is described in physics as "binding energy"; this is the amount of energy that must be supplied from outside in order to disrupt the complex unit, and to divide it into its individual components. If a complex unit consists of several elementary components, we can define binding energies for all conceivable ways of dividing the initial unit into two or more new structural units. Stable structures have large binding energies, indicative of the upper limit of the energy perturbations that they can withstand. The binding energies of molecules in solids or liquids, and of atoms in crystals or molecules, are much smaller than the typical binding energies of electrons and nuclei in atoms; the latter are in turn much smaller than the binding energies of protons, neutrons, or other elementary particles inside nuclei. Physical phenomena involving the formation and disruption of the weaker bonds (e.g. changes in the shapes of solids or liquids, phase changes between the solid, liquid and gaseous states, chemical reactions, etc.) can be triggered by small amounts of energy that are easily available; these phenomena are, therefore, much more frequent and usual than those pertaining to the stronger bonds (e.g. nuclear disintegrations).

The strength of a bond between two or more persons can be measured by the rate at which it contributes reward toward the satisfaction of the needs of each participant. In order to disrupt the bond, an amount at least equivalent to this "binding reward" must be supplied from another source. The stability of a social unit can be therefore gauged by the size of the binding reward that it represents for its constituents. The binding reward represents the emotional attachment of a person to another individual, to his family, or to larger social units such as his church, city, or nation.

People are organized in social units of various sizes and degrees of cohesion, and it is mainly through interactions within, or among such units that human needs are satisfied. From the nature of human needs, as discussed in terms of the respective need functions in the previous section, it is clear that a family unit is the most natural structure for filling the largest part of the needs of a man, a woman, and their children. The giving needs of the man are directed primarily to the woman, and also to the children, while the giving needs of the woman are directed primarily to the children. The binding reward and, therefore, the stability of the family unit can be very high, since it can cover a large part of the needs of everyone involved.

In addition to the family unit, people form a variety of other social structures, each characterized by a certain binding reward per member, equal to the average amount of reward needs that it fills for each participant.

Examples of such social structures are schools, religious institutions, villages, towns, cities, or nations. The degree of involvement and the stability of an individual's connection with any such unit can be measured by the binding reward that the unit represents for him, compared to the amounts of reward that may be available to attract him out of the unit.

For the average person, large social units usually represent a much smaller binding reward than family ties or other relationships at a close, personal level. Most prominent events in human societies revolve, however, around large structural units such as nations, political movements, and professional, educational or religious organizations. This state of affairs is similar to that observed in the realm of physics, where the most frequent and noticeable physical phenomena are the ones involving the weaker bonds, that can be rather easily perturbed. Since large social units contribute relatively little reward for each individual, they have enough inherent instability to generate big and dramatic events, involving the large number of people that they affect.

Social and historical events that occur at the level of large social units are directly motivated by the rather small percentage of human needs, whose satisfaction is left outside the area of private, personal relationships. It is, however, clear that even small variations in the satisfaction of needs at the level of close personal interactions will be quickly reflected on a magnified scale at the level of the large structural units. Although the macroscopic picture of human societies does not reveal at first sight much of what occurs in the private, personal lives of their constituents, this is in effect what drives the large human structures in their noticeable and often dramatic actions.

Since interactions at the secondary level of large social units are directed at needs that are left unsatisfied at the primary level of personal interactions, intense reliance of a culture on such secondary level need satisfying devices may be often an indication of a high degree of reward deprivation. In societies where existing living patterns lead to ineffectual need satisfaction at the primary level of personal and family interactions, people may tend to become intensely involved, as partisans or as adversaries, with large social units such as political movements, nations or churches. In such instances, secondary level events and interactions may be used as a prime vehicle of need satisfaction, rather than as a fine adjustment and as a controlling device superimposed on primary level need satisfaction. This mode of operation may be prone to severe instabilities, since secondary level events can assume huge dimensions and may involve large numbers of people. In societies that function in such an unstable manner, unsatisfied needs may quickly generate severe external or internal convulsions in the form of wars or revolutions.

The quantitative impact of a group or an institution, such as a government or a religion, on the members of a large population can be approximately estimated using statistical methods. The actual impact in terms of contributing need satisfaction or of prohibiting need satisfying actions will have different reward contents for each individual. Assuming a statistical normal distribution for the reward content we can estimate the average from the percentage of the population that are affected to a significant enough degree so as to be easily identifiable, in addition to that percentage that are affected to a degree below a lower limit that we consider negligible. Thus, for example, the average need deprivation that a police state imposes on its citizens can be deduced from the percentage of people that spend a substantial part of their lives in ways determined by the state, whether by losing their life, living as prisoners or being members of the policing force. As another example we can consider the case of a population in which one segment wishes to ensure for themselves a higher average need satisfaction than that available to the rest. In order to impose this deviation from the normal statistical distribution of need satisfaction that would have been reached otherwise, the privileged segment must exert authority over the rest of the population to a degree adequate to deprive them of the amount of need satisfaction in question. Following the same reasoning as in the previous example we can estimate the number of "substantially affected people" (police, prison inmates, etc.) that will result from the artificially imposed distribution of need satisfaction.

ON THE DECISION MAKING PROCESS—CONFRONTATION BETWEEN INDIVIDUALS OR GROUPS

Existing human needs are translated into actions and rewarding events through the decision making process. As a guide in discussing the factors that enter in human decisions, we introduce the decision ratio d_x, defined as

$$d_x = \frac{R_x}{\bar{R}_x} \tag{9}$$

where R_x is the expectation value for reward from course of action x, and $\bar{R}_x$ is the average available alternative need satisfaction, expressed as the reward that the person could obtain for an amount of effort equivalent to that required by course of action x. The expected reward is

$$R_x = \sum_j e_{jx}R_j - \sum_k e_{kx}^* R_k \qquad (10)$$

where e_{jx} is the estimated probability that event j will follow from course of action x, e_{kx}^* is the estimated probability that event k, which would have occurred otherwise, will be cancelled as a result of course of action x, and R_j, R_k are the reward contents of events j and k, as defined in Equation (6). The average alternative need satisfaction is

$$\bar{R}_x = \varrho \bar{t}_x \qquad (11)$$

where $\bar{t}_x$ is the overall effort required by course of action x expressed in terms of equivalent time, in a manner that will be discussed shortly, and ϱ is the average reward that the person can obtain per unit of effort, through the various experiences available in his environment. The effort $\bar{t}_x$ depends, in general, on the necessary financial and material means, and on the time duration and difficulty of the required physical or mental work. All these quantities can be appropriately translated into equivalent time. Financial and material requirements can be expressed in terms of the average time that the person must spend on activities irrelevant to his needs in order to acquire them. The actual time duration of the required work can be also adjusted so as to account for the various degrees of difficulty of the physical or mental work involved. When we say that a certain type of work is harder than another one, we implicitly mean that in the first case we can only work for shorter periods of time and we require longer periods of rest than in the second case. By combining the required resting time with the actual working time we can obtain an equivalent time length for all degrees of required physical or mental effort. The total effort $\bar{t}_x$, expressed in units of time, will be referred to in this discussion as the time effort required by course of action x.

The decision ratio d_x will be close to unity for courses of action with expected need satisfaction close to the average alternative satisfaction available. Whenever d_x is larger than unity the expected satisfaction is better than average; if d_x is much smaller than unity the proposed course of action is disadvantageous and should be rejected.

The formalism introduced above can be applied to the analysis of confrontations between individuals or groups with conflicting objectives. The price that must be paid for a contested objective x, in money and other material goods or in time and effort requirements, can eventually be translated into equivalent time efforts $\bar{t}_{x1}$ and $\bar{t}_{x2}$ for each of the two contestants. We also have the respective values for the expected reward R_{x1} and R_{x2}, as well as the equivalent alternative need satisfaction $\bar{R}_{x1}$ and $\bar{R}_{x2}$ available to each contestant. For contests between groups, these quantities can be computed to correspond to the average individual member of the contesting groups. These parameters determine the value of the decision ratios d_{x1} and d_{x2} (Equation (9)).

In order to have a contest at all, d_{x1} and d_{x2} must have values indicating that the pursued objective is worthwhile for both contestants. The winner of the confrontation can be predicted if one of the decision ratios is substantially larger than the other; the contestant with the higher decision ratio can afford to make a bigger effort and overpower his opponent, who will be the first one to quit at the point where his decision ratio will become low enough to make alternative ways of need satisfaction preferable to the further pursuit of the contested objective. The factors that decide a confrontation are the capabilities of the contestants, reflected in the values of the corresponding time efforts $\bar{t}_{x1}$ and $\bar{t}_{x2}$, as well as their motivation and willingness to pursue the contest. A very powerful and able contestant may lose a confrontation, if his motivation in the contest is low owing to small expected need satisfaction (low R_x), or to favourable available alternatives (high $\bar{R}_x$).

Acknowledgments

The author wishes to thank Dr. Lawrence Stark of the University of California, Berkeley for his valuable help during many interesting discussions. This work was supported through a Special Fellowship (GM 38,419) from the National Institute of General Medical Sciences.

References

H. F. Blum, "On the origin and evolution of human culture." *Am. Sci.*, **51**, 42–7 (1963).

L. Brillouin, *Science and Information Theory*. Academic Press, New York (1956).

H. Helson, *Adaptation-Level Theory*. Harper'and Row, New York (1964).

W. Heron, "The pathology of boredom." *Sci. Am.*, **196**, 52–6 (1957).

A. Katz, *Principles of Statistical Mechanics; The Information Theory Approach*. W. H. Freeman, San Francisco (1967).

H. J. Morowitz, *Energy Flow in Biology*. Academic Press, New York (1968).

A. Parducci, "The relativism of absolute judgements." *Sci. Am.*, **219**, 84–90 (1968).

E. Schrödinger, *What is Life?* Cambridge University Press, Cambridge (1946).

C. E. Shannon and W. Weaver, *The Mathematical Theory of Communication.* University of Illinois Press, Urbana (1949).

G. C. Theodoridis and L. Stark, "Information as a quantitative criterion of biospheric evolution," *Nature,* **224**, 860–863 (1969).

Stability and social change

A. M. YOUNG

U.S.A.

Summary

The author's experiments with helicopter stability are briefly recounted to establish that, despite the complexity of the problem, stability has three forms, known in aerodynamics as phugoid, neutral, and catastrophic. These types, which depend on whether feedback is negative, neutral, or positive, are then applied to the socio-economic field and the implications explored.

INTRODUCTION

Admittedly, the subject of stability is very complex and has endless ramifications which make efforts to simplify rather presumptuous. Further, the sensitivity of the stability of a system to factors whose importance do not at first appear (as, for example, economic and ecological stability), render the subject one in which increased knowledge brings a sense of humility. One realizes that the isolable system is artificial and cannot be obtained in practice.

Nevertheless, the solution to the problem continues a challenge. One could say, since it is the main problem of a living creature to survive, that this survival depends on mastering within appropriate limits how to regulate itself so that it can continue to *be*, that is, to maintain itself in dynamic equilibrium with its environment.

This equilibrium is fantastically complicated for even the simplest creature. Chemically, it must maintain a proper metabolism, regulate its food intake, its fuel consumption, its breeding cycle, its migrations. Just to stand up requires the continual exercise of muscular activity, regulated by cybernetic feedback which would confound a computer.

Complicated, therefore, as the subject is, as living creatures we instinctively achieve a mastery of cybernetic regulation that probably far transcends our conscious ability to analyse, and this competence should give us the confidence to tackle a subject that otherwise might seem hopelessly involved.

I would like, therefore, to approach the subject in a rather down to earth fashion. I would like to describe the work I did some 30 years ago on helicopter stability. The subject at that time was like an unexplored continent, and even if what I have to say may seem naïve in today's professional world, perhaps you will be amused in the way you would be with any account of early explorations.

HELICOPTER STABILITY

I might begin with my first encounter with the fact of helicopter instability, which did not occur until I had already spent 10 years of my life on trying to build a rather ambitious half-size prototype which never flew. Like most early helicopter attempts, my efforts were first directed to construction, the problem of configuration, of rotors, the mechanical problems of engine and transmission, and, as I found at a cost of great efforts, the problem of stress. It never occurred to me that flight stability was important, or even a problem. But the time came when after years I at last succeeded in getting a mechanical construction that held together under full power long enough to give promise that the mechanical problems could at last be set aside.

I then tried free flight, using for this purpose electrically driven models of the simplest possible type, for my years of apprenticeship had taught me to avoid complexity as the plague.

To my utter surprise, free flight was attended by a most disconcerting pendular instability which would wreck the model after two or three swings. Seeking to correct this I attempted a solution in the form of a small pendulum attached to the control plate in such manner that, if the fuselage tipped, the control plate would be held horizontal by the pendulum

When tested in flight, there was no difference; the model still swung about wildly. The pendulum did not remain vertical, but swung with the fuselage, and did not make the anticipated compensation. It became clear that the fuselage started to move horizontally as soon as it tipped. This horizontal acceleration tipped the pendulum just as much as the fuselage.

After many false steps I eventually hit upon the solution, an "aperiodic" pendulum, or one with no period, consisting of a horizontal bar linked to the controls and rotating with the rotor. Such a pendulum was unaffected by acceleration, and held position long enough to keep the rotor horizontal even when the fuselage was artificially tipped.

This provided the solution I needed and made it possible to add remote controls. By this means the model could be made to respond to the will of the operator, but in the absence of control by the operator, would remain stable.

While this seems simple in retrospect, it did not seem so at the time, and it was necessary for me to make some more rather fundamental, yet simple, investigations which I bring up at this time in the hope that they will be of interest in the question of stability in general.

The investigations to which I refer had to do with the complete spectrum of which could be called the pendular aspect of stability. Normally, a pendulum is supported a distance above its centre of gravity, and the period of the pendulum is proportional to the square root of this distance. In the case of the bar, the "pendulum", if such I may call it, is supported at its C.G. (centre of gravity). What happens if the pendulum is supported below its C.G.?

Obviously, it will fall over. This illustrates what is called in aircraft practice "catastrophic" instability. The opposite arrangement, with C.G. below the support, being given the name "phugoid" instability (Figure 1). Taking another simple illustration (Figure 2), the three states, catastrophic, neutral, and phugoid, are illustrated by a ball on an inverted bowl, a ball on a flat surface, and a ball inside a bowl. It might be thought that the ball in the bowl is stable, but this is not so in dynamic systems in which energy is available to cause self excitation.

To explore this spectrum of three possible configurations on the helicopter, it was necessary to make a helicopter with the rotor below the C.G.

The difficulties of landing a helicopter with the rotor below the fuselage were overcome by making small, hand-launched rubber band models. In fact, I could use the same model for both conditions, winding the rubber band one way for C.G. up and the other for C.G. down. To my surprise, the C.G. up version flew with beautiful stability, and it was not until I made longer tests that the tendency to catastrophic instability became manifest, partly because there is a tendency of the rotor to aerodynamically neutralize

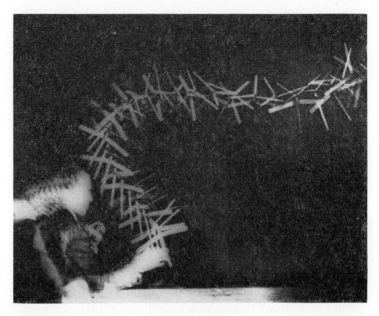

FIGURE 1   Phugoid instability in helicopter model with rotor above
centre of gravity

the effect of C.G. up, and partly because it takes a rather long time for the
C.G. up catastrophic instability to manifest (Figure 3)*.

In order to counteract the torque, it is necessary to have either another
rotor turning in the opposite direction, or torque vanes which also turn in
the opposite direction, but more slowly than the rotor.

This arrangement of rotor and vane makes it simple to obtain *neutral*
stability, since the rotors can be one above and one below the C.G. This
configuration has perfect stability (Figure 4).

I said that, so far as practical helicopter design is concerned, the existence
of a spectrum of stability from pendular to catastrophic is academic, because

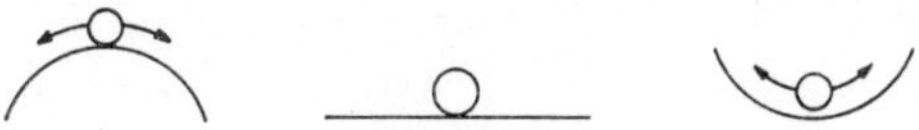

FIGURE 2

* The stroboscopic photos show a later version of the models in which the torque vane
alone was moved to change the C.G./rotor relationship.

to build a helicopter in which the C.G. coincided with the rotor is so impractical that is has never been attempted.

However, the concept of this *range of stability* has a very wide application. It applies in many fields as widely removed from aerodynamics as radio circuitry and even the behaviour of electrons in the atom.

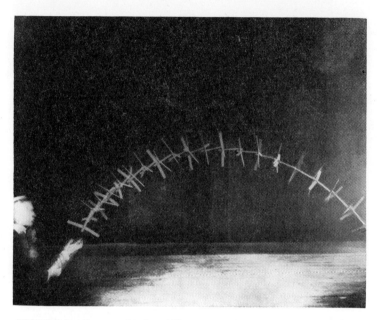

FIGURE 3   Catastrophic instability—centre of pressure above centre of gravity

We can begin with the airplane itself. Here phugoid instability is the one that is most likely because, unless the designer gives it special attention, the C.G. is likely to be behind the centre of lift, because the centre of gravity tends to be at the geometrical centre, and centre of lift tends to be well forward of this. The opposite disposition, when C.G. is forward of centre of lift, has application in the case of a dart or other form of projectile. In this case, there is no wing, and the tail surface points the dart in the direction of motion, as contrasted with the airplane, in which the horizontal tail surface holds the airplane so that the wing maintains a positive angle with respect to the wind. Hence, what would be catastrophic instability for an airplane is stability for a dart. The airplane must maintain level flight

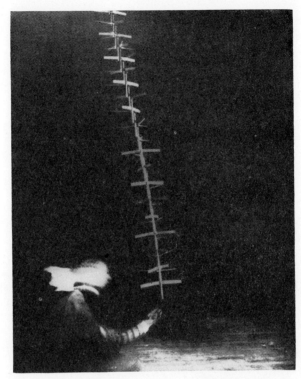

FIGURE 4   Stable configuration—centre of pressure at centre of gravity

indefinitely, whereas the flight of the dart is short; the airplane is propelled by the engine, whereas the dart depends on the initial impetus given it when thrown.

ECONOMIC AND SOCIAL STABILITY

This has significance in economic stability. Ordinarily, economics is subject to cyclic fluctuations. The law of supply and demand produces periods of oversupply. Prices then fall, discouraging production, which, in turn, causes scarcity. Prices then rise and encourage greater production, which causes oversupply, and the cycle repeats. This cyclic fluctuation is analogous to the phugoid instability of an airplane. But nowadays governments seek to regulate economics to prevent such fluctuations, and there has been considerable success. Starting with Roosevelt's concept of "priming the pump", there as been in the United States since the thirties an increasing tendency on the part of the governments to "spend for prosperity" to such an extent that today a very considerable part of the productive output of industry is paid for by the Government. Military expenditures, government research, roads, and moon shots have pushed production and employment to all time highs.

I will not presume to say that this has gone too far, but I would like to point out from what I know about stability in general that there is at least an analogy that may help reveal interactions in economics that have hitherto been neglected, and possibly throw light on economic prediction.

Let us return to the airplane. It consists of a lifting surface and a tail surface. In order to hold the wing at a positive lifting angle, the tail must push down, it must be at a negative angle. This disposition provides a self-regulating feature which insures that fluctuations in wind direction are accompanied by centre of pressure movement which neutralizes the wind fluctuations. To illustrate, let me cite a helicopter rotor blace, in which these considerations are highly critical (Figure 5).

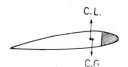

C.L.

C.G

FIGURE 5   Rotor blade

The helicopter rotor blade is a long, flexible, airfoil shaped structure which sweeps through the air at high speed. Its great length and flexibility make its angular position depend almost entirely on aerodynamic and centrifugal forces and very little on its own structural stiffness. Hence, the first requirement is that its centre of gravity coincide with or be slightly forward of the centre of lift (C.L.). This disposition insures that a sudden increase of lift will cause a decrease of angle, or at least no increase, since if it caused an increase the blade would lift more and start oscillation ("weaving" or flutter).

A second requirement for stability is that the position of the centre of lift should not move forward with angle. For most airfoil contours, the centre of lift does move forward with increased angle, banning them for helicopter use. Hence, helicopter blade contours are generally what is known as symmetrical sections, in which the centre of lift does not move. But even small differences in blade shape will show up in flight and cause the several blades of the rotor to "track" slightly differently, causing vibration, etc. To counteract this each blade is provided with a small metal trim tab, which can be bent up or down like the airplane tail to match the blades to one another (Figure 6).

FIGURE 6   Rotor blade (second requirement for stability)

Long practice has shown that it is better to bend the tabs up than down. The reason for this is that an *upturned* tab (which supplies a down force) creates a stable gradient for the centre of lift. It tends to make the total centre of lift move back with increased angle of attack (by moving back it reduces the angle).

In other words, like the airplane, the control should supply negative lift. Translated into economic terms, the control agency should be either neutral or negative; it should not create a force in the same direction as the prosperity it desires to produce.

This reads on "spending for prosperity". The original "pump priming" proposal of President Roosevelt was intended to be withdrawn when the pump got started, but spending for prosperity—if we can trust the aerodynamic analogy—would appear to create the combination of factors that leads to instability of the catastrophic variety. Why?

Because, when the control supplies lift, it also supplies a moment which reduces the lift of the lifting agent. In the dart or the projectile, this is desirable, but the dart has a finite life—it ends its career by plunging into the ground. In other words, the stability situation for sustained flight involves three factors: a force-producing factor, a control, and an environment. The purpose of the control is to maintain the force constant against fluctuations of the environment. To do so it must correct excesses by exerting a force in the opposite way to the change due to circumstance. (In the ideal case control is governed by an artificial horizon or other invarient that is not subject to circumstantial changes.)

In these difficult times there is no lack of reformers who see the need for changes, but in view of the subtlety involved in even the most simple instances of stability, it is of concern whether a proposed reform has the possibility of success. Indeed, it would appear that much of the present predicament is due to the reforms of the past. Should we not, therefore, before rushing to new reforms, try to understand better the way control is successfully achieved?

I have heard it advocated that the courts must be brought up to date "to conform with the times". Museums, formerly the repository of past achievements, strive to go modern. Even the church strives to gain popularity by concessions to the new morality.

Such a policy, in which the control function, normally directed to counter excesses, is revered, is good up to a point. It annuls the cyclic fluctuation which we described as phugoid and tends to produce neutral stability. But if it goes beyond this, it can create the conditions for the instability of the catastrophic kind.

Even this need not be serious. As noted before, catastrophic instability can be quite slow, and if slow enough, there is no occasion for concern. Death itself would appear to be the price paid by the organism for the desirable specializations in which it invests to meet environmental challenges. In other words, a civilization need not be expected to last forever, and if its instability does not cut its life span below expectancy, no harm is done.

Hence, the need again for sober appraisal. I recall attending a conference on research some ten years ago at a university. The head of the Aerodynamics Department, in an after-dinner speech, was explaining how the military, industry, and the universities were working together instead of competing and yapping at one another. "This new state of affairs was", he said, "ideal— the universities never 'had it so good'." I could not resist, when comments were invited, saying that the speaker as an aerodynamicist should be the first to realize that the state of affairs he described could lead to catastrophic instability.

But time has not borne me out. The universities, industry, and the government continue to enjoy this working arrangement. There does not appear to be a dissenting voice. While the lack of competition expands engineering departments out of all proportion to the work done, this is paid for by the military. Meanwhile, more engineers are needed, which requires more education and larger universities. The larger staffs turn out more research, which calls for more expenditure and more industry.

This harmony within the triplicity can be attained only by ignoring what we could call the larger picture. For the airplane whose flight is not corrected by its control this is the hard ground. It is only because the attraction of gravity leads to this dead end that self-regulation is important. The sociological picture is not so simple—it is not so easy to see what corresponds to the ground. I suspect that the student protest movement may epitomize the larger reference.

It is of sufficient power that it may either hasten the approach of the dead end, or provide the necessary correction. In any case, it may well be a symptom of a more general citizen-wide dissatisfaction with the self-reinforcement between industry, universities, and government.

Cybernetics as a model for political science: a critique

L. R. KERSCHNER
California State College, U.S.A.

Summary

Recent theoretical developments in political science have rested heavily upon cybernetic models. This dependence has many times been implicit but unacknowledged by the authors, and there have been explicit and acknowledged theories as well. The most prominent works in the latter category have been those developed by Karl Deutsch, David Easton, and Morton Kaplan. The bulk of this application of the cybernetic model has been heuristic in nature rather than mathematically precise. There has been little or no attention paid to the problem of operationalizing the models nor do authors and commentators involved appear to find much need for this process. The purpose of this paper would be threefold: (1) a description of the present state of cybernetics in political science, (2) a critique of the difficulties in these applications, and (3) suggestions for further research and development in this area with an optimistic prediction for the future.

INTRODUCTION

Cybernetics, the study of control and communication through man and machine, was first developed as a separate science in 1948 by Norbert Wiener, the Massachusetts Institute of Technology mathematician[1]. Taking the word "cybernetics" from the Greek word for "steersman", he regarded it as symbolizing the art of the pilot or, literally, "steersmanship". Wiener was apparently unaware that the term appears quite frequently in Plato's writings, where it is used both in the literal sense of steersmanship and in the meta-phorical sense of the art of guiding men in society, or specifically, the art of government[2]. The term was similarly used by André-Marie Ampère[3] in 1843 in his monumental effort to classify all knowledge. The word went generally unnoticed and Wiener apparently did not know of Ampère's application.

Recent theoretical developments in political science have rested heavily upon cybernetic models. This dependence has many times been implicit but unacknowledged by the authors, and there have been explicit and acknow-ledged theories as well. The most prominent works in the latter category have been those developed by Karl Deutsch, David Easton, and Morton Kaplan.

The bulk of this application of the cybernetic model has been heuristic in nature rather than mathematically precise. There has been little or no attention paid to the problem of operationalizing the models nor do authors and commentators involved appear to find much need for this process.

In one sense this is a very parochial paper, for political science as it is conceived here is almost exclusively an American discipline. There are some 16,000 political scientists in the world, of which there are 15,000 in the United States and several hundreds in Europe and the remainder are distributed among the rest of the countries[4]. In another sense, it is a catholic paper for the questions it raises are essential to the application of cybernetics to the social sciences.

CYBERNETICS

Cybernetics may be defined as the scientific analysis and control of animate or inanimate systems of organization based upon their methods of communi-cation. Emphasizing the essential unity of all systems, it disregards apparent differences in the construction of men and machines, and stresses such obvious functional similarities as neural connections and vacuum tubes.

Although automation and automatic machinery are constructed on cyber-netic principles, cybernetics is not, as many popularizers assume, restricted to the science of automatic control machinery. "The word cybernetics", G. T. Guilbaud[2] has complained, "now finds itself associated with robots, with electronics, and so on. Indeed, as an adjective, cybernetics threatens to go the way of atomic and electronic in becoming just another label for the spectacular."

Norbert Wiener and other cyberneticians conceive of cybernetics as a new science deserving a name of its own because they recognize in the concept of control an idea common to all the separate sciences[17]. As Karl Deutsch, a noted Yale political scientist, points out[5]: "Communication and control are the decisive processes in organization. Communication is what makes organizations cohere; control is what regulates their behaviour. If we can man the pathways by which information is communicated between different parts of an organization and by which it is applied to the behaviour of the organization in relation to the outside world, we will have gone far toward understanding that organization. This will be true of an organization composed of cells in an organism, or of machines in an automatic communications network, or of human beings in a social organization."

Deutsch argues that information itself has material reality. The development of this idea is, he says[6], "significant for wide fields of natural and social science. Information is indeed the 'stuff that dreams are made of'. Yet, it can be transmitted, recorded, analysed, and measured. Whatever we may call it information, pattern, form, gestalt, state description, distribution function, or negative entropy, it has become accessible to the treatment of science. It differs from the 'matter' and 'energy' of nineteenth century mechanical materialism in that it cannot be described adequately by their conservation laws." But information[6] "also differs, if not more so, from the 'idea' of 'idealistic' or metaphysical philosophies, in that it is based on physical processes during every single moment of its existence, and that it can and must be dealt with by physical methods. It has material reality. It exists and interacts with other processes in the world, regardless of the whims of any particular human observer; so much so that its reception, transmission, reproduction, and in certain cases its recognition, can be and sometimes have been mechanized."

Information theory, entropy, and feedback are the dominant concepts of cybernetics. The characteristic of cybernetics that distinguishes it from the disciplines from which these concepts are borrowed is the assumption that both natural and mechanical phenomena can be controlled on the basis of a unified approach, i.e. cybernetics, which is[7] "the essential unity of the set of problems centering around communications, control, and statistical mechanics whether in machine or in living tissue". Some wax even more enthusiastic. In the dramatic words of F.H.George, cybernetics is[8] "the attitude that recognizes, and emphasizes, the resemblances between organisms and man constructed machinery, and points out that even though the

17 Rose, Cybernetics III

materials used may differ, a theory of their operation is essentially the same. It implies that organisms are essentially constructable ... it implies a whole philosophy of science and, taken in the broader social context, a human philosophy of life."

W. Ross Ashby draws the conclusion that what[9] "cybernetics offers is a framework on which all individual machines may be ordered, related, and understood".

The essential thesis of cybernetics, then, is the assumption that man, machine, and society are very similar in structure and can best be understood and led through the study of their control and communication facilities. A second assumption is that messages of control between man and machine, machine and man, and machine and machine will play increasingly larger roles in society. Cyberneticians consider as parallel not only the nervous system and communication machines, but also all forms of behaviour to the extent that they are regular, determinate, or reproducible[9].

This parallelism between man and machine also distinguishes cybernetics from its parent sciences. However, more is implied by a science than the recurrence of a theme; control and communication are the prime object of study. The problems involved in this study are problems also found in biology, medicine, industry, or political science[17].

CYBERNETICS AND SOCIETY

Cyberneticians do not stop with the parallel between man and machine; they take the obvious step to finding parallelism between society and machine. Society, they conclude, can be better understood and described through cybernetics, for* "the social system is an organization like the individual ... it is bound together by a system of communication ... it has the dynamics in which circular processes of a feedback nature play an important part". The application of cybernetic analysis to man and society leads to certain theoretical conclusions about the nature of man and society, conclusions whose implications are important to this study.

---

* See Wiener[1], p. 33. He is not as certain about the applicability of cybernetics to society as his more enthusiastic fellows such as George and Ashby. A critique of the application of cybernetics to the social sciences can be found in Donald G. Macrae[10]. He defines cybernetics as "...the analytic study of the isomorphisms of communication structure in mechanisms, organisms, and societies".

Karl Deutsch claims that cybernetics provides for social sciences and philosophy a new model for thought much as they have been provided with scientific models for thought in centuries past. He notes that the Egyptian pyramid provides the model for the hierarchy, the wheel was the inspiration for the wheel of fate, and the balance wheel the symbol for law and justice[11].

This transfer of basic concepts of mechanism to all aspects of life was encouraged in the days of Newton. Although the classical notion of mechanism was metaphysical in that no mechanism as perfect as the ideal had ever been constructed, it nevertheless contributed to a notion as to how the universe was run. It implied a certain philosophical flavour from which it could not be divorced. For example, mechanism implied that the whole was equal to the sum of its parts. Furthermore, mechanism took from astronomy the assumption that things could be run in reverse just as it was possible to predict the movement of the stars forward and backward throughout the centuries. It is this concept that Wiener refers to as reversible Newtonian time and to which he opposes the Bergsonian concept of irreversible progress time[1,7].

The implications in the concepts of permanent function and design of Newtonian reversible time vitally affected political, social, and philosophical thought during the classical age of mechanism, or what is known in philosophy as the "age of reason". The clock model which implied the reversibility of time and permanence of function excluded assumptions which became more and more necessary as the modern world progressed[6]. "The notion of irreversible change, of growth, of evolution, of novelty, and of purpose all had no place in ... the age of reason."

Mechanism as a model for political and philosophical thought was replaced in the nineteenth century by the concept of organism. This theory was a marked improvement over that of mechanism since organism's behaviour was irreversible; it had a significant past and a history. However, organism was only partly self-determined for it was supposed to follow its own peculiar "organic law" which governed its birth and death. Organism was a more subtle concept than early mechanism, but it suffered from severe restrictions. The fact that the interior of the organism remained unanalyzable, that the organism could not be broken into its component parts and studies, left the theorists of the nineteenth century with only one solution—that of vital force or vital spirit.

Nineteenth century vitalists were unable to come to any realistic conclusions as to the content or structure of the organisms they studied. Although the "purpose" of organisms appeared to be a state of mature perfection or reproduction, vitalists were unable to determine what followed this mature state[6].

Models based on classical organism proved useful in biology, economics, psychology, and even in education by directing man's attention to the problems of interdependency and growth; however, their successes were severely limited by the inadequacies of their system. Classical organism models as a basis for thought were superseded later in the nineteenth century by models based on the concept of process. These incorporated within themselves concepts of change of law and structure founded on the assumption that there is a discoverable direction to the process as a whole. According to Deutsch[6], "the diverse models of historical process elaborated by these men (Hegel, Marx, Bergson, Toynbee) often contain notions of non-reversible change, of evolution through conflict, of some underlying relation between conflict and harmony, and even of overall purpose, or at least recognizable direction".

However, these theories of process and historical evolution were equally devoid of an ability to analyze the internal structure of their models. When pressed, some theorists fell back to talk of "super races" or spoke of evolution as a process of exposure of already pre-existing patterns. Others, like Marx, believed that they had discovered the key to the historical process and knew the end to which the world was evolving. They assumed that there were unchanging elements and laws which, once understood, indicated the direction of progress and history[6].

To Deutsch, such concepts of historical process should have been able to conceive of evolutionary movement which would provide for adjustment to changes in environment or to a new environment. The establishment of a fixed goal merely distorted the model as a tool of analysis. For him, evolution is[6] "an open-ended process containing the possibility of self-disruption or self-destruction as well as of a change of goals".

Until the beginning of the World War II these three models—classical mechanism, classical organism, and historical process—contributed to both philosophy and social science their own world views. Now cybernetics goes far beyond these concepts and provides a new model: a world view which supposedly supersedes not only classical mechanists and organicists but also modern day materialists and Marxists[6].

Cybernetics claims to be the new scientific means by which the world is to be ordered, understood, and controlled[1]. "... any organism is held together in their (sic) action by the possession of means for the acquisition, use, retention, and transmission of information."

Cybernetics appears to offer little that is new to those who assume that any recourse to a man–machine analogy is merely a reconstruction of eighteenth century mechanism. However, the assumptions of the mechanistic analogies of the eighteenth century were based on concepts of the universe drawn from Newtonian physics. This view was essentially deterministic and assumed that all causes and effects were directly linked and that the past had a distinct effect, indeed, a control, over the future. Theories derived from Newtonian mechanics were equally deterministic. Cybernetics, however, is not deterministic. It, with its assumptions that events are not eternally determined but are only likely to happen, owes its heritage to the new physics. Cybernetics asserts that systems are capable of change, innovation, self-destruction, or goal achievement, all of which are possible within differing degrees of probability.

Eighteenth century mechanical devices did not operate on the basis of sensing apparatuses, were not purposefully oriented and did not benefit from feedback responses. Tde clock work analogies and the dancing figures on the top of music boxes have little in common with the modern digital computer. The machines of cybernetics, in contrast, are self-optimizing and goal seeking; they are capable of knowing when their goals have been achieved. The new computers have sensory apparatuses, are purposefully oriented, and benefit from feedback responses; in other words, they are parallel to the animal system.

Demonstration of the functional analogy between the communication and control systems of animal, machine, and society may be the unique contribution of cybernetics to the understanding of the universe.

However, philosophical discussions of the implications of cybernetics for the social sciences are not enough[12,13]. The question is to what extent has cybernetics been specifically applied to political science and with what results. The applications to date have been largely, if not exclusively, theoretical and, in a way, almost solely heuristic.

CYBERNETICS AND POLITICAL SCIENCE

They are part of the general revolution in political theory that has been termed the "behavioural persuasion". This new paradigm has been well summed up by Gabriel Almond in a Presidential Address to the American

Political Science Association[4]. The "behaviouralists" seek nothing less than a theoretical explanation for the phenomena of government that will rival Einstein in its explanatory impact. It is to be a theory, at the grand level, which will permit conceptualization of interactions in any possible political system. It will be based on notions of comparative analysis and it will include middle-range and low-level theories as well. The norms of the science will be those of all science—hypothesis; validation; replicability; predictability—and ultimately control. (This raises the sticky question of control for what end.) It owes its philosophical base to the logical-positivists and presents itself as non-normative. This does not mean value free nor does it imply that the influence on the abandonment of a personal ethic in order to be a scientist but there is a claim to a need to suspend and perhaps modify that ethic in the process of research.

It assumes that statements of statistical probability about social phenomena are meaningful; that there are patterns of behaviour in political affairs which are predictable and that these patterns either are discoverable or conceptually impossible. There is a tacit assumption that the only type of political analysis that is meaningful is comparative analysis. Normative questions about good government are subsumed under a relativistic and ethical bias that doubts it knows what "good" is and is suspicious of those, who in the past dogmatically stated "the good"! There is an ethical bias in favour of pluralism in political systems and a reluctance to give up the role of evaluating political systems. Evaluation is not, however, to take place along a spectrum that says the Federalist model is perfection (or the Marxist model) or any other model but evaluation on the criteria of the theories that ask questions about "input" structures, conversion functions, output structures, system feedback and system capability and answer these questions in statistical terms and not in the binary, black–white, on-off judgments of all the traditional schools.

Political scientists have been forced to rethink the received wisdom of the past; to question actual operation rather than be satisfied with describing institutional relationships; to develop comparative techniques; to avoid the pitfalls of ideological and valuative considerations in comparison and to generally support the goals that Almond enunciated. Nevertheless, you cannot now use cybernetics to study political systems other than as a heuristic guide for research. Why not?

Two of the pioneers in both the development of the behavioural approach and the application of cybernetic ideas to political science have been Karl Deutsch and David Easton. Deutsch in his book *The Nerves of Government* takes an explicitly cybernetic model and applies it to foreign policy decision making[14]. Easton's *A System Analysis of Political Life* develops what are essentially the basic notions of cybernetics and elaborates a theory about the entire political system[15].

Both of these men have served to forward most of the goals that Gabriel Almond set out in the quotation that I read to you. Most but not all. There is one basic area of concern—one Achilles' heel to this entire process. That is the low level of conceptualization in political science itself. The terms, concepts, and constructs of the discipline are so weak that they cannot support the sophistication of the cybernetic models.

Abraham Kaplan in his magnificent work *The Conduct of Inquiry: Methodology for Behavioural Science* has explicated term, concept and construct in a most useful manner[16].

He notes that there are three types of terms, notational, substantive, and auxiliary. Auxiliary terms play a minor role in the language of discourse, substantive terms are essential to conceptual content but notational terms are fundamentally abbreviations and can be replaced. However, notations are not only dependent on the process of conceptualization but may in fact aid in that process—a good notation, such as found in chemistry may be very powerful but a notation, complex as it may be, does not guarantee profundity. Kaplan notes[16], "Behavioural science has suffered often from the illusion that a commonplace formulated in an uncommon notation becomes profound-rich with scientific promise." A notation may generate ideas and have certainly done so but it must have backing[16]. "Nothing is easier than to say 'Let $y = f(x)$' but nothing is gained if we do not have the faintest idea of how to solve the equation. Substantive terms remain fundamental."

Concepts permit the classification of a subject into meaningful divisions, i.e. scientifically useful. Thus, we conceptualize in such a manner as to provide data, the most useful of which tell us[16] "more about our subject matter than any other categorical sets."

Collective terms or group concepts pose even more critical methodological problems. They have both ideological and scientific importance and their denotations and connotations only serve to further confuse social science. As Kaplan notes[16], "From a methodological point of view, the most serious shortcoming of collective terms is the continuous temptation they hold out to commit the sin of reification. Though they are constructs or theoretical terms, they invite treatment as indirect observables, as if they designated

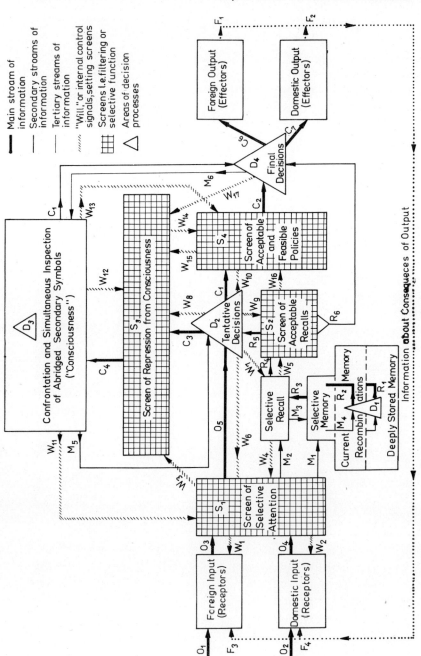

FIGURE 1   A crude model: a functional diagram of information flow in foreign policy decisions (from Deutsch[14], p.258)

individuals of a larger and more elusive kind than those ordinarily encountered in experience."

We can illustrate the magnitude of the above problems by turning to some of the diagrammatic representations that Deutsch and Easton used to explain and illustrate their work.

First, let us look at Deutsch's functional diagram of information flow in foreign policy decisions (see Figure 1). The first problem that we confront is the understanding of what is included in the sets foreign and domestic inputs as a major conceptual task. Assuming that we can distinguish between the two main categories, what constitutes relevant foreign inputs? For years the nation–state was perceived as the only relevant actor in foreign inputs. We are far more sophisticated today and automatically include corporations, organizations, groups (such as this one), and Aunt Mary's letters to Cousin Paula in Poland. This expansion of the set "foreign inputs" only serves to further complicate the issues for it merely increases the number of terms and concepts whose connotations and denotations are obscure and ambiguous.

Lest you think that it is only foreign policy that poses such problems let me note that "domestic inputs" have similar problems. We do not know what a "party" is; ideological considerations aside (where party in the Soviet Union and the United Kingdom are totally different conceptions) we have

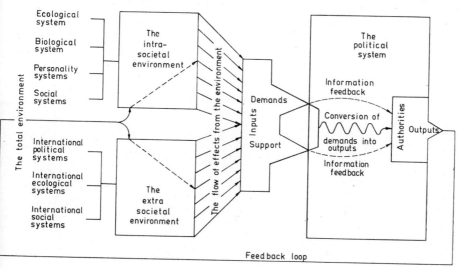

FIGURE 2   A dynamic response model of a political system
(from Easton[16], p.30, Diagram 1)

trouble distinguishing between so-called parties and interest groups. "Public opinion", a term often used as a domestic input to foreign policy poses still further methodological problems. We do not know what the collective "public" means and "opinion" opens up whole vista of arguments about held and expressed opinion, etc.

Professor Easton's diagrams make the situation still clearer (Figures 2, 3, 4, and 5). Figure 2 defines seven types of systems, four domestic and three international. It would be superfluous to point out that these labels do not provide categorization. It is understood that the old biological categories we learned in school are increasingly inadequate but still they provided more meaningful sets than these.

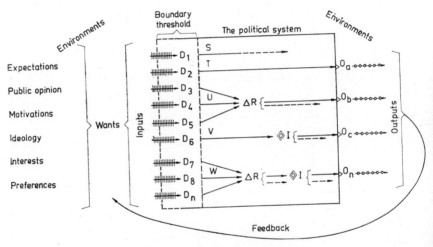

FIGURE 3   Types of demand flow patterns
(from Easton[16], p.14, Diagram 3)

Legend and expalnations

Environments: These include the intra- and extra-societal environments indicated on Table 1, in Chapter 2.

Boundary threshold: This is shown as a broad band, indefinite as to limits, in order to indicate that it matters little whether we interpret the conversion of wants as taking place in the environments or in the system.

Wants: By definition this term refers to expectations, opinions, motivations, ideology, interests and preferences, out of which demands arise or by which demands are shaped.

Conversion points:

Symbol	Reference	Interpretation
┼┼┼┼┼┼►	D_{1-n}	Voicing of demands: The shaded arrows represent the points of entry and inflow of demands. They indicate that varying wants have been voiced as demands. The letters D and their subscripts identify different demands.
──► ----►	S to W	Flow channels and patterns: The solid arrows represent the channels along which demands flow, and the broken arrows suggest the disappearance of the demands. The letters identify the five basic types of flow patterns that demands may take.
△	R	Reduction and combining points: Once a demand is part of the political processes, it may be modified or combined with others, thereby reducing the total number of demands in the system.
		Reducing units: These are not shown but may consist of any individuals or groups in the system. Typically, in modern systems they take the form of parties, opinion leaders, elites, interest groups, legislators, administrators, and the like.
◈	I	Conversion to issues: At some stage demands are transformed into issues; from these a selection is ultimately made for conversion to outputs.
▷ ○-○-○-○►	O_{a-n}	Conversion to outputs: Demands in their original or processed form are turned into decisions and accociated actions. The subscripts identify different outputs. The circled arrows represent the flow of the outputs into the environments.
		Output units: Outputs are produced and implemented by the authorities.

Feedback: Although this is shown as a single line, in fact it represents extremely numerous feedback channels. They represent the paths taken through the environment by outputs as they influence prior wants and demands.

Figure 3 lists six wants: expectations, public opinion, motivations, ideology, interests, preferences—need I comment? Figures 4 and 5 also illustrated add to the case. The terms, constructs, and concepts he uses are so ambiguous and have so many connotations and denotations, are subject to so many conceptual categories that they have lost meaning—they do not carry any information! And this in a cybernetic model! Reduction of such terms to a notational form (probably mathematical) for use in some type of algorithm is presently impossible.

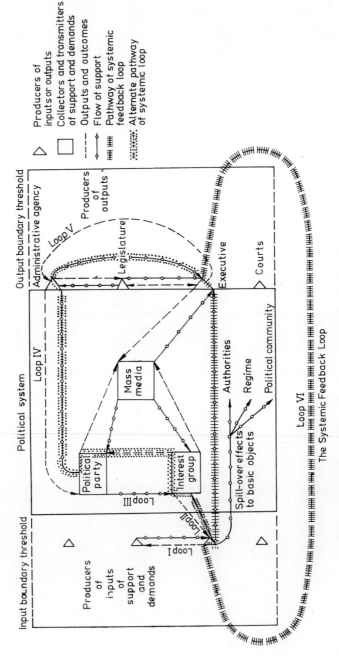

FIGURE 4   Multiple feedback loops of a political system (from Easton[16], p.374, Diagram 5)

Does not cybernetics have anything to contribute to the development of political science? Of course, and my critique has the great danger of falling into the "paradox of conceptualization". "The proper concepts are needed to formulate a good theory, but we need a good theory to arrive at the proper concepts." (Kaplan[16].) W.S.Jevon's noted as early as 1892 that[16]

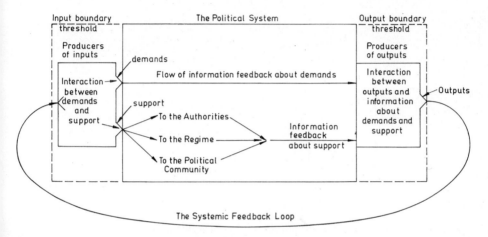

FIGURE 5   The systemic feedback loop
(from Easton[16], p.378, Diagram 6)

"almost every classification which is proposed in the early stages of a science will be found to break down as the deeper similarities of the objects come to be detected." There is almost a dialectical relationship (if my eastern colleagues will excuse me) between the development of theory, new concepts, rejection, further development, improved theory, new concepts, rejection, etc.

Cybernetics' main contribution to political science has been to highlight the essential bankruptcy of the language used as well as providing a guide for new conceptualization. We must now turn to this labourious task of developing categories, terms, and concepts that enhance our theoretical development and provide better logical categories. There is no doubt that these developments are taking place and the mathematization of political science is on the way—much is owed to cybernetics in creating the theoretical climate that made this necessary.

References

1. N. Wiener, *Cybernetics, or Control and Communication in the Man and the Machine*, Wiley, New York (1948).
2. G. T. Guilbaud, *What is Cybernetics?* Grove Press, New York (1960), pp. 1–7.
3. A. M. Ampère, *Essai sur la Philosophie des Sciences, ou Exposition Analytique d'une Classification Naturelle de Toutes les Connaissances Humaines*, Bachelier, Paris (1843), p. 140.
4. G. A. Almond, "Political theory and political science", in *Contemporary Political Science: Toward Empirical Theory* (Ed. I. de Sola Pool), McGraw-Hill, New York (1967), pp. 4, 13–15.
5. K. W. Deutsch, "On Communication Models in the Social Sciences", *Public Opinion Quart.*, **16**, 367 (1952).
6. K. W. Deutsch, "Mechanism, teleology, and mind", *Phil. Phenomenol. Res.*, **12**, 181–96 (1951).
7. N. Wiener, *The Human Use of Human Beings*, Houghton Miffllin, Boston (1950), p. 12.
8. F. H. George, *Automation, Cybernetics, and Society*, Philosophical Library, New York (1959), p. 45.
9. W. Ross Ashby, *An Introduction to Cybernetics*, Wiley, New York (1957), p. 2.
10. D. G. Macrae, "Cybernetics and social science", *Brit. J. Sociol.*, **2**, 135–49 (1951).
11. K. W. Deutsch, "Mechanism, organism, and society: some models in natural and social science", *Phil. Sci.*, **18**, 234 (1951).
12. F. S. C. Northrop, "The neurological and behaviouristic psychological basis of the ordering of society by means of ideas", *Science*, **107**, April, p. 411–16 (1948).
13. M. Jonas, "A critique of cybernetics", *Social Res.*, **18**, No. 1, 172–92 (1954).
14. K. W. Deutsch, *The Nerves of Government*, The Free Press of Glencoe, New York (1963).
15. D. Easton, *A System Analysis of Political Life*, Wiley, New York (1965).
16. A. Kaplan, *The Conduct of Inquiry: Methodology for Behavioral Science*, Chandler, San Francisco (1964).
17. S. Bert, "The irrelevance of automation", *Cybernetica*, **1**, No. 4, 280–295 (1958).

Subjective information theory, thermodynamics, and cybernetics of open adaptive societal systems

GEORGE G. LAMB

Northwestern University, Evanston, Illinois, U.S.A.

Summary

Wiener (1954) and Weaver (1959) discuss three levels of communication problems.

Level A. How accurately can the symbols of communication be transmitted? (Shannon's technical problem).

Level B. How precisely do the transmitted symbols convey the desired meaning? (The semantic problem).

Level C. How effectively does the received meaning affect the conduct in the desired way? (The behavioural problem).

Jaynes (1957) pointed out that in subjective information theory at Level B; in the expression for uncertainty or entropy $= -\Sigma p_i \ln p_i j$; the first p_i deals with the "interpretative" part of the information, the power of the controlling paradigms and the second, $\ln p_i$, deals with the substantive or factual part of the information. Level C involves societal change. Conceptually change involves work to overcome resistance to the change, and this involves potential and kinetic energy. Generalized energy is expressible as an "intensity factor" or generalized force times a conjugate "extensive factor" or generalized displacement. Generalizations of thermodynamic concepts of energy, entropy, informenergy, societal energy, negentropy, goal gap ratio, and rate of change equations provide an operationalizable framework for analysis of societal change. These latter concepts will be discussed from a basic scientific, philosophical point of view, developing "translating equations" between statistical thermodynamics and sociodynamics (or life) through subjective information theory.

INTRODUCTION

Boltzman (1872), Planck (1900), Gibbs (1902), Tolman (1938), Shannon (1948), Weaver (1949), Wiener (1954), Jaynes (1957), Brillouin (1962), Polonsky (1965), Tribus (1966), Lamb (1968), Galting (1968), Soukup (1968), and Anschutz (1968), and many others have dealt with inter-relations between thermodynamics, statistical mechanics, and information theory.

Since the function $S = -\Sigma p_i \ln p_i$ has been accepted as a measure of entropy, or of our "uncertainty" or ignorance about the state of a system, there has been a gradually developing emphasis upon subjective information theory in searching for more understanding of "Gibb's paradox" concerned with this equation.

Weaver (1949) and Wiener (1954) suggest three levels of communications problems.

Level A. How accurately can the symbols of communication be transmitted? (Shannon's technical problem).

Level B. How precisely do the transmitted symbols convey the desired meaning? (the sematic problem) (linguistics; bio-chemical genetic).

Level C. How effectively does the received meaning affect the conduct in the desired way? (the effectiveness, or behavioural, problem) (Lamb, 1968, 1969).

Shannon and Brillouin specifically rule out levels B and C and extensive developments dealing with flow of information through channels resulted. Jaynes (1957), Tribus (1966) and Lamb (1969) point out that the first p_i in the above entropy expression deals with the "interpretive" part of the information; and the second, $\ln p_i$, or $\ln (n_i/\Sigma n_i)$, deals with the substantive or factual part of the information, and suggest the term "subjective information theory". This includes levels A and B.

OPEN ADAPTIVE SOCIETAL SYSTEMS

Gibb's classical and Planck's quantum thermodynamics dating from 1900 deal primarily with *closed systems* in Gibbsian uniform ensembles, micro-canonical ensembles, canonical ensembles; but refer also to *open systems* or grand canonical ensembles. To solve Gibb's paradox there is need for hypo theses to guide in choosing probabilities and phases for different states that agree equally with our partial knowledge of the precise state of the actual system. This leads to the hypotheses of equal *a priori* probabilities and random *a priori* phases for micro or quantum mechanic states of the system, and the ergodic hypothesis has been assumed to justify the mathematical formulations. Subjective information theory presents an alternative approach to this problem.

Bertalanffy (1968, pp. 121–2) points out: "There is, therefore, a fundamental contrast between chemical equilibria and the metabolizing organisms. The organism is not a static system closed to the outside and always containing the identical components; it is an open system in a (quasi-) steady state, maintained in a steady state by the exchange of component material and energies, in which material continually enters from, and leaves into, the outside environment. The definition of the state of the organism as steady state is valid only in first approximation, insofar as we envisage shorter periods of time in an 'adult' organism, as we do, for example, in investigating metabolism. If we take the total life cycle the process is not stationary but only quasi-stationary, subject to changes slow enough to abstract from them for certain research purposes, and comprising embryonic development, growth, aging, death, etc. Such consideration proves especially useful in areas accessible to quantitative formulation." He refers to dynamic equilibria, energy concepts and rate equations in the growth of organisms and suggests these concepts apply to open system of a higher nature.

Due primarily to the development of language, man's accumulated knowledge, mass education, and the great advances in electronic communications systems facilitating interrelations between knowledge and societal man anywhere in the real world; our behavioural systems of man should be considered as *open adaptive systems* with the *real universe* as the environment. Can insights from subjective information theory, thermodynamics and cybernetics of global open adaptive systems help us formulate quantitive inter-relationships that will help us understand change in our very complex open adaptive societal systems at many levels which make up the real world in which we live?

Figure 1 presents a simplified comprehensive model of the real world and man's knowledge about it. The amount of understanding at the *why* level or the predictive "power of the controlling paradigms" for each discipline is represented roughly by the breaks in the vertical bars in the third row between the double line labelled "abstract theory" and the triple line labelled the "real world".

In thermodynamics a truly open system in the real physical world might be described as a black box with input and outputs to the environment,

SPECTRUM OF KNOWLEDGE								
REAL WORLD RANDOM DATA (ENTROPY)	1	2	3	4	5	6	7	8
KNOWLEDGE (NEGENTROPY) (PARADIGMS)	PHILO.	MATH.	PHYS. SCI.	LIFE SCI.	SOCIAL SCI.	HUMAN-ITIES.	ARTS.	RELIG.
ABSTRACT THEORY	POWER OF CONTROLLING PARADIGMS.							
PRACTITIONERS ENGINEERS. M.D. BUS. MGT POLITICAL DECISION MAKERS								
REAL WORLD								

FIGURE 1   Simplified comprehensive model of the real world and man's knowledge of it

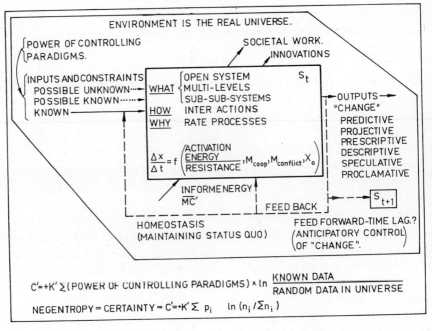

FIGURE 2   Cybernetics of open adaptive societal systems

similar to those described by Pask (1965), but the true environment should be considered the real universe. Similarly in subjective information theory at levels A, B, and C, a truly open system in the real societal world might be described as a black box with inputs and outputs to the environment, with the true environment considered as the real universe, including concepts of man's informenergy and negentropy or knowledge about it.

Figure 2 illustrates a complex, but simplified, black box, input–output, feed back, feed forward, multi-state representation of a societal system open to the real universe as its environment. This model is applicable to the study of change in open adaptive societal systems. For the input items the power of the controlling paradigms represents the first, or interpretive, p_i of the negentropy expression, i.e. the probability that our knowledge can predict future out comes. This is related to the classifying of change in the output as predictive, projective, prescriptive, descriptive, speculative, or proclamative. The general systems model allows simultaneous representation of both goal models and system models Etzioni (1967) showing both "structure" and operationalizable "process" for any societal system. This also aids clarity as to what system levels are involved and as to whether these are being discussed at the *what*, *how*, or *why* level of understanding.

THERMODYNAMICS AND SUBJECTIVE INFORMATION THEORY

In quantum thermodynamics entropy (uncertainty, *disorder*) may be expressed as

$$\text{entropy} = -K \Sigma p_i \ln \frac{\text{number of quantum states filled in system}}{\text{number of quantum states that might be filled in the universe}}$$

$$= \textit{disorder}, \text{ or uncertainty} = S = -K \Sigma p_i \ln p_i$$

In discrete socio-dynamics Lamb (1969), negentropy (certainty or order) might be expressed as

$$\text{negentropy} = +K'\Sigma(\text{power of controlling paradigms}) \ln \frac{\text{known data}}{\text{random data in the universe}}$$

$$= \textit{order}, \text{ or certainty} = C' = K' \Sigma p_i \ln \frac{n_i}{\Sigma n_i}$$

where (power of the controlling paradigms) is expressed as the subjective probability that the predictions are correct.

This formulation implies that man is quite ignorant, which is consistent with recent statements by Eccles (1968) and MacIver (1969). Man knows only a little of all that might be known about man himself and about the real societal universe. Our huge iceberg of organized knowledge is floating on an ocean of disordered or unknown data.

For an open system in the inanimate universe the denominator in the entropy expression is the total number of quantum states that might be filled in the universe. This is an almost infinite number of unknown discrete states as postulated in quantum theory. For an open behavioural system in the societal universe the denominator in the negentropy expression is similarly an almost infinite number of unknown random discrete items of data. How can we make use, in the real world, of equations with very large, mostly unknown denominators?

Jaynes (1957, p. 630) gives a summary of the assumptions and mathematical derivations of the following equation dealing with subjective uncertainty, subjective certainty, and the total number of possible choices or micro states of a system, keeping in mind that p_i deals with the interpretive part and $\ln n_i$ and $\ln \Sigma n_i$ deal with the substantive part.

$$H(p_i \cdots p_n) = \ln(\Sigma\, n_i) - K' \Sigma\, p_i \ln n_i = -K' \Sigma\, p_i \ln p_i$$

uncertainty = total number − certainty = Gibb's paradox
                    of micro states
                    in real world

or uncertainty + certainty = total No. of micro-states in the real world. Dividing by the right-hand expression

$$\frac{H(p_i \cdots p_n)}{\ln(\Sigma\, n_i)} + \frac{K' \Sigma\, p_i \ln n_i}{\ln(\Sigma\, n_i)} = 1$$

$$\frac{\text{subjective}}{\text{uncertainty}} + \frac{\text{subjective}}{\text{certainty}} = 1$$

In an open universe system if the n_i are discrete, Σn_i is very, very large; our state of ignorance is very large. The denominator $\ln(\Sigma n_i)$ will be very large compared to $K' \Sigma p_i \ln n_i$, and our subjective and absolute certainty or predictability will be very small. Yet our thermodynamics formulations are significant and relevant to the specific tasks of inquiry dealing with technological change in the real world. Why?

Fast (1962, p.68 ff.) discussing entropy and thermal energy gives some insight.

"The chance of encountering *exactly* the most probable distribution of thermal energy micro-states in a given macro-state becomes smaller as Σn increases. On the other hand, the fraction of micro-states belonging to the *nearly* exponential distributions continues to increase as Σn becomes larger... The exponential and nearly exponential distributions together comprise the overwhelming majority of all the microstates... One can even go a step further and take the micro-state to include exclusively the pure exponential distribution, although this comprises only a small fraction of all micro-states." Khinchin (1957) discusses the mathematical foundation of information theory.

A pragmatic approach based upon a thermodynamic analogy to give some further insight into the matter is as follows. If we are primarily interested in studying societal change, we are most interested in the changes brought about by the differences in levels of informenergy possessed by individuals in society and the results of groups of such individuals getting together either by joint motivation for co-operation or joint motivation for conflict in bringing about societal change.

The subjective certainty about change between (system state)$_1$ and (system state)$_2$ is equal to

$$(\Sigma p_i \ln n_i)_2 - \ln (\Sigma n_i)_2 - (\Sigma p_i \ln n_i)_1 + \ln (\Sigma n_i)_1$$

If $(\Sigma n_i)_2$ and $(\Sigma n_i)_1$ are so large that the difference between n_{i2} and n_{i1} has negligible effect on the (Σn_i) then the (Σn_i) may be assumed equal, and they cancel out in the above expression because they have opposite signs. Then subjective certainty $= \Sigma p_i \ln (n_{i2} - n_{i1})$.

This is comparable with the method used in dealing with change in chemical thermodynamics and amounts to assuming an empirical reference point or zero point. This procedure is justified by experimentally verified chemical thermodynamics, and is used in problem solving in this field in the real world. The intuitive justification appears to be based on verified "near decomposibility" or sub-systems unitization into spheres of strong inter-actions interconnected by weak interactions for energy subsystems into macromotion kinetic energy, thermal energy, and electronic and nuclear energy as illustrated in Figure 3.

Figure 4 summarizes some of the inter-relations through equations dealing with entropy, negentropy, disorder, order, intensity factor, extensive factor,

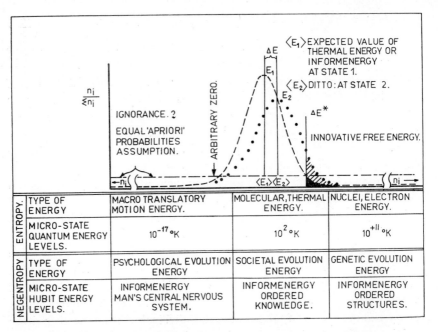

	ENTROPY		NEGENTROPY
TYPE OF ENERGY	MACRO TRANSLATORY MOTION ENERGY.	MOLECULAR, THERMAL ENERGY.	NUCLEI, ELECTRON ENERGY.
MICRO-STATE QUANTUM ENERGY LEVELS.	10^{-17} °K	10^{2} °K	10^{+11} °K
TYPE OF ENERGY	PSYCHOLOGICAL EVOLUTION ENERGY	SOCIETAL EVOLUTION ENERGY	GENETIC EVOLUTION ENERGY
MICRO-STATE HUBIT ENERGY LEVELS.	INFORMENERGY MAN'S CENTRAL NERVOUS SYSTEM.	INFORMENERGY ORDERED KNOWLEDGE.	INFORMENERGY ORDERED STRUCTURES.

FIGURE 3   Spectrum of energy or informenergy microstates. Subsystem decomposability: dimensional analysis

	ENTROPY		NEGENTROPY	
TYPE: DYNAMIC SYSTEM	THERMODYNAMIC.	STATISTICAL DYNAMIC.	SUBJECTIVE INFORMATION THEORY	SOCIO-DYNAMIC.
TYPE:ENERGY	THERMAL ENERGY. $\frac{E}{E_0}=\frac{T}{T_0}\cdot\frac{S}{S_0}$ *	QUANTUM ENERGY. $E=\frac{3N_0\,h\nu}{e^{h\nu/kT}-1}$	INFORMENERGY. MOTIVATION times KNOWLEDGE = $\overline{MC}'$ *	SOCIETAL ENERGY. $\left(\frac{E-S}{S}\right)_1\cdot\left(\frac{\Delta C'}{C_0}\right)$ $\left(\frac{E-S}{S}\right)_2\cdot\left(\frac{X-X_0}{X_0}\right)$ *
DISORDER	ENTROPY=S. UNCERTAINTY.	ENTROPY=S. UNCERTAINTY.	ENTROPY=S. UNCERTAINTY.	
ORDER			NEGENTROPY=C' CERTAINTY = C'	NEGENTROPY=$(\Delta C'/C_0)$ ORDER=$((X-X_0)/X_0)$ *
EXTENSIVE FACTOR	$\Delta S=-k\sum p_i\,\ln(n_2-n_1)$*	$S=-\sum p_i\,\ln(n_i/\sum p_i)$	$C'+K'\sum p_i\,\ln(n_i/\sum n_i)$*	$\Delta C'=+K'\sum p_i\,\ln(n_2-n_1)$*
INTENSITY FACTOR	T, TEMPERATURE	$\theta=d\varepsilon_i/dS_i$	M = GOAL GAP RATIO*	M_{coop}, $M_{conflict}$ *
RATE OF CHANGE EQUATION.	$\frac{\Delta x}{\Delta t}=f\left(\frac{e^{-\Delta E^*/kT}}{R},T,P,X_0\right)$*		$\frac{\Delta x}{\Delta t}=f\left(\frac{e^{-\Delta\overline{M}C^*/K'M}}{R}\,M_{coop},M_{conflict},X_0\right)$ *	
CONSTANT.	BOLTZMANN'S k 1.38×10^{-16}	PLANCK'S h 6.62×10^{-23}	I HUBIT, 0,1 HUMAN CODE	$K'=\dfrac{\sum HUBITS\ IN\ PARADIGM.}{I\ HUBIT}$ LANGUAGE.

CHANGE: RESISTANCE: ENERGY { INTENSITY FACTOR: $\left(\dfrac{T/T_0}{(E-S)/S}\right)$ EXTENSIVE FACTOR { ENTROPY: DISORDER. / NEGENTROPY: ORDER.

TRANSLATING EQUATIONS: THERMODYNAMICS TO SOCIO-DYNAMICS OR LIFE.

FIGURE 4   Summary

energy, informenergy, rate of change formulations in the general areas of thermodynamics, statistical mechanics, subjective information theory, and socio-dynamics. The principle translating equations between thermo-dynamics and socio-dynamics or life are outlined with heavy borders.

MEASUREMENT AND DIMENSIONAL ANALYSIS

For study of change in complex societal systems utilizing concepts of Inform energy, goal gap ratios, negentropy, rate of change formulations, with consciously assumed selected reference points (the status quo of society on any societal attribute might do), ratio scales to provide dimensionless parameters, logarithmic transformations, and probabilities based on subjective information theory, may be used heuristically to formulate operationalizable propositions to determine if they are significant and relevant to specific tasks of inquiry (Wartofsky, 1968, p. 171; Quade, 1968, p. 143; de Jong 1967).

In *Dimensional Analysis for Economists* de Jong (1967) cautions against nonsense correlations and describes pitfalls that may be encountered when dealing with equations which are automatically homogeneous dimensionally (re pure index numbers or ratio scales). "... considerations lead to advocating the following course for an econometrican (social scientist) wishing to make use of the possibilities offered by dimensional analysis. It is necessary for him initially to write the equation that must be investigated in absolute variables, not in their relative changes. He should then put the thus written equation to a test of dimensional homogeneity. If this equation turns out not to be dimensionally homogeneous it must be regarded as false, and there is no point in testing it by statistical methods. [The problem of causality is not solved by statistics but by (power of the controlling paradigms of) the special science investigating the phenomena.] If it appears to be dimensionally consistent, the equation may well make sense from the viewpoint of economic (social science) theory. If it is impossible to check the meaningfulness of the equation by means of theory directly, there is, none the less, good cause for checking it statistically: one may even say that there is then all the more reason to do so. When in this case for statistical reasons it appears to be necessary for the equation to be rewritten in a form containing only the relative changes of the variables, (i.e. ratio scales) no objection can, of course, be made to this."

Dimensional analysis has been a mainstay in engineering analysis of very complex physical systems since Reynolds in 1883 first used it to help understand the apparently simple transition from laminar to turbulent flow of water in pipes. (Some 80 years later, we still do not have a completely sound theoretical analysis of turbulent flow of fluids.) However, dimensional analysis has aided greatly in planning experimental procedures and in interpreting the results statistically so that our ability to analyse, design and predict the performance of airplanes, rockets, hydraulic turbines, etc., is excellent. This work has also aided greatly in our development of theory. The procedure used above is essentially that described in the last two sentences on the de Jong quote, and appears to have great promise in the study of change in complex societal systems. It should be guided by "strong inference and multiple hypotheses" and by understanding of the limited power of the controlling paradigms in many disciplines at this time, i.e. by using an innovative, iterative, trial and error approach with some consideration as to a generalized cost/benefit appraisal to clarify the appropriate scale of experiment and to balance the urgent demand for results now, versus the likelihood of serious failure to attain the goals set, or even to move towards goals diametrically opposed to these we seek.

LEVEL C: THE BEHAVIOURAL PROBLEM IN COMMUNICATIONS

Weaver's Level C, The behavioural problem, involves societal change. Conceptually change involves work to overcome resistance to the change, and this involves potential and kinetic energy. Energy is expressible in generalized terms as an 'intensity factor' or generalized force times a conjugate 'extensive factor' or generalized displacement.

Extending early intuitive ideas of Leibniz (1750) and Mayer (1842), thermal energy from the sun is the prime source of potential energy leading to change in our world, with temperature as the "intensity factor" and entropy *(disorder)* as the "extensive factor". This potential energy is transformable into heat, kinetic energy, electrical energy, chemical energy, biochemical energy, various types of physical and societal changes, etc.

It is here postulated that informenergy is the potential energy leading to change in our human behavioural world, with "goal gap ratio" or motivation as the "intensity and factor" and negentropy *(order* of structure of knowledge) as the "extensive factor". As an example from the behavioural world, econometrics has been developed over the last hundred years in terms of C. Menger's (1883) economic behavioural model of man. Although econometrics does not use the terminology of informenergy, societal energy, and negentropy, its empirically based formulations are consistent with these concepts (Lamb, 1969), and in measurement it does use ratio scales, empirical zero points, logarithmic transformations, and rate of change formulations in understanding and exerting some degree of anticipatory control of societal change. Stevens (1968) postulates that the use of ratio scales and empirical zero points is inconsistent. In both econometrics and thermodynamics quantitative relationships have been verified in the real world.

What is verification? How can we verify our controlling paradigms to develop understanding and some degree of anticipatory control of change in societal systems in the general systems spectrum? T. S. Kuhn (1962) states: "Verification is like natural selection: it picks out the most viable among the alternatives in a particular historical situation." He points out that K. Popper (1959) denies the existence of any verification procedures at all, placing the emphasis upon falsification. This led some to conclude that all history is unverified myth and hence irrelevant to the scientific study of current problems of societal change. But Kuhn observes that it is in the joint verification–falsification processes that the probabilistic comparison of theories plays its central role. J. R. Platt (1964) advocates "strong inference and multiple hypotheses". By this he means Baconian interconnecting theory by the conditional inductive tree, proceeding from alternative hypotheses (possible causes) through crucial experiments, to exclusion of some alternatives and adoption of what is left; or in an engineers language by using an innovative, iterative, trial and error approach guided by dimensional analysis.

RATE OF CHANGE FORMULATIONS FOR INTER-ACTING SUBSYSTEMS

To aid in developing working solutions to the problems of change in society some understanding of mutual causality and rate of change equations are needed for analysing and providing some degree of anticipatory control for societal changes.

Jaynes (1968) says that "... one needs to incorporate information not only over a space region at one instant of time but over a *space–time* region; and the partition function gets generalized to a partition functional over functions defined in this region—with further mathematical development I believe it will be possible to find equally general treatments of highly nonlinear phenomena...".

A generalized formulation for rate of change can be made meaningful for various types of societal change if the domain as well as the mapping "f" are specified with reference to operationalizable theoretical and empirical concepts.

A generalized irreversible thermodynamic rate of change equation

$$\frac{\Delta X}{\Delta t} = f\left(\frac{e^{-\Delta E^*/kT}}{\text{resistance}}, \text{ temperature, pressure, } X_0\right)$$

may be rewritten to apply to the real behavioural world of man (Lamb, 1968)

$$\frac{\Delta X}{\Delta t} = f\left(\frac{e^{-\overline{MC'^*}/K'M}}{\text{resistance}}, M_{\text{cooperation}}, M_{\text{conflict}}, X_0\right)$$

where the informenergy exponential term is similar to the Arrhenius velocity constant involving an energy of activation (thermal energy, $\Delta E^* \cdot kT$; or informenergy, $\overline{\Delta MC'^*}/K'M$) which is related to "free energy" possessed by the entities of the micro system (Lamb, 1968, Figure 4, 1969, Tables 3, 4).

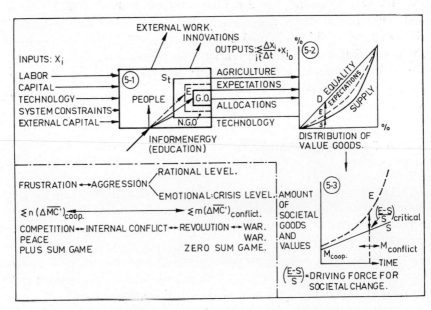

FIGURE 5 Operationalizable dynamic societal systems analysis: nation level. G.O.: government organization: authoratative allocation of values. N.G O.: non-government organizations. E: intellectual elites

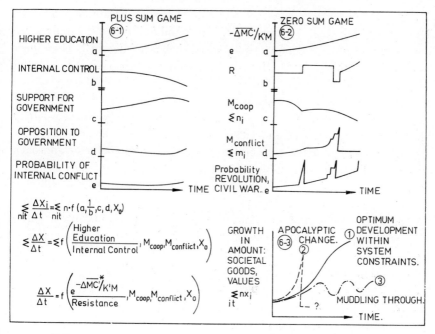

FIGURE 6   Societal dynamics: generalized rate of change formulation

M_{coop} and $M_{conflict}$ are related by the frustration–aggression hypothesis of social theory. These "intensity factors" of informenergy and societal change energy may be stated in generalized form as goal gap ratios: $(E - S)/S$:

$$\frac{\text{(goal sought times the expectations of attainment) minus (status quo)}}{\text{(status quo)}}$$

Upshaw in Blalock (1968) discusses measurement of cognitive, behavioural, and affective attitudes (or goal gap Ratios) and the use of ratio scales. Moses (1967) describes how to develop a standard scale for comparing the intensity of international conflict. X refers to any attribute of society involved in change. Resistance may represent inertia, conflicts, or other constraints on the system.

Figure 5 presents an "operationalizable dynamic societal systems analysis model" at the the level of the nation, as a cybernetic extension of the more usual verbal model. The details of the dynamic model may be altered within the framework of Figure 2, to apply to the inter-nation level, the international level; or to any level of structure and process within a nation, including the level of the individual. Figures 5–1, 5–2, 5–3 and 6–1, 6–2, 6–3 supply some structure and process details inside the black box of Figure 2. These may help in interdisciplinary studies and discussions by providing a common language at the pre-supposition level.

Societal systems are very highly complex with multitudeness interactions and many levels; and the powers of our controlling paradigms are woefully weak. However, the principle of "near decomposability" of subsystems can be consciously applied in an innovative, iterative, trial and error approach guided by dimensional analysis in a manner somewhat analogous to its use in engineering analysis and design in the better understood, but still very complex space programs. Perhaps we can ultimately progress from a state comparable with that of the alchemists with high goals and little understanding of change in the real world, to a level of understanding of man and his innovative capabilities to eventually bring about societal changes in the real world guided by mutual understanding of the goals and methodologies of humanists, social scientists, physical scientists, engineers, politicians, and all of the people in the world. A mutual understanding of the factors underlying curves 1, 2, 3 of Figure 6–3 may help.

Figure 6–2 illustrates how the rate equation may be applied to an example of conflict within a political system. Time is the abscissa and curves *a*, *b*, *c*, *d* represent the effects of the parameters in the rate equation when they are summed for discrete intervals overtime, leading to the summation curve "*e*". This last is the probability of a coup occurring overthrowing the government.

Lamb (1968, 1969) postulated that an increase in informenergy, attained by increased educational levels in a country, increased exponentially the capability for innovative change which could be applied through, either "motivation for co-operation" or "motivation for conflict", to bring about societal change, curve "*a*". Curve "*b*" illustrates the government's authorative power of internal control exerted by police power, censorship, barring public meetings, etc. Curve "*c*" illustrates the support of the government by the people with M_{coop} as the index based upon Figure 5–2. Curve "*d*" illustrates the opposition to the government with $M_{conflict}$ as the index, built up at an emotional frustration level by rising expectations, perceived injustices, protest meetings, confrontations, strikes, etc. (Figure 5–3). Curve "*e*" is the summation $\Sigma f(a, 1/b, c, d)$ illustrating the probability of a coup overthrowing the government.

Lamb (1969) based upon, on the scene, observations outlined in some detail how specific actions appeared to lead to the shapes of the curves in Figure 6–3 which did result in a coup overthrowing the government. With variations in detail similar examples have occurred in other countries in recent years. Ironically these activities were sparked by idealistic protests by university students against the discrimination shown by a majority against a minority, but ended in civil wars approaching race genocide of the minority. Detailed content analysis of speeches and actions of leaders, of press, radio and T.V. communications, and changes in societal attributes (Figure 5–2, 5–3), and graphical presentation of the parameters in the rate equation might hopefully increase the understanding of all people of the importance of the expectation goal gap, the frustration-aggression hypothesis, and dangers of poorly directed internal control.

Of course the generalized rate of change formulation can be made meaningful for the analysis of societal change of a co-operative (or plus sum game) type (Figure 6–1). This could be applied to analysis of economic development, socialization, modernization, education, etc., if the domain as well as the mapping "*f*" are specified with reference to pertinent operationalizable theoretical and empirical concepts.

Figure 6–3 illustrates the importance of understanding the dynamics of these factors upon rate of growth in the amount of any type of societal good we wish to consider. Curve 1 illustrates what we might attain if man had enough understanding or informenergy to provide optimum development within global, open adaptive system constraints. Curve 2 illustrates apocalyptic change—history is a myth—destroy the establishment—the world will become perfect by use of simplified slogans-approach. Curve 3 is more typical of man's past and present influence in carrying out societal change; perhaps a long-term upward trend, but with many frustrating ups and downs due to inadequate understanding of the dynamics of change in the real world.

Many analogies might be cited, but perhaps the operation of changing nuclear energy into heat in a nuclear reactor is fairly well known. Design, construction, and operation are optimized by the use of control rods. If the control of the neutron flux driving force by the rods is optimum, curve 1 of Figure 6–3 results. An urgent demand for more heat may be met by withdrawing the rods, but, if the demands exceed the constraints of the system and the rods are completely withdrawn, curve 2 may result; the carefully developed structures and processes are destroyed. If the rods are not adequately controlled, heat may be inadequately controlled and the fluctuations may lead to alternating euphoria and frustrations among the ultimate beneficiaries, curve 3.

SUMMARY

From a behavioural viewpoint models of man and his societies should be considered as adaptive, learning, open dynamic systems with both feedback and feed forward interrelations and possibly long time lags; at the bio-electromolecular, physiological, central nervous system, psychological, sociological, economic and political levels, including the interrelations between the various levels.

Subjective information theory appears to provide "translating equations" between thermodynamics and human socio-dynamics or life, which show promise as heuristic devices to study societal change in the behavioural world.

It is hoped that the "global framework for analysis of societal change: basic pre-suppositions" presented at a simple abstract level will help to reduce some of the communication gaps between physical scientists, engineers, social scientists, and humanists, by providing some insights that will help mutual understanding of, and motivation for co-operation in change in our highly complex real societal world. Man, whose studies of change in the physical world have made our world an open, adaptive system by technological developments such as instantaneous electronic communications and the industrial "horn of plenty" should be able to learn eventually how to carry out similar near miracles by studying change and conflict in behavioural societal systems. However our present level of understanding of change in man and in his societies calls for humility, extensive co-operative efforts, and some patience. Increase in "empathy", a "scientific humanism", or the "the golden rule" of several universal religions, still appear to be the soundest very broad generalizations for guidance in an overcrowded world dedicated to societal change. Oversimplification and ambiguity may be advantageous in developing innovative ideas, but they lead to confusion, frustration, and conflict in evaluating and carrying out societal change.

John R. Gardner (1968) in "No easy victories" asks: "How can we preserve our aspirations (without which no social betterment is possible) and at the same time develop the toughness of mind and spirit to face the fact that there are no easy victories?"

References

H. Anschultz, "Prospects for the development of the psychocybernetics of intelligent behavior." *Proc. 1st Ann. Symp. Am. Soc. Cybernetics*, pp. 111–123' Spartan Books, Washington, D.C. (1968).

L. Bertalanffy, *General System Theory*. G. Braziller, New York (1968).

L. Brillouin, *Scientific Uncertainty and Information*. Academic Press, New York (1964).

Sir J. Eccles, *Seminar, N.U. Soc. for Comparative Studies* (1969).

A. Etzioni, "Some dangers in 'valid' social measurement." *Ann. Am. Acad. Political Social Sci.*, **323**, 1–15 (1967).

J. D. Fast, *Entropy (The Significance of the Concept of Antropy and its Applications in Science and Technology)*. McGraw-Hill, New York (1962).

J. Galtung, "Entropy and the general theory of peace." *Proc. Intern. Peace Research Assoc.*, *2nd Conf*. Van Gorcum, Assen (1968).

J. W. Gardner, "No easy victories." Editorial. *Science*, **162**, 3851 (1968).

E. T. Jaynes, "Information theory and statistical mechanics. I." *Phys. Rev.*, **106**, No. 4, 620–30 (1957).

E. T. Jaynes, "Principles of statistical mechanics—the information theory approach." Book review. *I.E.E.E. (Inst. Elec. Electron. Engrs.), Trans. Inform. Theory*, 611 (1968).

J. de Jong, *Dimensional Analysis for Economists*. North-Holland, Amsterdam (1967).

A. I. Khinchin, *Mathematical Foundations of Information Theory*. Dover Publications, New York (1947).

T. S. Kuhn, *The Structure of Scientific Revolutions*. University of Chicago Press, Chicago. (1962).

G. G. Lamb, "Engineering concepts and the behavioral sciences." *Gen. Systems Res.*, **13**, 165–9 (1968).

G. G. Lamb, "A framework for analysis of societal change: basic pre-suppositions." *4th Interam. Congr. Chem. Engrs., Buenos Aires, Argentina* (1969).

R. M. MacIver, "Politics and society." *Saturday Rev.* (Ed. D. Spitz), May, p. 26 (1969).

C. Menger, *Problems of Economics and Sociology* (Transl.). University of Illinois, Urbana (1963).

L. E. Moses, *et al.*, "Scaling data on inter-nation Action." *Science*, **156**, No. 3778, 1054–9 (1967).

G. A. Pask, "The cybernetics of evolutionary processes and of self-organizing systems." *Proc. 3rd Intern. Congr. Cybernetics, Namur, 1961*, p. 27 (1965).

J. R. Platt, "Strong inference". *Science*, **146**, No. 3642, 347–53 (1964).

J. Polonsky, "La cellule vue comme un système cybernétique naturel à la lumière des récents progress enregistrés en électronique quantique". *Proc. 3rd Intern. Congr. on Cybernetics, Namur, 1961*, p. 684 (1965).

K. Popper, *The Logic of Scientific Discovery*. Basic Books, New York (1959).

E. S. Quade and W. I. Boucher, (eds.), *Systems Analysis and Policy Planning*, Elsevier, London (1968).

C. E. Shannon and W. Weaver, *The Mathematical Theory of Communication*. University of Illinois Press, Urbana (1949).

M. Soukup, "Toward a general social systems theory of dependence: introduction of entropy of behavior". *Proc. Intern. Peace Res. Assoc. 2nd Congr.*, Vol.1, *Studies in Conflicts*. Van Gorcum. Assen (1968).

S.S. Stevens, "Measurement, statistics, and the schemapiric view". *Science*, **161**, No.3844, 849 (1968).

R.C. Tolman, *Principles of Statistical Mechanics*. California Institute of Technology Press, Pasadena (1938).

M. Tribus, *et al.* "Why thermodynamics is a logical consequence of information theory". *Am. Inst. Chem. Engrs. J.*, 245–8 (1966).

H.S. Upshaw, "Attitude measurement". In *Methodology in Social Research* (Ed. Blalock). McGraw-Hill, New York, pp.60–111 (1968).

M.W. Wartofsky, *Conceptual Foundations of Scientific Thought*. MacMillan, New York (1968).

W. Weaver, *The Mathematical Theory of Communication*. University of Illinois Press, Urbana, pp.95–117 (1949).

N. Wiener, *The Human Use of Human Beings*. Doubleday, New York (1954).

On random decision processes with complete connections

M. MALITZA

University of Bucarest, Rumania

and C. ZIDĂROIU

Centre of Statistics
Rumanian Academy of Sciences, Rumania

Summary

Since about 1960 there has been a great deal of interest in the class of stochastic sequential decision problems in which the stochastic element is Markovian. The purpose of this paper is to introduce the concept of random decision processes with complete connections, which are a generalization of Markov decision processes and to indicate the results which have been obtained in this domain. The significance of this generalization is relevant in the applications to the social and economic sciences because in these fields the phenomena and the processes have a great complexity.

INTRODUCTION

The notion of chain with complete connections has been introduced in probability theory by Onicescu and Mihoc[8]. These authors have set themselves the aim to define a very broad type of dependence wich takes into account the whole history of the evolution and thus including as a special case the Markovian one. Important contributions to the theory of chains with complete connections are due to Doeblin and Fortet and refer to the period 1937–1940. Other Rumanian researchers have systematically used methods of functional analysis in the development of this theory. The theory of chain with complete connections, which remains a Rumanian creation, can be applied to the mathematical learning theory[5].

The purpose of this paper is to introduce the concept of random decisions processes with complete connections.

DEFINITIONS

Let us consider a set T, where T is either Z or N. Further, let (X, x), (W, ω), (D, d) be three measurable spaces, $\{u_t (.; .; .)\}_{t \in T}$ a family of mappings of $W \times D \times X$ into W and $\{{}^t P (.; .; .)\}_{t \in T}$ a family of real-valued functions on $\omega \times d \times x$ such that

$$(i) \ \{(w, d^{(n)}; x^{(n)}) : u_t (w; d^{(n)}; x^{(n)}) \in B\} \in W \times D^{(n)} x \times {}^{(n)}$$

for any $t \in T$, $n \in N^*$ and $B \in w$, where

$$u_t (.; d^{(n)}; x^{(n)}) = u_{t+n-1} (.; d_n; x_n) \circ \cdots \circ u_t (.; d_1; x_1)$$

$$\text{for} \quad x^{(n)} = (x_1, \ldots, x_n) \in X^{(n)} \quad \text{and} \quad d^{(n)} = (d_1, \ldots, d_n) \in D^{(n)}.$$

(ii) ${}^t P (.; .; .)$ is a transition probability function from $(W \times D, \omega \times d)$ to (X, x) for every $t \in T$.

Definition 1. A system $\{(W, \omega), (D, d), (X, x), u_t, {}^t P\}$ of measurable spaces, mappings and transition probability functions satisfying (i) and (ii) is a random decision system with complete connections.

Definition 2. A random decision system with complete connections

$$\{(W, \omega), (D, d), (X, x), (u_t)_{t \in T}, ({}^t P)_{t \in T}\}$$

is called *homogenous* if the mappings u_t and the probability transition functions ${}^t P$ do not depend on $t \in T$, that is

$$u_t (.; .; .) = u (.; .; .); \ {}^t P (.; .; .) = P (.; .; .)$$

A homogenous random decision system with complete connections will be denoted $\{(W, \omega), (D, d), (X, x), u, P\}$.

AN EXISTENCE THEOREM

We have the following existence theorem:

Theorem 1. If $T = N$, for a given random decision system with complete connections, a given $w \in W$ and a given sequence $d = (d_1, d_2, \ldots)$ where

$d_n \in D$ for every $n \in N$ there exist a probability space (Ω, K, P_w^d) and a sequence of random variables $(\xi_n)_{n \in N^*}$ defined on Ω and with values in X such that

$$P_w^d (\xi_1 \in A) = {}^0P (w; d_1; A)$$

$$P_w^d (\xi_{n+1} \in A \,|\, \xi_j, 1 \leqslant j \leqslant n) = {}^nP(u_0 (w; d^{(n)}; \xi^{(n)}); d_{n+1}; A) \, P_w^d - a \cdot s$$

for any $n \in N^*$, $A \in x$, where $\xi^{(n)} = (\xi_1, \ldots, \xi^n)$ and $d^{(n)} = (d_1, \ldots, d_n)$.

Proof. We take $\Omega = X^{N^*}$ and we set

$$\xi_n(\omega) = x_n, \qquad n \in N^*$$

if

$$\omega = (x_n)_{n \in N^*}$$

We put for any $n > 1$

$$P_w^d (\xi_1 \in A_1, \ldots, \xi_n \in A_n)$$

$$= \int_{A_1} {}^0P (w; d_1; dx_1) \int_{A_2} {}^1P (u_0 (w; d_1; x_1); d_2; dx_2)$$

$$\cdots \int_{A_n} {}^{n-1}P (u_0 (w, d^{(n-1)}, x^{(n-1)}), d_n, dx_n)$$

and

$$P_w^d (\xi_1 \in A_1) = {}^0P (w; d_1; A_1)$$

where $A_1, \ldots, A_n \in x$. According to a well-known theorem (see [6]) there will be a probability P_w^d on $\mathcal{K} = \mathcal{X}^{N^*}$ satisfying the desired relations. An analogous proof may be given in the case $T = Z$.

THE ASSOCIATED MARKOV DECISION SYSTEM

Let us consider the sequence of random variables $(\xi_n)_{n \in N^*}$ on the probability space (Ω, K, P_w^d) constructed as in the previous theorem.

Let $(\zeta_n^w)_{n \in N^*}$ be a sequence of W-valued random variables defined on the probability space (Ω, K, P_w^d) by

$$\zeta_n^w = u_0 (w; d^{(n)}; \xi^{(n)}), n \in N^*.$$

where w is a fixed point in W. We have

$$P_w^d (\zeta_1^w \in B) = {}^0P (w; d_1; {}^0B_w(d_1)),$$

$$P_w^d (\zeta_{n+1}^w \in B\zeta_j^w, 1 \leqslant j \leqslant n) = P_w^d (\zeta_{n+1}^w \in B|\zeta_n^w)$$

$$= {}^nP (\zeta_n^w; d_{n+1}, {}^nB_{\zeta_n^w} (d_{n+1})), n \in N^*$$

where

$$^tB_w(d) = \{x : u_t (w; d; x) \in B\}$$

for $B \in \omega$, $d \in D$, $w \in W$ and $t \in T$. Let us set

$$^tQ (w; d; B) = {}^tP (w; d; {}^tB_w(d))$$

It is easy to see that for any $t \in T$ and $d \in D$, $^tQ (w; d; B)$ is a transition probability function from (W, ω) to itself. Therefore we have Theorem 2.

Theorem 2. The sequence $(\zeta_n^w)_{n \in N^*}$ of random variables defined on (Ω, K, P_w^d) is a simple Markov chain with state space (W, ω), transition probability functions $(^tQ)_{t \in T}$ and initial probability distribution concentrated at w.

Proof. Obvious.

The following may be given.

Definition 3. The system $\{(W, w), (D, d), (^tQ)_{t \in T}\}$ is the associated Markov decision system of the random decision system with complete connections $\{(X, x); (D, \mathscr{d}); (W, \omega), u_t, {}^tP\}$.

From definition 2 it follows that the associated Markov decision system of a homogeneous random decision system with complete connection reduces to $\{(W, \omega), Q\}$, where the transition probability function Q is defined by

$$Q (w; d; B) = P (w; d; B_w(d))$$

with

$$B_w(d) = \{x : u (w; d; x) \in B\}$$

THE ASSOCIATED OPERATORS

Let $B (W, \omega)$ be the Banach space of all real-valued bounded and w-measurable functions defined on W with the uniform norm

$$\|g\| = \sup_{w \in W} (g(w))$$

For any $t \in T$ and $d \in D$ we define on the Banach space $B (W, \omega)$ the linear operator

$$(^tU(d) g) (w) = \int_X {}^tP (w; d; dx) g [u_t (w; d; x)]$$

For any $n \in N^*$ let us set

$$^tU^n = {}^{t+n-1}U_0 \cdots {}_0 {}^tU$$

Let us remark that for every $B \in w$

$$({}^t U(d)) \chi_\beta (w) = \int_X {}^t P (w; d; dx) \chi_B [u_t (w; d; x)] = {}^t P (w; d; {}^t B_w(d))$$

$$= {}^t Q (w; d; B)$$

It follows that

$$({}^t U(d) g) (w) = \int_W {}^t Q (w; d; dw') g (w')$$

DECISIONS AND STRATEGIES

Definition 4. A *decision function* $\delta(w)$ is a w-measurable mapping from the measurable space (W, w) to (D, d) which takes its values in a given space $D(w) \subset D$.

Definition 5. A N-strategy δ is a choice of N decision functions

$$\delta = \{\delta_0(\cdot), \ldots, \delta_{N-1}(.)\}$$

where $\delta_i(w) \in D_i(w) \subset D$, $0 \leqslant i \leqslant N - 1$, with given $D_i(w)$

Definition 6. A strategy δ is a sequence of decision functions

$$\delta = \{\delta_0(\cdot), \delta_1(\cdot), \ldots\}$$

where $\delta_i(w) \in D_i(w) \subset D$, $i \geqslant 0$, with given $D_i(w)$.

For any $w_0 \in W$ we associate to any N-strategy δ a "gain"

$$C_0^\delta(w_0) = [U^N(\delta) g] (w_0) = U (\delta_{N-1}(\zeta_N^{w_0})) \circ \cdots \circ (U (\delta_0(\zeta_1^{w_0})) g (w_0)$$

where

$$\zeta_n^{w_0} = \begin{cases} w_0 & \text{for } n = 1 \\ u (w_0, \delta_{n-2} (\lambda \zeta_{n-1}^{w_0}); \xi_{n-1}) & \text{for } n \geqslant 2 \end{cases}$$

Definition 7. A strategy δ is called admissible if the following conditions are valid.

(i) We have $\delta_i(w) \in D_i(w) \subset D$ for any $1 \leqslant i \leqslant N$ and $w \in W$, where $D_i(w) \subset D$ are given spaces. These spaces may be find in every concrete problem.

(ii) There exist the limit

$$C_n^\delta(w) = \lim_{N \to \infty} [U_n^N(\delta) g] (w)$$

for any $n \in N^*$ and $w \in W$, where

$$[U_n^N(\delta) \, g] \, (w_0) = U \left(\delta_{N-1} \left(\zeta_{N-n+1}^{w_0}\right)\right) \circ \cdots \circ U \left(\delta_n \left(\zeta_1^{w_0}\right) g\right) (w_0)$$

(iii) We have

$$C_n^\delta(w) = (U \left(\delta_n(w)\right) C_{n+1}^\delta) \, (w)$$

for every $n \in N^*$ and $w \in W$.

We denote by Δ the set of all admissible strategies.

Definition 8. A strategy $\tilde{\delta} \in \Delta$ is an optimal strategy if we have for any $w \in W$

$$C_0^{\tilde{\delta}}(w) = C_0(w)$$

where

$$C_0(w) = \sup_{\delta \in \Delta} C_0^\delta(w)$$

is a "maximum gain".

Definition 9. A strategy $\tilde{\delta}_\varepsilon \in \Delta$ is an ε-optimal strategy if we have for any $w \in W$

$$C_0^{\tilde{\delta}_\varepsilon}(w) \geqslant C_0(w) - \varepsilon, \, w \in W$$

Definition 10. A strategy $\delta_\varepsilon \in \Delta$ is uniform ε-optimal if

$$C_n^{\tilde{\delta}_\varepsilon}(w) \geqslant C_n(w) - \varepsilon$$

uniformly with respect to n and w $(0 \leqslant n \leqslant N < \infty)$, where

$$C_n(w) = \sup_{\delta \in \Delta} C_n^\delta(w)$$

We have the following theorem

Theorem 3. If there exist an uniform ε-optimal strategy for every $\varepsilon > 0$ then we have for any $0 \leqslant n \leqslant N - 1$

$$C_n(w) = \sup_{d \in D_n(w)} (U(d)) \, C_{n+1}(w)$$

and

$$C_N(w) = g(w)$$

Proof. Let us consider a strategy $\delta \in \Delta$ such that $\delta_n(w) = d$. Therefore, we have

$$C_n^\delta(w) = [U \left(\delta_n(w)\right)] \, C_{n+1}^\delta(w) \leq [U(d)] \, C_{n+1}(w) \leq \sup_{d \in D_n(w)} [U(d)] \, C_{n+1}(w)$$

It follows that

$$C_n(w) - \varepsilon \leq C_n^{\tilde{\delta}_\varepsilon}(w) \leq \sup_{d \in D_n(w)} [U(d)] \, C_{n+1}(w)$$

Therefore

$$C_n(w) \leq \sup_{d \in D_n(w)} [U(d)] \, C_{n+1}(w)$$

In an analogous way it is possible to obtain the relation

$$C_n(w) \geq \sup_{d \in D_n(w)} [U(d)] \, C_{n+1}(w)$$

These relations prove the theorem.

References

1. Derman, C., On sequential decisions and Markov chains, *Man. Sci.*, **9** (1962), 16–24.
2. Derman, C., Markovian sequential control processes, Denumerable State Space, *J. Math. Anal. Appl.* **10** (1965), 295–302.
3. Dreyfus, S.E., Some types of optimal control of stochastic systems, *J. SIAM Control*, Sér. **A, 2, 1** (1964), 120–134.
4. Fleming, W.H., "Some Markovian optimization problems", *J. Math. and Mech.*, **12, 1** (1963), 131–140.
5. Iosifescu, M., Theodorescu, R., Random processes and learning, Springer, Berlin-Heidelberg-New York, 1969.
6. Loève, M., *Probability Theory*, D. Van Nostrand Co. Inc., New York 1960.
7. Maitra, A., *Dynamic Programming for Countable Aaction Spaces* (preliminary report), AMS, 36, 2 (1965), 735.
8. Onicescu, O., Mihoc, G., Sur les chaînes statistiques, *C.R. Acad. Sci. Paris*, **200**, 511–512.

The importance of a cybernetic approach to the study of the natural languages

F. VANDAMME

University of Ghent, Belgium

Summary

In the simulation process of some aspects of the natural language, we begin from the idea that language is a specific kind of a communication system. In making theories about this system, we are obliged to start from data in connection with the effective use of this communication system. However, the appearance of disturbances may deform the ideal activities of the communication system. We can bring the competent language users into an ideal position, having minimal disturbance, to determine an approximation of their ideal speech production and speech recognition. Taking this into account we can make hypotheses about their recognition-and-production-competence-system. By simulation of this recognition-and-production competence, we found that both subsystems possess widely divergent characteristics; this strengthens the hypothesis of those linguists and psychologists who assert that recognition-and-production system are two independent subcomponents of the communication system which the language is. However, it is clear that these subcomponents are not without feedbacks with each other. This conclusion can also be taken as an important argument against them (i.e. Chomsky), who are trying to describe the language system as a competence which would bridge both competences; this is not necessary if, indeed, possible.

INTRODUCTION

For several years now we have been trying to shed some light on some aspects of the natural language by simulating them in a computer[1-4]. The main reason for this is that we believe that by simulating it is possible to construct a theory more exactly and also that the process of simulation itself is heuristically very important. We hope this paper will confirm this claim.

Before coming to the actual subject of this paper, it seems to us also worth while to say a few words here about the relation between the study of language and the social sciences. Edwin R. A. Seligman defines the social sciences as[5]: "Those mental or cultural sciences which deal with the activities of the individual as member of a group." Nevertheless further on, he does not classify linguistics under the social sciences, nor under the semi-social sciences, but unter the sciences with social implications. This is–in our opinion— a mistake. Linguistics is not only a science with social implications, but it even belongs to the social sciences. The kind of arguments to confirm this is sketched in the following quotation from Colin Cherry's article[6]: "But there is nothing I have, is essential to me": "Language is conventionally regarded by many people as the corpus of utterances of individual persons. This view seems to me to overlook the fundamental truth, which is that language is not spoken *by* a person; it is essentially spoken *between* persons. The conversation or dialogue is the atom of language, the smallest unit. Of course we can soliloquize or speak to ourself, but only after we have evolved our language through relations with our mother in childhood, through friends and all our social relationships..."

One can doubt if the dialogue is really the minimal unit. However, even in a more restricted point of view, viz. if one considers as the minimal linguistic unit the output of the emitter, directed to the receiver(s), then too *one has an activity of an individual (the emitter), directed to (an)other individual(s) (receiver(s))*. The formal characteristics of the output are deeply influenced by the expectations about the receiver's decoding-system, as will be shown later on. In some special cases, it is certainly true that the receiver can be identical with the emitter. This does not lessen the essential social characteristic of the minimal unit. Another argument is also that the linguist does not intend to describe the competences (viz. the ideal encoding and decoding-system) of a certain individual, but of a group. In other words, not the communication system of an individual (idiolect), but the general communication system of a group is aimed at.

An analogous point of view was taken by R. Jakobson[7] in his "The Saussurian course and linguistic vistas of today".

CYBERNETICS AND LANGUAGE COMPETENCE

The Notion "Competence"

Strongly simplified, one can model the communication process as follows. There is an emitter Z. The emitter emits its message through a channel K. In order to be able to emit its message, the emitter encodes its message by means of a certain code. Subsequently, the encoded message is brought through the channel K with or without noise. Then it is received by the receiver 0. The receiver 0 will decode the received message.

L. Apostel[8], taking into account this model, argues that in the process of making hypotheses about the communication system which is the language, one has to start from the effective use of the codes and on the basis of it to infer the code of the encoder and of the decoder. Of course, here the problem arises that more or less accidental factors and disturbances can interfere with ideal, careful use of the codes. So do for instance, the diversion of the attention, the limitations of the memory, etc. That the memory limitations have an important influence on the use of the codes (on the decoding and the encoding system) can be seen by the fact that by giving the emitter or the receiver a bigger memory, i.e. by permitting them to use a pencil and a notebook, they can encode or decode longer and more complex sentences. By bringing "language users" in an ideal environment with as few as possible disturbances and diversions, it will be possible to approach the ideal codes better.

Abstraction can be made of the impact of the limitation of the memory on the use of the codes, by hypothesizing that some principles may be infinitely applied in the ideal decoding and encoding system. However, such an hypothesis may only be made (a) if can be proved that the factual limitation in the application of the principle can be explained by factors which are external to the encoding and decoding system (i.e. characteristics of memory) and (b) if variations of these external characteristics imply a variation in the factual use of the decoding and encoding system. For, in this case it is more economical to hypothesize a principle that can be applied infinitely, than a plurality of systems, or a system quickly changing under these external characteristics.

The decoding or encoding system with abstraction made of the above-mentioned interfering elements—this does not imply that abstraction is made of memory as such, however, from the limitations of the memory—is called the decoding and encoding competence.

Feedback Relation Between the Encoding and the Decoding System?

It seems to us that the important cybernetic notion "feedback" plays an outstanding role in the relation between encoding- and decoding competence systems.

First of all it is obvious that between both competences such an interrelation must exist, so that most of what can be produced must admit for decoding and vice versa (see Figure 1).

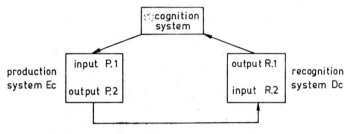

FIGURE 1   Recoding and encoding competences

In other words, the input P.1 of the production competence system Ec is mostly identical with the output R.1 of the recognition system Dc, after that the output P.2 which corresponds to P.1 is received as input R.2 and has been handled by Dc and vice versa. However, this is a too strong requirement. It seems to us more correct to require that, generally, there must be at least one R.1 which is identical with P.1, when P.2 is received as input R.2 and vice versa, the reason being that R.2 can be ambiguous.

We also think it obvious that this correspondence is only normally the case. For, it is a well-known phenomenon that the child who learns his first language, and an adult who is learning a foreign language, are sometimes able to understand sentences which they are not able to produce[9].* (Is the opposite also true?)

One can even ask, if sometimes the experience of some people which argue that they are not able to express what they intend to express, cannot be explained by the non-adaptation between the production and the recognition competence system of this people, viz. that in Figure 1: P.1 ≠ R.1.

---

* Also Chomsky argues that a child, producing speech in a "telegraphic style" can be shown to have an underlying fuller conception of sentence structure (unrealised in his speech, but actively involved in comprehension) as misplacement of the elements, he does not produce, leads to difficulties of comprehension, etc.

Chomsky explains the correspondence between the decoding competence (Dc) and the encoding competence (Ec) by introducing an overarching system. This is certainly not the only possible solution. We have already discussed a few alternatives in our review of Dik's work *Coordination*[10]. For instance, a rather trivial alternative would be to hypothesize Dc and Ec innate with such characteristics that they are adapted to each other.

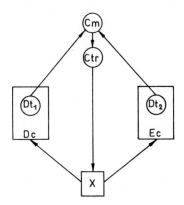

FIGURE 2   Complete negative feedback relation. Dc: decoding competence system. Ec: encoding competence system. Dt: detector. Cm: comparator. Ctr: control. x: general cognitive operation unit

A more interesting alternative, that we propose to discuss here is a solution, which does not make a call on specific innate language characteristics. It is a solution by introducing a complex negative feedback relation between Dc and Ec. In Figure 2 one sees a rough sketch of the proposed approach.

If a change occurs in system Dc and if the change in Dc causes a disjointing of correspondence between Dc and Ec, then a corresponding change in Ec must be made. The reverse is of course also true. Therefore every change in Dc and Ec is detected by the respective detectors Dt_1 and Dt_2. If a detector detects a change, then this change is investigated in the comparator, in view of the norm, viz. the correspondence between Dc and Ec. This investigation can, in principle be reduced to the investigation if the condition (a) or/and (b) is fulfilled. (a) The input P.1 of the production system Ec is identical—or at least that there is one output R.1 which is identical with input P.1. This, in the case where R.2 is ambiguous—with the output R.1 of the recognition system Dc, after that the output P.2, which corresponds to P.1, is received as input R.2 and has been handled by Dc. (b) There is at least (at least one, in case P. 1 can have several encodings by Ec) one output P. 2 which is identical with R. 2, when R. 1 which corresponds to R. 2 is introduced in Ec as P. 1. Of course, in this investigation a certain strategy must be followed. For, the sets of the possible inputs and outputs are infinite sets. Therefore, this investigation may be—and even must be, if one wants to make the task of the comparator efficiently handled—limited to the investigation (in view of the correspondence between Dc and Ec) of the output of Dc and Ec on the handling of which the change(s)—over a certain delay, i.e. since the last state of adaptation—in the system has a certain influence.

Perhaps this is also too big a task so that even here it will be necessary to use samples. If then a certain inadaptation between Dc and Ec is observed and if this inadaptation exceeds certain limits—perhaps this limit is different from person to person—then the Ctr (control unit) has to set in action the unit X. The control unit can maybe also set in action the unit X under external influence, viz. corrections made by the persons in his environment. This can also explain the evolution in Dc and Ec beyond the adaptation* between Dc and Ec.

The unit X is a general cognitive operation unit. This unit has here the duty to adapt Ec or Dc. For instance in case it adapts Ec, then it must do it taking into account (1) the changes in Dc, (2) the actual characteristics and the peculiar task of Ec, (3) the data given by Cm of inadaptation between Dc and Ec, and (4) the correction it observes, made by the people in his environment. The unit X makes on this basis a hypothesis for the adaptation of Ec (or respectively Dc) and on the basis of this hypothesis it changes Ec, viz. makes a few operations on Ec. So we get a change of Ec. This change is detected by Dt_2 and is communicated to Cm. The result of this investigation is again communicated to Ctr and if the adaptation is not sufficient, then the unit X is set in action again. This goes on till Dc and Ec are again sufficiently adapted to each other.

It seems interesting to me to introduce here a certain complication. If there occurs, for instance, a change Y_i in Dc and an inadaptation of Dc and Ec is a result of this change, then Dc, or Ec, or both can be changed so that a new equilibrium is reached. For instance, trivially the change Y_i can be deleted. As a consequence the system X has to make an evaluation of the observed change and on the basis of the result of this evaluation, it has to

---

* We became aware of this possibility in a discussion with L. Apostel, Parmentier, and M. De Mey in the work laboratory Communication and Cognition, at the State University of Ghent.

make an adaptation. A change which brings more generality, which permits the extention of communication or which is strongly awarded by the environment (in other words, evaluation on external or internal grounds) can be evaluated positively and therefore be conserved.

Perhaps the power of this approach will be seen more vividly in the following example.

There is some evidence in the common observation, that children understand the use of auxiliaries even when they do not produce them[11]. In other words, the auxiliary can already be incorporated in the decoding system, while it is still omitted in the output of the production. So the child will understand the sequence (1), but produces (2). Only later on the child* will produce (3).

(1) Who is that?
(2) Who 'at?
(3) Who is 'at?

Let us for the sake of simplicity hypothesize from the decoding point of view† the program II of "to be" as follows:

to be II:

$$X \sqcap Y$$
$$X = 1P \cdot N \cdot \text{be}$$
$$Y = 1S \cdot (Nv \ \text{Pron}) \cdot \text{be}$$

The significata structure of (1) will therefore be (4). "$\sqcap$" is a symbol for a property-assignment operation.‡

$$[\text{Who}] \sqcap [\text{that}] \tag{4}$$

---

* This is also clearly seen in the transcribed record of the Brown material. We are very thankful to R. Brown for having sent us this material.

† There is some evidence to identify the relation program II of "to be" with the one of the verbs in general, with this difference that in "$X \sqcap Z/Y$" (a part of the relation program II of the verb), $Z = \emptyset$ (see Vandamme[1]).

‡ Of course, "who" can further be analysed as

$$[\text{someone} \sqcap \ ?].$$

When considering the auxiliary as a verb with $Z = \emptyset$ (see footnote †), then one can explain the difficulties of the child to introduce the auxiliary in its output of the decoding system as follows. Z is always encoded by some words. However, when $Z = \emptyset$, then it can be an easy at hand solution to encode Z (a significatum $= \emptyset$) by an $\emptyset$-word category. This phenomenon can be strengthened by the fact that the child perhaps encodes Z by the verb and not "$\sqcap Z/$". Thus he considers "$\sqcap$ -/" as redundant. In this case, it is clear that, if $Z = \emptyset$, it is entirely superfluous to use a verb to express the $\emptyset$ significatum.

The child will encode (4) as (2). In order to be able to do that, (5) must be a possible sentence structure.

$$N_{(T)} \oplus \text{Pron}_{(K)} \tag{5}$$

Here T means to be the left argument of the operator "m" in the significata structure and K the right argument.

There will clearly be a certain inadaptation between the Dc and the Ec of the child, for Ec cannot produce (1), which can be decoded, and perhaps even (5), an output of Ec, cannot be decoded by Dc. The unit X, which is put in action, can for instance by "trial and error" or by comparison of the received corrections, with (2) and the analogous examples, introduce a new element. So it can, i.e. construct the structure (6). When the equilibrium be-

$$\text{aux} \oplus N_{(T)} \oplus \text{Pron}_{(K)} \tag{6}$$

tween Dc and Ec is not yet reached, then another modification in the structure can be made up to the point[13] that the structure (7) is reached

$$N_{(T)} \oplus \text{aux} \oplus \text{Pron}_{(K)} \tag{7}$$

CONCLUSION

The introduction in linguistics of (a) operations on programs—a concept which is already in many disciplines a common place—and of (b) negative feedback between the linguistic subcomponents, opens new perspectives in the study of language. The introduction of negative feedback even permits us to explain the data, i.e. that the decoding[12] capabilities of a person can be seriously damaged, while his encoding capabilities are in tact or vice versa—which indicate that language is composed of two relatively independent subcomponents, viz. the decoding and encoding systems.

Besides this, the introduction of the negative feedback is important on grounds that it indicates a way to guarantee the necessary adaptation between the decoding and the encoding system in a more economical way than the one which introduces (a) an overarching competence and (b) algorithms to get the encoding and the decoding systems from it.

Also a new look on the study of the ontogenesis of language is in this approach possible. For, the germs of a new approach to this problem—without postulating innate linguistic characteristics–appear.

References

1. F. Vandamme, "Partial simulation of some aspects of natural language", to be published.
2. F. Vandamme, "Sketch of a partial simulation of the concept of meaning in an automaton", *Logique et Analyse*, **9**, 372–87 (1966).
3. F. Vandamme, "Esquisse d'un essai de simulation de langage dans un automate en vue d'éclairer la notion 'signification'", *Le Langage*, La Baconnière, — (1966), pp. 223-226.
4. F. Vandamme, "Schets voor een gedeeltelijke simulatie van het betekenisbegrip in een automaton (Sketch of a partial simulation of the concept 'meaning' in an automaton)", *M. A. Thesis, State University of Ghent* (1966), pp. 251.
5. L. Sills, D. "Introduction", *International Encyclopedia of the Social Sciences*, Vol. 1, The McMillan Company, the Free Press, — (1968), p. XXI.
6. C. Cherry, "But there is nothing I have, is essential to me", *To Honor Roman Jakobson, Janua Linguarum*, Series Maior XXXI, Mouton, The Hague (1967).
7. R. Jakobson, "The Saussurian course and linguistic vistas of today", *Harvard University, Cambridge, Mass.*, Spring term (1967).
8. L. Apostel, "Epistémologie de la linguistique", *Encyclopédie de la Pléiade*, Sciences Humaines, Gallimard, Paris (1967), p. 1051.
9. N. Chomsky, "Formal discussion", in *The Acquisition of Language*, Vol. 29 (Eds. U. Bellugi and R. Brown), Monographs of the S.R.C.D., (1964), No. 1.
10. F. Vandamme, "Review of S. C. Dik's *Coordination*", *Commun. en Cognitie, State Univ. of Ghent*, **4**, 30–5 (1969).
11. "Open discussion", in *The Acquisition of Language*, Vol. 29 (Eds. U. Bellugi and R. Brown), Monographs of the S.R.C.D., (1964), No. 1.
12. R. Jakobson, "The role of phonic elements in speech perception", *18th Intern. Congr. Psychol., Symp. 23; Models of Speech Perception*, Preprint, Salk Institute for Biological Studies, San Diego, California (1966), pp. 12.

Towards a syntax-monitored semantic pattern recognition*

LUCIO CHIARAVIGLIO
and JAMES GOUGH, JR.

Georgia Institute of Technology, U.S.A.

Summary

The use of natural language as a facility in any system presupposes a knowledge of how natural language is understood. An attempt is made here to develop initially that semantics that is syntax-based (code-induced) through an algebra of ostension and thereby to monitor the cross-reference, the structure and the quantification of English noun phrases. An ostension is taken here as a *this* relation that relates the domain of interpretation of a language into expressions of the language which correspond to *this* quanta. Thus, for example, the expression "this runs" is taken as the value of the ostension which points to the running object. The Boolean structure on the set of expressions induces a corresponding Boolean structure on the set of ostensions, from which the indefinite and definite articles, the quantifiers, and number can then be derived by transformation. Verbs and other linguistic facilities of predication are taken into account by constructing the product algebras of the algebra of elementary ostensions. The structure which ensues from these considerations is homologous, if not identical, to a functional polyadic algebra. An attempt is made to develop the *this* relation within a generative grammar.

* The work reported in the paper has been sponsored in part by the National Science Foundation Grant GN-655.

INTRODUCTION

Semantics is sometimes thought of in terms of dictionary or thesaurus structures. It is intuitively evident that language possesses syntactic devices for the construction of complex expressions from simpler components and that many of these devices are designed to produce expressions whose mode of meaning bears systematic relations to the mode of meaning of the components. We use these devices because the constructions they afford are functionally related to constant and non-zero semantic transformations. Thus language may outrun any practical thesaurus or dictionary as the sole descriptor of its semantics. We normally make use of the semantics induced by the syntax in order to encode, decode, store, and retrieve language.

We wish to characterize systematically some syntactic devices for the English noun phrase which induce semantic transformations that can be identified and hopefully measured. Our program may be illustrated by means of a simple example which involves the semantics of reference and a transformation of the mode of reference.

Common nouns may be said to refer multiply or to have multiple reference (Geach, 1962; Hiz, 1968; Linsky, 1967; Quine, 1960). Within grammar there are many devices that use common nouns to form noun phrases that have a singular reference. The prefixing of the demonstrative "this" is such a constructive device; it may be viewed as a noun-phrase-forming operator that maps a subset of common nouns into the set of singular definite noun phrases. A constant transformation of referential mode is associated with this mapping—a transformation carrying us from multiple to singular reference. This simple example suggests some of the sets and structures that may be needed for the analysis of the described situation.

Firstly, there is a set of nouns, usually common nouns, that may be organized by a thesaurus into a set of terms. The thesaurus may well reflect some grammatical structures of the language such as compound-noun formation through attributive, conjunctive, disjunctive, and negative juxtaposition, etc. The thesaurus will also reflect some of the facts of the literature for which it was constructed. Hopefully, the thesaurus will go a long way towards organizing the nouns and the compounds it countenances into referentially equivalent subclasses. Thus, ideally, the terms in the thesaurus share no members. It is usually true that the terms of the thesaurus will have the same modes of multiple reference as the nouns and compounds from which they were constructed.

Secondly, there is a set of entities that is the domain of interpretation of the nouns and compounds and consequently of the terms in the thesaurus. We may say that the domain of interpretation is the left field of the reference relation and the nouns and compounds are the right field. The reference relation is many-many. Through a thesaurus we may obtain reference functions. These functions map the domain of interpretation into the set of terms.

Thirdly, there is a set of noun-phrase-forming devices. Many of these devices are referentially transparent. That is, the noun phrases formed by them are referentially invariant with respect to the substitution of referentially equivalent nouns and compounds. Such devices may be thought of as operating on terms so as to produce classes of referentially equivalent noun phrases. We may call these classes "terms".

Let T be the set of terms obtained in the manner outlined. We assume that the set of nouns, compounds, and noun phrases is closed under conjunction, disjunction, and negation; hence, T is a Boolean algebra under the induced operators. This assumption appears to us to be harmless, and it has the merit of simplifying subsequent exposition. At the price of some detours, we could deal with partial algebras.

We shall also assume that the thesaurus does not contain relative terms. Relative terms bring with them a set of complications which we do not wish to deal with here in detail. We shall indicate at the end of our presentation how to do so.

There is another assumption that we need to make with respect to T which has more drastic consequences than the ones just mentioned. We shall assume that T contains monadic quasi-terms. Quasi-terms are obtained by juxtaposing proper nouns to non-relative noun phrases and then considering the equivalence class of the resulting items. For example, consider the common noun "man" which belongs to some term in T. If we set in apposition to "man" a proper noun, say "Jones", we obtain "man Jones", which will be a member of some quasi-term. Quasi-terms will be thought of as equivalence classes of non-relative noun phrases with proper nouns in apposition. If the two component phrases and the two proper nouns of two such appositional complexes are equivalent, then the complexes are to be counted as equivalent and thus belong to one quasi-term.

Constructions such as "man Jones" appear artificial, though they are reminiscent of vocative-case constructions. They occur rarely and in very limited contexts. Further, while "that man Jones", "the man Jones", etc., may satisfy our grammatical intuitions, the phrases "that table Jones", "the man New York" undeniably run counter to them. It might be said that many of these constructions are felt as ungrammatical because the term co-occurring with the proper noun cannot be truly said of the object named by the proper noun. However, this explanation does not account for the seeming grammatical oddity of "man Jones" occurring without prefixed demonstratives, articles and the like. We might sweep aside the whole matter by baptizing quasi-terms with the respectable title of deep structure. We shall also suppose that we are not limited to proper nouns that may in fact occur in a thesaurus. We shall introduce dummy proper nouns as needed for the construction of quasi-terms. The only feature of the set of proper nouns that concerns us is the cardinality of this set.

If T is the set of terms and quasi-terms and X is a domain of interpretation of T, then the set of all functions from X into T, T^X, is the set of all possible ways of assigning referents in X to terms in T. If T is a Boolean algebra, then T^X is also a Boolean algebra under the pointwise definition of the operators. We may now use this algebra and algebras that are constructed from it in order to study some noun-phrase-forming devices and their allied semantic transformations.

ENGLISH DEMONSTRATIVES AND ARTICLES

Demonstratives possess several features that mark them as relatively primitive substantival symbols of the English language. Firstly, demonstratives may be used as vehicles of immediate reference to extra-linguistic objects, as in ostension, without the co-occurrence of nouns. Secondly, demonstratives may be prefixed to nouns to form a noun phrase which references a single object within the multiple reference of the noun. Thirdly, the reference of such a noun phrase may be made precise by the iterated use of demonstratives, as in the case in attribution. Consider the following sequence of noun phrases.

$$\text{This} \tag{1}$$

$$\text{This table} \tag{2}$$

$$\text{This brown table} \tag{3}$$

$$\text{This large brown table} \tag{4}$$

This sequence may represent the utterances made during repeated point-ings to an object in the vicinity of the speaker which the hearer had some difficulty in finding. An ostension may thus be regarded as a way of assigning an object to a demonstrative-indexed noun phrase. If the first ostension fails to perform the assignment for the intended hearer, the speaker may try again with a different phrase. The process is repeated with noun phrases that are systematically related in such a way that succeeding phrases in the sequence have increasingly narrower possible assignments.

In (1), "this" occurs by itself and thus may be thought of as a universal selective index (Peirce, 1955; Burks, 1949). It is an index in the sense that in the ostension it is used to mark the object in question. And it is universal in the sense that, apart from the purely extralinguistic limitations of point-ing, every item in the domain X can be correctly assigned to "this" by some ostension. The phrases (2) to (4), on the other hand, are such that only items that fall within nested subsets of X can be correctly assigned to them. These phrases represent increasingly particular selective indexes (Peirce, 1955).

A *caveat* must be entered here. It is clear that the demonstrative "this" is not an absolutely universal selective index since it is not neutral with respect to proximity to the speaker and with respect to the singular–plural distinc-tion. In English, some such phrase as "this or that or these or those" would be a closer approximation to absolute universality.

We may equate the set of all ostensions in which "this" is emitted with a selective index function, *SI*, in T^X whose value is the quasi-term "this i" for every item i in X. If we are dealing with absolutely universal ostensions and we take the demonstrative "this" to be the universal selective index, then we may say that "this" is correctly applicable to every item in X. The dummy proper noun "i" is redundant in this case, and the corresponding universal selective index function USI in T^X has as a value the term "this" for every i in X.

Similarly, the set of all particular ostensions of tables may be equated with a particular selective index function, PSI, in T^X whose value is the quasi-term "this table i" for every i in X. Thus described, the function PSI mirrors both correct and incorrect ostensions. This is as it should be, since we wish to assess the semantics induced by the syntactical facility of juxtaposing de-monstratives to terms independently of the facts that might render a partic-ular use of the resulting term correct or incorrect.

This situation is analogous to the algebraic formulation of the logic of first-order quantification. We deal there with propositional functions whose domain is a set X, which may be thought of intuitively as the set of objects being talked about, and whose ranges are in a Boolean algebra of propositions. The propositions may be true or false, much in the same way as the quasi-terms that are the values of the functions we are considering may be the result of the correct or incorrect use of terms.

Of course, we may identify within T^X what it is to make a correct use of a term. We can in fact say "not this" while ostending. If "this" is again taken as the universal selective index, then the corresponding function to "not this" is $\overline{\text{USI}}$. Thus the set of all correct ostensions of tables will be a function in T^X such that its value for every i in X is USI (i) if i is a table and $\overline{\text{USI}}$ (i) otherwise.

Let us consider again the phrase "this large brown table". *Ex hypothesi* this phrase was uttered in a terminal ostension which occurred in a sequence of four. We may represent this fourfold indexing accomplished by repeated ostension as an ordered quadruplet. Such quadruplets are elements of the product algebra $(T^X)^4$, the Cartesian product of T^X four times with itself:

$$\langle \text{USI}, \text{PSI}_1, \text{PSI}_2, \text{PSI}_3 \rangle \tag{5}$$

Since we are dealing here with attributive juxtaposition, (5) is equivalent to

$$\text{USI} \wedge \text{PSI}_1 \wedge \text{PSI}_2 \wedge \text{PSI}_3 \tag{6}$$

The function which maps elements such as (5) of a product algebra into elements of T^X of the form of (6) is a projection defined for any element in a product algebra as the infinum of the members of the element. Such projections are the semantic counterpart of attributive juxtaposition.

Aside from the syntactical facility of juxtaposing adjectives as in attribution, there are many devices that lead to the construction of general terms that may be suffixed to demonstratives and articles to yield noun phrases. Composite general terms may be formed with the aid of relative terms which in their turn may be formed by substantives and prepositions. General terms may be formed also by means of adjectival, verbal, substantival, and clausal juxtaposition. All of these cases will eventually require an extended separate treatment in order to identify the mappings that correspond to the semantic transformations induced via the syntax.

It is nevertheless possible to achieve a first level of analysis by representing all such cases as ordered n-tuples of values of the appropriate selective index functions. We may, as a first approximation, weight the terms in a thesaurus by the addicity of the noun phrase in which they occur. That is, we can associate to each occurrence of a term in a noun phrase the number of selective index functions which must be used in order to obtain the reference of the noun phrase.

Let us now consider some other types of noun phrases.

An indefinite singular such as

$$\text{A table} \tag{7}$$

is a function from X into T that has the value of the function USI for some one i in a finite subset of X, the subset of tables, and elsewhere the value of $\overline{\text{USI}}$. Let K be the subset in question, then since the phrase is indefinite, the i in K for which the value of the function allied to "a table" is to be equal to USI (i) is left unspecified. This may be achieved by considering a Boolean function of the values of selective index functions as follows:

$$\bigvee_{i \in K} (\text{USI}\,(i) \wedge (\bigwedge_{j \in K - \{i\}} \overline{\text{USI}}\,(j))) \wedge (\bigwedge_{i \notin K} \overline{\text{USI}}\,(i)) \tag{8}$$

If we keep track of suffixed nouns and adjectives as in (5) and enter the operator $\dot{V}$ for the exclusive disjunction we have

$$\dot{\bigvee_{i \in K}} \langle \text{USI}\,(i), \text{PSI}_1\,(i), \text{PSI}_2\,(i), \text{PSI}_3\,(i) \rangle \tag{9}$$

which is the form which corresponds to an indefinite singular with two adjectives in attributive juxtaposition to a common noun. An indefinite noun phrase neutral to the singular–plural distinction corresponds to a function whose values are of the form of (8) where we substitute the non-exclusive operator for the exclusive one.

A definite singular noun phrase such as

$$\text{The table} \tag{10}$$

is a function from X into T that has the value of USI for one i in X and elsewhere the value of $\overline{\text{USI}}$.

$$\text{USI}\,(i) \wedge (\bigwedge_{j \neq i} \overline{\text{USI}}\,(j)) \tag{11}$$

Definite plural noun phrases are allied to semantic functions whose values are of the form

$$\bigwedge_{i \in K} \text{USI}\,(i) \wedge (\bigwedge_{j \notin K} \text{USI}\,(j)) \tag{12}$$

As before, we may mirror some of the complexities of the phrase by keeping track of suffixed adjectives and nouns.

$$\langle \text{USI}\,(i), \text{PSI}_1\,(i), \text{PSI}_2\,(i), \text{PSI}_3\,(i)\rangle \tag{13}$$

$$\bigwedge_{i\in K} \langle \text{USI}\,(i), \text{PSI}_1\,(i), \text{PSI}_2\,(i), \text{PSI}_3\,(i)\rangle \tag{14}$$

Lines (13) and (14) represent the definite singular and plural respectively. Line (13) can be obtained from (9) by a cancellation transformation.

The semantic functions of the indefinite, definite, plural, and singular noun phrases are obtained as functions whose values are Boolean functions of the values of selective index functions. All of these in turn may be obtained as Boolean functions of the universal selective index function. Thus, besides the mentioned measure of complexity, monitored by the number of selective index functions to be evaluated, we may attempt to weight the terms in a thesaurus by means of Boolean measures on a product algebra of T^X. It is of importance to the development of such measures to ascertain the place of the limiting adjectives, the quantifiers, in the semantics of noun phrases. We now turn to this topic.

THE QUANTIFIER "SOME"

In algebraic logic it is profitable to think of quantification in terms of propositional functions. As previously mentioned, these are functions whose domain is a set and whose values are propositions. Quantification may then be viewed as mappings which generally transform propositional functions of a number of variables into propositional functions of fewer variables. In particular, the binding of all the free variables of some formula is regarded as a transformation of an appropriate propositional function into a constant function.

Similar ideas may be exploited in the case of limiting adjectives and terms. To each *bona fide* general term t in T we have allied a quasi-term ti. We may remind ourselves again that we are only dealing with non-relative terms. Thus, to each general term we have allied a selective index function, SI_t, that maps X into T. For each i in X the value of SI_t is the quasi-term ti. Since t is a non-relative term we have allied to it a function of one variable SI_t. The prefixing of the limiting adjective "some" to t yielding the term *some t* should result in a mapping Q of the function SI_t into the constant function $Q\,(SI_t)$ whose value for each i in X is the *bona fide* term *some t*.

An intuitive feeling for what the function $Q(SI_t)$ is may be obtained by considering the conditions under which the term t is correctly applicable or is true of items in X. If there is one item i_0 in X of which t is true, then *some t* has a non-null reference. It is not to be counted as a term equivalent to the standard null reference term "this and not this". Of course, we may not conclude conversely that if *some t* has a non-null reference, then t is correctly applicable to i_0. In other words, $SI_t(i) \leqslant Q(SI_t)(i)$ for every i. If X is finite, then $Q(SI_t)(i) = some\ t$ may be simply taken as $\bigvee_{i \in X} SI_t(i) = \bigvee_{i \in X} ti$. The assumption of the finitude of X is too restrictive; nevertheless, this assumption points to an essential feature of "some". The term *some t* is the least upper bound in the Boolean algebra T of the quasi-terms of the form ti.

Thus, in order to obtain the mapping Q that transforms selective index functions into constant functions, we need to postulate that the least upper bound of the range of the selective index functions exists in T. If T^X meets these requirements, then for any term t and allied selective index function SI_t we can describe the semantic function allied to the term *some t* as a new function $Q(SI_t)$ defined on X whose value is the least upper bound of the range of SI_t. It is clear that this function meets the intuitive requirements described.

The Boolean algebra T^X would be a monadic Boolean algebra with operator Q if Q were defined on the full set of functions T^X. This is not the case, since it generally does not make sense to prefix the limiting adjective "some" to arbitrary terms. For example, "some this" is not recognizably English, nor does it make much intuitive sense. On the other hand, if we extended the definition of Q to the universal selective index function, then the term "some this" would make formal and linguistic sense since it would be the value of $Q(USI)$ for each i. The term "some this" would be equivalent to the term "this". Such definitely non-English and counter-intuitive extensions of the operator Q are of importance to the introduction of Boolean measures on T^X.

We have glossed over some features of the English limiting adjective "some" that should be noted. We have treated "some" as if it were neutral to the singular–plural distinction. This is clearly not the case, for when "some" governs plural terms it is to be understood in the sense of more than one and when "some" governs singular terms it may be often understood as at least and at most one. These complications may be treated within the framework outlined by distinguishing a number of different operators which are analogous to Q.

SIGNIFICANCE FOR GENERATIVE GRAMMAR

Linguistically our ultimate aim is to incorporate the above syntax-induced semantical programming into a generative grammar and thereby to begin to appreciate the creative nature of grammar (Chomsky, 1965; Gough and Chiaraviglio, 1969; McCawley, 1968). Linguistic creativity is thus viewed as initiated in the base grammar of a language. Linguistic symbolism presupposes symbolic forces that create symbols possessing the properties of multi-referentiality and multiquantificationality (Gough, 1969). A basic classificatory potential thus resides in such symbolism. These forces also create indexical symbols of unique reference and quantification. Concatenation of these symbol categories generates the grammatical form PSI + NOUN, traditionally known as the noun phrase (NP), accomplishing, moreover, unique reference and quantification for the given noun.

Access to extralinguistic reality is provided grammatically by the code when the NP is paired with the USI as in $\langle$USI, PSI + NOUN$\rangle$, creating in the process the protosentential formula (THIS is THIS + NOUN). The protosentence results from the generation of the relationship between the first two ostensions as exemplified in (1) and (2). We regard this protosentential formula as the base structure of the NP (Bach, 1968). Hence, we have

$$
\begin{array}{c}
\text{NP} \\
| \\
\text{SeN} \quad \Rightarrow \quad \boxed{\begin{array}{c}\text{Non-zero}\\ \text{semantic}\\ \text{transformations}\end{array}} \qquad (15)\\
| \\
\langle\text{USI, PSI + NOUN}\rangle
\end{array}
$$

where SeN denotes the protosentence. This protosentence then represents the input for the non-zero syntactically induced semantic transformations outlined above. Grammatically, we generate the various modes of meaning of the NP such as definite and indefinite reference, singular and plural number as well as quantification through transformations on (15), and not simply by *fiat* through choice of selectional features (Jacobs and Rosenbaum, 1968). We attempt to realize and exteriorize in the grammar what it means for a NP to be definite or indefinite, singular or plural, and the like (Karttunen, 1968).

The noun sentence SeN also becomes our protosentential predication formula, either by a rule of the form

$$\text{SEN} \rightarrow \text{SeN} \qquad (16)$$

or a rule of the form

$$\text{SEN} \to \langle \text{NP, NP} \rangle \tag{16'}$$

$$\text{NP} \to \text{SeN}$$

so that we have

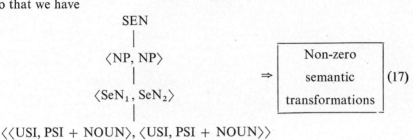

$$\langle\langle \text{USI, PSI} + \text{NOUN} \rangle, \langle \text{USI, PSI} + \text{NOUN} \rangle\rangle$$

where the relation between the ordered pairs of SeN's can now be realized again as, say, the BE relationship, thus giving us sentences of the form "A dog is an animal" after execution of the appropriate non-zero semantic transformations. The SeN's so ordered and related give us the protosyntactic, semantic formula $\langle \text{SeN}_1, \text{SeN}_2 \rangle$. Thus, the final meaning of a sentence such as "a child is an adult" must first be gauged against the backdrop of the semantics that resides in the protosentential formulae. This indicates how we intend to view grammar. It is a semiotic process that is triggered by symbol types and their syntactic functions which generate constant syntax-induced semantic transformations.

SUMMARY AND DISCUSSION

We have sketched an algebra of semantic functions for noun phrases as follows.

(a) Common nouns, hence general terms were assumed to refer multiply.

(b) The set of entities multiply referred to by a set of general terms was taken as the domain of the semantic functions whose values were the terms in question.

(c) To each term we allied a set of quasi-terms.

(d) The set of quasi-terms associated with a given term were taken to be the range of selective index functions, thus to each term we associated a unique selective index function.

(e) Every selective index function was seen to be recoverable as Boolean functions of the values of the universal selective index function and its Boolean complement.

(f) In a similar fashion particular selective functions associated with the articles and attributive juxtaposition were seen to be recoverable.

(g) The use of the limiting adjective "some" in the formation of noun phrases was seen to induce a transformation of selective index functions of general terms into constant functions whose value is the least upper bound of the range of the selective index functions.

(h) A generative grammar was chosen as the linguistic device incorporating the base structure of NP and the syntax-induced semantic transformations.

(i) The base structure of the English NP was interpreted as a protosentence consisting of an ordered pair of ostensions of the form $\langle \text{USI}, \text{PSI} + \text{N} \rangle$.

(j) The syntax-induced semantic transformations were interpreted as operating on the base structure of the NP.

We initially restricted ourselves to non-relative terms. If we wish to countenance relative terms of arbitrary addicity we need to consider the Boolean algebra of all functions from sequences of elements of X into T. If I is the set indexing such sequences we need to consider all functions from I into X, X^I, and all functions from X^I into T. T^{XI} is the ensuing algebra. In this algebra a single quantifier transformation will not generally reduce arbitrary selective index functions into constant functions. Suppose we have the relative term "brother of", the term "some brother of" still has one place open since it can give rise to terms of the forms "some brother of x" for any singular term x. In order to deal with these cases we would have to countenance polyadic quantification (Halmos, 1962).

We have discussed the syntax-induced semantics of a variety of types of English noun phrases within the guiding framework of algebraic systems that are closely allied to the monadic and polyadic algebras of monadic and polyadic quantification. If we stay close to the apparent realities of the English noun phrase it soon appears that we cannot have such fundamental algebraic properties as closure. It is thus convenient at times to force appropriate behaviour by *ad hoc* assumptions. One might go the whole way and make sufficient assumptions so as to obtain a polyadic algebra. Or one may stop at various half-way points and obtain a Boolean algebra, a product algebra, or a monadic algebra. We feel that the range of *ad hoc* assumptions that may be appropriate is to be decided, at least in part, by the applications envisaged. For example, we are presently testing indexing, storage and retrieval facilities that may be implemented by the syntax-induced semantics described in a product algebra. *A fortiori* semantic measures that may be introduced in such algebras will be rather gross. For it is impossible to reflect certain syntax-induced semantic transformations within them.

In conclusion we wish to emphasize that the ultimate aim of our approach is to elucidate those aspects of grammar that constitute man's first-line mechanisms for the structuring and processing of information.

References

E. Bach, "Nouns and noun phrases". In *Universals in Linguistic Theory* (Eds. E. Bach and R. T. Harms). Holt, Rinehart and Winston, New York (1968).

A. W. Burks, "Icon, index, and symbol". *Phil. Phenomenol. Res.*, **9**, 673–89 (1949).

N. Chomsky, *Aspects of the Theory of Syntax*. M.I.T. Press, Cambridge, Mass (1965).

P. T. Geach, *Reference and Generality*. Cornell University Press. Ithaca (1962).

J. Gough and L. Chiaraviglio "The referential structures of the English noun phrase". (To be published.) (1969).

J. Gough, (1969). "The syntax-based semantics of the English determiners ∅, A and THE", Paper presented at *Southeastern Conf. on Linguistics, Florida State University, Tallahassee, Florida, 1969*.

P. R. Halmos, *Algebraic Logic*. Chelsea, New York (1962).

H. Hiz, "Referentials". *Univ. of Penn. Transformations and Discourse Analysis Papers*, No. 76 (1968).

L. Karttunen, "What makes definite noun phrases definite?". *The Rand Corp.*, p. 3871 (1968).

L. Linsky, *Referring*. Humanities, New York (1967).

J. D. McCawley, "The role of semantics in a grammar". In *Universals in Linguistic Theory* (Eds. E. Bach and R. T. Harms). Holt, Rinehart and Winston, New York (1968).

C. S. Peirce, "Logic as semiotic: the theory of signs". In *Philosophical Writings of Peirce* (Ed. J. Buchler). Dover Publications, New York (1955).

W. van O. Quine, *Word and Object*. M.I.T. Press, Cambridge (1960).

Resource allocation for university information services

H. D. BAECKER

University of Calgary
Canada

Summary

To-date university library services have been financed out of block grants and provided at no charge to the user. Professional library staff have been able to assess and monitor the cost of retrieval requests, and so modify the scope of the search. At the same time the scarcity of trained staff serves to limit the costs incurred. Automated information retrieval systems will enable staff and students to originate retrieval requests from remote terminals, and those users will in general have no conception of the work, and hence costs, incurred, by specific requests. We must therefore determine whether open access to information is so precious to the university community that its demands must be satisfied at any cost, or whether financial constraints are to be placed upon access to the information system. In the case of fact retrieval, as opposed to document retrieval, systems it will also be necessary to determine cost guidelines for the assessment of the validity of new information to be added to the data bank. The advent of total information systems of a self-regulating nature, replacing current piecemeal human systems, will have far-reaching effects on the structure and function of the university community.

INTRODUCTION

"The increase and diffusion of knowledge" has long been taken as the major aim of university institutions, and the university library plays a central role in both these functions. In order to be in a position to increase knowledge the scholar and researcher must first determine the current state of his field, and this is largely accomplished by means of literature searches. Subsequently his quantum of increase is deposited in the library as a journal paper or book. Diffusion is also accomplished by literature searches initiated by students, but quantitatively their demand for specific documents nominated by a teacher outside of the library system is more important.

Traditionally it is the right of academic staff to make retrieval requests freely of library staff. This does not at all mean that all requests are satisfied. Making cynical generalisations, libraries are far more concerned about the scale of their acquisitions programme than about the scope of their retrieval services, in any case they are chronically short of money, so there has never been any question of expending the resources necessary to satisfy the request made. The priority accorded retrieval requests has depended upon extraneous, institutional, factors and upon the personal interests of the library staff, the individual user has become accustomed to conducting his own searches, so rationing himself by his own resources and needs.

The advent of electronic data banks with remote interactive access facilities promises a new era for university library services, and it is the aim of this paper to explore a few of the consequences.

THE TWO FORMS OF RETRIEVAL

Before going any further let us be clear that the term "information retrieval" covers at least two very different operations. These are document retrieval and fact retrieval.

Document retrieval is characterized by questions of the form, "find me all publications in English since 1960 regarding the chemical composition of Jupiter", whilst a query to a fact retrieval system might be "is nicotine present in the Jovian atmosphere?" Although we often want the answer to the latter form we are in the habit of getting there via the former, if only to establish for ourselves the validity of the answer.

Initially the electronic systems will be for document retrieval, save in specialized areas, and we shall concentrate on these for the moment.

THE ELECTRONIC LIBRARY

In its idealized but feasible form the electronic library of tomorrow is interfaced to the user by an input keyboard, like a typewriter, and a cathode ray tube display for the presentation of information in alphanumeric character form. After logging in, that is, identifying himself as an accredited user, the user submits one or more retrieval requests.

Within the system each document would bear a number of descriptors by which it could be found. Some descriptors, such as date and language, would be universal, others would be present only if relevant to the particular document. Thus our previous request might be typed in as

CHEMISTRY AND JUPITER AND L (ENGLISH) AND DATE (> 1960)

The system would now find all the documents for which these descriptors were applicable, and would list them by author, title, and source. The user can then request summaries to be displayed of these papers that interest him, and finally he could request microfilm or page copies of any that were of real interest to be run off and mailed to him.

Let us assume also that we have surmounted the hurdle of devising and agreeing upon a standard classificatory scheme for descriptors, and for describing documents, so that a request issued at library A means the same as one issued at library B.

THE COST OF RETRIEVAL

In a manual retrieval system the searcher can at any time decide that the quest is fruitless because the search parameters have been ill-chosen, and can refer back to the originator. Or it may be that the search parameters were ill-chosen because too many documents satisfy them, again a reason for requesting redefinition of the search. If the user disagrees with the opinion of the library professional he always has the option of arguing the point, or, finally, of getting to the stacks himself and conducting his own search. As long as the texts exist the user can, as a last resort, disregard the retrieval service of a conventional library and can go it alone.

An electronic retrieval system for general use will also have to have programmed in some parameters to limit the cost of searches, else any user could tie up system resources. But it will be a very long time indeed before we can design a system so versatile that the user can argue his case for the application of more liberal parameters in this instance with the system itself. Of course we always have the out that the frustrated user can apply to the system management for a higher priority, or whatever, but should there be any volume of such users then the system has failed, the operating expenses of staffing the user contact service will climb too high.

Unfortunately, by the time a good portion of the library contents have been mechanized, the user's present last resort will have vanished, there will be no stacks left for him to attack on his own. This highlights the point that we have no true idea of the current costs of university library retrieval, simply because most users do their own searching and their expenditure of time and effort is not costed.

It may well be that we decide that unrestricted access to information is so precious to the university community that we must provide it at any cost. In that case we should be aware that present costs do not form a reliable guide to the costs likely to be incurred under an electronic system, both because of the ease of initiating searches under the latter and because of the large proportion of the actual costs of the former that are not made explicit at present.

Alternatively, we may restrict each user to a budget. Here two different types of access must be considered, as I have pointed out elsewhere[1] in relation to the ordinary computing needs of university members. On the one hand we have the student and also members of academic staff pursuing personal or departmental research not sponsored by an outside funding agency. On the other we have sponsored research, most obviously by government or industry but also by granting agencies such as SRC, SSRC, MRC, NERC, etc., in Britain, NRC and MRC in Canada, CSIRO in Australia, and so on. Really we should also include charities such as the Ford Foundation in this latter category.

Library access for the student and academic is a right, so each person would have to have a certain automatic and inalienable budget for library access provided out of the university budget merely by virtue of his existence in this status. The scale of these personal budgets is open to debate. However, it is clear that both students and staff will require explicit instruction in the utilization of the electronic library service, yet another burden on the curriculum, so that they may disburse their budgets to advantage. This not only involves instruction in the mechanics of the interface used to access the library but also in the principles underlying the library's classification system.

Clearly work on sponsored research must be on a true case cost basis, with all retrieval requests charged for explicitly. It may come as a surprise to the sponsoring agencies when it is determined what proportion of the university information resources are consumed on their account. The proportion will not change much probably, from that now, but it will be explicit for the first time.

FACT RETRIEVAL

Eventually we will get to fact retrieval services. As far as retrieval requests are concerned the costs and rules do not differ from document retrieval. But unlike document retrieval a fact retrieval system will have a far higher social and financial cost for acquisitions, the formation of the data base. The only acquisition costs of document retrieval will be the purchase of the document, with its descriptors, in machine readable form, for by the time university library services are automated publishers will supply documents ready for machine entry, and either the publisher or an independent body will have similarly coded the descriptors for that document according to one or more common coding schemes. All a library has to decide is the scope of its acquisitions policy.

But additions to the data base of a fact retrieval system are far more complex. Rarely may facts have to be purchased, but what of determining the validity of a given datum? But first let us consider another problem, the scope of the data base.

It is almost certain that no university will be able to afford to maintain a universal encyclopaedia of all public knowledge. It will have to determine the purpose and scope of the data base it maintains locally. Given a new datum, how is it determined whether it is within that scope? Some are easy, a new measurement of fabric shrinkage is implausibly related to Roman history. But is turbulence in the upper atmosphere really without influence upon endemic disorders of grazing stock? Are we really sure? Is not this what a university is all about, always ready to question the accepted patterns of relationships?

Any administrative decision about the scope of a given data base will arbitrarily circumscribe the lines of enquiry open to the users of that data base. Of course the user of the particular facility will be intellectually aware that he is operating upon a subset of the available information, but he would have to be superhuman to overcome the unconscious assumption that he is operating with the total relevant universe of discourse. And when from time to time he becomes aware of the limitations, what then? His data base will be extensible by others, via telecommunications equipment, but at what cost?

Now let us return to the validity problem. A new datum has to be vetted for admission to the data base. How? By whom? And if it is found to contradict some existing element of the data base, which has the higher validity? Once admitted to the data base, do we set the system to mull over the relation of the new datum to the existing data, seeking to establish new relationships or to elicit obscure contradictions? To what extent and at what cost?

CONCLUSIONS

The introduction of programmed information systems in universities will require us to become explicitly aware of the costs incurred by information retrieval and dissemination, which is not the case under current systems. Political decisions will have to be made about the value of the various possible scopes of information systems and the consequences of the decision made will have to be evaluated and accepted in full.

Further, fact retrieval systems will require vetting procedures for accessions to the data base, and the form of vetting and composition of the "tribunal" will themselves raise major problems, as will the accession of data inconsistent with the prior contents of the data base.

Reference

1. H.D. Baecker, "To remove the gloom from university computing", *New Univ.*, **2**, No. 1 (1968).

Cybernetics: its impact on the processes of learning, politics, and production

ALICE MARY HILTON

The Institute for Cybercultural Research
U.S.A.

Summary

The impact of cybernetics as a philosophy (C_p) is distinguished from the impact of cybernetics as a science (C_s). The impact of C_s is more evident than the impact of C_p though the latter may eventually be of greater significance. The applications of C_s are revolutionizing the production process. Prognosis is further increasing dramatic changes and their chaotic consequences until the impact of C_p makes itself felt. The applications of C_s to the learning process are discernible in the area of research, with C_p making some headway. The impact of C_p or C_s on the education of the young is minimal. The impact of cybernetics on the political process—which, in its broadest sense, includes the entire complex spectrum of man's relationships with his fellow man—is barely beginning. The technological applications of C_s have been enormously important (though rarely acknowledged) particularly in international relations; but there is as yet no discernible evidence that sorely needed C_p has made any impression. When human thought absorbs the insights of C_p as readily as it accepts the technological applications of C_s, then the improving quality of human life may, at last, match the increasing quantity of produced goods.

INTRODUCTION

Discussing the impact of cybernetics, one needs to remember that cybernetics is both modern science—just coming of age this year—and ancient philosophy. For the great philosophers and theologians and poets of the ages have known that everything is part of a *uni*verse—the vast complex system composed of myriads of subsystems and entities, all related in extremely complex and intricate patterns.

The young science (which will hereafter be designated C_s) has found many applications in the two brief decades of its existence, but the ancient philosophy (hereafter designated C_p) is still only rarely applied and expressed save, perhaps, in the thoughts of theologians and poets. (Even our contemporary philosophers are more likely to concern themselves with fractional minutiae than with the magnificence of the grand design of a cybernetic and dynamic universe.) Yet, never has there been a time when completeness ought to concern us more. And never has such a concern been more "practical" than now that a human being has actually set foot upon the moon, which surely demonstrated that we are part of an intricately connected universe, a universe that is holistic, or, to use another word, wholesome.

Calling our troubled, turbulent world "wholesome" might seem incongruous. But though it is undeniably troubled, turbulent, perhaps even disintegrating, the universe is "whole", simply because it is all there is. Its troubles might be healed, its chaotic turbulence channelled into creative energy, and its grinding wheels made to mesh harmoniously, when C_p influences the minds of men. For admittedly, dramatic as the impact of C_s (and its technological applications) has been in the two decades since its birth, one must search patiently and optimistically to find much evidence of C_p. That is not so surprising in a period of young excitement and brashness. A philosophy grows slowly; it must wait quietly for its historical era to come of age. For there can be little doubt that this is the era of cybernetics—the "age of cyberculture"—and imperceptible as the impact of C_p seems, it is—from the long-range point of view of human history—perhaps even more significant than C_s. It is not unusual for a philosophy to be accepted less impetuously than a science and its technologies. The ideas, for example, of Newton, and other mathematicians and philosophers of Enlightenment, had immediate and dramatic impact in the invention of instruments and machines—or what can be quickly translated into the tangible.

Societies always can quickly recognize the tangible. But the impact of the philosophy, of quantification and, more important, of a universe human reason can understand took hold only slowly. When it did, the consequences were enormous; man was freed both from fear of the incomprehensible forces of the unfathomable supernatural and the shackles of his own incompetence. Perhaps man has not become much more competent in running his life than he was before the "Age of Enlightenment", but his faith in the human capacity to learn was kindled then, and it is still shining bright.

With the philosophical acceptance of quantification and the increasing success and popularity of inductive logic—still the bases of modern scientific investigation—came the devaluation of human judgment, diminishing faith in divine guidance, and the decline of the criteria of quality and taste. In fact, some technologically advanced societies went overboard on quantification; they developed a preposterous faith in "objective measurement" and complete disdain for what they deprecatingly call "subjective value judgments", which means a person's ability and willingness to make decisions based upon his personal judgment, his integrity, and his sense of value and taste, and to take full responsibility for his judgments. Inevitably, perhaps the esteem of quality declined as sheer quantity increased in importance. Why "objective measurements" should be superior to human judgment is not quite clear. On the contrary, it seems obvious that indiscriminate number worship is as dangerous a fanaticism as unexamined faith in witchcraft, rain gods, or demons.

In a society where the philosophical acceptance of quantification and inductive logic has led to such preposterous aberrations as the belief that knowledge—not merely information can be quantified and measured by "objective" tests, one can only hope for the rapid decline of such misplaced faith and a growing awareness of the complexity of the dynamic system we call the universe. That cybernetics—C_p—will have its day seems probable. The question is what kind of day! Will there be a broad base of real understanding of this philosophy? Or will it merely a vogue, followed and imitated by many but rarely understood, that deteriorates into a vulgar fad and soon is preposterously abused without ever serving a good purpose, until it finally declines. There are some indications that we are moving in this direction. The *Manhattan (N.Y.) Telephone Directory*, for example, lists about twenty titles that use (and more often abuse) the word cybernetics, including the Cybe-Tape Co, Cybertronics, Inc., Cybern-Education, and Cybervex Systems. There is even a best-selling book on "psycho-cybernetics".

History shows many precedents of such ideological cycles: from the rise of an idea from obscurity to popular acclaim until it swells to preposterous proportions and, like an overblown balloon it finally bursts or else, forgotten in a quiet corner, it shrivels. Were such ideas nothing but hot air from the beginning? It is hard to be certain and there are no comparison charts for the potential and actual achievement of ideas. Only one thing is certain as long as living human societies are dynamic systems: if an idea were ever to reach perfection and such a state could be maintained, the system would become static, and, as every cybernetician knows, it would be dead. For change is the life-blood of a living system.

Even though C_p is not yet a popular philosophy, the technical applications of C_s demonstrate beyond doubt that the universe is indeed whole, complex, and, therefore, an indeterminate, but rational, structure of a dynamic character. In other words, modern technology proves the universe to be not merely three- or four-dimensional, but multi-dimensional, and most probably infinite-dimensional. This does not, of course, surprise mathematicians and ought not to be news to poets, theologians and philosophers.* And it is almost taken for granted in an exasperatingly casual fashion by the most intelligent and thoughtful of students who, therefore—unless they are exceptionally kind and patient with their elders' "hang-ups" on fractionization and quantification—drop out from our better universities.

In order to make the impact of cybernetics, which is a vast and all-pervasive universe of discourse, manageable, and the discussion orderly, I shall examine the impact of cybernetics in three areas, confident that we are all fully aware of the fact that these areas—or fields—are not walled off but melted into one another and, together, encompass the spectrum of life in a social system. For the sake of convenience, the three fields are: (1) the production process, which includes the production of goods and the provision of services; (2) the learning process, including the furthering of human knowledge, i.e. research, exploration, discovery, and invention, as well as the transmittal of knowledge and information to the young that is usually called education, though it is all too often merely training; and (3) the political process which is broadly defined as the area of man's organized relationships with his fellow man. In all areas, we shall be concerned with the impact of cybernetics, C_p *and* C_s, and bear in mind that C_s has barely come of age and perhaps has not yet melded with C_p into a harmonious whole.

ON THE PRODUCTION PROCESS

The impact of cybernetics—C_s—on the production process has been the most dramatic, far-reaching, and widely recognized. It has been enthusiastic-

---

* The great success of the physical sciences has led biological and social scientists and philosophers to adopt many of the methods that were so successfully applied to physics. Unfortunately there seems to be a considerable time lag. Hence, at a time, when the phy-

ally heralded and desperately feared. In fact, the impact of cybernetics on the production process has been confined almost entirely on the application of the theory of automata—which is merely one of the many applications of cybernetics—and the resulting "automatic" technology. The popular mistake of confusing a science with a single application of a science, need not be elaborated here[1]. Cybernetics—C_s or C_p—is not often comprehensively applied in the management of firms that produce goods and services, and cybernetics is also almost completely ignored as a thinking tool in managing the economic system in the western nations. The few attempts to construct economic models have suffered from lack of funds and interest[2]. In the Soviet Union, interest in this thinking tool has been somewhat more extensive. Kosygin, for example, admonished scientists to pay more attention to the use of scientific tools in solving economic problems at the first All-Union Conference of Scientific Workers[3-5] held at the Kremlin on June 14, 1961. The West has not lacked brilliant men, for example Stafford Beer, who pointed out that cybernetics is indeed a fine "thinking tool" for problems of the production process and that to this thinking tool, automation is irrelevant[6]. If cybernetics is not extensively enough applied to the management of production, one application of cybernetics has certainly had enormous impact on the methods and tools of production. This is the process known as "automation" or cybernation.

In Stafford Beer's classification of systems, a production system (the company) is probabilistic and "exceedingly complex", but automation is classified as deterministic and complex[7]. The company has shown no great fervour of reorganizing itself in accordance with cybernetic ideas. Tables of organization are shuffled here and there, divisions that have been autonomous become more directly controlled by headquarters, as improved information-processing facilities make this practical. But these are small inroads of C_p, confined to the top echelons of management and the upper regions of think tanks and consultants which the company often maintains for the sake of prestige and decoration rather than use. The technological offspring of C_s—twice removed via the theories of automata, control, information, communication, etc.—is most appropriately called cybernation. It has had enormous impact in the technologically advanced nations. So great has been the impact of technical innovation in the production process (cybernation)

---

sicists have already forgotten determinacy, it is stubbornly embraced by social scientists and philosophers. For the former it is, of course, unworkable, and for the latter quite unphilosophical.

that it has had enormous socio-economic consequences. Societies are so unprepared to cope with these consequences—predictable though they are—that we have been witnessing a decade of desperate efforts to encourage ever more sophisticated cybernation and sing its praises and simultaneously declare solemnly that nothing has changed at all.

Every cybernetician is perfectly aware of the continuum of change, including technological change. But to assert that a *continuum of change* is synonymous with *no change* is preposterous. The reason for this preposterous effort is the lag between technological applications of C_s and acceptance of C_p. Lacking the acceptance of C_p—or even any attempt to understand the relationship between technology and its purpose—we persist in a social ethos that began to decline with the earliest introduction of labour-saving devices. Obviously all machines are labour-saving—or, rather, labour-performing—devices, and cybernated systems are the most efficient of all machines known to man.

In the long continuum of technological change, the purpose of technology has always been the *dis*employment of human beings[8,9]. But in the technologically advanced nations, the social ethos of toil and effort as the sole prerequisites for rewards, both spiritual and material, is deeply ingrained. This social ethos regards highly the virtues of individual strife and personal deprivation, which was important for the creation of capital for investment and expansion[10]. Understanding the relationships that make up the universe is not so highly regarded. Action is prized, contemplation disdained, leisure suspect. Quality is understood only when it is measurable, which means not at all. This is about the state of the technologically advanced nations, particularly the United States which is probably the most Puritan nation in the world, with the Soviet Union and the People's Republic of China close runners-up. In the United States, we are as busy inventing labour-saving devices as we are trying to find busy-labour for those whose drudgery the devices are supposed to relieve. The result is obvious: there are more products and there are fewer nasty chores for people to do, but also fewer opportunities for them to earn the purchasing licences required to obtain the products. And nobody is as yet willing to reorganize the toil-purchasing licence-buying cycle because the social ethos, let alone the socio-economic process of distribution, is lagging far behind technological advance. Thus social disharmony is inevitable.

I have concluded that a nation does not change its social ethos or its institutions because it adopts a more suitable philosophy, but that the philosophy will pervade the society's thinking when the old social ethos atrophies from disuse, is buried in hypocrisy, or drowned in ridicule. A new social ethos grows slowly—it is adopted even later than applied. And social institutions are changed—or transformed—because the stark reality of the prevailing situation demands change. Change is the basic characteristic of a living system. The only alternatives are in the way change is brought about: by an orderly revolution, i.e. evolution, with some continuity in form while contents alter; or by violent revolution, the destruction of form with almost inevitable chaos. The latter is far less efficient than the former in bringing about fundamental change and usually brings about far less *real* change.

In practical terms, when a society so improves its production methods that increasingly fewer producers are needed to produce increasingly numerous products, there are few alternatives for restoring a semblance of harmony to the production-distribution balance. The most sensible alternative—and, therefore, most rarely used—is to welcome man's release from drudgery and scarcity and to invent new social methods of balancing supply and demand—of leisure and work as well as of products and purchasing licences. Secondly, the society can limit productivity and extend meaningless busy-labour. Thirdly, the society can devise means of disposing both of surplus production and surplus producers. In the United States, we have employed a combination of all three methods, with a tiny proportion of the first and a heavy dose of the third. The war in Viet Nam has proved to be an efficient—though surely neither sensible nor moral—means of disposing of surplus production and at least keeping potential producers out of the labour pool[11-13]. With the increasing unpopularity of the war, the second alternative is gaining in preponderance. Productivity is limited by fiscal policy—building is effectively curtailed, for example, as soon as interest rates rise—and the proliferation of busy-labour on every level and in every field becomes astounding.

The puritan ethos does not decline gracefully or gently but, like a pierced balloon with an imploding vacuum. For all the desperate, often foolish, almost invariably futile search made by our best young people for a new ethos and for the rebirth of morality, the vacuum is not likely to be filled for reasons that will become obvious when we discuss the impact—or lack of impact—of cybernetics upon the education of the young.

ON THE LEARNING PROCESS

The impact of cybernetics upon the learning process has been quite spectacular in most areas of scientific research. C_s has had the more dramatic effect; every self-respecting research worker thinks he must use a computing machine—whether he knows how or not, whether he needs it or not, and whether it makes sense or not. In other words, in a gadget-loving era, the technological applications of C_s are enthusiastically adopted in the accumulation of information that often is confused with the extension of knowledge. The fact that this confusion is so prevalent is evidence that C_p is lagging far behind. But it is also true that there is a beginning of the dawning understanding of cybernetics—C_p. Scientists from all disciplines have been meeting at the computing centres and, although disciplines seem to proliferate and narrow, there is increasing understanding of relationships among disciplines. But we must not overrate this. It is more important that the great scientists have always known that knowledge cannot be divided into fractions. It is universal and encompassing. Even at the zenith of disciplinary division, there were always the great minds that could not be confined to narrow disciplines. Since the beginning of this century, the reunification of science has begun with the reunification of logic and mathematics in the epoch-making work of Bertrand Russell, a philosopher–mathematician in the best tradition of man's search for knowledge and meaning[14].

Unfortunately, the impact of cybernetics—science or philosophy—on the learning process, as far as the education of the young is concerned, is appallingly small. For practical purposes it is non-existent. We hear a great deal about "teaching machines" and "programmed learning". But invariably such "innovations" turn out to be mere gadgets. The most "sophisticated" are nothing but typewriters with colored keys connected to short-circuit television screens, or question-and-answer books, or combinations of both. In the United States the process of educating the young is beset by two formidable handicaps. First, we do not have an education system at all. We have a training system that, until recently, prepared young people fairly competently to earn a living. We have no institution or system that teaches them how to live. And we have never tried to teach them to think and to understand a complex, dynamic universe. As long as there was room for expansion, young people could be kept busy conquering the West and the lack of an education system was not apparent. Training institution provided adequate preparation for the varacious demands of industrialization. Now, the frontier has met the Pacific Ocean, industrialization is highly advanced, and cybernation provides us with a virtually bottomless pool of tireless, obedient, efficient slaves. The puritan ethos was well suited to life on the frontier, but we have not been able to adapt to a life of ease with our crystalloid machine slaves. And we are faced with disaster. Our young people—particularly the brightest among them—feel the lack of proper education and, quite rightly, I think, protest against the misguidance the society inflicts upon them. Some rebel by staying in school, grimly setting out to get a diploma, if education is not available. They soon become cynical and hard, and nobody knows how they will develop in another decade or two. They will probably be competent technicians but unimaginative and rigid—or quite useless in a society which already has too many technicians and far too few philosophers and poets. Others rebel by escaping into dissent or drugs. Either way, the best are lost to us—permanently, if we cannot find a way to introduce cybernetics into the teaching process and thus create an education system.

Unfortunately, those among intellectuals and young people who are philosophically most attuned to study cybernetics, have been repelled by the overemphasis on some of the secondary applications (in production as well in some aspects of the political process, as we shall see presently) and misled by definitions of cybernetics such as one given in the latest edition of *Webster's Dictionary*[15] which, erroneous and primitive though it is, has spread through the mass media. Those who really are philosophically most attuned to C_p are almost violently prejudiced against the very word.

There is a glimmer of hope. A few, very few, among the brightest teachers have become interested in cybernetics and have wholeheartedly embraced its philosophical implications[16]. The same, not surprisingly, is true among theologians[17].

ON THE POLITICAL PROCESS

Has cybernetics had any impact upon the political process? Without doubt the technological applications of C_s—the means of communications, space explorations, for example—have been significant both in domestic and foreign policy. A world linked by instant, global television is qualitatively different from a world in which news takes months to traverse an ocean. People still differ in their way of life and (perhaps even increasingly) in their living standards. But the enormously important new political phenomenon—directly resulting from the applications of C_s—is that in the most remote corners of the world people are becoming aware of the differences and inequities of their living standards as well as of the universal nature of human desires and aspirations. This fact has an irreversible consequence: human beings no longer believe that the scourge of misery is inevitable; they know with increasing certainty that change is possible and that their misery is not only *not inevitable* but that it is *unacceptable*.

In a large country like the United States the impact of instant communications on domestic politics is said to be dramatic. In a national election, results in the Eastern states are known through the nation hours before the polls close in the West. A bandwagon effect seems inevitable, and politicians are endlessly arguing about its importance for their candidate. But since there is little evidence of an "easternization" of American politics, there is some doubt of its impact. Although there has been talk of building models of the political process, there is so little rational understanding of this process that the impact of C_p is not considerable. Couffignal says there is a mutual influence between man and his environment[18], in other words a cybernetic relationship. But though cybernetics offers us the thinking tools to further our understanding of political processes, we lack the philosophy to use this powerful tool wisely.

The Department of Defense has used mathematical (i.e. cybernetic) models extensively—successfully in the development of tactics, but (as results demonstrate) unsuccessfully for devising intelligent strategy. Tactics are, of course, less complex than strategy. But more important, strategy requires more than technique; and C_p is at least as remote from the thought processes of the military as it is from those in institutions that are less liberally endowed with vast computing centers.

PROGNOSIS FOR THE FUTURE

The prognosis of the future impact of cybernetics in all fields is indeterminate though the trend is dismal. But a trend is not inevitable or irreversible. Cyberneticians must take the lead in reversing the trend. Who knows better how dangerous a continuing imbalance between proliferating applications of C_s and dwarfing of C_p is to us all! In a world where the mediocre hide in minutiae and trivia, it is much easier to speak of gadgets and tricks than of grand designs and philosophy. Roger Revelle observes that "our technology has outpaced our understanding, our cleverness has grown faster than our wisdom", and Omar Bradley feared that "ours is a world of nuclear giants and ethical infants". Neither can be denied. But the cybernetician who is by nature and definition a scientist–poet–philosopher must show to the myopic tree watchers the majesty of the woods.

References

1. A. M. Hilton, *Logic, Computing Machines, and Automation*, I.C.R. Press, New York; The Macmillan Company, London (1963), pp. 3–4.
2. A. M. Hilton, "Job yield versus investment, an I.C.R. study of optimum job yield versus investment of public and/or private funds in various types of industries", *The Feedback*, **4**, Nos. 1–4 (1966).
3. A. N. Kosygin, Address at *First All-Union Conference of Sci. Workers, Kremlin, Moscow*, (1961); also reported in *Pravda*, 15 June (1961) and A. I. Berg, in *Cybernetics in the Service of Communism*, Vol. I, Moscow, Leningrad (1961); Transl. into English by the Office of Technical Services, U.S. Dpartment of Commerce, Washington, D.C., JPRS, 14,592 (1961), p. 23.
4. V. D. Balkin, "Cybernetics and economics". In *Cybernetics in the Service of Communism*, Vol. I, Moscow, Leningrad (1961), pp. 256–79.
5. A. I. Kitev, "Cybernetics and control of the national economy", in *Cybernetics in the Service of Communism*, Vol. I, Moscow, Leningrad (1961), pp. 280–300.
6. S. Beer, "The irrelevance of automation", *Cybernetica*, **1**, No. 4, 280–95 (1958).
7. S. Beer, *Cybernetics and Management*, I. Wiley, New York (1959), p. 18.
8. A. M. Hilton, "Full employment and human tasks", *Data Processing*, July, pp. 33–6 (1964).
9. A. M. Hilton, "Of work and labor". *Data Processing*, September, pp. 41–2 (1964).
10. M. Weber, *The Protestant Ethic and the Spirit of Capitalism* (Translated T. Parsons), Charles Scribner's Sons, New York (1958).
11. A. M. Hilton, "Cyberculture—in the transition from a war- to a peace-time economy", *Fellowship*, May, pp. 3–9 (1964).
12. A. M. Hilton, "Cybernation, weaponry and war, and esaclation in Vietnam", *The Feedback*, **2**, No. 6, pp. 2–5 (1965).
13. A. M. Hilton, "Can we afford peace in Vietnam?", *SSRS*, Spring (1969).
14. B. Russell and A. N. Whitehead, *The Principia Mathematica*, Vols. I–III, Cambridge University Press, Cambridge (1910–13).
15. *Webster's Seventh New Collegiate Dictionary*, G. & C. Merriam, Springfield, Mass. (1961), p. 206.
16. A. M. Hilton, "Cybernation and its impact on American society", in *Technology and the Curriculum* (Ed. P. W. F. Witt), Teachers College Press, Columbia University, New York (1968).
17. A. M. Hilton, "The human spirit and the cybercultural revolution", *CNR News, New Rochelle, New York*, **43**, No. 2, pp. 8–16 (1966).
18. L. Couffignal, *Les notions de base*, Gauthier-Villars Editeur, Paris (1958), p. 52.

Self-regulation of internal states*

ELMER E. GREEN, ALYCE M. GREEN
and E. DALE WALTERS

Research Department, *The Menninger Foundation*
Topeka, Kansas, U.S.A.

Summary

This paper is concerned with the development and use of tools and techniques for investigating states of internal awareness, psychological and physiological, which until recently have been considered unapproachable by scientific means. Experimental subjects have been trained by physiological feedback methods in the voluntary control of normally unconscious physiological functions which represent three major neuroanatomical regions, craniospinal, autonomic, and central. Subjects who have been most successful have demonstrated control by volitional relaxation of striate muscle tension down to the "zero" region, by volitional increase of temperature in the hands as much as 5 °C in two minutes, and by volitional increase in percentage of alpha rhythm up to 100% alpha over 10 second epochs, while speaking, with eyes open. The purpose of this physiological training is to enhance and make possible the study of those psychological states which appear as functional concomitants of a passive peripheral nervous system and an "alpha-activated" central nervous system. This on-going project has significant implications for psychology, psychosomatic medicine, psychiatry, education, and research in creativity.

* This study was supported in large part by Grant MH 14439, National Institute of Mental Health.

We thank Mr. Rex Hartzell and the personnel of the Biomedical Electronics Laboratory for their great assistance in the design, construction, and maintenance of feedback apparatus.

In recent years scientists in every nation have come to realize that self-regulation is of primary importance if we hope to establish an ordered society. The long-range political implications of a population of self-regulating individuals and the effects on our possessions-oriented society would be salutary, even if not welcomed by everyone. In advertising, for instance, where success depends on setting up strains in the personality which can be relieved (they tell us) only by buying a particular brand of merchandise, people who could regulate their own biological and emotional responses to perceptual stress would be a new, and perhaps difficult-to-manipulate factor. In the domain of social science, it goes without saying that the person with voluntary control of his own behavior (or who at least could curb the excesses of his responses) would not only *not* be a problem, but would make it easier for others to attain a stable, and yet creative, life.

INTRODUCTION

The title of this paper is "Self-Regulation of internal states", but a more descriptive title might be "Voluntary control of internal states, psychological and physiological". Although it is not possible to define in an operational way the meaning of the word "voluntary", it goes without saying that all of us have a *feeling* of voluntary control, at least part of the time, regardless of the psychophysical and metaphysical implications of that feeling. Few people realize, however, that that feeling, or intuition of freedom, has significance in respect to the so-called involuntary nervous system, the autonomic nervous system, nor do they realize that the "psychophysiological principle" when coupled with volition makes it possible to regulate a number of involuntary functions, and at least theoretically to regulate in some degree every physiological function of the body.

The psychophysiological principle affirms that "every change in the physiological state is accompanied by an appropriate change in the mental-emotional state, conscious or unconscious, and conversely, every change in the mental-emotional state, conscious or unconscious, is accompanied by an appropriate change in the physiological state". This closed Newtonian-type principle, when coupled with *volition*, which is at present of indeterminate origin, makes possible a psychosomatic self-regulation. Whether volition has origin beyond the physiological matrix, is the essence of the mind-body problem, but this is not of concern in the present paper. It is sufficient that research using feedback techniques has demonstrated that self-regulation of a number of internal states, psychological and physiological, is relatively easy to achieve[1-6].

For about 200 years, medical doctors serving with the British Army or Civil Service in India sent back reports of a few self-regulating people. The doctors claimed that these unusual individuals, called yogis, could regulate a large number of so-called involuntary physiological processes, such as heart rate, or pain. This unusual degree of control was obtained, they said, through long practice of specific mental, emotional, and physical disciplines.

In some parts of the Western world there was great interest in such reports, and by 1910 in this century, Johannes Schultz (in Germany) had developed a Western system of self-regulation by combining various ideas from his medical research, especially hypnosis, with concepts from yogic methods. Although Freud gave up the use of hypnotism in therapy because its results were too unpredictable, it occurred to Schultz that the major defect with hypnotism might lie in the fact that the patient was not in control of the situation and therefore resisted, in various ways, the doctor's instructions. Schultz combined the free will, or volitional aspect of yoga with some of the techniques he had worked with, and eventually developed the therapeutic system to which he gave the name "autogenic training"[7], that is, self-generated or self-motivated training. The research which I shall discuss today carries this development one step further and combines the conscious self-regulation aspect of yoga and the psychological method of autogenic training, with a modern technique called physiological feedback. This feedback, of physiological information, generally consists of providing visual or auditory displays which show the subject, or patient, what is happening in certain functions of his body as he attempts to control them.

I do not wish to say much more about autogenic training, but it is worth mentioning that after a patient learns to relax, somewhat in the manner of Jacobson's *Progressive Relaxation*[8], he learns to regulate blood flow in various parts of the body. This is followed by exercises in the control of heart rate, and, if necessary, the patient eventually focuses his control effort (under medical supervision) on the functional correction of psychosomatically sensitive areas, such as the gastrointestinal tract. Gradually, as emotional and physiological harmony is obtained in distraught patients, the therapy moves into the psychological areas important in general psychiatry. In spite of a significant amount of success, autogenic training (though over fifty years old) is almost unknown in the United States, and in the book *Autogenic Training*[7], by Schultz and Luthe, of 604 references, only 10 are in English.

Although autogenic training has had a measure of success, it is handicapped by the fact that it normally takes a great deal of time for the subject, or patient, to learn how to do it. And this is where feedback techniques come into the picture. In our laboratory and in others throughout the United States, new techniques are being developed for rapid achievement in self-regulation. Before discussing training experiments, electronic devices, and significance, however, I wish to focus attention on the neurological systems which are involved.

MAJOR PSYCHOPHYSIOLOGICAL CONCEPTS

Figure 1, a schematic diagram of the nervous system, is arranged to indicate brain areas associated with conscious functions on the right, and unconscious functions on the left. The entire nervous system is contained within the large circle, and the central nervous system (CNS), brain and spinal cord, is represented by the smaller circle. The peripheral nervous system (PNS) is the ring surrounding the central nervous system and is divided by the vertical line into the autonomic *involuntary* nervous system on the left, and the craniospinal *voluntary* nervous system on the right. The central nervous system is divided by the vertical line into the archipallium, the old brain (which man shares with the other vertebrates) and the neopallium, the new brain, whose most significant development is in man (dolphins notwithstanding).

The dashed line is to be visualized as a continuously undulating boundary between conscious and unconscious processes, as attention shifts from one brain region to another. For instance, after we have learned to drive a car, many of the striate muscular activities upon which so much attention was lavished at first become unconscious, and eventually it is possible, when the mind is preoccupied, to drive through miles of traffic without awareness.

On the other hand, the involuntary nervous system is not necessarily involuntary. If we concentrate attention on our right hand for a few seconds, the blood vessels in it will involuntarily constrict or dilate, depending on our previous conditioning, owing to tensing or relaxing of smooth muscles embedded in blood vessel walls. After training in temperature control, however, many subjects can increase or decrease the volume of blood in the hands at will. Consciousness of the specific neural pattern involved is not obtained, any more than there is consciousness of the neural network in the voluntary nervous system which causes the arm to move from side to side, but in both cases, autonomic and craniospinal, the desired behaviour is ob-

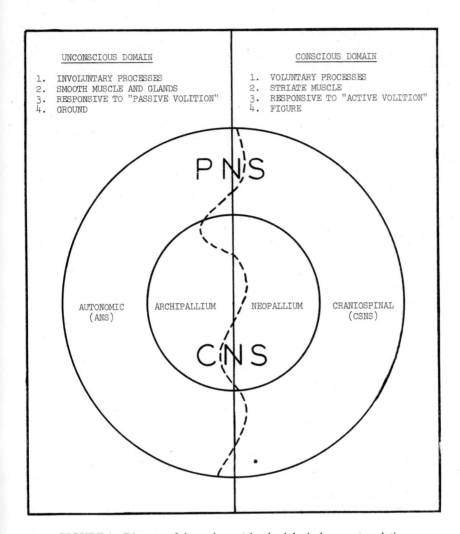

FIGURE 1 Diagram of the major psychophysiological concepts, relating the conscious–unconscious domain to the various sections of the central (CNS) and peripheral (PNS) nervous systems. The solid vertical line separates the nervous system into functional subregions and the dashed line (conceptually visualized to be in continuous undulatory movement) separates the conscious and unconscious areas

tained through visualization of the desired event accompanied by volition. The significant difference in controlling these two systems, is that for the voluntary nervous system, *active* volition is used, and for the involuntary nervous system it is necessary to use *passive* volition. It must be admitted that this last, passive volition, sounds like a contracdition in terms. How can anyone have passive volition? It is paradoxical, but after learning to use passive volition it seems quite reasonable, though not easy to put into words. Passive volition might best be described as detached effortless volition.

A RELAXATION EXPERIMENT WITH FEEDBACK

Generally, the control of striate muscle is developed with feedback of information from special sense organs, especially the eyes, and as errors are detected voluntary control is gradually developed, but in one area of striate muscle control there is essentially no perceptual feedback. This is in the reduction of muscle tension down to zero[9]. If an electromyographic (EMG) electrode is placed on the skin surface, over the dorsal muscle of the forearm, for instance, it will usually detect a continuous firing of motor fibres, even though visible signs of tension may not exist and somatic or muscular feelings of tension may not exist. If the EMG signal is made visible to the subject through external feedback, however, he can learn to turn it off.

Figure 2 is a schematic diagram of such a feedback arrangement by means of which experimental subjects have quickly learned to reduce muscle tension in the forearm down to zero. The signal from an EMG electrode on the forearm is amplified, rectified, and then fed back to the subject by a meter. Instruction to the subject is to bring the meter needle down to zero. With this arrangement, seven out of twenty-one subjects were able to achieve either zero firing or single motor unit firing in less than twenty minutes of a single session. This is a phenomenal performance which only one subject could do without feedback. He, oddly enough, had practiced yogic meditation for a number of years. Eleven of the twenty-one subjects were able to achieve *low* tension levels with feedback but could not reach single-motor-unit firing in twenty minutes. Three of the subjects did not seem to succeed at all. They, incidentally, gave evidence of strain due to the experimental setup.

Of the seven subjects who approached zero levels in less than twenty minutes, five reported body–image changes, making such statements as: "My arm feels like a bag of cement", "My arm feels like a ton of lead", "It feels

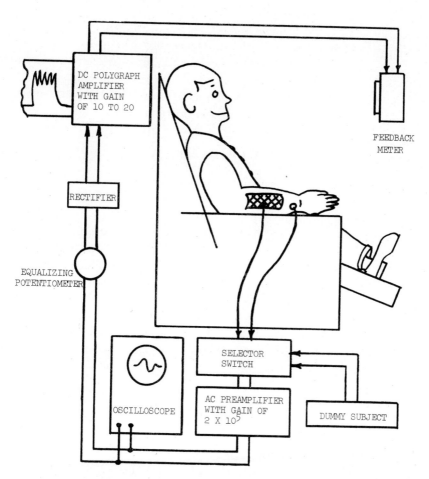

FIGURE 2   Block diagram of E.M.G. feedback system. Viewing distance of the meter is about five feet. The large "active" forearm electrode is referenced to a small disc electrode placed over the bony styloid process. A ground electrode on the subject is sometimes used in order to reduce sixty-cycle noise. The dummy subject is used for calibration of the system. It is an electrical stimulus generator whose biphasic rectangular pulses are rounded off with a choke and capacitor so as to produce trains of triphasic pulses (seven per second, each of twelve milliseconds duration) very similar in appearance to single-motor-unit firing, as shown on the oscilloscope[3]

like it is moving away from me", "I had to look at it to see if it was still in the same place", etc. In naïve subjects in a proper setting (reclining chair, quiet room, dim lights, etc.), relaxation generally spreads over a large part of the body, but we have found that a normal subject can learn, with a little practice, to dissociate his right forearm from the rest of his muscular system so that he can tense his left arm, leg muscles, or neck muscles, without causing any significant increase of tension in the right arm[3].

TRIPLE TRAINING PROGRAM WITH FEEDBACK

Preliminary experiments with EMG feedback and with autogenic training led to our present project in which college men are being trained in the simultaneous (1) reduction of muscle tension in the right forearm, (2) increase in temperature in the right hand, and (3) increase in percentage of alpha rhythm in the EEG record. Feedback of muscle tension is from a circuit of the type already described. Temperature feedback is initiated from a thermistor taped to a finger of the right hand. Percentage-of-alpha feedback is achieved by allowing the subject to watch a meter whose scale shows the average percentage over a continuously computed ten-second epoch. That is, the meter continuously tells the subject what his average percentage has been over the preceding ten seconds. More immediate feedback in alpha is obtained, of course, as the average rises or falls in response to the on-going EEG signal.

Figure 3 shows a pilot subject wired up for a training session. Skin resistance, skin potential, photoplethysmographic response in one finger, temperature of the adjacent finger, eye movement (EOG) (not visible), right forearm EMG, and left and right occipital EEG, referenced to the vertex, are being recorded. A respiration gauge is hidden by the psychophysiological research jacket which we constructed for reducing "the electric chair effect" in this type of experiment. The individual signal wires plug into sleeve and collar pin-blocks molded of silicone rubber. Fine shielded cables sewn into the jacket lead to a thirty-six-pin miniature connector (in the hem) which is snap-attached to a flexible cable, carrying the various signals to the main control room fifteen feet away.

The meters and their arrangement for this triple training program are shown in Figure 4. The experimenter, at the right in this figure, is able to switch on any of the feedback meters which give the subject, in the reclining chair, information about forearm muscle tension, finger temperature, and percentage of alpha. The behaviour of these three physiological variables is shown by the three bars of light on the black panel in front of the subject. Each bar, becoming taller or shorter in correspondence with the behaviour

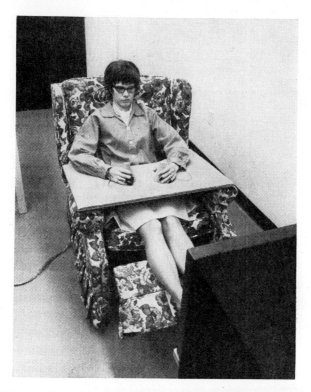

FIGURE 3   Pilot subject "wired" for a training session. The arm board standardizes the placements of the subject's forearms and hands and helps in achieving relaxation. The blotter-covered cones are moveable, and in addition to allowing the subject to find the most comfortable position, they stabilize the hands for the various physiological measurements

of a physiological variable, is literally the readout mode of an optical projection-type meter. The bars of light, one-half inch wide, can reach a maximum height of five inches, and give the subject an easy-to-see indication of physiological behaviour and control. The feedback circuits are arranged so that (1) at complete relaxation (zero muscle tension) the left bar rises to the top, (2) a temperature increase of about 5°C causes the second bar to rise to the top, and (3) 100% alpha rhythm over a period of ten seconds causes the third bar to rise to the top. Each bar reaches its maximum height if the subject achieves maximum success in controlling the corresponding physiological variable.

A training sequence involves eight sessions, two per week, each of about two and one-half hour's duration, including forty minutes for wiring. The time of only six sessions is devoted to training, however, since a number of

FIGURE 4   The experimenter switches feedback meters (bars of light in front of the subject) on and off as a training session progresses. On the experimenter's control panel are five edge-type meters which give a continuous indication of the subject's behaviour in five physiological variables. Even though subjects will be trained and tested in five variables, it is planned that no more than three feedback meters will be switched on at any one time

psychological tests are given to each subject, mainly to determine his inward–outward orientation, which is hypothesized to be significantly related to his success in voluntary control of internal states. The tests include (1) the *Eysenck personality inventory*, for determination of extraversion–introversion, (2) the *James I–E scale*, for determining internal versus external control of behaviour, (3) the *rod and frame test*, for determination of field dependence or independence, (4) the flexibility scale, F_x, of the *California personality in-*

ventory, (5) the *Thurstone concealed figures test*, for estimating flexibility of closure, (6) a *visual autokinetic test*, for determining ego closeness (to the environment)[10], (7) an *afterimage test*, which seems to be related to internal awareness, and (8) a *recall test*, for determining relationship between recall and percentage of alpha. The last two tests are of our own construction.

A typical training session has several distinct phases. After the subject is comfortably seated he closes his eyes and relaxes for three or four minutes while various recording machines are adjusted. Then the EMG signal is calibrated by having the subject squeeze a hand dynamometer to produce a one-kilogram force while the recorder and feedback circuit is adjusted. In this way, all subjects produce an equal EMG response for equal tension regardless of the exact electrode placement, skin thickness, etc. Training typically consists of the following phases.

(1) Relax with eyes closed, no feedback, for three minutes.

(2) Relax with eyes open, no feedback, for four minutes.

(3) Maintain relaxation and visualize warmth with eyes open, no feedback, for four minutes.

(4) Maintain relaxation and warmth, and establish a quiet innerfocused and alert state of mind, no feedback, for four minutes.

(5) Training with *muscle tension* feedback meter; three minutes with autogenic phrases for relaxation initiated by the experimenter, followed by four minutes of practice without phrases. Relaxation phrases, of which about eight are used, follow a typical pattern, Three such phrases are: "I feel quite quiet." "My feet are heavy." "My ankles, my knees, my hips, feel heavy and relaxed."

(6) Training with muscle tension and *warmth* meters; three minutes with several autogenic phrases for warmth initiated by the experimenter, followed by four minutes of practice without phrases. A typical warmth phrase often emphasizes both relaxation and warmth. For instance: "My hands are heavy and warm."

(7) Training with muscle tension, warmth, and *percentage-of-alpha* feedback meters; three minutes with autogenic phrases for alpha enhancement initiated by the experimenter, followed by four minutes of practice without phrases. For control of percentage of alpha we have devised autogenic-like phrases that focus attention inward, away from the outside world, and emphasize the quiet, but alert mind, as in the practice of Raja Yoga.

(8) Twenty minutes of free practice with three meters.

(9) With feedback meters switched on, subject attempts to maintain periph-

eral nervous system passivation and central nervous system alpha-activation during discussion and interview, about twelve minutes.

For five experimental subjects whose training records have been almost completely evaluated, it was found that relaxation results were essentially the same as those reported above for the seven out of twenty-one subjects who achieved unusually low tension levels in a single session. It should be noted that as attention shifts to warmth control and alpha control in the first two or three training sessions, subjects find that deep relaxation is difficult to maintain. In later sessions, control of relaxation improves. Zero levels were not observed in any of the five subjects, but all reached very low levels of tension and, when interviewed, reported significant body–image changes, including one comment: "I felt I was floating above the chair."

In respect to warmth, subjects succeeded to an encouraging, though not remarkable, degree. The average voluntary increase in temperature of the finger for the group was about one and one-half degrees centigrade after three or four training sessions. One pilot subject (not a member of the three-

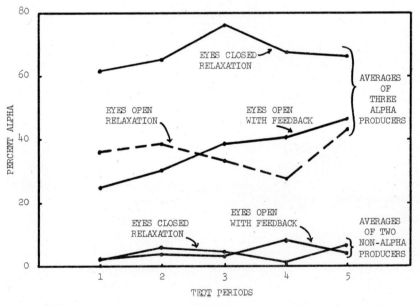

FIGURE 5 Avergage percentages of alpha rhythm under various conditions of eyes-open, eyes-closed, with and without feedback. Point 5 of the dashed line was raised unusually high by one subject who produced 79% alpha

variable training group) when working only with the temperature meter, is able to produce a change in hand temperature of 5°C in two and one-half minutes, after being requested to increase the meter reading. Training experiences have convinced us that for warmth control, practice at home for fifteen to twenty minutes per day during the one-month training period, using autogenic-type phrases and visualizations, will enhance the efficacy of the feedback sessions in the laboratory and will, of course, make it possible for the skill that is developed to be more easily applied in normal life. Warmth control does not seem to have any unusual body-image effects, but rather is accompanied by a feeling of tranquil well-being.

Average percentages of alpha for subjects on whom data reduction is complete, are shown in Figure 5. The two upper solid lines show the average results of three alpha-producing subjects, with closed eyes, and with open eyes, using feedback. The two lower solid lines show the average results of two non-alpha-producing subjects (less than 10% alpha), also with closed eyes and with open eyes (feedback). The dashed line shows the average results of the three alpha-producing subjects during relaxation without feedback, but with their eyes open. Visual examination of the records of additional subjects suggests that the increase in percentage-of-alpha in the eyes-open feedback situation is not a chance occurrence for alpha producers, but we are not yet prepared to offer statistical evidence. It will be noted that the two "non-alpha" producers give a slight indication of an increase in percentage of alpha with training. If this tendency is borne out with additional subjects, a future experiment may seek to determine the extent to which the percentage curve of non-alpha subjects can be raised.

An especially interesting finding was that in the *delayed* recall test of prose stories, the subjects who produced the highest percentages of alpha rhythm in their EEG patterns while they were recalling and speaking, remembered the most material, but since we have completed data reduction for so few subjects we have no feeling of certainty about the significance of this finding. An important observation is that every subject who learned to produce a relatively high percentage of alpha rhythm with open eyes and while being interviewed by the experimenter, was a natural high-level alpha producer with closed eyes.

A tentative summary of our *physiological* findings with about sixty subjects over a period of three years in both feedback and autogenic training studies, indicates that (1) relaxation of muscle tension down to extremely low levels is quite easy to learn with feedback of EMG signals, but not nearly so easy with autogenic phrases alone, (2) control of warmth is aided by feedback and in some cases phenomenally, but does not generally become easy with just a few practice sessions, and (3) increase in percentage of alpha rhythm with eyes open, and while talking to the experimenter, is easy to learn by feedback methods for those subjects who normally have a high percentage of alpha rhythm (above 30% when their eyes are closed), but is not easy for subjects who do not normally produce alpha rhythm with closed eyes.

A tentative summary of our *psychological* findings are (1) body–image changes, reaching a feeling of disembodiment in some subjects, seem to be associated with very low levels of muscle tension, (2) a general feeling of tranquillity is usually reported in conjunction with significant increases in hand temperature, but an accompanying drowsiness tends to interfere with the alert inner-focused state which is associated with the production of alpha rhythm, (3) a poised non-drowsy reverie is generally associated with a high percentage of alpha, and appears to facilitate recall processes, and in addition, (4) hypnagogic, awake, dream-like images have been observed by a number of pilot subjects in conjunction with periods of theta rhythm and low-frequency alpha waves.

VOLUNTARY CONTROL OF FREQUENCY OF ALPHA AND PERCENTAGE OF THETA

With the above findings in mind, we are selecting the most talented of our alpha rhythm producers for more advanced experimentation in alpha frequency lowering and conscious theta wave production. In connection with this we will test several methods of bringing the subjects to focused awareness during these physiological conditions in order to study the associated states and contents of consciousness.

The main goals of our research, it should be mentioned, are related only indirectly to the peripheral nervous system, and are focused mainly toward voluntary control of the central nervous system so that subjects can experience, and we can study, the states of awareness which are associated with the conscious control of alpha and theta rhythms in the brain. The reason for working at first with the peripheral nervous system, is because it is relatively easy to learn the rudiments of passive volition therein. Central control is not easily attained, and very few people can, without previous practice in passive volition, significantly lower the frequency of their basic alpha rhythm, or consciously increase the percentage of theta rhythm in their EEG pattern. The last two items, lowering of alpha frequency and increase in percentage of theta, are associated with a developing awareness of normally unconscious processes[11,12]. In this connection, it is interesting to note that pilot work, with three subjects who have practiced meditation, indicates that effort toward the voluntary control of internal states, if persisted in, is accompanied by extensions of perception, and appears to lead to what some people have called "altered states of consciousness".

Feedback in frequency of alpha and percentage of theta is obtained by switching on a fourth and a fifth bar of light on the subject's feedback panel. The fourth bar of light is arranged so that a change in the frequency of alpha from 12 Hz to 8 Hz causes the bar to rise from the bottom to the top. The fifth bar rises to the top when the subject produces continuous theta waves for a ten-second period. One pilot subject could essentially do this, and could communicate verbally during trains of theta.

AUDITORY FEEDBACK

In addition to the visual display of EEG data, we are beginning pilot studies in which auditory feedback of delta (0.5–4 Hz), theta (4–8 Hz), alpha (8–13 Hz), and beta information (13–26 Hz) is used. For this we have constructed a stereo–audio feedback system in which the frequencies in each EEG band are multiplied by 200. Separate banks of EEG filters for signals from the left and right occiputs control both frequencies and amplitudes of audio oscillators, whose signals when recombined, give a pleasant modernistic biological music, which we call "the music of the hemispheres". Just below the experimenter's hand in Figure 4 are eight switches which individually control the auditory feedback to the two ears in each of the four EEG bands. When training with auditory feedback, the subject and experimenter will both wear stereo headphones.

Although auditory feedback is expected to be useful in training subjects in awareness of internal states associated with alpha and theta bands, especially in early stages of training, it seems to be so internalized that the subject cannot easily verbalize. We are hypothesizing, therefore, that a visual tie-in will be useful in attempting to enhance both consciousness and the ability to communicate while in the alpha-theta border region. As already mentioned, each auditory component of the stereo system can be presented singly to the appropriate ear, but in addition a monaural arrangement makes it possible to provide both ears with feedback of any component or combination of components, from either left or right occiput. Thus, visual and auditory feedback can be used together.

SIGNAL HANDLING AND RECORDING

Feedback of physiological information involves a number of real-time signal-handling steps, and in order to present percentage and frequency of EEG data, we have had to construct small single-purpose computers. Computing, recording, and signal-handling gear is shown in Figure 6. The most important physiological signals are recorded, raw, on the tape machine in the background for back-up in case of polygraph malfunction. Recorded information includes (1) the various physiological signals already mentioned, (2) heart rate, which is obtained from the photoplethysmograph signal, (3) percentages of delta, theta, alpha, and beta waves, from either right or left occiputs, whichever is selected, (4) event markers which show the presence of EEG signals meeting specific criteria for amplitude, frequency, and duration, in each of the four EEG bands, for either left or right occiput, (5) continuous tachometer-like readout of frequencies in each of the four EEG bands, for left or right occiput, (6) event markers controlled by a voice-sensitive relay, to indicate the exact times of the subject's verbalizations, and (7) event markers controlled by the experimenter to indicate specific phases of the training program. Our greatest single hardware difficulty at present is with an obsolete six-channel polygraph, on which are recorded those data whose loss will least seriously jeopardize our work.

SIGNIFICANCE

If a successful training procedure develops out of this combined physiological and psychological research with feedback techniques, it is anticipated that it will be of significance in the fields of psychology, psychosomatic medicine, psychiatry, education, and research in creativity.

(1) Psychology has long suffered, at least in the United States, from the exclusion of "attention" and "consciousness" because these words could not be operationally defined. Now it is hoped to help reinstate these once-abandoned concepts through the use of feedback techniques, and even more, reintroduce *volition* into experimental psychology. Volition has been largely ignored in the United States for seventy years, since the days of William

FIGURE 6 Computing for on-line feedback of physiological variables and for automatic data reduction is an essential feature of a voluntary controls project. Immediate knowledge is needed by the experimenters concerning a subject's performance in order to efficiently modify various training procedures, especially in the early phases of research

James. Johannes Schultz, be it noted, is a German, and Roberto Assagioli, the author of *Psychosynthesis*[12], in which volition is of great significance, is an Italian. Carl Jung, of course, was a Swiss.

(2) Psychosomatic medicine is an obvious area for application of feedback techniques. In the last ten months, for instance, several of our subjects have

reduced or eliminated chronic headaches through the use of autogenic phrases and a portable temperature feedback device which they were able to work with at home for two weeks. One of these subjects has stopped using medication and has been free from headaches for over six months. She also taught herself to increase the temperature of her feet at night, and was able to alleviate a long-standing insomnia problem.

In appropriate situations, starvation and absorption of tumors through blood flow control would be an interesting psychosomatic area in which to work. The elimination of warts through hypnosis, a well-established fact, is possibly a function of blood flow control.

(3) Psychiatrists will be able to develop in many patients a deep reverie in a short period of time through the use of feedback techniques for deep relaxation, and if they use EEG feedback during interviews with selected cases, as we have done with each experimental subject, an increased amount of normally unconsciousness material of analytic value should be recoverable.

(4) Education has need of a method for teaching control of attention, but until now no way of gauging central processes was available. The control of attention can be learned through EEG feedback techniques, and if it should prove to be a fact that better recall is associated with higher percentages of alpha rhythm, then it may be feasible to teach students how to put themselves into that psychophysiological state which facilitates recall. The pain of an education could be lessened, and mental blocks during examinations, for instance, could perhaps be avoided.

(5) Creativity is one of the fascinating areas of modern research and it is interesting to note that the psychological state associated with hypnagogic-like imagery has been reported by many outstanding thinkers as the condition in which their most valuable ideas came to them. To describe this state, they have used such phrases as "the fringe of consciousness", "the off-conscious", "the transliminal mind", "the threshold of consciousness", and "reverie". Feedback of EEG signals certainly has bearing in this area, and it is not difficult to imagine a research program in creativity in which brain-wave feedback is used for voluntary induction of that psychophysiological state, in the alpha–theta border region, which is associated with such descriptive statements.

References

1. B. B. Brown, "Recognition of aspects of consciousness through association with EEG alpha activity represented by a light signal", *Psychophysiol.*, in press (1969).
2. E. Dewan, "Communication by voluntary control of the encephalogram", *Proc. Symp. Biomed. Eng.*, *Milwaukee*, Marquette University, Wisconsin (1966).
3. E. E. Green, E. D. Walters, and A. M. Green, "Feedback technique for deep relaxation", *Psychophysiol.*, **6**, 1969, 371–7.
4. J. Kamiya, "Operant control of the E.E.G. alpha rhythm and some of its reported effects on consciousness", in *Altered States of Consciousness: A Book of Readings* (Ed. C. T. Tart), Wiley, New York, London (1969).
5. T. Mullholland and S. Runnals, "The effect of voluntarily directed attention on successive cortical activation responses", *J. Psychol.*, **55**, 427–36 (1963).
6. D. P. Nowlis and J. Kamiya, "The control of electroencephalographic alpha rhythms through auditory feedback and the associated mental activity", *Psychophysiol.*, in press (1969).
7. J. H. Schultz and W. Luthe, *Autogenic Training: A Physiologic Approach in Psychotherapy*, Grune and Stratton, New York (1959).
8. E. Jacobsen, *Progressive Relaxation*, University of Chicago Press, Chicago (1938).
9. J. V. Basmajian, "Control and training of individual motor units", *Science*, **141**, 1963, 440–1.
10. H. M. Voth and H. Mayman, "Diagnostic and treatment implications of ego-closeness–ego-distance: autokinesis as a diagnostic instrument", *Comp. Psychiat.*, **8**, No. 4, 203–16 (1967).
11. B. K. Anand, G. S. Chhina, and B. Singh, "Some aspects of electroencephalographic studies in yogis, *Electroencephalog. Clin. Neurophysiol.*, **13**, No. 3, 452–6 (1961).
12. A. Kasamatsu and T. Hirai, "Science of Zazen", *Psychol.* **6**, 86–91 (1963).
13. R. Assagioli, *Psychosynthesis*, Hobbs, Dorman and Co., New York (1965).

Creative work and computer structures

Z. L. RABINOVICH

Institute of Cybernetics, Kiev, U.S.S.R.

Summary

Automation of creative work processes is presented in the form of man—machine systems, using heuristic and formal methods. The "technological" peculiarity of such systems is examined, and the place of computers in the scheme is evaluated, particularly as regards the problem of "intellect". The construction of complex computer structures as cybernetic tools requires the use of special computer design methods.

CREATIVE PROCESS OF INFORMATION PROCESSING AND ITS AUTOMATION

The term "creative process" will mean—in this paper—any information processing executed even though partially in a non-formalized way in order to create a new information structure (creative work object). For all that the process of information processing *entirely* executed by the system of formulated rules (i.e. which is determined with the detailization sufficient for its realization by the computer) is considered completely formalized and so non-creative. Thus, unlike the latter, the creative process of information processing (in this interpretation) consists in *the variable non-formalized arriving at the solutions and in actions corresponding to this solution* in conformity with the results of the preceding steps and the aims in view.

For example, a usual problem compiling process together with problem solution already forms a creative process, though not clearly expressed. Moreover, the steps of arriving at the solution here if not formalized (selec-

tion or compilation of the solution method, writing a program in an algorithmic language, trial read-out analysis, program correction, etc.) are creative, but actions execution steps (automatic translation of a program and its
fulfilment by the computer, including trial read-out) are completely algo-
rithmized. This process will be more creative if the solution algorithm is
unknown beforehand and the program is compiled in separate successive
portions in conformity with the preceding results. Finally, especially creative is the artistic creation work, where not only steps of arriving at solutions
are non-formalized, but also the steps of actions execution in conformity
with these solutions, i.e. the whole process is non-formalized (though there
may be the elements of formalization as rhythm and rhyme restrictions in
poems, for example).

However, this does not mean that this process is the most complicated
one of creative processes. Quite the opposite, the process of the scientific
creative work may appear more complicated just because of these strong
restrictions in arriving at solutions (which must satisfy certain validity criteria); at the same time this fact gives the opportunity for certain formalization of this process.

Summing up these considerations it is possible to define the general
scheme of the creative process as the sequence solution (ϱ) on the operations (δ) of creative object construction and these very operations, executing
these solutions, i.e. this scheme may be given as follows:

$$\varrho_1, \delta_1; \varrho_2, \delta_2; \ldots; \varrho_i, \delta_i; \ldots; \varrho_{n-1}, \delta_{n-1}; \varrho_n, \delta_n$$

Each of the indicated pairs is the dependence

$$\delta_i = \varrho_i\left(S_{i-1}, M\left(S_{l<i-1}\right), M(C), M(K), M(Z)\right)$$

$$S_i = \delta_i\left(S_{i-1}, M(Z)\right)$$

where S_{i-1} and S_i are the situations arrived at the $(i-1)$th and ith steps;
$S_{l<i-1}$ a set of situations (creative object states) arrived at the $(i-2)$th
steps; $M(C)$ a set of aims; $M(K)$ a set of the approach to the aims criteria;
and $M(Z)$ the totality of fixed knowledges of the information processor.

It is impossible to express a priori in a formal way the dependence ϱ_i because of the creative process definition mentioned above. The term ϱ_i shows
that arriving at the decision on actions δ_i on the coming ith step of the process (including working out of a formal method of its arriving at if it is possible) depends on the estimate of the results got on the $(i-1)$th step, i.e.

on the situation S_{i-1} estimate, but also in comparison with preceding situations $S_{l<i-1}$.

The estimates and arriving at the decision are executed in accordance with the criteria ($M(K)$) determining the degree of aims arriving ($M(C)$) and with the totality of knowledges ($M(Z)$) use. The solution (δ) end the situation (S) are essential variables here, and moreover, they differ from each other by different degrees of approximation to the set aims ($M(C)$). However in the time of working out of the solution ϱ, the criteria $M(K)$ and even aims $M(C)$ can change, but the principal aim cannot change cardinally as it will already mean the substitution of this creative process by a new one. Besides, knowledge $M(Z)$ is enriched if it has foreseen a possibility of remembering characteristic features of the creative process being realized. Thus, the process of arriving at the decision on any ith step, characterized in general by the dependence ϱ_i, is a two-staged process. Its first stage on the ith step is the analysis and estimate of the results of execution of actions δ_{i-1} (realizing the ϱ_{i-1}th solution), and the second stage is the working out of the plan of the next stage of actions δ_i (program), for example, determining of the sequence of information processing concrete operators. The stages of working out of the solution do not change the state of the creative object themselves. These states are changed only under the influence of the executive process δ, on each stage (δ_i) of which a new state of the creative object—situation S_i, is working out in accordance with solution δ_i on the basis of situation δ_{i-1} using the knowledges $M(Z)$.

The creative process whatsoever is, as a rule, of a heuristic character. Really, the author–executor of the process chooses (in every step of the process) the solution δ_i in the multi-dimensional space of solutions using heuristic methods—in the sense of the indefiniteness of arriving at the aim with these methods. It should be noted that the heuristic process of information processing can also be non-creative (in the given interpretation) and it will take place in case the heuristic process is completely formalized.

The expediency and possibility of automation of this or that concrete creative process depends first of all on its aims and its kind. These two factors (expediency and possibility) are not contradictory. Really, for the process can even partially be automatized it must be formalized in a certain degree. It is worst of all to formalize such a creative process which is connected with a huge variety of sets of solutions, actions, knowledges, and mainly, in which the criteria of arriving at the aim are of an emotional character. But the processes processing these features, artistic creative work, for example, relate solely to the prerogative of the creator, and the automation of these processes is not expedient (but this fact does not except the necessity of simulation of these processes in order to investigate them).

The creative processes that it is useful to automate (fully or in part), have, as a rule, clear criteria of arriving at the aim, which can be formally expressed. Technical creative work, scientific researches, long-term planning, etc., refer to processes of this kind. However, though it is useful and possible to automate the above, while executing this automation there appear essential difficulties, connected with the examination of a large number of variants. In partial automation these difficulties are overcome on the basis of reasonable compromises in distribution of the creative process functions between different processors of information—men and computers.

First of all it is possible to note the essential difference in possibilities of formalization of the process of arriving at the solution ($\varrho = \varrho_1, \varrho_2, ..., \varrho_n$) and the process of transformation of the situation ($\delta = \delta_1, \delta_2, ..., \delta_n$). The first process is, in the whole, less formalized, especially as regards the choice of the solution ϱ_i itself. But as to the estimation of the situation, obtained on the preceding stage (S_{i-1}), on the basis of which this solution is arrived at, there are real possibilities of automation unless the criteria are especially emotional (in the true sense of the word).

Thus, automation for process ϱ, considered as the auxiliary means of accelerating the arriving at the decision, means facilitating the estimation of the received situation and simplifying the use of the knowledge $M(Z)$ (extraction of the necessary information), etc. Such an automation in no way restricts the display of the creative abilities of a man, and on the contrary, it releases him of the auxiliary formalized work and reserves for the intuitions only the highest spheres of the creative process, promoting to its more effective influence on the course and the results of this process.

The second process (δ) is undoubtedly easier for automation, as at each step it already consists of executing definite actions in accordance with the decision arrived at, i.e. in the work of the *chosen* sequence of operators δ_i at the situation S_{i-1}. However, there may also appear essential difficulties connected with the examination of a large number of variants and depending on the character of the creative process the range of the automation role varies from the main one to the insignificant auxiliary one, but the trend in the possibility of automating this process is very strong. Thus, when supporting the indicated trend it is obvious that the greater weight of the process δ in comparison with the process ϱ in the whole process of information processing favours the possibilities of automation. On the other hand, with this trend the possibilities for the automation of a creative process are promoted with its steps quantity reduction, when arriving at decisions on stages ϱ_i about the large stages of actions δ_i corresponds to the compiling of the whole program δ in the process ϱ_1 as a limiting case of one step. If the stages of the formalized sequence of actions are short (i.e. the rate of the non-formalized interference of the process is high) it is quite natural that the possibilities of such a process are less.

Thus, the whole method of automation of creative processes (if it is expedient, of course) consists in dismembering the whole process into subprocesses of arriving at decisions (ϱ) and transformation of situations (δ), and in picking out (within these subprocesses) formalized sections, which would be fully realized by means of automatic information processing. Moreover, for different possibilities of automation of subprocesses ϱ and δ it should be expected that the transitions from the first subprocess steps to the steps of the second one will coincide with the boundaries of the corresponding non-automatized and automatized areas of the general creative processes.

COMPUTER INTELLIGENCE AND THE QUESTION OF DEVELOPMENT OF COMPUTER STRUCTURES

Requirements for automating facilities which at present are still completely insufficiently adapted for participation in creative problem solution follow the main idea indicated. These requirements must include two main parts of the problem.

(1) The corresponding development of information processing methods that would allow the extension of the scope of efficiently formalized sections of creative processes.

(2) The corresponding establishment of possibilities of the efficient realization of the man–computer dialogue regime, that just appears in the automated of a creative process, consisting of *separate* steps of subprocesses ϱ and δ.

Both these requirements are essentially reflected in the computers structure. Moreover, following the above concepts we also consider the computer structure, the so-called internal software (all kinds of data including standard computational and auxiliary algorithms selected in the computer structurally, i.e. in the hardware and in long-time memory of *any* kind). The present problem of computers structures development can be defined in general as the problem of the "computer intelligence" increase. The word "intelligence" in this application is convenient as it includes a great number of computer useful properties, which became of great significance owing to the increase of computer qualification in solution of complicated logical problems on symbol and numerical information processing (creative processes automation problems predominate over these problems). However, in application to the computer the concept of "intelligence" naturally acquires some simplified interpretation; that is why it would be provided with the epithet "computer".

The following computer properties will be considered to belong to computer intelligence.

(a) Rich knowledge and data (constants, concepts, all kinds of standard algorithms); convenient use of this knowledge and its enrichment (by means of learning, for example).

(b) Logical perfection of information processing methods in the computer and its ability for self-organization of a computational process, which are secured by a certain structure of the auxiliary algorithm.

(c) The grade of the computer's comprehension of input algorithmic high level languages. The levels of development of these properties do determine the level of "computer intelligence".

It is clear that the totality of these properties imitates in the computer variant such properties of man intelligence as erudition, ingenuity, speed of information processing, perception of input information. It should be noted that man intelligence is far from being exhausted by these properties but they appear to be the most important from the point of view of increasing the computers possibilities in creative processes automation. Of great importance is the fact that the increase of computer intelligence (in this interpretation) provides the increase of efficiency of computer mathematical utilization process in general, i.e. in solution of all kinds of problems. This is possible because of the essential simplification of man–computer interaction at the expense of the computer intelligence increase. It naturally influences the efficiency of the problems solution, and especially the solution of problems that are of creative character, solved in the regime of high man–computer interaction in the dialogue, when man takes an active part in the general process of problem solution as a direct information processor (in nonautomatized sections of the subprocesses ϱ and δ).

Of great interest and importance from the standpoint of man–computer interaction is property "$\dot{c}$". With sufficient intelligence this property means nearness of the operative program language (about the so-called program level of the internal language—see below) to the input algorithmic language which is the language of initial programs, and it removes or reduces the language barrier and consequently the man–computer translation mediation. The authors of a great number of works on this subject which recently appeared (mainly Soviet and American, and also English, French and German) consider this factor to possess at least the following advantages.

(i) Simplification of translation systems and possibility of using a number of algorithmic languages as the input languages for a given computers.

(ii) Securing of analogy in mapping of information processing in the operative and initial programs.

(iii) Retention of the initial program property in the operating program.

(iv) Securing of conditions for high efficiency of execution of standard algorithms, foreseen by the input language.

(v) Simplification of the operating system, especially with the regimes of multi-program and multi-processor information processing.

(vi) Securing of the possibilities for further development of algorithmic languages without an excessive complication of the translation system.

The first two considerations especially influence the simplification of man–computer interaction in the process of mathematical utilization with all possible consequences which are of great importance for the creative information processing regime; the third consideration stimulates programming in algorithmic languages; the fourth and the fifth considerations and also all the preceding factors facilitate the organization and increase the efficiency of the computational process in general.

The last consideration is of great importance from the standpoint of automation of the creative problems solution process, for the further development of algorithmic languages towards their rapprochement with natural languages should considerably simplify the organization of the man–computer dialogue and promote the possibilities of its conducting by people having no other preparation than the specialization in those problems which they solve together with the computer.

The cardinal stage in the development of algorithmic languages causes the increase of the gap between these and internal languages (this gap is absorbed by the translation systems), and this fact in its turn will stimulate the further development of internal languages which again allows to develop algorithmic languages, and so on. Thus, the man–computer interaction level should constantly increase, and it is of paramount importance for creative processes automation.

The problem of computer structures adaptation for creative problems means first of all a corresponding development of their internal languages, as they include the most characteristic features of the computer intelligence ((a), (b), and (c)). There are really fixed in the internal language, as quantities identificators and standard algorithm, all the input data, all the concepts acquired by the computer in the process of learning, all means of organization and control over the conventional process, as auxiliary algorithms identificator, and, at last, all the input information that is directly used in the computer. The internal language is one that the computer "understands" directly executing algorithms written in it with the help of their interpretation. Moreover, the interpretation is defined as the process of the concurrent transformation of the algorithms from the high program level of the internal language (ϱ), through the intermediate levels $R_1, R_2, \ldots, R_k$ to its level of micro-order signals (M) (determining already the execution of corresponding micro-operations):

$$A_m = J_{R_K \to m} \{J_{R_{K-1} \to R_K} \{J_{R_1 \to R_2} [J_{P \to R_1}(Ap)]\}\}$$

where the index of algorithm A means the level of the internal language, in which it is expressed in the process of information processing, and $I_{\alpha \to \beta}$ – the stage which means the transformation of the algorithm from level α to level β.

Thus, man does not notice the interpretation process in the computer as well as the problem solution of computation itself. That is why the internal language, which is the interpreted one, is regarded as the language understandable by the computer. In the sense of this term it is of no importance that the computer itself translates from the input into the internal language with the help of the program translator (as the man in order to understand the text in an unknown language translates it with the help of a dictionary and a certain system of rules). The development of internal languages in the direction of the increase of the computer intelligence causea a characteristic development of systems of their interpretation. These questions in connection with the problem of approaching the internal languages to the algorithmic languages have already been described in literature[1,2]. That is why there will, only, be submitted the idea of the indicated development of computer structures in connection with the problem of their intelligence increase.

The internal language is developed in two directions. The first direction is the usage of main facilities on its program level, including large extended algorithmic programming languages constructions which, of course, should correspond to the character of automated creative processes. This provides the distribution of tasks to the computer without their essential transmission and detailing. This fact is of great importance for attaining high efficiency, for facilitating and conveniently conducting a creative process in the man–computer dialogue regime, in that widespread case (involving even the common process of problems preparation for their solving in the computer), when the programs of automated sections of the process are not known beforehand and are defined by man as regards non-formalized sections.

The second direction is the usage of the lower level of the branched network of macro- and micro-facilities, providing high efficiency of different standard (conventional and auxiliary) algorithm realization, including the algorithms of interpretation of the high program level facilities. The characteristic functional features of systems of interpretation of the internal languages, developed in such a way, are as follows.

(a) Corresponding detailing of large operations (including the operations on processing of symbol information) and different standard procedures (including that, conducting over the files).

(b) The current analysis of programs in order to find the next feasable operation and to define its contents—depending on the types of operands.

(c) The current accomodation and addressing of information in the computer memory.

Thus, the developed interpretation systems, in comparison with trivial, possess a new analyzing part (functions (b) and (c)) and an essentially extended traditional actuating part (function (a)). The increased complexity of the computers structure increases the necessity of formalization of their design, which appears to be a difficult creative process realized in an automated way by the man–computer system. Formalized and automatized computer design is carried out by the cybernetic methods on the basis of consideration of the information processing process as a multilevel one. In this realm there appears a special "push–pull" link between cybernetics and its devices—computing techniques, the link which promotes their mutual development.

References

1. V.M.Glushkov and E.L.Rabinovich, "O nekotorygh problemagh razvitia algoritmi-
chiskigh struktur vychislitelnygh mashin", *Sb. Kibernetika na slughby kommunizmu*
(1966).
2. V.M.Glushkov, S.B.Pogrebinsky, Z.L.Rabinovich, and A.A.Stogny, "Some questions of d.c. structures in connection with the systems of their softwares", *J. Cybernetics* (1967).

Cybernetics and warfare

JOHN VOEVODSKY

Cybernetica Research Corporation
Stanford, California, U.S.A.

Summary

Warfare is demonstrated to be an orderly and repetitive behavioural event by cybernetic analysis of Vital Statistics of the U.S. Civil War, World Wars I and II, the Korean War, and the Vietnam War. The repetitive behavioural pattern of past wars suggests that the U.S. is in a decision period where the Vietnam War is either settled at the present levels of violence or another major escalation will be forthcoming. No attempt is made to explain the processes which result in the behavioural orderliness. The data of all five wars are seen to fit very closely the same, simple mathematical laws.

INTRODUCTION

During the last 100 years, the United States has fought four major wars to conclusion: the Civil War, World War I, World War II, and the Korean War. For the past eight years, we have been engaged in a fifth and not yet concluded war, the war in Vietnam, which has occupied our minds, our troops, and our resources longer than any other war in our history.

And yet, despite its record duration, the Vietnam War appears to be progressing, as of this writing, in the same orderly manner as our four previous wars. For an inquiry into the repetitive behavioural patterns of nations at war, particularly of the United States, our allies, and our enemies during the last 100 years, reveals that we and the enemy are acting today in the same way as we have acted in the past. Because of this orderliness of our behaviour, it now appears that we may be at a crisis point in the Vietnam War where either a settlement is possible or another major escalation is indicated.

This orderly manner in which the Vietnam War and the previous wars have progressed is based on an examination of the phenomena—the vital statistics—of modern armed conflict by means of cybernetic analysis. Thus, it is an identification and demonstration of the orderly progress of warfare that is the primary concern of this paper, together with the derivation of equations that express mathematically the relationships among the vital statistics of warring nations.

The present investigation is purely of an exploratory nature, it should be emphasized; and no pretence is made that it is possible at present to explain fully and in detail all the factors which result in the orderly progress of warfare.

All such endeavours, though, however bravely undertaken and whatever their results may be, have a theoretical origin. This research is no exception. In fact, it has two origins: one in the quantitative behavioural concepts of the psychologist S.S.Stevens[1] and the other in the cybernetic concepts of the mathematician Norbert Wiener[2]. In essence, Stevens shows that quantification of behaviour is readily achieved by the assignment of numerals to distinguishable behavioural events in the career of living systems. These behavioural events become the system variables, which are time variant. The system variables, in addition, appear to have the characteristics inherent in linear second-order feedback-control systems of the type first conceived by Wiener. Furthermore, the work on the quantitative nature of warfare performed by L.F.Richardson[3] and F.W.Lanchester[4] supports these general observations.

THE VITAL STATISTICS OF WAR

The quantitative behavioural data which best describe modern warfare fall into three categories: battle strength, battle casualties, and battle deaths. By coincidence, these are the vital statistics of war, because nations habitually count their troops, assess their attrition, and record the results of combat for current and historical uses. From the point of view of the analyst, though, these particular items of data have a value in addition to their ubiquity. They have an advantage over other war statistics, because they appear to be remarkably stable and accurate, since in most cases they have stood the scrutiny of countless researchers over long periods of time.

It should be further emphasized that only official government sources are used for the statistics in this analysis, with two exceptions. French and German battle deaths and casualties during World War I were taken from Winston S. Churchill's compilation of official records[5]. Union and Confederate statistics for the Civil War were taken from Thomas L. Livermore's compilation of official records[6].

The basic vital statistics, battle strength, battle casualties, and battle deaths, unless carefully defined, may mean different things to different analysts. In this analysis, the numbers used for all wars represent only Army personnel, officers, and enlisted men, reported at the specified instant of time that is under consideration. This applies whether the troops are Union, Confederate, French, German, British, or American. In the case of the Vietnam War, however, numbers of total Department of Defense forces, which includes Army, Air Force, Navy, Marine Corps, and Coast Guard, are used separately and in addition to the numbers used for the Army personnel.

For the United States Army, battle strength is the total number of officers and enlisted men at any instant, t, deployed in the battle zone. For the Vietnam War, the battle zone is considered to be South Vietnam, and the number of Army personnel in South Vietnam at any instant is considered to be the Army battle strength[7]. This does not include Army personnel who are off shore or are in any other location such as Thailand.

Army battle strength for the Korean War is the total number of Army personnel on the Korean Peninsula at any instant (see Department of Defense[8], data is taken from Table 3); for World War II, it is the total number stationed outside the continental limits of the United States at any instant of time[9]; for World War I it is the total number in France, at any instant (see Ayres[10], p. 15). Similarly, British Army battle strength is the total number of British Army personnel in France at any instant of time during World War I (see Ayres[10], p. 14). Comparative statistics for German Army battle strength during World War I were not available in suitable form.

For the Civil War, the Union Army battle strength is the total number of personnel on the Union rolls at any instant, and the Confederate Army battle strength is the total number of personnel on the Confederate returns at any instant (see Livermore[6], p. 47). Of all the war statistics included in this analysis, the Civil War strength data show the widest fluctuations and are considered the least reliable of all the data.

Army battle casualties for the Vietnam War[6]*, the Korean War[11]†, and World War II[12]‡ are the accumulated totals from the beginning of the particular war up to any instant of time, t, of all Army personnel killed in action, dead as the result of wounds or injuries received in action, wounded or injured in action, missing in action, captured by the opposing forces, or taken into custody as internees by the authorities of a neutral country. The term "in action" characterizes a casualty status in which an individual suffered death or injury as a direct result of enemy action, either while engaged in a battle, going to it, or returning from it. Excluded from United States Army battle casualties are injuries or deaths that resulted from exposure to the elements or from diseases.

Army battle deaths for the Vietnam War, the Korean War, and World War II are the accumulated totals from the beginning of the wars up to any instant, t, of Army personnel who were killed in action, died as a result of injuries or wounds received in action, or declared dead while missing in action.

For the United States Army World War I, the time variants in the battle casualties are not known. The time variants in battle deaths are known. Total U.S. battle casualties at the end of World War I include dead, wounded, missing and prisoners (see Ayres[10], pp. 120–2††). Similarly, mutually

---

* Only 1% of battle casualties are classified as missing and prisoners. This is the lowest percentage of all wars considered.

† Of all battle casualties recorded, approximately 10% were listed as missing in action, captured, or returned.

‡ All theaters and campaigns, including the Army Air Corps officers and enlisted men, are grouped in U.S. Army casualties, except from 7 December 1941 to 10 May 1942. During this period three non-combat divisions were captured and held for the duration of the war. This resulted in 30,838 casualties and 13,847 deaths being listed as having occurred in the single month of May 1942. This accounting procedure thus caused the only significant statistical anomaly noted in all the data. Hence these data were excluded. About 9.3% of all battle casualties are classified as missing or captured.

†† Battle deaths include only deaths from action. They do not include deaths from diseases and privation. Battle deaths for the month of May 1917 were estimated as 400, the month of April as 100, and the month of December as 800. With these estimates, a 4.4% difference exists between total battle deaths of 48,909 reported on page 122 and the accumulated total deaths on page 120. Total battle casualties at the end of the war were 286,330 of which 7347 were classified as missing in action of taken prisoner. 230,074 were the total wounded. The rest were killed. As in the Vietnam War, negligible casualties are classified as missing and prisoners, about 2.6%. No reasonable explanation for this similarity has been forthcoming.

caused British versus German[13]* and French versus German[5] battle casualties include dead, wounded, missing and prisoners. Only the U.S. Civil War Battle casualties, which included dead and wounded, exclude missing and prisoner because the data was unavailable[6]†. The interested auditors of this paper should consult the original sources cited for more detailed definitions of battle strength, battle casualties, and battle deaths.

The British-German and French-German World War I and U.S. Civil War vital statistics should be considered as approximations. Differences exist in the data for each war which must be considered by the analyst as measurement error. The size of the error, unfortunately, is not known at this time. Also, when the analyst compares the errors between wars, he should assume that part of the errors are due to differences in accounting procedures. The errors that might occur in the United States data for the Vietnam War, the Korean War, the World War II, however, can be considered the smallest, since statistics for the three wars are compiled by the same government, are close together in time, and major changes in accounting procedures do not appear to have been made. No detailed studies have been made of the exact accounting methods employed by the other governments because of the exploratory nature of this research. The data have been taken more or less on faith from official sources, except where noted. The reader should be assured,

---

* The British list a total of 2,441,673 casualties, including missing and prisoners, and 2,177,484, excluding missing and prisoners. Thus, approximately 11% of the total were classified as missing and prisoners. Similarly, the total German casualties, including missing and prisoners, is 1,680,396, of which 1,313,421 were wounded and killed. Thus, approximately 22% have been classified as missing and prisoners mostly in the last year of the war. Finally, comparative statistics between Great Britain and Germany are not available for 1914. These data are assumed small in comparison with the total losses.

† For certain battles, listed on pp. 140 and 141, Confederate strength on the battle field for a particular battle (not battle strength) had to be estimated and was assumed to be one half of the known Union strength. This in general proved to be the case throughout the war. Estimates of Confederate battle casualties, when their derivation was necessary, were made by multiplying the Confederate battlefield strength by 0.123, which is the average Confederate casualty per soldier engaged in thirty battles of which twelve were defeats and eighteen were victories. Estimates of Confederate battle deaths, when made necessary, were derived by multiplying Confederate battle casualties for that battle by 17.6%, which is the average for twenty-nine battles. Estimates of Union battle deaths were made by multiplying Union battle casualties by 17.5% which is the average for thirty-seven battles. Union and Confederate missing, and prisoners were not available.

however, that when conclusions are drawn, he will be alerted to the possible error in the base statistics so that he may discount the conclusions to the degree he chooses.

METHOD OF ANALYSIS

A mere compilation in tabular form of these three items of data, arrayed over time, reveals very little about the progressive nature of the statistics for a particular war, the relationships that exist between opposing forces in a particular war, or the relationships that exist among the statistics of different wars. Yet it is an identification of these significant relationships that is being sought in this analysis through a graphic and mathematical manipulation of the three sets of vital statistics. Thus, here are identified and separated out for examination the relationships between battle casualties and battle deaths, between battle strength and battle casualties, between opposing forces (the effect of their coupled statistics), and between battle strength and time. Other by-products, such as the effectiveness of weapons systems, can also be identified.

In order to accomplish this purpose of identifying significant relationships, the standard scientific method of analysis is followed. The published statistics were gathered and put into the form dictated by the theories of Stevens and Wiener. For example, one important feature of the dictated form is to record accumulated totals over time. Any two sets of these data, thus compiled, define co-ordinate points. Semilog paper is used to plot the relationship of the statistics to time, and loglog paper is used to plot the relationship of one vital statistic to another. This is done because semilog and loglog paper best illustrate the respective exponential and power relationships that were found to exist.

The connection of one data point to another on the graph paper, of course, results in two types of lines. The exponential functions produce curves and straight lines. The power functions produce straight lines. In presenting these data graphically a suitable mean line has been drawn through the data points by inspection. Owing to the exploratory nature of the research, it is considered unnecessary to employ more rigorous methods of curve fitting.

Thus, it must be said that the basic method, or scheme of analysis, is not materially different from that followed in any other responsible scientific investigation. What is different here are the items chosen for analysis, the uniqueness of their arrangement, and the results of their manipulation.

BATTLE DEATHS AND BATTLE CASUALTIES

Identification of the mathematical relationship between battle deaths and battle casualties is the first of the four equations presented here to demonstrate the orderly progress of warfare. The relationship is shown in Figure 1

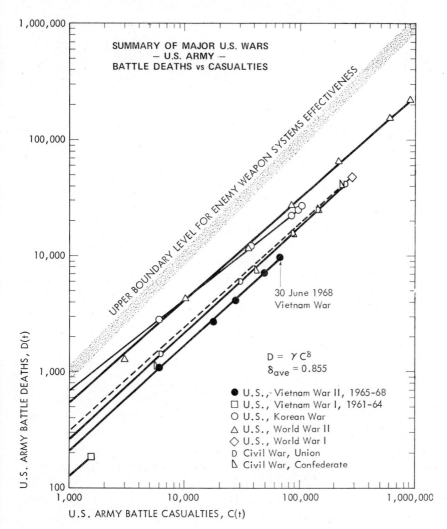

FIGURE 1   U.S. Army battle deaths plotted versus battle casualties for the major U.S. wars

by a graphic representation of a summary of the United States Army statistics for the Vietnam War, the Korean War, World War II, World War I,
and the Civil War (both Union and Confederate sides). In order to avoid a
confusion of lines and symbols, however, the British and German statistics
for World War I are not shown in Figure 1, even though they portray an
identical relationship to the ones actually shown.

This relationship between battle deaths and battle casualties can be described mathematically from an inspection of the plotted curves by a power
function

$$D = \gamma C^\delta$$

where D is the battle deaths at any instant, t; C is the battle casualties at the
same instant, t; and γ and δ are constants, which as a by-product define the
net effectiveness of the enemy's weapons system over the effectiveness of all
countermeasures designed to protect troops. γ and δ define a family of curves, or levels, between the battle deaths and battle casualties for each war.
This formulation permits the analyst to view a coalition of nations as one
weapon system.

Since the time-variant nature of the United States Army battle casualties
for World War I is not known, but the final battle casualties and the time-
variation in battle deaths are known, the slope given to the dashed line in
Figure 1 that is drawn from the final casuality point is the average slope,
δ_{ave}. This average slope was computed by adding the slopes for the Union
and Confederate sides of the Civil War, the United States in World War II,
and the United States in the two phases (to be defined later) of the Vietnam
War and dividing the sum by five.

Quite automatically, the formulation also establishes the upper boundary
of enemy weapons system effectiveness. On the graphs, Figure 1 and Figure 2, this maximum effectiveness boundary represents points where, at a
given time, all battle casualties are also battle deaths. Hence, any data point
which falls above this boundary represents the physically impossible condition in which more fatalities than casualties occur. The main point here is
that the purposes of the weaponry is to destroy the enemy's fighting ability
by killing his troops. Therefore, the relationship of deaths to casualties is
one index of weapons effectiveness. The upper limit of weapons effectiveness,
by this definition, is when casualties equal deaths.

In no war has a sudden improvement in enemy weapons system effectiveness been more noticeable than in the Vietnam War, represented sepa-

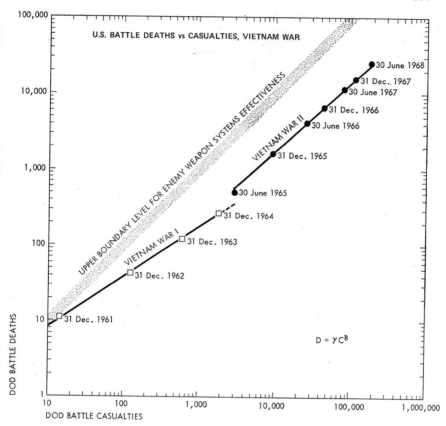

FIGURE 2   U.S. Department of Defense battle deaths plotted versus U.S. Department of Defense battle casualties for the Vietnam War

rately in Figure 2 in terms of Department of Defense battle deaths to battle casualties. Here, a smoothly progressive and constant relationship is observed to have been maintained from December 31, 1961, through December 31, 1964, which for convenience's sake is identified as Vietnam War I. In the year 1965, though, a significant change in the relationship occurred, which has held constant through June 30, 1968. This second phase of the war is identified as Vietnam War II.

The enemy weapons system effectiveness level on which Vietnam War I was fought is entirely different from the level on which Vietnam War II is being fought. That these two effectiveness levels are under other major

United States war levels is the net result of the effect of the enemy and the countereffect of our modern medical treatment, helicopter evacuation service, and other new protective systems.

These are modern times, though, and this particular enemy theoretically has access to an even more sophisticated weapons system than he is now employing. It thus appears possible that the Vietnam War could suddenly escalate to levels experienced during the Korean War and World War II and become Asian War I merely through the introduction of tanks, air power, missiles, and/or Chinese troops. An escalation in enemy weapons system effectiveness might also occur simultaneously through the employment of Chinese- and Soviet-directed tactics and strategies.

What can happen and what might happen in Vietnam in terms of battle deaths to battle casualties relationships, however, will lie somewhere between the present level and the upper boundary of weapons system effectiveness as shown in Figure 1 and Figure 2. The potential for change in the future, thus defined, lies within a limited range.

BATTLE STRENGTH AND BATTLE CASUALTIES

Identification of the mathematical relationship between battle strength and battle casualties is the second of the four equations presented to demonstrate the orderly progress of warfare. This relationship is shown in Figure 3 by a graphic representation of a summary of United States Army statistics for the Vietnam War, the Korean War, World War II, World War I, and British participation in World War I. Statistics for the Civil War are not included, because the strength figures as a function of time for both sides are known to be of questionable accuracy.

Once again a relationship pattern, one that is common to all wars analysed, is immediately discernible from an inspection of the plotted curves. This pattern, too, can be described by a power function

$$S = \alpha C^{\beta}$$

where S is the total Army strength at any instant, t; C is the Army battle casualties at the same instant; α and β are constants, which in combination define the intensity of the fighting in the battle zone. α also represents the theoretical initial battle zone strength at the moment the first battle casualty is sustained. In this sense, α is a battle-preparedness coefficient and β is the replacement coefficient.

The equation, however, represents other conditions. It states that the number of Army troops in a battle zone at a given instant is primarily determined by the battle casualties. It also states the converse. In other words, it implies that each new casualty causes the influx of new troops by a predictable amount and, conversely, that new troops produce additional casualties. This is evident, because if a simple mathematical manipulation (the logarithmic derivative) is taken, then

$$\frac{dS}{S} = \beta \frac{dC}{C}$$

results. From Figure 3, β is seen to be less than 1, where β varies very roughly from 0.57 for the Korean War, 0.38 for World War II, 0.37 for the British experience in World War I, and 0.36 for Vietnam War I and II. If β were zero, then battle strength would be a constant, α, equal to the initial fighting strength. Thus β is, then, the replacement coefficient, where the strength, when doubled in the battle zone, causes the casualties to go up roughly by nine times for all wars considered, except for the Korean War, where they went up roughly by four times.

While it is acknowledged that consideration of five data points, in this case five wars, is not necessarily proof of the existence of a phenomenon, an examination of the relationships between wars suggest that two important conclusions can be drawn.

The first is that there are limits in strength build-ups and casualties a nation will sustain, beyond which it either accepts defeat, changes its leadership, or acquires new allies. This idea is graphically illustrated in Figure 3 and Figure 4 by a lower boundary level, which defines the points where battle casualties and battle strengths are equal.

This line, in effect, represents a boundary to the right of which a nation cannot seem to pass and still sustain its own war effort. For example, Great Britain at the end of World War I suffered roughly two million battle casualties with a total strength in France at the end of the war of two million soldiers. Since the population of Great Britain at the time was 60 million, this represents 3.33% of her 1918 population. It is revealing to note that 3.33% of the United States population (110 million during World War I) is 3.67 million combat troops, or casualties, which is the point where the United States experience in World War I intersects the lower boundary when it is extended as shown by the dashed lines in Figure 3.

Furthermore, if the two United States wars in Asia, the Korean War and

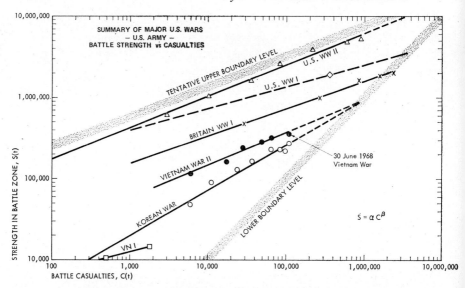

FIGURE 3   U.S. Army battle strength plotted versus U.S. Army battle
casualties for the major U.S. wars

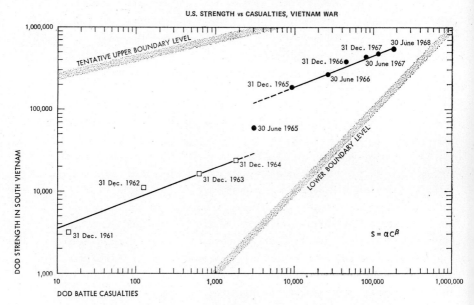

FIGURE 4   U.S. Department of Defense battle strength in South Vietnam plotted versus U.S. Department of Defense battle casualties

the Vietnam War, are extended in the same manner, they intersect with each other and with the lower boundary level at the same point, 850,000 casualties and men. Also, the estimated absolute ceiling on the number of men physically fit for active war service for the United States during World War II was between[14] 15 and 16 million, which again is the intercept of the extension of the United States World War II with the lower boundary level. This point represents 11.4% of the United States population of 131 million in 1940.

The second conclusion that can be drawn from an examination of the relationship of battle strength to battle casualties over five wars is that there appears to be an upper boundary level, or limit on the degree of mobilization that a nation's citizens will consent to as they prepare for and participate in a major war. This upper level becomes a sloping line when it is represented on the graph, which in this instance is drawn backward from the point where all potential soldiers could become casualties. The angle of the line is drawn according to a slope that is the average for all wars analysed. This average slope is $\beta_{ave} = 0.38$.

If one assumes that, as during World War II, 11.4% of the United States population represents the maximum number of soldiers we could prepare for combat, then our present 200 million population would produce a potential reservoir of 22.8 million men for an Asian war. The data show, however, that a nation does not mobilize all its potential fighting men at once. It characteristically mobilizes gradually as casualties are incurred. Therefore, this gradual mobilization, mathematically represented by $\beta_{ave} = 0.38$, appears to be a behavioural characteristic of warring nations: to maintain a balance between the maintenance of combat-eligible men in their normal productive activities in the society and the complete mobilization and commitment to battle of these same men in an effort to protect the nation's way of life.

Finally, when the strength to casualty relationship is applied to the Vietnam War, as illustrated in Figure 4, it may be clearly seen that a jump in activity occurred in 1965. This was the point at which the United States escalated its strength, expressed mathematically by changing α to a higher level of effort, in response to the change in enemy weapon system effectiveness. For the past two and a half years the relationship of strength to casualties has not changed materially. Since the data point for June 1968 is slightly to the left of the mean line, one can conclude that the United States battle strength is being kept down in comparison to the casualties received.

This means that slightly more casualties are being inflicted by the enemy than United States strength calls for. Furthermore, since the data point for June 1968 is so close to the lower boundary level, this second phase of the Vietnam War is shown to be one of the most intensely fought wars the United States has ever experienced.

RELATIONSHIP BETWEEN OPPOSING FORCES

Identification of the mathematical relationship between strength to strength, casualties to casualties, and deaths to deaths for opposing armies for a particular war is the third of the four equations presented to demonstrate the orderly progress of warfare. (The French versus German Armies; for the British versus the German Armies during World War I; for the Union and Confederate Armies during the Civil War.) Analyses for the other wars were not made, because data on enemy forces in the Vietnam Wars, and Korean War, and World War II were either not available or were not in suitable form.

Here, too, a discernible relationship can be deduced from the resulting curves, which can be described by a power function

$$Y = jX^k$$

where X and Y are identical statistics at the same instant of time for opposing forces. The coupling coefficients are j and k. In all cases studied, however, k is found to be almost equal to 1. In fact, k varies between 0.95 and 1.04. Thus, by setting k equal to 1, the coupling relationship assumes the simpler form of

$$\frac{dY}{dX} = j$$

This equation states that if one side changes its war variables, a similar change occurs on the other side. Lanchester has defined j as the exchange ratio, i.e. the ratio between those combatants lost on one side to those combatants lost on the other. Also, an increase in troops on one side results in an increase in troops on the other. This ratio also is intuitively expected because when two armies come together in combat, firing begins almost simultaneously from both sides. When the combat ends, the firing ends simultaneously on both sides. If a large battle occurs, both sides suffer large

losses at the same time. This is true regardless of whether the battle is classified as a success, a failure, a defeat, a rout, or a victory.

Historically, the Germans have been accused of dividing their casualty
statistics in half for political purposes. This may or not be the case. What is
important is that the casualty data for both sides have essentially the same
shape. The Civil War also shows this expected characteristic of similarity
in shape, and even in magnitude for the casualty statistics. Thus the most
important point to be realized here is that if the analyst is interested in when
a war begins and when it might end, as indicated by a leveling of hostilities
(measured by strengths, casualties, and deaths), he can determine this from
the casualty data of only one of the two combatants. True, the other side
might have a higher or lower strength ratio, or casualty ratio, or kill ratio,
but the leveling of hostilities occurs simultaneously and in like manner on
both sides. The reader should be cautioned, however, that this conclusion is
based on observation made of only two wars and within these two wars on
only six relationships. They are: Union and Confederate strength, Union
and Confederate casualties, Union and Confederate deaths, Frecnh and
German casualties, British and German casualties, and British and German
deaths. Thus, on this basis one may conclude that opposing warring nations
have similar behavioural patterns over time during a war even though the
ratios between statistics may be different.

As this conclusion applies to the Vietnam War, one can say: if the coupling
constants do not change, then the levelling of hostilities (as measured by the
vital statistics of warfare) is clearly discernible from the United States statistics alone. If, on the other hand, the North Vietnamese escalate the war,
the first indication to the United States will be a rise in casualties above projected levels. The coupling coefficients will then have been changed by the
enemy and a new and bigger war will have begun.

BATTLE STRENGTH AND TIME

Identification of the mathematical relationship between Army battle strength
and time is the last of the four equations presented to demonstrate the orderly
progress of warfare. Since battle deaths are related to battle casualties and
in turn are related to battle strength, the relationship between casualties
and between deaths and time can be established by means of algebraic mani-
pulations once the mathematical relationship between battle strength and
time is known.

If the behaviour of warring nations can be characterized by linear second-order feedback-control systems equations of the type first considered by Wiener and supported by the work of Richardson, Lanchester, and others[15,16], then the solutions are exponential in nature.

The general solution for a second-order system is

$$S = A + B\,e^{\lambda_1 t} + C\,e^{\lambda_2 t}$$

where A, B, C, λ_1, and λ_2 are characteristic constants of the system. For the wars studied it is found that the first exponential term quickly disappears, while the strength is less than 10% of the ultimate forces. The remaining 90% of the ultimate fighting force is characterized by only one time constant. Thus, if the analyst is concerned only with the last 90% of a war, first-order differential equations appear to describe accurately the time-variant nature of the vital statistics. Second-order equations appear to be needed only when the beginnings of wars are to be analysed. Since the Vietnam War is found to be in its terminal stages, the first 10% of wars have not been analysed.

To develop these ideas, one considers first the case of Vietnam War II, shown in Figures 5a and 5b. S denotes, in this case, the total Department of Defense strength in South Vietnam at any instant, t. The variation of battle strength, S, with time, t, is shown in Figure 5a. It is seen that if the conditions which have been acting in a particular manner over the past three years continue in an unchanged manner, the battle strength, S, approaches an upper limit, say S_∞, the ultimate number of forces that are to be engaged. By extrapolation in Figure 5a, one finds that S_∞, to a good approximation, is 600,000 Department of Defense personnel. To obtain a simple analytical representation for the function S, one finds, as shown in Figure 5b, that $\log(S_\infty - S)$ varies linearly with time, i.e. the curve $\log(S_\infty - S)$ versus t is a straight line. If $-1/\tau$ denotes the slope of this line and if S_0 denotes S at some initial time, t_0, the equation for the line is

$$\log\left[\frac{S_\infty - S(t - t_0)}{S_\infty - S_0}\right] = -\frac{t - t_0}{\tau}$$

or, equivalently,

$$\frac{S(t - t_0)}{S_\infty} = 1 - \left(1 - \frac{S_0}{S_\infty}\right)e^{-(t - t_0/\tau)}$$

Generally, for the wars analyzed here the initial strength, S_0, is much less than the final strength, S_∞, at least by a factor of 10. It is, therefore, reason-

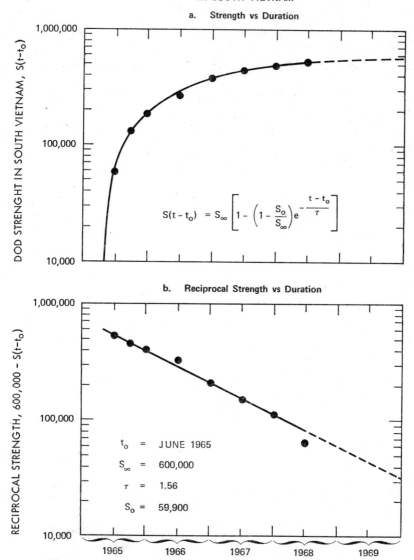

THE TIME VARIATION IN TOTAL DOD STRENGTH
IN SOUTH VIETNAM

a. Strength vs Duration

DOD STRENGHT IN SOUTH VIETNAM, $S(t-t_o)$

$$S(t - t_o) = S_\infty \left[1 - \left(1 - \frac{S_o}{S_\infty} \right) e^{-\frac{t - t_o}{\tau}} \right]$$

b. Reciprocal Strength vs Duration

RECIPROCAL STRENGTH, $600{,}000 - S(t - t_o)$

t_o = JUNE 1965

S_∞ = 600,000

τ = 1.56

S_o = 59,900

1965   1966   1967   1968   1969

FIGURE 5 (a) U.S. Department of Defense strength in South Vietnam plotted from June 1965 to June 1968, where 600,000 is estimated to be the strength of the ultimate forces to be engaged. (b) The difference between the strength of the ultimate Department of Defense forces engaged, 600,000, and the actual Department of Defense strength engaged in South Vietnam at a particular instant plotted versus time from June 1965 to June 1968 able to assume that the ratio of initial strength to final strength is much less than one and the above expression may be expressed in the simpler form of

$$\frac{S\,(t - t_0)}{S_\infty} = 1 - e^{-(t - t_0/\tau)}$$

The constant, τ, which has the dimensions of time and is referred to as the time constant, characterizes the variation of troop strength in the battle zone, S, with respect to time. For the case of Vietnam War II, as shown in Figure 5b, one finds that $\tau = 1.56$ years, i.e. in the first 1.56 years, 63% of the troops that are to be committed to the battle zone will have been committed. In the next 1.56 years, 86% of the troops will have been committed; and in the next 1.56 years (yields a total of 4.68 years), 95% of the ultimate forces will have been committed. If the coupling relationships are assumed valid, then the enemy's strength in the battle zone will have increased by the same percentages.

In like manner, the battle strength to time relationship, plotted as the fraction of ultimate forces engaged in the battle zone, is shown in Figure 6a by a graphic representation of a summary of the United States statistics for the Vietnam War, the Korean War, World War II, and World War I (including the British Army). Figure 6a has been constructed in the same manner as Figure 5a in the light of the last equation. Here the strength of the United States Army in the battle zone has been chosen for the variable S. S_∞ for each war is estimated. For Vietnam Wars I and II, Korean, and British World War I, S_∞ can be estimated by inspection from a graph of strength versus time for each war in the same manner, as $S_\infty = 600,000$ is observed for Department of Defense strength in Vietnam War II in Figure 5a. The estimated value for the United States Army in these cases is as given in Figure 6a.

Not so obvious is the ultimate strength that could have been mobilized by the United States in World War I and Wolrd War II. In these two cases the wars ended before the curves became sufficiently horizontal to determine by inspection the value of S_∞. Thus, for World War II a value of 16 million is chosen for S_∞, because this was estimated to be the absolute ceiling on the number of men who could be considered physically fit for active war service at that time[14]. Similarly, an S_∞ value of 3,670,000 was chosen for United States participation in World War I, because it was the same percentage of our population in France as Great Britain's 2 million soldiers in France was of her total population in 1918.

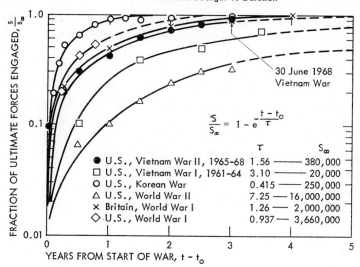

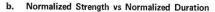

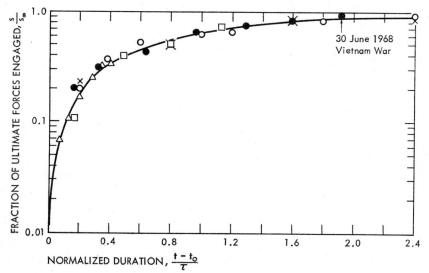

FIGURE 6 (a) Normalized battle strength expressed as the fraction of ultimate forces engaged plotted versus years from the start of the war for the major U.S. wars. (b) Normalized battle strength plotted versus normalized duration for each war analysed

If one chooses arbitrarily the initial time, t_0, such that S_0/S_∞ is at least less than 0.10, the variation of S/S_∞ for the different wars can then be plotted, and is shown in Figure 6a. The time constants for the different wars can then be determined.

The last equation shows that $S(t - t_0)/S_\infty$ is the same function of the parameter $(t - t_0)/\tau$ for all wars. This means that all wars can be brought together and represented by a single line when S/S_∞ is plotted against $(t - t_0)/\tau$ for each war. That this is true, is shown in Figure 6b for all wars analyzed.

This derivation and demonstration, in effect, shows that if the battle strength is expressed in terms of the percentage of ultimate forces to be engaged and is plotted against the time constant for each particular war, all wars studied can be expressed by a single mathematical relationship. Thus, each war forms a pattern over time and then history repeats each pattern.

Figure 6b allows comparison between the Vietnam War and all other wars analysed. Where the Vietnam War stood, with respect to all other wars as of June 30, 1968, and every other six-month interval back to June 30, 1965, can be seen by the black data points. In sum it can be seen that 86 % of the troops to be committed by both sides had been committed by June 30, 1968. It can also be seen that the rate of change from now on should stay minimal, providing those conditions that have been acting over the past three years continue to act unchanged in the future.

Deviations of the actual data points from the theoretical curves can be traced to a number of causes, such as the effects of elections, weather, and influenza epidemics. However, the major phenomenon seen here is the remarkable stability and trueness-to-course that, in general, wars follow over long periods of time. Instead of complete chaos, which is the expected characteristic of the conduct of human affairs, the exact opposite condition seems to exist when the human affair is warfare. When viewed in the manner demonstrated here, wars appear to become remarkably orderly events.

IMPLICATIONS FOR THE VIETNAM WAR

Because of the orderliness of our behaviour, the implication of the Vietnam data is that we, the United States, our allies, and our enemies, as of this writing, are approaching a violence level, where either a settlement is possible or another major escalation is indicated.

What prompts this statement is the shape of the curves for each of the previous wars and the shape of the curves for the Vietnam War. The shape of the curves for the past wars, and particularly the manner in which they level off, suggests that peace is negotiated when death, casualty, and strength exponentially approach the horizontal.

The overall leveling of these vital statistics can be seen in the British and German Armies during World War I, leading to a conclusion in November 1918 and for the Union and Confederate Armies, leading to a conclusion in April 1865. The same levelling occurred in the Korean War and led to a conclusion in July 1953. An identical pattern can be traced in the first phase of the Vietnam War, which ended December 1964. It can be further noted that the Korean War and the Vietnam War are relatively close together in time and place; thus their comparability is best of all the other wars.

If these variables for the second phase of the Vietnam War coninue to level in the latter half of 1968 and during the first half of 1969, then the past pattern will have repeated itself for the sixth time in our history.

As of this writing, since most of the principal nations of the world are supplying money, material, men, or some combination of the three, indeed, in reality, a global decision period is imminent.

Acknowledgments

I thank for ideas and encouragement Mr. Sidney Burr Brinckerhoff, Fellow, Company of Military Historians; and Professors Ronald Grant (Physiology), Ernest R. Hilgard (Psy-(Psychology), Krishnamurty Karamcheti (Aeronautics and Astronautics), James McGregor (Mathematics), Robert C. North (Political Sciences, Studies of International Conflict and Integration) of Stanford University; and Dr. Samuel C. McIntosh, Research Associate, Aeronautics and Astronautics, Stanford University; and Dr. S. L. Waleszczak, Chief Scientist and RADM E. R. Zumwalt, Jr., Director, Systems Analysis Division, Office of the Chief of Naval Operations. For all interpretations of the data, however, I am solely responsible.

References

1. S. S. Stevens, in *Handbook of Experimental Psychology* (Ed. S. S. Stevens,) Wiley, New York (1966), pp. 1–49.
2. N. Wiener, *Cybernetics*, M.I.T. Press, Cambridge, Mass. (1962), pp. 95–115.
3. L. F. Richardson, *Arms and Insecurity*, Boxwood, Pittsburgh (1960), pp. 1–36.
4. F. W. Lanchester, *Aircraft in Warfare; The Dawn of the Fourth Arm*, Constable, London (1916).
5. W. S. Churchill, *The World Crisis*, Vol. III, Scribner, New York (1924), p. 39.

6. T. L. Livermore, *Numbers and Losses in the Civil War in America: 1861–1865*, Indiana University Press, Bloomington (1957), pp. 75–141.
7. Department of Defense, Office of the Assistant Secretary of Defense (Public Affairs), *Vietnam Weekly Casualties, Statistical Summary*, June (1968).
8. Department of Defense, Office of the Comptroller of the Army, Program Review and Analysis Division, *ROK and UN Ground Forces Strength in Korea, 31 July 1950– 31 July 1953* (1964).
9. Department of Defense, *Annual Report of the Secretary of the Army—1948*, GPO, Washington (1949), p. 295.
10. L. P. Ayres, *The War with Germany—A Statistical Summary*, 1st edn., GPO, Washington (1919).
11. Department of the Army, Office of the Assistant Chief of Staff, *Battle Casualties of the Army, 30 September 1954*, CSGPA-363.
12. Department of the Army, Office of the Adjutant General, Statistical and Accounting Branch under the direction of the Program Review and Analysis Division of the Office of the Comptroller of the Army, *Army Battle Casualties and Non-battle Deaths in World War II, 7 December 1941–31 December 1946, OCS Report Control Symbol* CSCAP(OT) 87, pp. 10, 95.
13. The War Office, *Statistics of the Military Effort of the British Empire During the Great War, 1914–1920*, H.M.S.O., London (1922), pp. 358–62.
14. G. C. Marshall, *Biannual Report to the Chief of Staff of the U.S. Army, July 1, 1943– June 30, 1945,* GPO, Washington (1945), p. 101.
15. J. Voevodsky, "A mathematical representation of time-variant quantitative behavior", *J. Psychol.*, **68**, 129–40 (1968).
16. J. Voevodsky, L. M. Cooper, A. H. Morgan, and E. R. Hilgard, "The measurement of suprathreshold pain", *Am. J. Psychol.*, **80**, 124–8 (1967).

The epicosm model of the material and mental universes

STUART C. DODD

Department of Sociology, University of Washington
Seattle, U.S.A.

Summary

Let cosmos $= U^0 = 1 =$ the universal set of all namable elements, n in number, and let them be called "actants". *Hypothesis 1.* If n actants interact, reiterantly, randomly and ceaselessly, then they will always be forming and unforming compound actants, each in its own life-cycle, by trying out all their n^n possible combinations, or permutations, or repetitions, and thus operating the cosmos and all its parts largely by the "key" self-reiterant processes (i.e. $2n$, n^2, 2^n, n^n)—as uncreated creators of all that was, or self-made makers of all that is, forever working towards greater fulfilment ($= n^n$) of what may be. More exactly: if all n actants thus interact, they form the cosmos overall at a fixed creation rate, C, in 8 levels of organization, each a normal distribution with its average life-cycle in one eon or log century of time—all as more fully hypothesized in the epicosm model.

SPECIFICATIONS

The specifications for this epicosm model of the cosmos are as follows. The model tries to state the following.

(A) A *semiotic system* which describes, extensionally in terms of sets and elements, man–symbol–thing systems. So some of the model's symbols (concepts, scales, operation signs, etc.) become some of its substantive variables. (See Rows A and B of the Reiteratings Matrix appended as Exhibit D.)

(B) A *stochastic system* which explains probabilistically how each state yields the next by reiterant operations. (See Row B of Exhibit D.)

(C) A *self-reiterating system* which predicts continually its own self-creating ($= 2^n$), and self-fulfilling ($= n^n$) (See Row C of Exhibit D.)

(D) A *testable system* which controls, by indices above 99%, (1) its reliability in descriptive reobserving, (2) its reproducability from explanative antecedents, and (3) its agreement with predicted outcomes. (See last section, Exhibit D).

FEATURES

The features of the epicosm model in five versions (A)–(E) follow herewith.

(A) *Popularly stated*, the core epicosm hypothesis helps to describe the cosmos thus (in either four or eighteen words).

If all n	ACTANTS' INTERACTS	occur in n^n ways,
then they continually	ORGANIZE COSMOS	and all its parts.

Here: cosmos   = the set of all things namable;
       actant   = any thing namable as its element;
       interacts   = any repeatings, combinings or permutings of actant
                      elements or sets of them;
      to organize $\approx$ to interact $\approx$ to build
      continually $\approx$ ceaselessly $\approx$ without start or stop;
      occur $\approx$ happen $\approx$ reiterate;
      parts $\approx$ pieces $\approx$ samples $\approx$ aspects
(n is estimated by the model as $C_n^7 = 10^{77} = 2^{256}$ real and rising primal actants in the 7-level universe, so $n^n = 2^{2^{264}}$).

(B) *Algebraically stated*, the epicosm equation helps explain cosmic growth thus:

$$U^0 = 1 = a/ct$$

This says: "The universal set of cosmic actants is unitary ($U^0 = 1$). It builds up to level t as the number of actants a_t (in logs), which equals the constant creation rate, $c (= \lg^2 10 \doteqdot 11)$, if multiplied by the time taken, $t (= 1, 2, 3, 4, 5, 6, 7, 8)$, so $c = a/t$."

(C) *Geometrically stated*, the Mass–Time Triangle (M.T.T.) graphs the epicosm model in Exhibit A. It shows cosmic self-control, or complexity, H, as an area or product of actants $\times$ interacts, of abscissa $\times$ ordinate, of

$A \times \lg A$, of $n \times \lg n$ (so $H = n \lg n = \lg n^n$ = a self-power or fulfilmentl of possibilities in bit units).

Exhibit A pictures the cosmos (i.e. the n actants) if organized, or built up, as self-products, into seven real levels and one top imaginary level. This top level measures all symbols or speech acts of society. This integrates all communicated mental activity with all other cosmic activity—perhaps the first non-mystical mathematical model to achieve operationally such integration of mind and matter. (See Exhibits A and B for details.)

Four inductive steps discovered the M.T.T. as follows.

(1) Plotting masses of actants found the interlevel quantum jump ($C_n = 10^{\pm 11}$ tons).

(2) Plotting these against their time sequence, t, found high correlation ($r_{nc \cdot t} = \pm 1.0$).

(3) Plotting masses against levels found their constant log creation rate, ($= \log C_n = c/1 \approx 11$).

(4) Plotting $\pm c$ found the isosceles triangle (M.T.T.) or normal-curve-in-logs, which the central limit theorem proves to synthesize *all* distributions of means of actants in the cosmos.

By deductive steps, one can read off averages from the M.T.T., for each level in turn, its smallest mass and size, frequency and age, number of actants and interacts, degree of organization and complexity, and rate of cosmic evolution and devolution. All these are hypotheses deduced from the epicosm system, $a/ct = 1$, ready for further empirical testing.

(D) *Technically stated*, the Epicosm theory helps cosmic predicting as follows (see EpiDoc 128).

If all n actants, or things namable, interact
= the core hypothesis
and do so randomly, reiterantly and ceaselessly,
= 3 postulate hypotheses
thus forming and unforming in life-cycles
= the universal cyclic hypothesis
all combinations, permutations or repetitions
= the combinatoric hypothesis
in all their possible n^n ways.   = the fulfillment hypothesis
Then they form the cosmos and all its parts
= the core consequence hypothesis
as a vast normal probability distribution,
= the normal consequence hypothesis

organized in 8 levels of complexity, $a_t = ct$
$\qquad\qquad$ = the 8-levels consequence hypothesis
at a creatant rate, c, of actants $c = \log C_n = \lg^2 10 = 11.03522$
$\qquad\qquad$ = the creatant consequence hypothesis
organized one level per eon or log century of time, t,
$\qquad\qquad$ = the eon-century consequence hypothesis
by compounding self-reiterant processes, $K^s = 2n, n^2, 2^n, n^n$
$\qquad\qquad$ = the Key reiterants hypothesis
—all as spelled out further in the epicosm modelling
$\qquad\qquad$ = the residual epicosm hypothesis.

(E) (1) *Statistically* stated, the Epicosm modelling applies the theory of stochastic processes to the cosmos, if cosmos is defined as the unit universal set, $U^0 = 1$, of all things namable. By this definition, or semiotic operation, everything in the cosmos reappears as a fraction of one. Then in the future tense, everything can be, in principle, measured as a probability or proportion of unity. Every science then seeks to discover the precise amounts and relations and systems of compounded probabilities of its actants (or "phenomena-viewed-as-sets"). Since every probability density function adds up to one by definition, these stochastic functions express alternative and specifiable ways of analysing the infra-structure of any set up to, and including, the cosmos. Stochastic formulas then portray cosmic phenomena as *the probable acts of cosmos*.

(2) Thus the binomial and normal distributions arise from the simplest intra-acting of a set of n elements $(= n^0 = 1)$ with itself n times when structured into its two half-lives:

$$(n^0)^n = (\tfrac{1}{2} + \tfrac{1}{2})^n = (p + q)^n = 1^n = 1 = (n^0) = (n^n)^0 = 1 \text{ set.}$$

(3) In polar co-ordinates, $e^{\theta i} = \cos\theta + i\sin\theta = e^{2\pi n i} \ (= 1^n = 1 = U^0$ for integer n). This on-going unitary cosmos, $U^0 = 1$, is analyzable into cycles of a cohort of actants. Thus as $e^{2\pi n t i} = 1^{nt} = 1$ the cycles are of size or radius n, and t in number. This is hypothesized to measure cosmic activity as n actants, and cosmic time as t cycles.*

Then their product, activity × time (in erg seconds), or $A \cdot t$ or $n \cdot \lg n \, (=H)$ can measure the complexity of the universe as an area in the mass–time

---

* n and t are ordinarily taken as finite, representing a finite slice, or sample, of a potentially infinite number of interacts. When n and t are infinite, one is then talking about "the eternal cosmos", and not about the current finite slice of its constant and ceaseless on-going.

triangle, defined by any specified n and t (such as "the spatial universe", "the material universe", "the living universe", "the mental (i.e. verbal) universe", etc.).

(4) All this stochastic interpretation of the unit cosmos, $U^0 = 1$, may go far towards explaining the cosmos causally by combinatoric processes, themselves products of reiteratings, K^s, of actants. If this semiotic hypothesis holds up, man can say: "Reiterant interactions of actants seem to describe the contents of the cosmos, as $U^0 = 1 = a/ct$; and explain their continual creation as the characteristic function of a single random process, i.e. $E e^{2\pi n i}$, and predict their future as the Gompertz entropic growth and decay curve of cosmic evolution and devolution, i.e. $p_t = 1 - q^{2^t}$. All these and other stochastic submodels are semiotic hypotheses that spell out the epicosm modelling in detail—which is largely awaiting exploration.

IMPLICATIONS

The implications of the epicosm model, too manifold for full discussion here, may be suggested by the notes below.

(1) The whole epicosm modelling has been formally systematized in a tight semiotic theory of 32 hypotheses, for eventual publication and wider testing. (See EpiDoc 42.)

(2) Over a hundred tests of fit, averaging above 99.5% of agreement, have been run between the model's formulas and major constants of mathematics and the physical sciences, e.g. G of gravity, C, light, F, Faraday's constant, in one series; $e = 2.7182$, $c_y = 0.5772$, $i = \sqrt{-1}$, 0, 1, 2, 4 in another series, etc.

(3) Lists of many further testable fits await funding to execute.

(4) Two technical hypotheses of high promise seem to be: "If the reiterating matrix (see Exhibit D) is systematically explored and tested, cosmologists will gain measurably in explaining and predicting cosmic activity."

(5) "If the key periodic table for generating cosmic constants (EpiDoc 144) were similarly expanded and fitted, cosmologists could measurably improve cosmology."

(6) Two highly controversial, yet important, physical hypotheses are: "Epicosm theory is more able than current physical theory to account for *negative entropy* whereby the cosmos, with no external source of energy, yet builds up the stars, galaxies, and all other organized entities to their current state."

(7) "If *antilog time* scales, $_at$, were appropriately substituted for the present standard sidereal time scales, t_s, where $_atdef = e^{ts}$ or $\ln_a t = t_s$, then the universe would reappear as non-expanding consistently with the red shift and all other empirical facts. This calls for semantic, not hardware, testing. This antilog time hypothesis seems not only to produce a constant universe but it also seems fully to solve the problem of creation, whether gradual or sudden bang, by predicting and postdicting an eternally existent, and overall constant, on-going.

Five hunches, for example, expect that epicosm modelling might help (8) to explain anomalies of quasars, (9) to systematize subatomic particles, (10) to develop a unified field theory, (11) to predict fission of photons into gravitons, (12) to generate curved space and gravity from a random state of completed entropy; etc.

Note four Epicosm hypotheses of human import.

(13) One hypothesis expects that on our Earth total evolution will accelerate in verbal and mental ways more than in physical or physiological ways.

(14) Another hypothesis expects that inner-directed or self-governing systems whether in atoms or cells, persons or nations, tend to gain compared with outer-directed systems.

(15) Based on the physicists estimate of 10^{78} particles in the universe, the mass–time graph expects well over a hundred billion, 10^{11}, Earth-like planets with conditions suitable for humanoids to have evolved on them.

(16) Finally, a summarizing hypothesis expects that human systems, in common with all systems, will tend with sufficient time towards fuller trying out and consequent greater fulfillment ($= n^n$) of their potentialities. This leaves great freedom for men to hasten or hinder, to redefine or alter such fulfillings as they desire. The design of the cosmos and all its parts including man seems to tend toward mutually compatible self-fulfillments.

APPENDIX 1: EXHIBIT A EXPLAINED

Exhibit A graphs the cosmos overall as a unit isosceles triangle or normal curve on log co-ordinates. Its internal structure is pictured (by these loglog units) as a hierarchy of eight nested triangles with a common apex. Their eight base lines represent the eight levels of increasing complexity into which cosmic activity (i.e. phenomena) seems currently organized. These ascending levels seem to evolve in eight successive log-time periods. They go from the state of completed entropy at the bottom (Level G) to the mental activity of

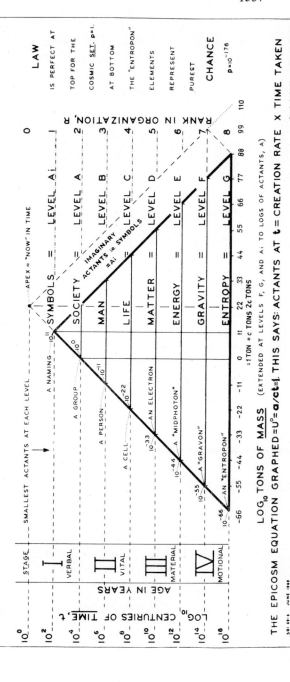

EXHIBIT A

symbols used by society at the top (Level Ai). The graph therefore shows the evolving of cosmic action (or phenomena measured in erg seconds) within each first half-life of every cohort of cosmic action elements (called "actants").

The co-ordinates in the graph of this mass–time triangle are in units of common log cycles here. The abscissa is measured in metric tons (convertible into erg seconds). When generalized, it represents the amount of activity, a, or number of actants at any level, t. Then the ordinate simultaneously represents (a) the rank in complexity of the level from 1 to 8 (in units of the creatant, $c = \lg^2 10 = 11.03522 \doteqdot 11$); (b) the degree of organization (as a log of the activity); (c) the amount of interaction of the actants (in log cycles of self-products); (d) the correlated time, t (in logs of centuries ago).

Then the equation for the two sides of the mass–time triangle in logs is $-a_c = \pm ct$. This says that the cosmic activity (a_t) or number of actants at level t equals the creatant, c, or rate of organizing that activity, times the period (t) it took. This equation for the cosmos, $= U^0 = 1 = a/ct$ (when the cosmos is extensionally defined as the universal set ($= U^0$) of all namable elements) summarizes the epicosm model.

The mass–time triangular distribution can be interpreted when re-graphed as a log transformation of the normal probability distribution of all actants in the cosmos. To show this, take natural logs of the normal equation, transforming it to a parabola, i.e. $\ln(y) = \ln(e - x^2/2) = -x^2/2$ and then take bits-logs transforming the parabola into the M.T.T.'s straight-line sides, i.e., $\lg \ln y = \lg |-x^2/2| = 2 \lg x - 1$ or $T = (\pm)2M - 1$ where $T = \lg \ln y$ = time and $M = \lg x$ = mass.

Viewing the cosmos or universal set of all actants (or phenomena) as a normal distribution is supported by the central limit theorem and the binomial theorem. The former says in effect that properly adding all distributions of actants in the cosmos together must yield a normal distribution. The binomial theorem says that n rounds of full interacting, or self-multiplying, of the rising and falling halves* of the cosmos (as $(p + q)^n = 1^n = 1$) will also yield a unit normal distribution. Thus, the cosmos, if built of randomly interacting primal elements (or like elements at any level) will organize itself continuingly as a normal distribution *if looked at through these symbols or concepts of randomly interacting halves.*

Thus, an extensional and semiotic re-viewing of the cosmos opens up vast vistas for science and for human understanding of everything around and

---

* Or halves of any set where $p = q = .5$ and $n^0 = (n^0/2 + n^0/2) = p + q = 1$.

within us. For this normal cosmos entails for every properly specified actant, or compound of them, a unique and computable and absolute probability of occurrence. Every science is then seen as the re-search on how best to specify actants in its field by the most fruitful empirical techniques of observation *and* semiotic* techniques of symbolizing. The epicosm modelling is largely a semiotic inquiry to find more fruitful concepts—such as "actants", "interactants", and "reiterants", etc., seem to be.

A dual interpretation of the mass–time triangle—in its static versus dynamic aspects—should be well understood. Just as the formula for the circular circumference, $2\pi n$, can be graphed either as one circle of radius n or as n circles of unit radius, or just as "a set of elements" should be seen *both* as a unitary set *and* as a plurality of elements, just so the epicosm formula, $a = ct$, and its graph (the M.T.T.) should be viewed *both* as a static picture at one date of eight cohorts of actants varying over eight different phases of their life cycles†; *and* also as a dynamic picture at eight dates of one cohort of actants evolving through eight successive phases of its life-cycle.

Further interpretations of this normal cosmos when viewed through log units are tabled as readings from the full mass–time graph. These estimate, for each of the eight levels of cosmic organization, its probable minimum, median and maximum of equivalent mass, time span, age, length, number of actants $(= A)$, degree of organization $(= \lg A)$, degree of complexity $(= A \lg A \text{ or } \lg A^A)$, fulfillment $(= A^A)$, and rate of organizing $(= A/\lg A)$ or average speed of evolving and devolving.

Thus, the epicosm model's induction of a normal cosmos seems fruitful for many important deductions—all as hypotheses to be tested, of course.

APPENDIX 2: EXHIBIT B EXPLAINED

Exhibit B plots all material entities in the cosmos by their mass cross-classified against their rank in organization. It tells how the epicosm model was developed by inductive steps. When actants were listed by increasing weight, an important periodicity emerged. Equal intervals of eleven log cycles, 10^{11}, a factor of one hundred billion, were observed between the smallest entities at each of the four most observable levels of organized actants. (See the four dots in Exhibit B.) The threshold actants at the successive levels of matter, life, man, and society fitted well to the straight

---

* Semiotics is the science of man–symbol–thing relations or systems.

† Or first, and rising, half-life cycles, more exactly.

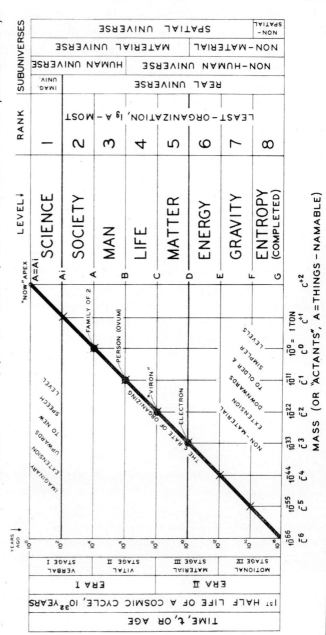

PLOTTING MATERIAL ENTITIES BY MASS vs. ORGANIZATION RANK

BY S. C. DODD, UNIV. OF WASH., SEATTLE 98105

SD 69-27 EPI DOC 155 JUNE 1969

THIS DEVELOPS: 1) A CARDINAL SCALE OF COSMIC ORGANIZATION (IN BITS, lg A), THE ORDINATE;

2) EXTENDIBLE TO AN 8 LEVEL UNIVERSE (WHERE t=8, AS BELOW);

3) CORRELATED WITH PAST TIME PERIODS (OR AGES, t, TO DATE);

4) YIELDING A CONSTANT LOG GROWTH RATE, c, (=LOG C_n = lg^{2}10=11.03522);

5) THEIR SYNTHESIS IN THE EPICOSM EQUATION, $a_t = ct$, WHICH SAYS: "COSMIC ACTIVITY, a, AT ANY LEVEL t, EQUALS ITS GROWTH RATE c, x TIME TAKEN, t."

diagonal line, *C*. (See Exhibit B.) This line measured a constant rate of organizing 10^{11} actants per level or per log century of time (since sequence in organizing showed a perfect rank correlation with log intervals of time). This rate of organizing is interpretable as the cosmic speed of evolving, i.e. a creation rate of a hundred billion ($= C_n \fallingdotseq 10^{11}$) actants organized per level or eon of time, if reckoned back from the present.

This "rate of evolving" hypothesis (that expects a constant ratio between interlevel jumps in organization of actants and their correlated time periods) was then explored further. It was dramatically found to hold if extended in this mass versus time graph both upwards and downwards and even sidewards in a symmetric and complementary downslope taken to measure a rate of devolving from an apex.

Details of these extensions, as hypotheses generalizing the rate of evolving index, *C*, to all levels of cosmic activity or phenomena, are developed in the 160 EpiDoc mimeographs or working notes prepared to date for checking and eventual publishing. Here these exhibits will simply sample these semiotic hypotheses which claim that better symbolizing can make better relations among actants and systems of them more observable and testable.

Glimpses of fruitful consequences of extending this constant creation rate*, *C*, upwards, downwards, and sidewards in the mass–time graph may be seen through the following four sentences that state four "extension hypotheses".

(1) If the constant creation rate, *C*, is extended upwards (by using complex numbers) through Level *Ai* in the mass–time graph, then all society's speech activity and consequent mental life will become more observable and testable as that special case of the epicosm formula, $a = ct$, for all cosmic activity, or phenomena, when $t = 1$ (i.e. the ever-current present century).

(2) If the constant creation rate, *C*, is extended downwards (by equating *C* to the speed of light) in the mass–time graph, then all the physical phenomena and laws involving radiant energy, or gravity, or completed entropy will become more observable and testable as those three special cases of the

---

* The rate of cosmic evolving, called the creation rate, *C*, was first estimated at 10^{11} actants organized one level upwards per eon of time by the best fit line (in the mass–time graph) to the four points representing the smallest material, living, human and societal entities, i.e. the electron, the cell, the fertilized human ovum, and two spouses. Later five "isotopes" of variants by other units or definitions have been discovered including the speed of light if re-expressed as 10^{11} mm per third of a second. Millimetres and thirds-of-a-second replace centimeters and seconds as units of length and time in Epicosm modelling because they yield simpler, more parsimonious and better systematizing formulas and laws.

epicosm formula, $a = ct$, for all cosmic activity when $t = 6$ or 7 or 8 (i.e. their formative period between ten billion and ten quadrillion years ago).

(3) If the constant creation rate, C, is extended downwards and rightwards from an apex (by using its opposite sign) in the mass–time graph, then the upper limit of actants in each level and the nature of all cosmic on-going as the concurrent life-cycling of all its actants, in cohorts by levels, will become more observable and testable. This is the reversed or devolving case of the epicosm formula, $a = ct$, for all cosmic activity when t rises from 1 to 8, measuring increase of positive entropy, or "heat death" or disorganizing of each cohort of actants in its second half life.

(4) If the constant creation rate, C, is extended by rotating it 90 degrees in the mass–time graphing, then all cosmic activity becomes more observable and testable as a vast normal probabilistic and stochastic process which, as t varies from 8 to 0, varies from purest chance or least predictability (with $p = (10^{-2c})^8 = 10^{-176} = 0$ at Level G) to perfect law or complete predictability (with $p = (10^{-2c})^0 = 10^0 = 1$ at Level A).

APPENDIX 3: EXHIBIT C EXPLAINED

Exhibit C is entitled "The mass–time triangle extended through the radiation spectrum". This graph enlarges and fills in the mass–time graph from the Level F for gravity through the energy Level E and up to the matter Level D. It shows that the action or phenomena of radiant energy and gravity in their varying degrees can be viewed as a special case (when $t = 5, 6, 7$ in $a = ct$) or representative sample of overall cosmic action and laws. One can either generalize to (i.e. induce) the cosmic law, $a = ct$, from this graph, or particularize (i.e. deduce) this graph in physics from the larger law of cosmic activity, $a = ct$.

This radiation spectrum graphs the wave lengths plotted against their frequencies for waves of radio and radar, visible light, X-rays, gamma rays, and cosmic rays up to the electron or threshold of matter.

The slope of the graphed line represents the speed of light which is $C = 3 \times 10^{10}$ cm/s. This becomes $C_n \approx 10^{11}$ mm/third-of-a-second when translated into millimeters and third-of-a-second in the simplifying and systematizing terms standardized throughout the epicosm modelling. For then, $C_n \approx 10^{11}$ becomes approximately the cosmic creation rate or ratio of actants organized one level upwards per eon of time, throughout the mass–time graph. Then, the graph measures the rate of organizing photon actants into

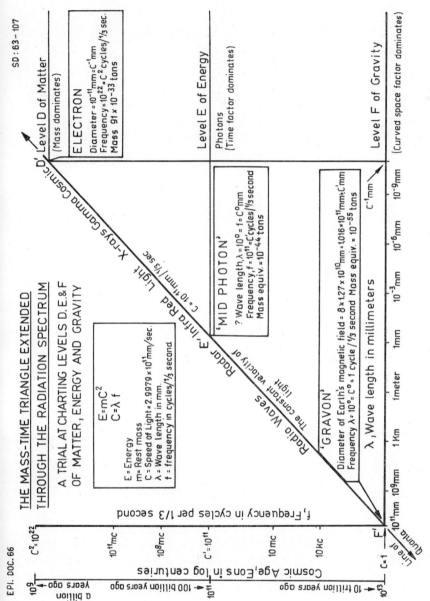

EXHIBIT C

SD : 63 - 107

EPI. DOC. 66

particle actants and the rate of organizing or creating photons (of about 1 mm wavelength) from the hypothetical gravons (of about C_n mm wavelength).

A useful consequence of equating the creation rate to the speed of light (in appropriate units of length and time) seems to be that the mass–time graph, if amplified as in Exhibit C, can be used to read off or predict the results of clean fission or fusion between photons and particles. Thus, when a laboratory's clean fission of a proton and its paired anti-proton into a pair of photons of exactly the same mass was published, the wave length and frequency of those resulting photons was read off correctly from the mass–time graph interpreted by Exhibit C.

Furthermore, the mass–time graph enables predicting clean fission and fusion between specified photons and the hypothesized lower levels of gravons as elements of gravity at Level F and entropons as elements of the state of completed entropy at Level G.

Thus, the epicosm modelling seems to offer powerful symbolic tools for analysing the activity of gravity and entropy where hardware tools are not at present adequate.

APPENDIX 4: EXHIBIT D EXPLAINED

Exhibit D is entitled "The reiteratings matrix, R_{rc}, for cosmists". It tells broadly how scientists, starting from scratch without even a language, can build models for the past, present, and future cosmos. Row A of this 4×4 reiteratings matrix tells how every symbol that man ever uses is built by the trio of acts called "reitering". Reitering is operationally defined in Row A as the intersect or product of three acts, namely *combining* a name and a thing named; *repeating* that naming among people, occasions, and contexts; without *permuting* or changing it. This trio of combinatoric speech acts seems to create every standardized and socialized and recurring symbol known or knowable to man.

Then Row B tells how four successive and cumulative rounds of reitering produce the four "key operators" and operations of all mathematics, logic, and language. Compounding these operations builds all *syntax*. Syntax in turn relates all symbols together producing all language and the communicated knowledge of man.

Row C, next, tells how the simplest and most probable self-reiterings of the four key operations form the four "key processes". These, when mixed and blent as sums and products, etc., seem to produce the regular entities and their formulas of whatever exists or happens around us and within us.

Finally, Row D organizes cosmic on-going or phenomena in four sub-models by tenses. These try to help explain the past causation of the cosmos; to describe its present contents; to predict its future consequences; and to control more and more of its compounding at any time. The synthesis of these submodels produces the epicosm model. This tells how the n cosmic actants, interacting in their n^n ways that tend to fulfil all their possibilities, continually organize the cosmos. Its summarizing epicosm equation, $U^0 = 1 = a/ct$, asserts for testing that the unitary cosmos, if defined as the universal set, U^0, of all things namable, is organized in eight levels or subsets of random and reiterant actants ($a_{t=8}$) which are ceaselessly and constantly formed and unformed by the creation rate (c) and the time taken (t).

EpiDoc # 152
Techn. Note 18
Univ. of Wash.
Seattle, Wash.

SD: 69-24
by S. C. Dodd
June 1969

THE REITERATINGS MATRIX, R_{rc}, FOR COSMISTS

(Expanded Version)

This 4×4 matrix offers, for criticism and testing, a methodological model, R_{rc}, of the cosmologist's speech acts when building a substantive model, $a/ct = 1$, for the cosmos. It describes the actions of the cosmist when he describes the actions of the cosmos. Both of these actions in this cosmic modelling transaction are hypothesized to be well explained and predicted by *reiterants*. Evidence on how reiterants help cosmists to model the cosmos is ordered in this Reiteratings Matrix as follows:

This reiteratings matrix in 4 rows, R_{r*}, state 4 operations, called 4 "reiteratings", which tell the cosmist how to produce:

SYMBOLS of all sorts from the
  4 factors of "reitering" (in Row A below)
SYNTAX and language from the
  4 rounds of reitering (in Row B below)
KEY RULES or formulas from the
  4 self-reiterings (in Row C below)
COSMIC LAWS or submodels from the
  4 log-self-reiterings (in Row D below)

This reiteratings matrix in 4 columns, R_{*c}, state 4 operations, called 4 "reiterings", for cosmists who build models for:

CAUSES of the cosmos in the past, in terms of
  repetitive reiterings mostly (in Col. 1 below)
CONTENTS of the cosmos at present in terms of
  combinative reitering mostly (in Col. 2 below)
CONSEQUENCES of the cosmos in future as
  permutative reitering mostly (in Col. 3 below)
COMPOUNDING in the cosmos at any time, as
  combinatoric reitering wholly (in Col. 4 below)

The 16 cells (called "reiterants" $= R_{rc}$), as a set-product of rows and columns, hypothesize that:

"REITERANTS CAN BEST MIRROR THE COSMOS TO MAN"

This hypothesis will be confirmed insofar as reiterants produce models of the cosmos that are more (1) comprehensive, (2) exact, (3) reliable, (4) explanative, (5) predictive, (6) controllative, etc., than rival methodologies.

Semiotic

HYPOTHESIS A: If the *4 sub-reitering acts* (italicized below) recur jointly, then any SYMBOL can recur—as most *liked* by ghe users.

	Col. 1	Col. 2	Col. 3	Col. 4	Col.
	The act of *Recurring*	The act of *Naming it*	The act of *Ordering it*	The act of *Reitering it*	Note 7 versions: ← in Lay terms
ROW A How Subreiterings produce **SYMBOLS**	REPEATS	COMBINES	PERMUTES	INTERACTS	← in Combinatoric
	a thing namable, i.e. an item or "It" called an "*Actant*" (in *Time*),	a name with a thing named among *People*,	the repetitions of that naming in diverse *Contexts*,	this trio as a product", or item, of speech *Behaviour*, i.e. any symbol,	← in Operational ″ ← in Dimensional [$B_s = APTC$]
	making it likely.	making it liked.	making them alike.	making it "enliked."	← in Likability Theory terms
	This rule Serializes It = "re-"	This rule Socializes It = "re-it-"	This rule Standardizes It = "re-it-er"	This rule Symbolizes It = a "re-it-er-ing"	← in Scientific term ← in "Reitering" terms

---

Semiotic

HYPOTHESIS B: If the *4 reitering acts* (italicized below) recur cumulatively, then any KEY OPERATING can recur—as most *alike* to the facts.

ROW B How cumulative reiterings produce **SYNTAX**	Reitering namings as in *listing* items forms	Reitering sets as in *adding* counted elements forms	Reitering sums as in *multiplying* forms	Reitering products as in *self-multiplying* a number forms	← In terms of: ← Math. operation
	A SET	A SUM	A PRODUCT	A POWER	← Algebra
	of elements called an "entity" e.g. $\{1, 2, 3, 4\}^0$ $= n^0 = 1$	of units called a "natural no." e.g. $1 + 2 + 3 + 4$ $= 10 = n^I$	of factors called an "intersect" e.g. $1 \times 2 \times 3 \times 4$ $= 24 = n^{II}$	of a base called a "log" e.g. $2 \cdot 2 \cdot 2 \cdot 2$ $= 2^4 = 16 = n^{III}$	← Units ← Technical name ← Examples
	This round 0 of reitering builds Qualitative speech. S^0 as in Language	This Round I of reitering builds Quantitative speech, S^I as in Mathematics	This Round II of reitering builds Relational speech, S^{II} as in daily Life	This Round III of reitering builds Systemative speech, S^{III} as in Scientific Laws	← 4 Rounds of ← Reiterings build ← Dimensional ← Speech, S^X, or ← Analysis

Semiotic
HYPOTHESIS C: If the *4 Self-reitering acts* (italicized below) recur pairingly, then any KEY FORMULA can recur—as most *likely* for prediction.

ROW C — How Self-reiterings produce Key Formulas, K^s

Self-sums form minimal	*Self-products* form maximal pairings, or a	*Minimal self-powers* form a	*Maximal self-powers* form a	← Self-reitering terms
PAIRINGS, $2n$,	SQUARING, n^2,	NORMING, 2^n,	FULFILLING n^n,	← Connotative terms ← Key terms
as simplest Repeating	as simplest Permuting	as simplest Combining	as simplest Full-Interacting	← Combinatoric terms
of n things, if taken 2 at a time.	of n things, if taken 2 at a time.	of n things, if put into 2 states.	of n things, if in any of the 3 ways.	← Operational terms
General formula $a = mn$	n^m	m^n	n^n	← General formulas
Minimal formula $= 2 \times 2 = 4$	$2^2 = 4$	$2^2 = 4$	$2^2 = 4$	← Minimal cases
Maximal formula $= n \times n = n^2$	n^n	n^n	n^n	← Maximal cases

Semiotic
HYPOTHESIS D: If the *4 log-self-reitering acts* (italicized below) recur empirically, then any SUBMODEL can recur—as best fits the cosmos.

ROW D — How Log-self-reiterings produce SUBMODELS of cosmos, $A = B^n$, or $A/B^n = 1$

Exponentiating $2n$ to the half-cycle base, $(e^{\pi i})$, forms Euler's	Exponentiating n^2 to the natural root-base, $(e^{-0.5})$ forms Gauss's	Exponentiating 2^n to q or the natural log base, (e), forms Gompertz'	Exponentiating n primal, real actants to n as log base forms Stirling's	Exponentiating time, t, to a Creation Rate, C, as a cosmic log base, forms Dodd's
Helical coil with n loops: $e^{2\pi in} = \text{cis } 2\pi n = 1^n = 1$ ($\text{cis } \theta = \cos\theta + i \sin\theta$)	*Normal* probability curve: $y = 1/u_1 (e^{0.5})^{n^2} = 1$ $(n = x)$ $(u_1 = \sqrt{2\pi \cdot 1} = 2.50662)$	*Entropic* growth and decay curve $y = e^{2^n}$ or $q_t = q_o^{2^n}$ so $p = 1$ ($n = t =$ no. of time units)	*Combinatoric* formula for interacts $n^n = e^n n!/u_n = e^{n \ln n}$ $(u_n = \sqrt{2\pi n})$ $= 2.50662 \cdot \sqrt{n}$	*Epicosmic* model, graphed in MTT, as $A_t = C_n^t = 10^{ct} = 2^{256}$; $t = 7$ or $a = ct \doteqdot 11t$ —in logs.
This epicosm submodel$_1$ helps in	This epicosm submodel$_2$ helps in	This epicosm submodel$_3$ helps in	This epicosm submodel$_4$ helps in	This epicosm master model may help men
EXPLAINING	DESCRIBING	PREDICTING	CONTROLLING	analyse and synthesize
the past ceaseless lif-cycling of all actants as they seem to form and unform at all 8 levels of an eternal universe.	the present random distribution of all actants as kept up by finite self-renewal at all 8 levels within an infinite (?) domain	the future reiterant evolution of all actants as successive pair-permutings at all 8 levels of a self-governing whole	at any and all times, a probabilistic design for actants, overall constant and unitary, at all 8 levels of a self-fulfilling cosmos	all cosmic interacts. Its hypothesis says: ACTANTS INTERACTS ORGANIZE COSMOS

ote on fitting this matrix to the MTT (=Mass-Time Δ):

This matrix above expands Level *Ai* for symbolic
stems in the mass-time triangle into 4 quadrants, if the
matrix rows translate into 4 powers of i in the helical
bmodel, $(e^{\pi i/2})^t = 1^t = \pm 1, \pm i$; $t = (1, 2, 3, 4)$ 4
ow A forms *symbols* $= i^1 = \sqrt{-1} = (e^{\pi i/2})$
as imaginary names of real things-named.
ow B forms *syntax* $= i^2 = i \cdot i = -1 \; (= e^{\pi i})$
as products of symbols, $i \cdot i$, of Operatings.
ow C forms key formulas $= i^3 = i \cdot i^2 = -i$
as names $(= i)$ for key processes of syntax.
ow D forms *submodels* $= i^4 = +1 = e^{2\pi i}$, each viewing
cosmos as a unit life-cycle (of 10^{32} years among
10^{176} primal actants??).

Note on fitting this matrix, R_{rc}, to data:

The 16 cells (called here "reiterants") in the matrix above need further tests of:

i) their reliability correlations with reobservings, requiring $r > 0.9$.
ii) their validity correlations with empirical facts, requiring $r > 0.8+$.
iii) their predictivity correlations with outcomes, $r > 0.7+$.
iv) their probability correlations with math. theorems, $r = 1.00$.
v) their agreement, above 99.6% when fitting cosmic constants.

Index to authors

This index refers to the authors of the papers given at the congress. A bold **I** preceding a page number indicates that the author's name appears in the first volume, a bold **II** the second, and a bold **III** the third.

Andrew, A.M.   **I** 265, **I** 359
Arés, L.   **I** 266, **I** 403
Arigoni, A.O.   **I** 266, **I** 383
Ashby Ross, W.   **I** 1, **I** 57
Auslander, D.M.   **I** 266, **I** 467

Baecker, H.D.   **III** 1096, **III** 1281
Bagley, J.D.   **II** 841, **II** 901
Bălăceanu, C.   **I** 265, **I** 266, **I** 281, **I** 441, **I** 491
Beck, M.S.   **II** 523, **II** 597
Beer, S.   **I** 1, **I** 65
Belis, M.   **I** 265, **I** 281, **III** 1095, **III** 1121
Benthall, J.   **II** 841, **II** 949
Bergmann, R.H.   **III** 1095, **III** 1097
Billeter-Frey, E.P.   **II** 683, **II** 715
Birch, P.R.   **II** 523, **II** 597
Bîrlea, S.   **II** 683, **II** 703
Bodington, S.   **III** 961, **III** 1073
Booth, A.M.   **II** 841, **II** 843
Botez, M.I.   **I** 265, **I** 347
Boulanger, G.R.   **I** 1, **I** 3
Brix, V.H.   **III** 1095, **III** 1107

Challier, L.   **I** 127, **I** 215
Chiaraviglio, L.   **III** 961, **III** 1019, **III** 1096, **III** 1267
Čobeljić, N.   **II** 683, **II** 753

D'Annunzio, A.   **III** 1095, **III** 1145
Didday, R.L.   **II** 841, **II** 849
Dimitrijević, M.R.   **I** 265, **I** 353
Dodd, S.C.   **III** 1096, **III** 1351
Drozen, V.   **I** 265, **I** 291

Ericson, R.F.   **III** 1095, **III** 1163

Fatmi, H.A.   **III** 961, **III** 1003
Favella, L.F.   **I** 266, **I** 497
Firnberg, D.   **II** 841, **II** 927
Foster, D.B.   **I** 127, **I** 139
Frederick, T.J.   **II** 523, **II** 613

Gambardella, G.   **I** 266, **I** 447
George, F.H.   **I** 1, **I** 113
Giolito, P.C.   **I** 266, **I** 497
Glushkov, V.M.   **I** 1, **I** 97
Goffman, W.   **III** 961, **III** 971
Goransky, G.K.   **II** 523, **II** 553
Green, A.M.   **III** 1096, **III** 1299
Green, E.E.   **III** 1096, **III** 1299
Greguss, P.   **I** 266, **I** 433
Gough, J. Jr.,   **III** 1096, **III** 1267
Gyergyek, L.   **I** 265, **I** 353

Hammer, P.C.   **III** 961, **III** 985
Harris, G.W.   **II** 523, **II** 641
Harrison, P.J.   **II** 523, **II** 597

Hatori, T.   **I** 127, **I** 245
Helvey, T.C.   **I** 127, **I** 201
Herman, G.T.   **II** 841, **II** 873
Hilton, A.M.   **III** 1096, **III** 1287

Irtem, A.   **III** 961, **III** 1087

Kabrisky, M.   **III** 961, **III** 1035
Kerschner, L.R.   **III** 1095, **III** 1215
Kleffman, T.E.   **II** 684, **II** 823
Klir, G.J.   **I** 127, **I** 155
Koenig, E.C.   **II** 523, **II** 613
Kogan, A.B.   **I** 265, **I** 275
Kvitashvili, A.   **I** 265, **I** 267

Lamb, G.G.   **III** 1095, **III** 1231
Legéndy, C.R.   **I** 265, **I** 309
Lévy, J.C.   **I** 265, **I** 339

Magureanu, R.   **I** 265, **I** 347
Majernik, V.   **II** 841, **II** 917
Malić, D.   **I** 127, **I** 149
Malitza, M.   **III** 961, **III** 1013, **III** 1095,
   III 1249
Mallary, R.   **II** 841, **II** 931
Mănescu, M.   **II** 683, **II** 741
Marazio, G.   **I** 266, **I** 497
Marinov, Ul.P.   **II** 684, **II** 813
Mashhour, M.   **II** 523, **II** 579
Masturzo, A.   **I** 1, **I** 87
Mays, W.   **I** 127, **I** 129
Meitus, W.Yu.   **II** 523, **II** 565
Merzer, L.   **III** 961, **III** 1061
Mira, J.   **I** 266, **I** 403
Mitchell, J.H.   **I** 266, **I** 505
Moore, G.P.   **I** 266, **I** 393
Muses, C.   **I** 127, **I** 175

Naplatanoff, N.D.   **II** 684, **II** 813
Nicolau, E.V.   **I** 266, **I** 441, **II** 841, **II** 887,
   III 961, **III** 963

Okumura, B.   **I** 266, **I** 393
Orr, D.A.   **II** 523, **II** 525

Pask, G.   **I** 1, **I** 15
Penaloza-Rojas, J.H.   **I** 266, **I** 393
Perez, A.   **II** 841, **II** 891

Pesonen, H.   **III** 961, **III** 1051
Popovici, A.   **II** 841, **II** 887

Rabinovich, Z.L.   **III** 1096, **III** 1319
Racoveanu, N.   **II** 683, **II** 777
Rahman, S.   **III** 961, **III** 1003
Reed, A.L.   **II** 684, **II** 823
Ricci, F.J.   **III** 1095, **III** 1131
Rubio, F.   **I** 266, **I** 403

Santesmases, J.G.   **I** 266, **I** 403
Scott, B.C.E.   **II** 683, **II** 793
Sharma, D.C.   **I** 266, **I** 467
Shen, D.W.   **II** 523, **II** 525, **II** 541
Sheridan, T.B.   **II** 684, **II** 803
Sister Stella Mary   **I** 127, **I** 223
Smith, J.U.M.   **II** 683, **II** 767
Spencer, D.C.   **II** 523, **II** 653
Stanley-Jones, D.   **I** 127, **I** 249
Stanoulov, N.   **I** 127, **I** 167
Steg, D.R.   **III** 1095, **III** 1145
Stoica, E.   **I** 266, **I** 491
Stojanović, R.   **II** 683, **II** 723
Stoodley, K.D.C.   **II** 523, **II** 597

Tallman, O.   **III** 961, **III** 1035
Taylor, W.K.   **I** 266, **I** 419
Theobald, C.E.   **II** 523, **II** 541
Theodoridis, G.C.   **III** 1095, **III** 1185
Traill, R.R.   **II** 841, **II** 861
Trontelj, J.K.   **I** 265, **I** 353

Vaida, D.   **II** 684, **II** 833
Vandamme, F.   **III** 1096, **III** 1257
Verduzco, R.H.   **I** 266, **I** 403
Voevodsky, J.   **III** 1096, **III** 1329

Walter Grey, W.   **I** 1, **I** 45
Walters Dale, E.   **III** 1096, **III** 1299
Wilcox, J.W.   **II** 683, **II** 685
Williams, D.C.   **II** 523, **II** 597
Winkelbauer, K.   **II** 683, **II** 783

Young, A.M.   **III** 1095, **III** 1205

Zabara, J.   **I** 265, **I** 299
Zannetos, Z.S.   **II** 683, **II** 685
Zidariou, C.   **III** 1095, **I I** 1249

Index to papers

This index was prepared from all the titles in the three volumes of the work, extensively cross-referenced. It is hoped that this will enable the reader to locate rapidly any paper or papers in which he is interested. A bold **I** preceding a page number indicates that the paper appears in the first volume, a bold **II** the second, and a bold **III** the third.

Ability, neural network learning **I** 265, **I** 267
 self-learning **I** 265, **I** 267
Adaptable neural nets, modelling of **II** 841, **II** 861
Adaptive control of engineering cybernetic systems **II** 523, **II** 525
Adaptive societal systems, thermodynamics and cybernetics of **III** 1095, **III** 1231
Algebra of the logical deductive intelligent activity **I** 266, **I** 383
Algol 60 implementation **II** 684, **II** 833
Algorithms, minimized graph-schemes of **II** 523, **II** 553
Allocation, optimum of personal presence **II** 684, **II** 803
Analysis, formal, for a general automaton **II** 523, **II** 613
Analysis, harmonic, in the visual pathway of higher mammals **I** 266, **I** 403
Approach, cybernetic, to the study of natural languages **III** 1095, **III** 1257
Artifacts and cybernetics **II** 841
Artificial intelligence **I** 1, **I** 3
 paradigm for **I** 841, **I** 901

Aspects of economic models, cybernetic **II** 683, **II** 715
Associative memory, mathematical model of **I** 265, **I** 291
Auditory system, spectral analysis performed by, **I** 266, **I** 447
Automatic classification by extraction of parameters from human ECG **I** 266, **I** 497
Automatic diagnosis and cybernetic medicine **I** 1, **I** 87
Automatic diagnosis by extraction of parameters from human ECG **I** 266, **I** 497
Automation and cybernetics **II** 523
 cybernetics and industry **I** 1, **I** 113
 of clinical diagnosis **I** 266, **I** 505
 of minimized graph schemes of algorithms **II** 523, **II** 553
Automaton, general, formal analysis of **II** 523, **II** 613
 self-optimizing **II** 841, **II** 843
Automotive batteries **II** 523, **II** 641

Basic design for "changing" of laws of nature cybernetically **III** 961, **III** 1087

Behavioural sciences, meaning of cyber-
netics in **I** 1, **I** 15
Biochemical cybernetics **III** 961, **III** 1067
Biocybernetical systems, humoral, dis-
orders in cerebral infarction **I** 266,
I 491
Biocybernetics **I** 265
Bioholography, model of information
processing **I** 266, **I** 433
Biosynthesis of steroid hormones, dis-
orders of **I** 266, **I** 467
Boolean operators in modelling of neural
sets **II** 841, **II** 861
Boole logic **III** 961, **III** 971
Brain, its information trapping device
I 265, **I** 309
visual illusions in **I** 266, **I** 419

Cat's visual system, models of nerve cell
interactions **I** 266, **I** 393
Cerebral infarction, disorders of effector
mechanism **I** 266, **I** 491
Change **II** 841, **II** 927
Classification of sorts of information in
cybernetics **I** 127, **I** 167
Clinical diagnosis, automation of **I** 266,
I 505
Clinical disorders, study by computer
simulation of **I** 266, **I** 467
Cognitive strategies and skill learning
II 683, **II** 793
Command and control system with high
traffic, response time distributions
II 523, **II** 541
Computer model, of the evolution of
DNA sequences **III** 961, **III** 1019
of frog's optic tectum **II** 841, **II** 849
Computer sculpture **II** 841, **II** 931
Computer simulation, of industrial opera-
tions **II** 683, **II** 767
study of clinical disorders by **I** 266,
I 467
Computer structures and creative work
III 1096, **III** 1319
Computers, neuron model acceptable by
I 265, **I** 339

Computing ability of a developmental
model for filamentous organisms
II 841, **II** 873
Concept, system in economic cycles
II 683, **II** 703
Conceptual usefulness of Boolean opera-
tors in modelling of neural nets
II 841, **II** 849
Considerations, theoretical and experi-
mental, of cybernetics, responsive
environments, learning and social
development **III** 1095, **III** 1145
Control, adaptive, of engineering cyber-
netic systems **II** 523, **II** 525
of man-machine systems **II** 523,
II 579
systems, cybernetic, design of **II** 523,
II 653
systems, management and cybernetics
II 683, **II** 685
Co-ordinated systems, information flow in
I 1, **I** 57
Creative work and computer structures
III 1096, **III** 1319
Cross-connection neuron network,
learning and self-learning ability
I 265, **I** 267
Cybernetic, approach to form recognition
problems in neurological clinic
I 265, **I** 347
approach to the study of natural lan-
guages **III** 1095, **III** 1257
aspects of economic models **II** 683,
II 715
"changing" of laws of nature **III** 961,
III 1087
control system for manufacturing and
distribution (design of) **II** 523,
II 653
engineering systems, adaptive control of
II 523, **II** 525
cytoblast **I** 1, **I** 65
medicine **I** 1, **I** 87
modelling and town planning **III** 961,
III 1073
sculpture of Tsai **II** 841, **II** 949

Cybernetic—*cont.*
systems to control production and distribution of automotive batteries **II** 523, **II** 641
Cybernetical systems, science as **III** 961, **III** 963
Cybernetics, a fundamental science and philosophy of "existence" **I** 127, **I** 215
and artifacts **II** 841, **II** 843
and automation **II** 523
and education **I** 127, **I** 201
and industry **I** 1, **I** 113, **II** 523
and information **II** 841, **II** 843
and management **II** 683, **II** 685
and natural sciences **III** 961
and philosophy **I** 127, **I** 129
and religion **I** 127, **I** 223
and social sciences **III** 1095, **III** 1096
and social structure **III** 1095, **III** 1107
and society **III** 1095, **III** 1131
and ternary logic **III** 961, **III** 1003
and warfare **III** 1095, **III** 1329
application of, in a planned economy management **II** 683, **II** 741
as a model for political science **III** 1095, **III** 1215
as a universal philosophical theory **I** 127, **I** 139
bio- **I** 265
biochemical **III** 961, **III** 1067
classification of sorts of information in **I** 127, **I** 167
definition and philosophy of **I** 127
economic consequences of **II** 683
economic, system concept in **II** 683, **II** 703
fundamental notion of **I** 127, **I** 245
impact on learning, politics and production **III** 1095, **III** 1287
meaning of **I** 127
in revolutionary systems **I** 127, **I** 175
in the behavioural sciences **I** 1, **I** 15
neuro- **I** 265
of evolving systems **III** 1095, **III** 1121

Cybernetics—*cont.*
of open adaptive societal systems **III** 1095, **III** 1231
organizational and human values of **III** 1095, **III** 1163
past and future in human development of **I** 1, **I** 45
six levels of **II** 841, **II** 931
social consequences of **II** 683
system concept in economic **II** 683, **II** 703
theoretical and experimental considerations of **III** 1095, **III** 1145

Decision processes, random with complete connections **III** 1095, **III** 1249
Design, of cybernetic control systems for manufacturing and distribution **II** 523, **II** 653
of cybernetic systems in industry **II** 523, **II** 641
Development of natural sciences, automation of **I** 1, **I** 97
Device, trapping of information in the brain **I** 265, **I** 309
Diagnosis, automatic, by extraction of uncorrelated parameters from human ECG **I** 266, **I** 497
clinical automation of **I** 266, **I** 505
Diagnostic recognition of structures **II** 684, **II** 813
Disorders of effector mechanism in cerebral infarction **I** 266, **I** 491
Distribution of response time in command and control systems **II** 523, **II** 541

Economic consequences of cybernetics **II** 683
Economic cybernetics, system concept in **II** 683, **II** 703
Economic models, cybernetic aspects **II** 683, **II** 715
Economic system, investment cycles and stability of **II** 683, **II** 753
Education and cybernetics **I** 127, **I** 201
Effector mechanism in cerebral infarction, disorders of **I** 266, **I** 491

Engineering cybernetic systems, adaptive control of   II 523, II 525

Entropy and philosophy   I 127, I 149

Epicosm model of the material and mental universes   III 1096, III 1351

Epidemic theory, application to the growth of science to   III 961, III 971

Error detection and correction in the control of man-machine systems   II 523, II 579

Evolution of DNA sequences   III 961, III 1019

Evolving systems, cybernetics of   III 1095, III 1121

"Existence", fundamental science and philosophy of   I 127, I 215

Extraction of uncorrelated parameters from human ECG, use of   I 266, I 497

Filamentous organisms, developmental model of   II 841, II 873

Fineware   III 961, III 1013

Form recognition problem in neurological clinic   I 265, I 347

Formal analysis for a general automaton   II 523, II 613

Foundations of ternary logic and cybernetics   III 961, III 1003

Frog's optic tectum, computer model of   II 841, II 849

Fundamental notion of cybernetics   I 127, I 245

process of information gaining   II 841, II 917

science of "existence", cybernetics   I 127, I 215

Games, strategies of co-operative   II 683, II 783

General automaton, formal analysis of   II 523, II 613

General systems theory and cybernetics   I 127, I 155

Gödel logic   III 961, III 971

Growth of science, application of epidemic theory to   III 961, III 971

Hardware   III 961, III 1013

Hardware, software, fineware   III 961, III 1013

Harmonic analysis in the visual pathway of higher mammals   I 266, I 403

Human development, past and future of cybernetics in   I 1, I 45

Human encephalogram (ECG)   I 266, I 497

interactions, quantitative approach   III 1095, III 1185

values and organizational cybernetics   III 1095, III 1163

Humoral biocybernetical systems in cerebral infarction   I 266, I 491

Illusions, visual, in brain   I 266, I 419

Impact of cybernetics on learning, politics and production processes   III 1096, III 1287

Industrial operations, computer simulation of   II 683, II 767

Industry and cybernetics   I 1, I 113, II 523

Information, and cybernetics   II 841, II 843

flows within co-ordinated systems   I 1, I 57

gaining, fundamental process of   II 841, II 917

management and cybernetics   II 683, II 685

processing, model of (bioholographic)   I 266, I 433

services of universities, resources allocation for   III 1096, III 1281

subjective theory of open adaptive societal systems   III 1095, III 1231

transmission, a model of internervous system   I 265, I 299

trapping device of brain   I 265, I 309

Information growth model   II 841, II 887

Intelligence, artificial   I 1, I 3

paradigm for artificial   II 841, II 901

Intelligent activity, logical deduction (algebra of)   I 266, I 383

Interactions in nerve cells of the cat's
    visual system **I** 266, **I** 393
Internal states, self-regulation of
    III 1096, **III** 1299
Inter-nervous system, model of informa-
    tion transmission of a **I** 265, **I** 299
Interneuronal spinal system in man,
    stochastic stimulation use of **I** 265,
    I 353
Investment cycles and stability of big eco-
    nomic systems **II** 683, **II** 753

Languages, cybernetic approach to natural
    III 1096, **III** 1257
    neurocybernetical approach to problem
    I 266, **I** 441
Laws of nature, "changing" of **III** 961,
    III 1087
Learning, impact of cybernetics on
    III 1096, **III** 1287
    method for systems dynamics **II** 523,
    II 597
    skill **II** 683, **II** 793
    theoretical and experimental considera-
    tion of **III** 1095, **III** 1145
Logical deductive intelligent activity
    (algebra of) **I** 266, **I** 383

Mammals, visual pathway in **I** 266,
    I 403
Man, spinal interneuronal system in
    I 265, **I** 353
Man-machine systems, control of
    II 523, **II** 579
Management, and cybernetics **II** 683,
    II 685
    cybernetic cytoblast **I** 1, **I** 65
    information and cybernetics **II** 683,
    II 685
    of planned economy and cybernetics
    II 683, **II** 741
    process and cybernetics **II** 683, **II** 685
Mathematical model of associative
    memory **I** 265, **I** 291
Mathematical systems, organization of
    III 961, **III** 985

Material universe, epicosm model of
    III 1096, **III** 1351
Meaning of cybernetics, in behavioural
    sciences **I** 1, **I** 15
    in revolutionary systems **I** 127, **I** 175
Measurement as a fundamental process
    of information gaining **II** 841,
    II 917
Memory, associative of **I** 265, **I** 291
    of robots **II** 523, **II** 565
Mental universe, epicosm model of
    III 1096, **III** 1351
Method, learning for system dynamics
    II 523, **II** 597
    of automatic diagnosis **I** 1, **I** 87
Minimized graph-schemes of algorithms,
    automation and synthesis of
    II 523, **II** 553
Model, computer, of evolution of DNA
    sequences **III** 961, **III** 1019
    computer, of frog's optic tectum **II** 841,
    II 849
    cybernetic aspects of economic **II** 683,
    II 715
    developmental of filamentous organisms
    II 841, **II** 873
    epicosm of material and mental uni-
    verses **III** 1096, **III** 1351
    for classification of visual images
    III 961, **III** 1035
    for political science, cybernetics of
    III 1095, **III** 1215
    informational growth of **II** 841, **II** 887
    mathematical, of associative memory
    I 265, **I** 291
    neuron, acceptable by computers
    I 265, **I** 339
    of information processing **I** 266, **I** 433
    of inter-nervous system information
    transmission **I** 265, **I** 299
    of nerve cell interactions in the cat's
    visual system **I** 266, **I** 393
Modelling, cybernetic of town planning
    III 961, **III** 1073
Modern technology, social aspects of
    III 1095, **III** 1097

Multi-level approach to adaptive control of engineering cybernetic systems **II** 523, **II** 525

Natural definition of similarity and typicality of taxonomic units **III** 961, **III** 1051
  languages, cybernetic approach to **III** 1096, **III** 1257
  sciences development (automation of) **I** 1, **I** 97
  sciences and cybernetics **III** 961
Nerve cell interactions in the cat's visual system **I** 266, **I** 393
Neural nets, modelling of **II** 841, **II** 861
  origin of visual illusions in brain **I** 266, **I** 419
Neurocybernetical approach to the problem of languages **I** 266, **I** 441
  contribution to the theory of agnosias **I** 265, **I** 281
Neurocybernetics **I** 265
Neuron model acceptable by computers **I** 265, **I** 339
  network learning and self-learning ability **I** 265, **I** 267
Neuronal brain organization, probabilistic ensembles in **I** 265, **I** 275

Open adaptive societal systems, thermodynamics and cybernetics of **III** 1095, **III** 1231
Optimization of big economic systems in socialist countries **II** 683, **II** 723
Optimum allocation of personal presence **II** 683, **II** 803
Organizational cybernetics and human values **III** 1095, **III** 1163
Organization of mathematical systems **III** 961, **III** 985

Paradigm for artificial intelligence **II** 841, **II** 901
Parameters for validation of time sharing **II** 684, **II** 823

Past and future of cybernetics in human development **I** 1, **I** 45
Pattern recognition, system of classes **II** 841, **II** 891
  syntax-monitored semantic **III** 1096, **III** 1267
Peripheral auditory system, short-time spectral analysis performed by **I** 266, **I** 447
Personal presence, optimum allocation of **II** 684, **II** 803
Philosophy and cybernetics **I** 127, **I** 129
  and entropy **I** 127, **I** 149
  of "existence", cybernetics as **I** 127, **I** 215
Planned economy management and cybernetics **II** 683, **II** 741
Political science, cybernetic model of **III** 1095, **III** 1215
Politics, impact of cybernetics on **III** 1096, **III** 1287
Positive feedback, rôle of **I** 127, **I** 249
Prediction of strategies in co-operative games **II** 683, **II** 783
Principle of probabilistic ensembles in neuronal brain organization **I** 265, **I** 275
Probabilistic ensembles principle in neuronal brain organization **I** 265, **I** 275
Problem of form recognition in neurological clinic **I** 265, **I** 347
Problem of language, neurocybernetical approach **I** 266, **I** 441
Problems of optimization of big economic systems **II** 683, **II** 723
Production, impact of economics on **III** 1096, **III** 1287
Production and distribution of automotive batteries, control of **II** 523, **II** 641
Properties of short-time spectral analysis performed by the peripheral auditory system **I** 266, **I** 447

Quantitative approach to human interactions and social phenomena **III** 1095, **III** 1185

Random decision process with complete connections **III** 1095, **III** 1249

Rational solutions from minimized graph-schemes **II** 523, **II** 553

Recognition of structures, diagnostic **II** 684, **II** 813

Regulation of steroid hormones, disorders of **I** 266, **I** 467

Relation between cybernetics and general systems theory **I** 127, **I** 155

Religion and cybernetics **I** 127, **I** 223

Resource allocation for university information services **III** 1096, **III** 1281

Response time distributions in a command and control system **II** 523, **II** 541

Responsive environments, theoretical and experimental considerations of **III** 1095, **III** 1145

Robots with memory **II** 523, **II** 565

Rôle of positive feedback **I** 127, **I** 249

Sculpture, computer **II** 841, **II** 931

Sciences as a cybernetical system **III** 961, **III** 963

Self-learning ability and neuron network learning ability **I** 265, **I** 267

Self-optimizing automaton **II** 841, **II** 843

Self-organization and statistical theory **I** 265, **I** 359

Self-regulation of internal states **III** 1096, **III** 1299

Semantic, syntax-monitored pattern recognition **III** 1096, **III** 1267

Short-time spectral analysis preformed by the peripheral auditory system **I** 266, **I** 447

Simulation, by computer of certain clinical disorders **I** 266, **I** 467

by computer of industrial operations **II** 683, **II** 767

model of a system **II** 683, **II** 777

of robots with memory **II** 523, **II** 565

Skill learning and cognitive strategies **II** 683, **II** 793

Software **III** 961, **III** 1013

Software translation, implementing of **II** 684, **II** 833

Social aspects of modern technology **III** 1095, **III** 1097

Social change and stability **III** 1095, **III** 1205

Social consequences of cybernetics **II** 683

Social development, theoretical and experimental considerations of **III** 1095, **III** 1145

Socialist countries, optimization of big economic systems in **II** 683, **II** 723

Social phenomena, quantitative approach to **III** 1095, **III** 1185

Social sciences and cybernetics **III** 1095, **III** 1096

Social structure and cybernetics **III** 1095, **III** 1107

Society and cybernetics **III** 1095, **III** 1131

Spinal interneuronal system in man, stimulation by **I** 265, **I** 353

Stability, and social change **III** 1095, **III** 1205

of big economic systems and investment cycles **II** 683, **II** 753

Statistical theory and self-organization **I** 265, **I** 359

Steroid hormones, biosynthesis and regulation of **I** 266, **I** 467

Stimulation, stochastic of spinal interneuronal system in man **I** 265, **I** 353

Stochastic stimulation for studying the spinal interneuronal system in man **I** 265, **I** 353

Strategies, cognitive **II** 683, **II** 793

in co-operative games **II** 683, **II** 783

Structural computer model of the frog's optic tectum **II** 841, **II** 849

Structure of robots with memory **II** 523, **II** 565

Structures, diagnostic recognition of **II** 684, **II** 813

Study of certain clinical disorders by computer simulation **I** 266, **I** 467

Subjective information theory **III** 1095, **III** 1231

Symbiotic art and cybernetic sculpture **II** 841, **II** 949

Symbolic logic from Boole to Gödel **III** 961, **III** 971

Synthesis of minimized graph-schemes of algorithms **II** 523, **II** 553

System, big economic and investment cycles **II** 683, **II** 753

command and control with high traffic **II** 523, **II** 541

concept in economic cybernetics **II** 683, **II** 703

inter-nervous of information transmission **I** 265, **I** 299

of cat's visual and models **I** 266, **I** 393

of classes in pattern recognition **II** 841, **II** 891

peripheral auditory **I** 266, **I** 447

simulation model of **II** 683, **II** 777

Systems, adaptive control of large-scale engineering **II** 523, **II** 525

control of man-machine **II** 523, **II** 579

cybernetics of evolving **III** 1095, **III** 1121

learning method for determining dynamics **II** 523, **II** 597

open adaptive societal **III** 1095, **III** 1231

optimization of big economic **II** 683, **II** 723

organization of mathematical **III** 961, **III** 985

revolutionary with rapid or discontinuous shifts in standards **I** 127, **I** 175

Taxonomic units, similarity and typicality of operating **III** 961, **III** 1051

Ternary logic and cybernetics **III** 961, **III** 1003

Theory, statistical and self organization **I** 265, **I** 359

Theory of agnosias, neurocybernetical contribution to **I** 265, **I** 281

Theory of diagnostic recognition of structures **II** 684, **II** 813

Theory of size and intensity invariance of visual illusions in the brain **I** 266, **I** 419

Thermodynamics of open adaptive societal systems **III** 1095, **III** 1231

Time sharing, parameters of its validation **II** 684, **II** 823

Town planning and cybernetic modelling **III** 961, **III** 1073

Traffic in command and control systems **II** 523, **II** 541

Transmission of information, inter-nervous system model of **I** 265, **I** 299

Trapping device of information in the brain **I** 265, **I** 309

Tsai's cybernetic sculpture **II** 841, **II** 949

Uncorrelated parameters for human ECG in automatic diagnosis **I** 266, **I** 497

Universal philosophical theory, cybernetics as **I** 127, **I** 139

Universes, material and mental **III** 1096, **III** 1351

University information services, resource allocation for **III** 1096, **III** 1281

Validation, parameters of time sharing **II** 684, **II** 823

Visual images, classification model for **III** 961, **III** 1035

Visual system of cat, nerve cell interactions in **I** 266, **I** 393

Warfare and cybernetics **III** 1096, **III** 1329

Ways of automation of natural sciences development **I** 1, **I** 97

Yugoslav experience of optimization of big economic systems **II** 683, **II** 723